IRISH EDUCATION

THE MINISTERIAL LEGACY, 1919–99

ANTONIA McMANUS

The
History
Press
Ireland

For my mother and teacher May Murphy
Le fíor buíochas agus grá

First published 2014

The History Press Ireland
50 City Quay
Dublin 2
Ireland
www.thehistorypress.ie

British Library Cataloguing in Publication Data.
A catalogue record for this book is available from the British Library.

ISBN 978 1 84588 844 2

Typesetting and origination by The History Press

Contents

List of Abbreviations

ASTI	Association of Secondary Teachers, Ireland
BITE	Ballymun Initiative for Third-Level Education
CDVEC	City of Dublin Vocational Education Committee
CEB	Curriculum and Examinations Board
CEC	Central Executive Council
CHA	Catholic Headmasters' Association
CHIU	Council of Heads of Irish Universities
CICE	Church of Ireland College of Education
CITC	Church of Ireland Training College
CMCSS	Council of Managers of Catholic Secondary Schools
CMRS	Conference of Major Religious Superiors
CORI	Conference of Religious of Ireland
CPSMA	Catholic Primary-School Managers' Association
CSA	Commission on School Accommodation
DARE	Disability Access Route to Education
DCU	Dublin City University
DES	Department of Education and Science
DIT	Dublin Institute of Technology
DSP	Dalkey School Project
DT	Department of the Taoiseach
ECEA	Early Childhood Education Agency
ERC	Educational Research Centre
ESF	European Social Fund
ESRI	Economic and Social Research Institute
ESRU	Evaluation Support and Research Unit
FETAC	Further Education and Training Awards Council
FIRE	Future Involvement of Religious in Education
HEA	Higher Education Authority
HEAR	Higher Education Access Route

HETAC	Higher Education Training and Awards Council
HSCLS	Home School Community Liaison Scheme
IALS	International Adult Literacy Survey
ICSTI	Irish Council for Science Technology and Innovation
ICT	Information and communications technology
ICTU	Irish Congress of Trade Unions
IDA	Industrial Development Authority
IFUT	Irish Federation of University Teachers
IIE	Investment in Education
INTO	Irish National Teachers' Organisation
IT	Institute of Technology
ITEA	Irish Technical Education Association
IVEA	Irish Vocational Education Association
JAM	Junior Assistant Mistress
JMB	Joint Managerial Body
JCSP	Junior Certificate School Programme
LCA	Leaving Certificate Applied
LCVP	Leaving Certificate Vocational Programme
LEC	Local Education Committee
LFM	Language Freedom Movement
LUPC	Limerick University Project Committee
MCC	Manpower Consultative Committee
NAI	National Archives of Ireland
NALA	National Adult Literacy Agency
NAPS	National Anti-Poverty Strategy
NCAD	National College of Art and Design
NCCA	National Council for Curriculum and Assessment
NCEA	National Council for Educational Awards
NCPE	National College of Physical Education
NCTE	National Centre for Technology in Education
NCVA	National Council for Vocational Awards
NDP	National Development Plan
NEC	National Education Convention
NEPS	National Educational Psychological Service
NESC	National Economic and Social Council
NESF	National Economic and Social Forum
NIEC	National Industrial and Economic Council
NIHE	National Institute of Higher Education
NIHED	National Institute of Higher Education, Dublin
NIHEL	National Institute of Higher Education Limerick
NPC	National Parents' Council

NQAI	National Qualifications Authority of Ireland
NUI	National University of Ireland
NUJ	National Union of Journalists
OECD	Organisation for Economic Co-operation and Development
OEEC	Organisation for European Economic Co-operation
PCSP	Primary Curriculum Support Programme
PCW	Programme for Competitiveness and Work
PD	Progressive Democrat party
PE	Physical education
PEEP	Public Examinations Evaluation Project
PERB	Primary Education Review Body
PESP	Programme for Economic and Social Progress
PISA	Programme for International Student Assessment
PLC	Post-leaving Certificate course
REC	Regional Education Council
RTC	Regional Technical College
SERC	Special Education Review Committee
SNA	Special needs assistant
TAP	Trinity Access Programme
TBA	Teaching Brothers' Association
TCD	Trinity College Dublin
TEASTAS	Irish National Certification Authority
TIB	Technical Instruction Branch of the Department of Education
TUI	Teachers' Union of Ireland
TWG	Technical Working Group
UCC	University College Cork
UCD	University College Dublin
UCG	University College Galway
UL	University of Limerick
USI	Union of Students in Ireland
VEC	Vocational Education Committee
VPTP	Vocational Preparation and Training Programme
VTA	Vocational Teachers' Association
VTOS	Vocational Training Opportunities Scheme

Glossary of Irish Terms

Aireacht na Gaedhilge	Ministry for Irish
An Cheárd Chomhairle	Apprenticeship Board
AnCO (An Chomhairle Oiliúna)	Industrial Training Authority
An Gúm	Publishing section of the Department of Education for Irish material
An t-Oireachtas	The Irish legislature
AONTAS	National Association for Adult Education
Ár nDaltáí Uile (All our Children)	All our pupils
Buntús Cainte	Rudiments of Language
Buntús Gaeilge	Foundation Irish Programme
Ceann Chomhairle	Speaker of the House
Coimisiún na Gaeltachta	The Gaeltacht Commission
Dáil Éireann	Lower House of the Irish Parliament
Deontas	A grant
Fianna Fáil (Soldiers of Destiny)	Political party
Fine Gael (Family group of Irish)	Political party
Gaeltacht	Irish-speaking area
Gairm	Profession
Misneach	Courage
Oireachtas na Gaeilge	Gaelic League annual cultural festival
RTÉ (Raidio Teilifís Éireann)	Irish television station
Saorstát Éireann	Irish Free State
Sceilg	Rock or crag
Seanad	Senate
Sinn Féin (We ourselves)	Political party
Tanáiste	Irish Deputy Prime Minister
Taoiseach	Irish Prime Minister
TD (Teachta Dála)	Deputy – Member of Irish Parliament
Telefís Scoile	School Television

Acknowledgements

I wish to express my sincere gratitude to the staff members of the National Library of Ireland, the National Archives and Trinity College Dublin for their professional assistance and cooperation. I wish to acknowledge the debt I owe to those who have conducted research on various aspects of Irish education spanning many years, particularly Professor John Coolahan, Professor Áine Hyland and Ms. Susan M. Parkes.

I wish to record my gratitude to Ronan Colgan and Beth Amphlett of The History Press Ireland for their great courtesy and professionalism at all times.

I wish to thank my family for their keen interest in this book, and for their love and unstinting support, especially my husband Ken.

I'm dedicating this book to my mother and teacher May Murphy on the 25th anniversary of her death. *Le fíor buíochas agus grá.*

Introduction

This book studies Irish ministerial careers from 1919 to 1999, and analyses the contributions of the ministers to the advancement of education policy and practice, during their terms of office. It reviews the social and political factors that impinged on their decisions in the formation of those policies, from the impoverished ministry of John J. O'Kelly, who with great fortitude tried to revive the Irish language on a budget of £10,000,[1] to the cash-rich ministry of Micheál Martin, who had access to a £250 million Scientific and Technological Education Investment Fund.

Ireland in 1924 was described in the *Irish Catholic* as being in a 'pathological crisis' as the nation was 'convalescing from the fever and prostration of two wars'.[2] As one commentator remarked, 'There was little use for idealism and less scope for utopianism in the Irish Free State of 1923'.[3] But educational developments occurred even during the worst of times, for example the passing of the Ministers and Secretaries Act, which established the Department of Education, the Intermediate Education (Amendment) Act, the School Attendance Act and the Vocational Education Act.

But all was not well in the field of education. The language revival policy became synonymous with the education policy, and educational standards quickly plummeted, so much so that a writer to *The Bell* in 1947 commented that 'The policy of raising the standard of education has never been tried'.[4] An Irish National Teachers' Organisation (INTO) inquiry into the language policy revealed that it placed an undue mental strain on children, and that it had a deleterious effect on their education. Dr Johanna Pollak's report 'On Teaching Irish' confirmed that 'the children get an overdose of it'.[5] Doctoral research conducted in the mid-1960s confirmed the accuracy of the INTO's report, and served as a damning indictment of Ministers for Education who were prepared to put their nationalist aspirations before the educational welfare of Irish children.

The most striking feature of ministerial careers spanning eight decades was the continuity of educational plans. The language policy survived for 40 years, while plans to replace vocational schools resurfaced periodically over 63 years. The proposal to introduce local education committees (LECs) never failed to ignite controversy, from the time of the MacPherson Education Bill when in 1920 Cardinal Logue called for a national solemn novena in honour of St Patrick 'to avert from us the threatened calamity',[6] to the mid-1970s and mid-1980s when church opposition broadened out to include the Catholic and Protestant churches, and their respective education management bodies. In the 1990s, the churches just bided their time, as different Ministers proposed different options, ranging from county committees of education to LECs or regional educational councils. In 1997 Martin, who defended patrons' rights while in opposition, as Minister introduced executive agencies, and with that, the ghost of MacPherson was finally laid to rest.

Over the 80 years there were great failures and great successes. The greatest failure of a succession of Ministers for Education was their denial that there was excessive use of corporal punishment in industrial and reformatory schools, even when individual cases were brought to their attention. When the Kennedy Committee received an open admission of the abuse of children in Daingean Reformatory School, the department was forced by District Justice Kennedy to close the school down, but their report made no reference whatsoever to this incident lest it 'cause a great public scandal'.[7]

Ministers for Education, up to the late 1950s, did not see the need for widespread remedial provision. But Seán Brosnahan, the general secretary of the INTO, did and he denounced what he called 'one of the greatest crimes of our system … the callous disregard for subnormal and backward children' many of whom were 'condemned as fools and dunces'.[8] Even though the government signed up to the United Nations Convention on the Rights of the Child in 1992, the reality was that education provisions in Ireland for profound and severely handicapped children 'were limited if non-existent'.[9] It took a High Court judgment in the O'Donoghue case in 1993 to alter the situation, when the onus was placed on the Minister to provide educational opportunities for all students, whatever their disabilities. This ruling was complied with in the Education Act of 1998.

Another great failure of the earlier Ministers for Education was their inability to recognise the value of secondary education, or to take stock of parental demand for it. Free second-level education could have been introduced in 1947, at a time when 'for nine out of every ten Irish people, the primary school' was 'their only centre of learning'.[10] Donogh O'Malley earned iconic status when he did so 20 years later, and this marked one of the greatest successes in Irish education because of its enduring benefits. It is reasonable to attribute our unprecedented economic success of the 1990s, when Ireland was placed 'top in Europe for its educated workforce and second (after Germany) for the skills of the workers',[11] to O'Malley's 'free education' scheme.

Parents were practically excluded from the education system for over four decades. Éamon de Valera, who drew up Article 42 of the Constitution, played lip-service to the idea of setting up a parents' committee, because he said parents 'may not be educational experts, but they know where the toe pinches. Their judgment is often a great deal better and far wiser than a lot of these people who set themselves up as experts'.[12] While parents had representation on boards of management since 1966, they really had very limited powers. Significant change occurred when Gemma Hussey gave parents real power through the National Parents' Council (NPC). Parents empowered themselves on occasions. It was a mother whose son had special needs who established what was eventually called St Michael's House. It was parental demand that led to the growth of All-Irish schools, and it was parents who set up the Dalkey School Project (DSP), Ireland's first multi-denominational school, and they did so despite strong official resistance. Subsequent Ministers were enthusiastic supporters of multi-denominational schools.

The composition of boards of management was one of the most contentious issues from the 1970s to the 1990s, as power-sharing proved to be difficult for those who traditionally enjoyed a monopoly of it. But teaching unions fought their corner, and after 12 years the Association of Secondary Teachers of Ireland (ASTI) won a fair representation on boards of management of secondary schools. After 7 years they and the Vocational Teachers' Association (VTA) got representation on the boards of management of community schools. But a hornet's nest was opened following the publication of the 1997 Education Bill, which diluted the powers of the owners or patrons of schools. It led to representatives of almost every religious faith in the country coming together on the lawn of the Church of Ireland College of Education (CICE) to protest against the proposals on the management of schools. It was a defining moment and their protest was successful.

The Catholic hierarchy and religious authorities maintained considerable influence in Irish education. On two occasions bishops' representatives were invited to participate on boards of management. On the first occasion, Faulkner went to great lengths to secure Cardinal Conway's support for the introduction of community schools. He even gave a greater weighting to representatives of the Catholic Church on boards of management at the expense of the Vocational Education Committees (VECs), and on the second occasion, the VECs invited representatives of the Catholic bishops to participate on the boards of management of their new community colleges. The religious authorities themselves found an ingenious way of ensuring that the religious ethos of their schools would be protected in the future, as they faced the prospect of steadily declining religious vocations. They set up trusteeships in the form of companies, with directors consisting of a number of lay Catholics, to carry out the patron's functions. It was to these companies that boards of management reported.

The ASTI became a powerful pressure group over the 80 years, while the INTO, under the leadership of its towering general secretary and Labour TD, T.J. O'Connell (who might have been Minister for Education himself except for the vagaries of politics), led the first teachers strike in 26 years with the Dublin teachers' strike of 1946. It lasted 7½ months, and Thomas Derrig would accept nothing less than unconditional surrender. At Archbishop McQuaid's request, the teachers returned to their classrooms in the knowledge that a special payment had been made to their colleagues who had worked during the strike. The ASTI led three strikes in 1920,[13] 1964 and 1969, but the two most successful strikes were those where the three unions united, as happened with the landmark pay settlement of 1980, and again in 1986 when the unions exulted in having 'already secured a moral victory in effectively toppling the former Minister for Education, Mrs. Hussey'.[14]

Patrick Hillery transformed Irish education in the 1960s by exposing the system to Organisation for Economic Co-operation and Development (OECD) scrutiny and to international influence. The Investment in Education Report which followed ensured that future policy making would be research based. He gained episcopal acceptance of comprehensive education and he provided a blueprint for the status of vocational schools, which had been perceived as 'just dead-end schools for dead-end kids'.[15] He also provided a signpost for the future Regional Technical College (RTCs). OECD studies of Irish education have continued, and their reports have provided indicators of comparative educational performance across a number of European countries, thereby ensuring that Ministers can never return to the complacency exhibited by a Minister in the past who claimed that 'our system of education approaches the ideal'.

Ireland's membership of the EEC in 1973 brought countless benefits to Irish education, particularly through the financial support received from the European Social Fund (ESF) during years of austerity in the 1970s and through the economic recession of the 1980s, and for co-funding of large-scale educational reforms in the 1990s.

Profound changes took place in higher education over 80 years. Participation rates rose spectacularly as Ireland moved quickly from a situation where a relatively small elite went into higher education, to something approaching mass higher education. Expansion was not confined to the university sector as numbers in non-university education soared due to funding from the ESF. Higher education suffered from a number of shocks over 30 years. The first one was O'Malley's surprise announcement of a merger between Trinity College Dublin (TCD) and University College Dublin (UCD) in April 1967; and the next one occurred in December 1974, when Richard Burke attempted to replace the binary system of higher education with a new comprehensive model; but the abolition of tuition fees for undergraduates in 1995 could not have come at a worse time for universities, struggling to cope with burgeoning numbers and few resources.

The non-university sector was not enamoured of the 1974 proposals either, but it was when Niamh Bhreathnach decided to raise Waterford RTC to Institute of Technology (IT) status, and to call time on the beleaguered National Council for Educational Awards (NCEA), that confusion reigned supreme. Martin provided a more coherent and effective system of certification and accreditation for the sector when he introduced the Qualifications (Education and Training) Act in 1999. But one of the finest achievements over 80 years was Bhreathnach's Universities Act of 1997, the first of its kind since the Universities Act of 1908 establishing the National University of Ireland.

As the international prestige of universities depended on their research achievements, it was a source of concern to universities to have it confirmed by Circa Group Europe in their comparative assessment of higher education research, that 'Public funding of higher education research in Ireland' was 'among the worst in Europe'.[16] Third-level colleges benefited enormously from a £150 million 3-year investment programme for scientific and other research in the late 1990s and plans were afoot for even bigger investments in research and technological development in the education sector. This had a knock-on effect on the Irish economy as it helped to improve Ireland's competitive advantage.

Another significant milestone was reached with the passing of the Education Act of 1998, to which five Ministers for Education made a contribution, namely O'Rourke, Brennan, Davern, Bhreathnach and Martin, and which provided the education system with a legislative foundation for the first time. However, many challenges still persisted in the education system, such as early school leaving and youth unemployment, an inadequate educational psychological service, poor participation rates by Traveller children, inadequate provision for part-time students in universities who still had to pay fees, and a lack of diversity in school provision in a country which now boasted a multicultural society.

However, the vast progress made over 80 years should be acknowledged, as an education system which was underfunded, undeveloped and uncoordinated for four decades, was now a vibrant, modern system, the kind of system Pádraig

Faulkner willed us to have in 1972, when he said:

> We in the business of education have for our raw material the nation's most precious asset, our children. Let us give them the opportunities they deserve, and a system for which they will thank us.[17]

Notes

1   Report of the Ministry of the National Language, August 1921, p.9.

2   *Irish Catholic*, 23 February 1924.

3   Patrick Lynch, 'The social revolution that never was' in Desmond Williams (ed.) *The Irish Struggle 1919-1926* (London, 1966), p.53.

4   Patrick O'Callaghan, 'Irish in schools' in *The Bell*, 14:1, 1947, p.63.

5   NAI *S7801* Dr Johanna Pollak, 'On teaching Irish', 1943.

6   T.J. O'Connell, *History of the Irish National Teachers' Organisation 1868-1968* (Dublin, 1969), pp.318–20.

7   *Dáil Debates*, vol. 504, cols 1181–2, 13 May 1999.

8   *Irish School Weekly*, 15 and 22 March 1952, p.127.

9   Áine Hyland, 'Primary and second-level education in the early twenty-first century' in Fionán Ó Muircheartaigh (ed.) *Ireland in the Coming Times: Essays to Celebrate T.K. Whitaker's 80 Years* (Dublin, 1997), p.174.

10 *Dáil Debates*, vol. 80, col. 1566, 6 June 1940.

11 Sweeney, *The Celtic Tiger*, p.117.

12 *Dáil Debates*, vol. 96, col. 2171, 18 April 1945.

13 £1,000 was placed at the disposal of the ASTI strike committee by the INTO in 1920.

14 *The Irish Times*, 20 February 1986.

15 *Sunday Independent*, 22 December 1957.

16 CIRCA Group Europe, *A Comparative International Assessment of the Organisation, Management and Funding of University Research in Ireland and Europe* (Dublin, 1966), p.iv.

17 *Dáil Debates*, vol. 259, col. 874, 2 March 1972.

1

The MacPherson Education Bill, 1919–20: 'It means Irish education in foreign fetters'

On 14 November 1919, against a backdrop of the War of Independence,[1] the British Government's chief secretary in Ireland, James MacPherson, attempted to introduce the MacPherson Education Bill. It proposed radical administrative and structural reform of the education system for all of Ireland. The Bill provided, inter alia, for the setting up of a central department of education, the establishment of an advisory board, the setting up of LECs and the imposition of a local rate for education.

The proposals sparked off a lively campaign of opposition by the Catholic hierarchy, as the proposed new structures threatened their managerial role. Individual members of the hierarchy attacked the Bill, claiming that it posed a threat to the spiritual welfare of their flock, and that it could undermine their national identity. The most outspoken critic of the Bill was Dr Foley, Bishop of Kildare and Leiglin, who asked the people to resist 'this latest brazen-faced attempt of a hostile government to impose on the mind and soul of an intensely devoted Catholic people, the deadly grip of the foreign fetters'.[2] In fact the Bill was simply attempting to substitute one type of British administration system with another.

On 9 December 1919, a Statement of the Standing Committee of the Irish Bishops on the proposed Education Bill contended that 'The only department which the vast majority of the Irish people will tolerate is one which shall be set up by its own Parliament'.[3] The Catholic Clerical School Managers considered that 'the only satisfactory education system for Catholics' was one 'wherein Catholic children are taught in Catholic schools by Catholic teachers, under Catholic control'.[4]

When the Education Bill was re-introduced in 1920, Cardinal Logue of Armagh issued a pastoral letter in which he called for a national solemn novena in honour of St Patrick 'to avert from us the threatened calamity', and he suggested that fathers of families should 'assemble in the parish church ... on Passion Sunday ... to register their protests'.[5]

The Bishop of Kerry, Dr O'Sullivan displayed his displeasure at the INTO's decision to support the Bill by forbidding a local school choir from partici- pating in a welcoming reception for INTO delegates to their annual congress. The INTO reacted by transferring the congress from Killarney to Dublin on 6 April 1920.[6]

Dáil Éireann, which had been established on 21 January 1919, with Sinn Féin as the main governing party, refrained from public comment on the MacPherson Education Bill, but a short minute recorded by the Ministry for Irish on 4 March 1920 stated that 'the Dáil will support the bishops in setting up and maintaining a national system of education'.[7]

The MacPherson Education Bill was withdrawn on 13 December 1920, a week before the Government of Ireland Act, which would partition Ireland, was passed into law, the latter Bill having been given priority.[8] However, the intense contro- versy surrounding the MacPherson Education Bill acted as a salutary reminder to future Ministers for Education in Dáil Éireann that a heavy price would be exacted if they ever interfered with the administrative structures of Irish education, and if they posed a threat to the managerial system.

The meeting of the first Dáil of 1919 was a historic event in itself, but it was remarkable for another reason. No Minister for Education was appointed by the president of the Executive Council, Éamon de Valera, when constituting his minis- tries. According to Cathal Brugha,[9] 'President de Valera had some definite reason for not appointing a Minister for Ed'.[10] One could conjecture that he hoped to avoid any involvement by the Dáil in public discussion on the contentious MacPherson Education Bill.

Responding to a resolution of the ard-fheis of the Gaelic League, a decision was taken by the Dáil in November 1919 to appoint a Minister for Irish. The Gaelic League was a powerful nineteenth-century language revival movement which had devised its own educational plans in 1918–19. It counted among its adherents and founding members future presidents, taoisigh and ministers for education. John J. O'Kelly, the president of the Gaelic League, was appointed Minister for Irish and his new role incorporated the duties of a Minister for Education. By August 1921, the threat posed by the MacPherson Education Bill had long vanished when de Valera sanctioned the appointment of O'Kelly (1872–57) as Ireland's first Minister for Education.

Notes

1 The War of Independence commenced on 21 January 1919, the day Dáil Éireann met for the first time. It lasted until 11 July 1921.

2 T.J. McElligott, *Secondary Education in Ireland 1870–1921* (Dublin, 1981), pp.134–5.

3 Statement of the standing committee of the Irish bishops of the proposed education bill for Ireland in *Irish Ecclesiastical Record*, 14 (1919), pp.505–7.

4 *Evening Telegraph*, 22 January 1920. The Catholic Clerical School Managers was founded in 1903 as the Clerical Managers of Catholic National Schools.

5 T.J. O'Connell, *History of the Irish National Teachers' Organisation 1868–1968* (Dublin, 1969), pp.318–20.

6 Ibid., pp.327–8.

7 *Dáil Éireann Minutes of Aireacht na Gaedhilge 4 March, 1920.*

8 *Hansard's Parliamentary Debates*, vol. 138, col. 213, 13 December 1920.

9 He was Acting President in the First Dáil, and later Minister of Defence.

10 *Dáil Éireann Minutes*, 10 October 1919, Nollaig Ó Gadhra, *An chéad Dáil 1919-1921 agus an Ghaeilge* (Coiscéim, 1989), p.162.

2

John J. O'Kelly (1921-22): '... towards the Irishising of Primary Education'

John J. O'Kelly[1] became Minister for Irish in very inauspicious circumstances. The War of Independence raged in the background and the Dáil had just been proscribed. His ministerial work had to be conducted mainly from his office in O'Connell Street, where he worked for a publishing firm. Furthermore, he had to substitute for the Speaker of the Dáil, while also fulfilling his duties as president of the Gaelic League. Despite his many commitments, and periods spent 'on the run' or in prison,[2] O'Kelly, who was assisted by Frank Fahy, was a productive Minister. He applied himself to his ministerial roles as Minister for Irish from November 1919, and as Minister for Education from August 1921 until the signing of the peace Treaty in December, following which he withdrew from the Dáil in January 1922, along with the anti-Treaty Sinn Féin members.

As Minister for Irish, O'Kelly produced two important reports, one in June 1920 entitled 'Report of Aireacht na Gaedhilge'[3] and another in August 1921, the 'Report of Ministry of the National Language'.[4] It was clear from the 1920 report that O'Kelly used his position in the Gaelic League to channel its Education Programme 1918–19[5] into the Dáil education programme.

In schools where teachers were unable to teach Irish, travelling teachers were to be provided. A scholarship scheme was to be devised with a view to increasing the number of travelling teachers. The Gaelic League offered eight annual scholarships to the total value of £100 to the Irish College in Dublin for the month of August. The Ministry for Irish recommended that the Dáil should sponsor a similar scheme, and finance a further eight scholarships to the value of £50 each to a preparatory training college for eight Gaeltacht residents, 'as a practical step towards the Irishising of Primary Education'.[6] Some of these ideas were to form the basis of an experimental system of preparatory colleges which were set up by the Ministry for Irish in 1920[7] in order to recruit native Irish speakers to primary teaching. The experiment failed, and a further attempt was made in 1921–22, which suffered a similar fate.

So close was the connection between the Gaelic League and the Ministry for Irish, that O'Kelly considered formally recognising the League as a department of the Dáil. The idea was abandoned due to financial considerations as a substantial sum of money had been provided for the teaching of Irish by the British administration. According to the 1917–18 report, the National Board paid a sum exceeding £14,000, in fees alone, for the teaching of Irish that year.[8] The annual budget for the Ministry was £10,000.[9] In the second report of 1921, this practical consideration featured once more, when it commented that 'The Dáil will be well advised in bearing constantly in mind that the alien Estimate for primary Education in Ireland this year exceeds £5,000,000'.[10]

The problem of poor school attendance was identified as the one which posed the most immediate threat to the successful implementation of the language policy. O'Kelly stated with some urgency that 'The Dáil must find a remedy to it'.[11] Another problem which beset the plans of the revivalists was the urgent need for the provision of suitable reading material and textbooks in Irish. The 1920 report rejected the proposal that a generous Dáil subsidy should be given towards the publication of standard works in Irish and of popular reading matter. This decision was ill-judged and proved to be short-sighted.[12] Referring to the shortfall in the supply of suitable textbooks for every grade of education, O'Kelly confirmed that 'practically every available writer of Irish is now at work to remedy this want'. He added reassuringly that 'the matter has now assumed a distinctly favourable aspect'.[13]

In both reports he emphasised the great level of public support for the language revival policy, and he was 'glad to be able to report that the language is advancing everywhere'.[14] Even though he believed 'the Church alone could restore and perpetuate the national language if only it so willed', he was happy to confirm that the Dáil department had taken counsel with most of the bishops in the Irish-speaking areas, and that all but two had promised 'their active co-operation in the revival of Irish'.[15]

It was not O'Kelly who took the first 'practical step towards the Irishising of Primary Education',[16] but rather an organisation which strongly supported this ideal – the INTO. They did so on foot of a resolution passed at their annual congress in 1920. They held the First National Programme Conference of Primary Instruction on 6 January 1921, in order 'to frame a programme, or series of programmes, in accordance with Irish ideals and conditions, and due regard being given to local needs and views'.[17]

Invitations to participate in the conference were sent to a select group of individuals and organisations but were only accepted by the Ministry for Irish, the General Council of County Councils, the Gaelic League, the National Labour Executive and the ASTI. As such it was an unrepresentative conference, but nonetheless the report of the conference made a special reference to the Professor of Education from UCD, Fr Timothy Corcoran SJ, who 'placed the benefit of his advice and experience at the disposal of the conference'.

The conference drew up a programme which confined itself to pruning the curriculum. The report recommended that the programme's obligatory subjects should be reduced to Irish, English, mathematics, history and geography (now one subject), needlework for girls (from third standard upwards), singing and drill. This meant the elimination of drawing, elementary science, cookery and laundry, needlework (in lower standards), hygiene and nature study as formal obligatory subjects, and the modification of the programme in history and geography, singing and drill. The status of Irish, both as a school subject and as a medium of instruction, was to be raised. Giving due regard to political sensitivities, it was stated that 'in the case of schools where the majority of the parents of the children object to having either Irish or English taught as an obligatory subject, their wishes should be complied with'.[18]

The most controversial changes were the proposals that Irish should be used as a medium of instruction, and that 'the work of the infant school is to be entirely in Irish', with no teaching of English. In the senior standards, Irish was to be the teaching medium for history, geography, drill and singing, and all songs in the singing class were to be Irish language songs. History was to consist of the study of Irish history only, with one of its chief aims being 'to develop the best traits of the national character, and to inculcate national pride and self-respect'.[19]

The INTO representatives had grave reservations about the policy and about the programme for infants in particular, which they expressed at the time, and which they would repeat again in 1926 and in 1934, when further amendments would be made to the programme. The influential advisor to the conference, Prof. Timothy Corcoran, described posthumously as 'the master builder in education',[20] was generally held responsible for this policy, although it should be noted that his advice was happily received by members of the Gaelic League especially, and won majority support. Professor Corcoran held the view that the infant stage was the ideal one for the purpose of language acquisition, and that the vital years for vernacular usage were those from the age of 3 years onwards, as the child's mind was at its most receptive. He believed that complete immersion in the Irish language would result in oral fluency, regardless of the fact that 90 per cent of these children came from English-speaking homes,[21] and despite the fact that there was no empirical research conducted to support his claim.

An INTO deputation was appointed from the First National Programme Conference to meet with O'Kelly, following the receipt of a resolution passed at a Central Executive Committee (CEC) meeting of the INTO, which stated that teachers who were 'unable to take up or fit themselves for the teaching of Irish, should not be penalised on that account'.

O'Kelly received the deputation and reassured them that their fears were ungrounded. He was prepared to give a guarantee that no undue hardship would be inflicted on any teacher who owing to his special circumstances was unable to fit himself for the teaching of Irish. This promise would be broken within a decade.[22] In April 1922, of the 12,000 lay teachers in national schools, only about 1,100 had bilingual certificates, and a further 2,800 had 'ordinary certificates', which were not regarded as satisfactory indicators of proficiency in Irish.[23] O'Kelly added ominously that teachers as a body should 'realise that they are the servants of the nation, and that the nation who employs and pays them, must have the right to specify the nature of the work they are to do'.[24]

After the split over the Anglo-Irish Treaty, the pro-Treaty government kept in existence a Dáil cabinet in an effort to keep open 'the door to rapprochement with the de Valera wing of the anti-treaty movement'.[25] There were two Ministers for Education in January 1922. Michael Hayes succeeded O'Kelly as Minister in the Dáil, and he had responsibility for intermediate and higher education. Finian Lynch was Minister in the Provisional Government and he had responsibility for primary education. As soon as the Provisional Government was in place, T.J. O'Connell,[26] who had been general secretary of the INTO since 1916, submitted a summary of O'Kelly's guarantee and presented it to Hayes. Hayes passed on this letter to Lynch, who replied to O'Connell on 18 January 1922. He stated that he had read O'Kelly's response to the deputation from the INTO, and that he concurred with the guarantee given.

O'Connell knew only too well that inspectors interpreting this guarantee might not be as sympathetically disposed towards these teachers as the foregoing three ministers for education clearly were.[27]

INTERMEDIATE EDUCATION CONFERENCE

In parallel with the developments in the primary sector, O'Kelly summoned a Conference on Intermediate Education on 22 August 1921 under the authority of Dáil Éireann.[28] The conference was requested to examine 'the position of Intermediate education and lay down a suitable programme, to be introduced in the schools in an independent Ireland'.

It recommended that the study of Ireland, the Irish language and Gaelic culture should be at the centre of the secondary-school curriculum. It proposed that all examination papers should be made available bilingually, except for English, mathematics and science, that the history and geography papers should be such as to make it possible for students to obtain full marks on questions relating to Ireland or directly affecting Ireland, and that for history and historical geography, in which the honours paper only was available, the questions should be set so as to enable a candidate to obtain 50 per cent of the marks allotted to the papers, on answers relating to Ireland or directly affecting Ireland. Prizes of books, medals and cups were to be offered to encourage proficiency in Irish, but there was to be no compulsion on pupils to answer papers in Irish.

Lynch accepted these recommendations in February 1922, with one exception and that was 'that the modern literary group should have Irish a compulsory with English an optional subject'.[29] He requested the intermediate board to issue a circular to schools informing them of the new changes. He was anxious that secondary-school students presenting for the June 1922 examination would have the right to answer the intermediate certificate examination questions in Irish if they so wished.[30] However, only thirty out of the slightly more than 10,000 candidates who took the examination, answered either wholly or partly in Irish.[31]

Following on from the conference, a more specialised Dáil Commission on Secondary Education was established in September 1921. This was more representative than the First National Programme Conference on primary education. In addition to the organisations represented in the earlier conference, the commission included nominated representatives of the universities, the Church managerial organisations, the Christian Brothers and eighteen persons 'of wide experience in education, along with 2 students representing the student bodies of the university colleges of the National University of Ireland'.[32] The commission sat from 24 September 1921 to 7 December 1922. In the absence of O'Kelly, Hayes chaired the proceedings and Fahy acted as secretary. The terms of reference for the commission were 'To draft a programme which would meet the national requirements while allotting its due place to the Irish language'.

Fahy, in opening the proceedings, emphasised the importance which the Ministry attached to the terms of reference and to the view that the schools were the prime agents in the revival of the Irish language. He stated that the ultimate object of the commission was the revival of 'the ancient life of Ireland, as a Gaelic state, Gaelic in language and Gaelic and Christian in its ideals'.[33]

The commission appointed six members to deal with the main curricular areas, and gave them a mandate to outline courses and programmes for each subject. Interestingly, the commission consulted headmasters and teachers and sought their suggestions and opinions on the draft courses, which were dispatched to all secondary schools in December 1921. Its interim report of 10 December was favourably received, and in particular its announcement of the introduction of 'open courses' as opposed to the traditional set texts. The *Irish School Weekly*, the teachers' journal, saw this as a progressive move. It said, 'The reversal of this cast-iron policy cannot begin a moment too soon. It has worked untold injury to many generations of Irish children'.[34]

Professor Corcoran, who was a member of the commission, was described by a fellow member as a 'forceful educationalist' who 'dominated the commission'.[35] He was requested to produce a report on English studies. He did so and his Memorandum on English Studies was adopted with only slight amendments, as the commission's report on English studies.[36] As one of the leading exponents of the language revival policy, Corcoran attempted yet again to lessen the role of English in school courses. He favoured English being made an optional subject in secondary schools. Consequently, the commission recommended that schools eligible for State grants should offer Irish or English. This recommendation was later adopted as government policy.

It also recommended the introduction of two new examinations, a junior leaving certificate and a senior leaving certificate, which was what the Molony Committee had recommended in 1919.[37] For the award of the junior leaving certificate, six subjects were to be required, including Irish or English. In his memorandum, Corcoran put forward a very modest aim for English studies when he claimed that 'Power to write for practical use, is the aim of English studies in Ireland'.[38] His bias against Anglo-Irish literature was reflected in the absence of any Anglo-Irish writer from the list submitted for English studies in the commission's final report. He made no secret of his aversion to this type of literature.[39] He approved of teaching English through translations of European classics as they were emptied of English thought.[40]

The report of this commission was never published. It was forwarded to the Minister, Eoin MacNeill, on 7 December 1922 as a collection of subject committees' reports, outlining 'a policy on the curriculum regarding which there is substantial agreement among the members'.[41] While some of its proposals, such as oral examinations in Irish, were omitted, other recommendations formed the basis of the programme for secondary schools which came into operation on 1 August 1924.

John J. O'Kelly commenced the language revival policy using the schools and teachers as the prime agents of that revival. He did so as the War of Independence raged and as Irish cultural nationalism flourished. His colleagues in the Gaelic League warmly welcomed it, the Catholic Church approved of it, as did the majority of the Irish public, and the minority who did not, remained silent.

The INTO were to the fore in initiating and promoting the national programme, while Professor Timothy Corcoran, as academic advisor, was its chief architect.

How O'Kelly set about achieving his objective does not stand up to scrutiny. He did not tackle the school attendance problem, and he rejected a proposal that the Dáil should subsidise the publication of popular Irish literature. He was also over-optimistic in his assessment of the shortfall in the supply of textbooks, as he claimed that the matter was under control.

His dedication to the revival policy cannot be disputed as he supported the First National Programme Conference and summoned the Conference on Intermediate Education. He made two attempts to introduce preparatory colleges, and while both were unsuccessful, they provided the inspiration for the preparatory colleges which were introduced in 1926.

Notes

1   O'Kelly was familiarly known as 'Sceilg', having been born on Valentia Island, County Kerry, facing Sceilg Mhicil.

2   *Dáil Éireann Minutes of Proceedings of the first Dáil of the Republic of Ireland 1920-21*, 17 September 1920, p.277; 11 March 1921, p.265.

3   Report of Aireacht na Gaedhilge, June 1920.

4   Report of Ministry of the National Language, August 1921.

5   NLI Ms. 9798 Gaelic League Education Programme.

6   Report of Aireacht na Gaedhilge, p.2.

7   Valerie Jones, *A Gaelic Experiment: The Preparatory System 1926-1961* (Dublin, 2006), p.8.

8   The National Board allowed Irish to be taught for fees outside school hours from 1879.

9   Report of Aireacht na Gaedhilge, p.3.

10 Report of Ministry of the National Language, p.9.

11 Ibid., p.1.

12 Report of Aireacht na Gaedhilge, p.3.

13 Report of Ministry of the National Language, p.5.

14 Ibid., p.8.

15 Ibid., pp.1–3.

16 Report of Aireacht na Gaedhilge, p.2.

17 National Programme of Primary Instruction: The National Programme Conference (Dublin, 1922), p.3.

18 Ibid., p. 4.

19 Ibid., p.5.

20 Joseph O'Neill, 'Prof. T. Corcoran – the educationist' in *Studies*, 32 (1943), p.158.

21 Brian Ó Cúiv, 'Education and language' in D. Williams (ed.) *The Irish Struggle 1916-1926* (London, 1966), p.162.

22 *Irish School Weekly*, 28 January 1922, p.77.

23 Report of the Department of Education 1924-25, p.21.

24 Op. cit., p.77.

25 D.H. Akenson, *A Mirror to Kathleen's Face: Education in Independent Ireland* (Dublin, 1975), p.27.

26 T.J. O'Connell was general secretary of the INTO from 1916 to 1948. He was leader of the Labour Party from 1927 to 1932. He was an effective opposition spokesman on education from 1922 to 1932.

27 *Irish School Weekly*, 28 January 1922, p.77.

28 *Irish School Weekly*, 1 October 1921, p.104.

29 Ibid.; Coolahan, *Irish Education: Its History and Structure.* (Dublin, 1981), p.75.

30 *Times Educational Supplement*, 14 February 1922.

31 Department of Education, Report of the Council of Education: The Curriculum of the Secondary School 1962, p.62.

32 The NUI was established under the Universities' Act of 1908, and had three constituent colleges: UCD, UCG and UCC.

33 *Times Educational Supplement*, 1 October 1921.

34 *Irish School Weekly*, 10 December 1921.

35 Joe O'Connor, 'The teaching of Irish testament of a pioneer' in *Capuchin Annual* (1949), p.209.

36 John Coolahan, 'The secondary-school curriculum experiment 1924-42: the case of English' in Vincent Greaney and Brendan Molloy (eds) *Dimensions in Reading* (Dublin, 1986), p.47.

37 This was one of two committees set up in 1918, the other one was the Killanin Committee on primary education. The Molony Committee (Vice-Regal Committee) was set up to consider the problems of the intermediate sector. The proposals from both committees were included in the MacPherson Education Bill of 1919.

38 Ibid.

39 Revd T. Corcoran, 'Education through Anglo-Irish literature' in *Irish Monthly*, 51 (1923), p.242.

40 Revd T. Corcoran, 'How English may be taught without anglicising' in *Irish Monthly*, 51 (1923), p.269.

41 Dáil Commission on Secondary Education: Subject Committee Reports (unpublished), quoted in Coolahan, *Irish Education*, p.75.

3

Michael Hayes and Finian Lynch (1922): 'to teach the teachers Irish overnight'

But in Ireland in 1922 there was no State and no organised forces. The Provisional Government was simply eight young men in the City Hall standing amidst the ruin of one administration with the foundations of another not yet laid, and with wild men screaming through the keyhole.[1]

Following the departure of O'Kelly from the Dáil, two Ministers were appointed to replace him, namely Michael Hayes (1889–1976) representing the Dáil, and Finian Lynch (1889–1966) representing the Provisional Government.

Amid the growing excitement that accompanied the handover of power from the British Government to the Dáil in February 1922, there was simmering unrest among the ranks of the secondary-school teachers. On 24 February, a deputation from the sub-committee of the Conference of Intermediate Teachers met Hayes. They requested increased grants for secondary education and an overdue pay increase for secondary teachers. The teachers were unfortunate insofar as the MacPherson Education Bill had included provision for their salaries and pensions, but the government decided to link improvements in teacher salaries to the successful advancement of the Education Bill.[2]

As secondary schools were mainly privately owned, a salary was paid to them by their employers who were either Christian Brothers, nuns, or in the case of the minority churches, clergymen or laymen. In 1920 a strike was called by the Cork branch of the ASTI, a month before the June examinations, and just as the Catholic Church was winning the campaign against the MacPherson Education Bill.

Satisfactory terms were negotiated between the Catholic Headmasters' Association (CHA) and the ASTI, and between the Christian Brothers and the ASTI, on 29 May 1920.[3]

Shortly afterwards, 600 members of the INTO occupied the offices of the national education commissioners, and they won an interim salary award, to be paid before 30 July rather than September.[4] The ASTI failed to obtain their interim grant, as 'the Government, in view of the impending political changes refused to discuss it'. On this occasion, the deputation got a promise from Hayes that the interim grant would be paid, and he hoped to have the amount at least doubled.[5] In fact, the ASTI had to wait until February 1925 for the introduction of a State incremental salary scheme, which was backdated to September 1924.[6]

DISBANDMENT OF THE NATIONAL BOARD

As soon as the report of the First National Programme Conference had been accepted, Lynch issued Public Notice No. 4. He did so on the day the Irish Free State took over responsibility for national education. He ordered that from the following St Patrick's Day, Irish was to be taught or used as a medium of instruction, for not less than 1 hour each day in all schools where there was a teacher competent to teach it. The new programme came into operation for all national schools on 1 April 1922,[7] despite the inordinate number of teachers who were unqualified, and the fact that less than half of the inspectorate were proficient in Irish.[8]

The *Irish School Weekly* of 11 February hailed the news of the appointment of a new chief executive officer, Pádraic Ó Brolcháin, as 'one of the most sensational occurrences in Irish education circles for many years'. Ó Brolcháin informed the commissioners of national education of the government's intention to disband them. In so doing he set out the new direction for Irish education policy, which was to strengthen 'the national fibre by giving the language, history, music and tradition of Ireland their natural place in the life of Irish schools'.[9]

Another important appointment was that of Joseph O'Neill[10] as secretary of the department, with effect from 1 May 1923. On 8 June he was one of two new commissioners to be given responsibility for intermediate education; the second one was Proinnsias Ó Dubhthaigh.

O'Connell, as general secretary of the INTO, rejoiced at the demise of the 'authoritarian national board'. It was disbanded on the orders of Lynch, a man who had been dismissed by the board for participating in the Easter Rising.[11] O'Connell was overwhelmed by the realisation that 'One word of the Minister of Education unmade it'.[12]

The INTO received a morale boost when addresses were delivered by the two Ministers at their 1922 congress. Hayes informed the delegates that 'It was through the teachers and the schools that the ideal of a Gaelic Ireland was to be attained, and real progress educationally in Ireland could only proceed along Gaelic lines'. Lynch reassured them that 'They would expect of the inspectorate friendly co-operation with the teachers'. These words were ironic in light of subsequent events.[13]

Issues discussed at the congress included a call for training colleges to be affiliated to the universities, and for the introduction of a Compulsory School Attendance Act.[14] A resolution was passed unanimously, calling upon the government to set up a representative commission of inquiry into Irish education. Another resolution was passed calling for a conference to be convened between the educational authorities and representatives of the INTO, to devise an educationally efficient and acceptable system of inspection.[15]

The *Freeman's Journal* of 22 April conveyed a sense of national pride when it reported that 'The 1922 Congress, in truth, bore the impress of an emancipated teaching profession'. It added that if anyone wanted evidence of the changes for the better that the peace Treaty brought to Ireland, he could have found it at the Teachers' Congress of April 1922.[16]

In his address to the teachers, Lynch gave details of the summer courses which would be provided to assist them to gain fluency in the Irish language. He said that it was the government's intention to close the schools for 3 months to allow teachers to attend these courses. Plans to do so came to fruition and O'Neill reported that all national schools had been closed for 3 months from 30 June to 25 September 1922, to allow teachers to attend Irish courses. The courses cost about £76,000, but they were attended by approximately 12,000 teachers and students, despite the unsettled conditions which prevailed in the country at the time.[17] An instructor on the summer courses recalled the 'extravagantly courageous decision' the Ministry took 'to teach the teachers Irish overnight', and how patriotic teachers sacrificed their 'long summer holidays of 1922 … to the forlorn hope of learning a difficult language before the schools reopened'.[18]

According to an ASTI survey, 33 per cent of secondary teachers had no knowledge of the Irish language.[19] In July 1922, as the Civil War raged, a series of university courses for secondary teachers was given through the medium of Irish, on lines suggested by the Gaelic League in its Education Programme 1918–19.[20] The ASTI was not satisfied with either the location of the courses or with the quality of some of them, so it provided its own in-service courses for teachers. It did so each summer from 1926 to 1929, when the department stopped subsidising them.[21]

In the training colleges, the month of June was devoted to study of the Irish language, literature and literary history.[22] Special courses in Irish were also held for the inspection and organising staffs in the department. Eight senior inspectors out of fourteen transferred to the North of Ireland, following the reorganisation of the primary inspectorate by Ó Brolcháin. Inspectors with no knowledge of Irish were offered immersion courses or lengthy spells in the Gaeltacht, those with a fine command of the language were promoted, and new inspectors were recruited who had a good working knowledge of Irish.[23]

At the First National Programme Conference, representatives of the INTO voiced the opinion that the proposal that Irish should be the medium of instruction for infants was both impracticable and premature.[24] This soon proved to be the case and teachers' initial enthusiasm for the policy waned as they struggled to implement it. Some believed that 'a decline of interest had set in as a result of the Civil War and through the discovery that Irish was a difficult language to learn'.[25] Others believed that the language policy was flawed as 'English had more to offer' and Irish had 'no international value outside philology'.[26]

The INTO adopted a resolution in March 1924 to reconvene the National Programme Conference. The teachers had understood that the new programme was to be an ideal which could be achieved, at the soonest in 5 years' time.[27] It now seemed to them that the principle, originally agreed to by the Education Ministry, of using Irish as a medium of instruction only when the pupils were able to benefit from it, and the teachers were competent to teach through it, was an 'amiable fiction' which quickly vanished as inspectors placed undue pressure on teachers in their missionary zeal to revive the language.[28]

Disillusionment was also setting in at the failure of the government to set in train the promised Compulsory School Attendance Bill. The president of the INTO, John Harbison, had called on the Ministry to do so in April 1922, as only 69 per cent of the country's children were in daily attendance at school, compared to 90 per cent in Scotland and 85 per cent in England.[29] No action was taken, so once again the INTO took the initiative.

An INTO deputation to the Minister for Education in the Irish Free State Government, Eoin MacNeill, pressed him to make the Ministry responsible for the conference.[30] MacNeill agreed to this and a notice convening the Second National Programme Conference was published in June 1925.

The Second National Programme Conference was given a narrow brief, which was to consider 'The suitability of the National Programme of Primary Instruction ... and to make any recommendations ... as regards any alterations which may seem desirable'.

The membership of the conference, which was chaired by Fr Lambert McKenna SJ, was more representative than the First Conference. Catholic and Protestant school managers were represented, as were the INTO, the County Councils and the Gaelic League, along with eleven nominees of the Minister and university representatives. The conference's many recommendations commenced with a statement on the centrality of religious instruction in the school curriculum.[31]

Their report of 1926 endorsed the programme of 1922. The principle of teaching infants through the medium of Irish was re-affirmed but one modest change was allowed – English could be used before 10.30 a.m. each morning and after 2 p.m. Members of the conference confirmed that they were influenced by Professor Corcoran from whom 'they received authoritative evidence'. Corcoran remained a firm believer in teaching infants through the medium of Irish.

The report recommended two courses in Irish, a higher and a lower course for senior classes during the transition period. Those who adopted the alternative lower course in Irish and the higher course in English, were expected to advance gradually towards the higher course in Irish. The higher course was to be taught only in those schools where the teachers were fluent in the Irish language.

To allow for the demands of teaching through Irish, the requirements in subjects such as mathematics, history and geography were reduced. Algebra and geometry were made optional in all one-teacher schools, and in all classes taught by women. Rural science was added for certain sizes of school, as a compulsory subject.[32] This report was accepted as the official departmental policy in May 1926 by John Marcus O'Sullivan as Minister for Education.

Michael Hayes and Finian Lynch could not have achieved this as the country was plunged into a brutal Civil War, in which Lynch played a commanding role. During their brief period in office, they raised the morale of teachers with their infectious enthusiasm for the language policy. It was a time when national pride had been restored following the handover of power by the British Government. The demands of Public Notice No. 4 and the national programme placed a great burden on teachers, but Hayes and Lynch provided Irish courses for them and closed the schools to allow them to attend. Patriotic teachers rose to the challenge as they attempted to learn a difficult language before the schools re-opened.

Idealism and over-optimism clouded the judgment of the two 33-year-old Ministers, who should have taken steps, however tentative, to initiate a School Attendance Act. They would have left an important legacy to Irish education had they set up an education inquiry, as the INTO had called on them to do at their annual congress in April 1922, but in the circumstances prevailing at the time, perhaps that was expecting too much.

Notes

1 Tom Garvin, *1922: The Birth of Irish Democracy* (Dublin, 1996), p.94.

2 *Hansard's Parliamentary Debates*, vol. 123, col. 1016, 22 December 1919.

3 John Coolahan, 'The ASTI and the secondary teachers strike of 1920' in *Saothar* 10 (Dublin, 1984), pp.43–59.

4 *Freeman's Journal*, 14 July 1920.

5 *Irish School Weekly*, 4 March 1922, pp.197–8.

6 Coolahan, 'The ASTI and the secondary teachers strike of 1920', p.54.

7 NAI *S7801C* Irish language development in the schools.

8 John Coolahan and Patrick F. O'Donovan, *A History of Ireland's School Inspectorate 1831-2008* (Dublin, 2009), p.113.

9 *Irish School Weekly*, 11 February 1922, p.127

10 O'Neill was an experienced inspector at both first and second levels of the education system.

11 Ibid., p.126.

12 Ibid., p.131.

13 *Freeman's Journal*, 19 April 1922.

14 Ibid.

15 *Freeman's Journal*, 21 April 1922.

16 *Freeman's Journal*, 22 April 1922.

17 *Statistics Relating to National Education in Saorstát for the Year 1922-23* (Dublin, 1925), p.13.

18 O'Connor, 'The teaching of Irish testament of a pioneer' in *Capuchin Annual* (1949), p.210.

19 *Irish School Weekly*, 27 May 1922, p.488.

20 Brian Ó Cuív, 'Education and language' in *The Irish Struggle*, p.164.

21 John Coolahan, *The ASTI and Post-Primary Education in Ireland 1909-1984* (Dublin, 1984), p.72.

22 *Statistics Relating to National Education in Saorstát for the Year 1922-23*, p.13.

23 Séamus Ó Buachalla, *Education Policy in Twentieth-Century Ireland* (Dublin, 1988), p.347.

24 T.J. O'Connell, *History of the INTO*, p.347.

25 León Ó Broin, *Just Like Yesterday: An Autobiography* (Dublin, 1986), p.67.

26 Ibid., p.66. This was the view of P.S. O'Hegarty, secretary of the Department of Posts and Telegraphs in 1922.

27 O'Connell, *History of the INTO*, pp.348–551; National Programme of Primary Instruction, pp.30–2; *Irish School Weekly*, 10 January 1925.

28 O'Connell, *History of the INTO*, pp.354–5.

29 *Freeman's Journal*, 21 April 1922.

30 Op. cit., p.355.

31 Report and programme of the Second National Programme Conference 1925-26 (Dublin, 1926), p.2.

32 Ibid., p.7.

4

Eoin MacNeill (1922–25): '... wholly detached from practical affairs, living in the air as it were'

I have seldom seen a man more unfitted for action, less fit to lead others in a difficult crisis and less wise in his judgement of men ... Eoin MacNeill is meant for a scholar's life and that alone.[1]

Eoin MacNeill (1867–1945) replaced Michael Hayes as Minister for Education in the Dáil for 10 days, before becoming the first Minister for Education in the Irish Free State Government on 9 September 1922. He had written extensively on the subject of education and had been centrally involved in the educational work of the Gaelic League.[2]

The president of the Executive Council, W.T. Cosgrave,[3] selected MacNeill as Minister, possibly because of his scholarly credentials as Professor of Early and Medieval History at UCD (1909) and possibly because of his acceptability to the Catholic Church's high-ranking members. De Valera recognised the importance of this connection when he commented, 'Don't forget that the clergy are with MacNeill and they are a powerful force'.[4] The Catholic Church or indeed the minority churches had nothing to fear from MacNeill, a Minister who had 'a strong horror of state-made education'.[5]

Understandably, the Catholic Church found the idea of a State education system abhorrent and unpalatable, as it 'had gone through centuries of unpleasant relations with the Irish Government before Independence'. Not only that, but the Catholic Church was well aware of the pressures which the modern State had brought to bear on the Church in certain continental countries.[6]

MacNeill and members of the government had a tendency to quote from papal encyclicals in support of education policy. In the 1920s, education policy was influenced by the papal encyclical of Pope Leo XIII, *Rerum Novarum*, 1891, which 'set the limits of State supervision of education … that it must not go further than what is required, for the remedying of evils and the avoidance of dangers'.[7]

MacNeill and his successor, O'Sullivan, won the confidence and loyalty of the minority churches, who provided strong leadership when they encouraged their followers to co-operate with the new authorities. Archbishop John Allen Fitzgerald Gregg exhorted members of the Church of Ireland 'to co-operate with the new Government and to stop clinging to a way of life that had gone forever'.[8]

The General Assembly urged Presbyterians in the South 'to co-operate whole-heartedly with their Roman Catholic fellow-countrymen in the best interests of their beloved land'. In 1924 the Revd A. W. Neill, Moderator of the Synod of Dublin, appealed to Presbyterians in the Free State to 'concentrate on the business of building up our country's fortunes on sound lines'.[9]

The Jewish community also supported the government, and when one of its representatives approached O'Sullivan for financial assistance to build a new Jewish school in Dublin, the government contributed one-third of the cost of the building.[10] Under Article 8 of the 1922 Constitution, 'all recognised forms of worship' were 'placed on the same level, on grounds of fairness and prudence'. Article 10 of the Constitution entitled all school-going children 'to a free elementary education'.

Each of the churches welcomed denominational education, and harmony reigned between Church and State in Ireland in the field of education.[11] The Protestant schools played a major role 'in easing the very considerable strains … experienced by the Protestant community in the Free State'. The schools, to a certain extent, provided 'an ark to shelter Protestant children from the prevailing winds of cultural change that swept across the education system'.[12]

H. Kingsmill Moore, a Church of Ireland clergyman and principal of the Church of Ireland Training College (CITC), recalled a meeting which he, Archbishop Gregg and the president of the Methodist Church had with MacNeill during the Civil War. They entered wire cages where they 'found our Minister safe beneath the level of the ground'.[13] The purpose of the meeting was to lodge an objection to a situation 'in which Protestant children were being compelled to study Irish books written for Roman Catholic pupils'. Moore was appreciative of MacNeill's understanding of their predicament and added that 'On all occasions we have been treated with consideration, kindness and respect'.[14]

In October 1925, a further Protestant deputation, consisting of Moore, Gregg and the Bishop of Cashel, were the recipients of a generous offer by MacNeill of

a separate Protestant preparatory college. The function of the proposed preparatory colleges was to provide 'a thoroughly sound secondary education' in an
'atmosphere of Gaelic speech and tradition' to native Irish speakers and fluent
Irish speakers who wished to become teachers.[15] The deputation appreciated
'the generosity and the potentialities of the offer'.[16]

The preparatory colleges were opened in 1926, but in 1923 the numbers in the
CITC plummeted from 135 in 1922 to 98 by December 1923. This was due partly
to the loss of entrants from the North of Ireland as a result of the political parti-
tioning of the country, but it was also due to the Irish language requirement which
'for those whose mother-tongue was English made a four or five years' study of
the language necessary'. MacNeill came to their rescue by authorising a course of
not more than 1 year's study. The *Times Educational Supplement* concluded that this
was 'a concession which Irish language fanatics would not have made'.[17]

One decision taken by the government after Independence 'was taken as an
unkind move by Northern interests'.[18] This was the decision to close the National
Board's non-denominational training college in Marlborough Street, the majority
of whose students had been Northern Presbyterians. However, the Northern
Ministry of Education had established Stranmillis College in Belfast as a
non-denominational State training college, and 'it was presumed that in future
these students would train at Stranmillis'.[19]

MACNEILL SUPPORTS IRISH POLICY

The general secretary of the Gaelic League had so much confidence in the language
revival policy that he declared in July 1922 that 'there will not be the same necessity
for the teaching of Irish, under the League's auspices'.[20] Consequently, branches of
the Gaelic League declined from 819 in 1922 to 139 branches by 1924.[21]

MacNeill appeared vague on educational policy and was a reluctant supporter
of the language policy. He stated that 'The chief function of Irish education
policy is to conserve and develop Irish nationality'.[22] When he repeated this in the
Dáil,[23] O'Connell asked, 'Is the aim of his Department to make this country an
Irish-speaking country, or is the aim to make it a bi-lingual country?'[24] O'Connell
believed that the Minister seemed 'to be from his writings and statements, wholly
detached from practical affairs, living in the air as it were'.[25]

O'Neill as secretary was well placed to confirm that the policy aimed 'to redress
the balance and to make compensation' for the neglect of Irish culture within
the educational system in the past.[26] MacNeill was opposed to compulsory Irish,
but he was prepared to support the implementation of a policy he had inherited.

He was convinced that the Irish language could not be revived by relying on the schools alone to do so.[27] As far as he was concerned, attempting to do so was about as useful as attempting to put wooden legs on hens.[28]

MacNeill was also opposed to compulsion with regard to school attendance, but the Dáil adopted a resolution in November 1922 that 'the Compulsory Attendance Act should be amended'. O'Connell reminded MacNeill of this, and added that 'the scandal of attendance or want of attendance goes on'.[29]

The opposition parties repeatedly reminded MacNeill of several deficiencies in the education system as they proffered advice to him. While O'Connell requested action on the School Attendance Bill again in 1924, he was aware of the primitive conditions to which he was condemning poor, hungry children. He advised MacNeill to carry out a survey of school buildings and 'to make good the necessary accommodation'.[30] MacNeill attributed the situation 'to a grievous neglect of the public interest in the past'.[31] Thomas Johnson, leader of the Labour Party, suggested that MacNeill could possibly 'find means of raising a fund by the issue of Bonds' to provide school accommodation.[32]

O'Connell brought the question of school maintenance to MacNeill's attention, and the fact that the State grant of £2 per school was totally inadequate. He referred also to the sensitive issue of managerial neglect of school maintenance, to which MacNeill replied, 'The facts are exactly as stated by Deputy O'Connell'.[33]

In 1923 O'Connell urged MacNeill to 'go in for a bold policy of the amalgamation of schools'.[34] Two years later he called again for amalgamation 'as one direction in which he could secure economy and efficiency at the same time'.[35] He asked MacNeill what his policy was on amalgamation, only to be told that it was up to those 'who are responsible for the moral guidance of the community' to decide.[36]

There was ample evidence of poor educational planning. Many officials in the department lacked experience in school management, and had won their promotion to the top posts as a reward for being 'fervent exponents of the Gaelicisation policy'.[37] There was an over-supply of teachers for national schools in the 1920s,[38] yet O'Connell had to call on MacNeill in July 1924 not to appoint any more untrained teachers.[39] No report had been issued by the department since the foundation of the new State, and when reports were eventually published, they were 'two years in arrears'.[40]

O'Connell brought the concerns of teachers to MacNeill's attention, in particular with regard to the rating system of inspection. He pointed out that it was part of the inspector's duty to examine every subject that was taught. The teacher's annual increment was dependent on whether the report for a particular subject was marked 'good' or 'very good'. O'Connell's contention was that a general report would suffice, stating whether the teacher's work was satisfactory or very satisfactory.[41] MacNeill responded, 'I have not sufficient experience to base judgment on that question of the classification of teaching'.[42]

O'Connell had repeatedly requested that national school teachers should have the benefit of a university education.[43] In December 1922, MacNeill suggested that the teaching bodies and the universities should arrange an appropriate scheme. A year later the teaching bodies and the universities 'came to an agreement about a scheme', and the matter was referred to MacNeill. No action was taken[44] by the time MacNeill left office, even though the Labour Party had called for university education for teachers in its 1925 policy document on education.[45]

In contrast, students at the CITC had gained entrance to TCD as registered students, in September 1921. This entitlement was secured when the National Board and the Treasury supported the scheme put forward by the governors of the CITC for affiliation to the university.[46]

Dissatisfaction with the education system came to the fore in the Dáil in July 1924, with Professor Thrift[47] of TCD stating that 'The whole country is badly educated both in primary and secondary education'. He asked, 'Will the Ministry undertake to inquire into this enormously important question?' and added 'one thing that is wanted above all others is a system of sound primary education backed up by a system of applied education for use in ordinary life'.[48]

Despite the multiplicity of problems bedevilling the education system, MacNeill steadfastly refused to set up an education inquiry or a council of education. He did not consider that it was an opportune time to do so. He considered that the opinions expressed in the Dáil should be 'allowed to ferment for a short time'.[49]

CHANGES IN THE ADMINISTRATION OF IRISH EDUCATION

The *Irish Catholic* described the state of the country in 1924 as being in 'a pathological crisis' as the nation was 'convalescing from the fever and prostration of two wars'.[50] The Civil War ended on 30 April 1923, and W.T. Cosgrave's government had the unenviable task of administering a country in turmoil. As one commentator remarked, 'There was little use for idealism and less scope for utopianism in the Irish Free State of 1923'.[51]

MacNeill acknowledged as much when he said that the cost of the civil war, 'when the country was losing £1 million per week', prevented the government from making the improvements in the education system it undoubtedly would have made.[52] The Minister for Finance had to make some drastic cutbacks in public expenditure, including reducing primary teachers' salaries by 10 per cent in 1923, and lowering the old age pension by a shilling.

By 1924, however, legislation was prepared which would see changes in the administration of Irish education, and in the public examinations and curriculum of intermediate schools. Professor Mary Daly described the Irish education system before Independence as consisting of 'Three separate and uncoordinated elements – a system of national schools normally denominational ... an undeveloped, classically-orientated secondary system ... and the two universities accessible only to a few'.[53] In fact, there were three different types of schools – primary, secondary and technical – and they were all brought under the umbrella of the Department of Education on 1 June 1924. This occurred following the passing of the Ministers and Secretaries Act which established the Department of Education and reorganised the government into eleven different departments. In the Act, the former national schools were called 'primary schools' and the former intermediate schools became 'secondary schools'.

However, the establishment of the department did not result in a unified system because 'the three systems remained distinct and administratively incompatible entities'.[54] The department acknowledged that it had limited influence over the privately owned secondary schools. It exercised 'a certain amount of supervision through its powers to make grants to schools, as a result of ... inspections'.[55] But it exerted its power through the programmes for public examination, and through regulations concerning the qualifications of teachers who would receive State salary awards.[56]

In 1924 the government introduced a most significant alteration to Irish educational practice with the abolition of the system of allocating grants to secondary schools according to their pupils' examination results, known as payment-by-results. This system was replaced by a capitation grant for pupils who followed an approved course of study and had 130 attendances per annum. The abolition of the results fees removed one form of pressure from secondary teachers, but it was replaced by a different pressure, that of the public examinations, the results of which were published by the department.

Fr Seán Ó Catháin SJ regarded this as a 'grievous error' as it led to 'a deplorable spirit of rivalry ... schools advertised their annual successes as if they were purely commercial concerns'.[57] The practice of publishing the names of the schools was abandoned after some years, but the spirit of rivalry it generated lingered on.[58] Managers of schools were required to hold entrance examinations at the beginning of each school year, which students had to pass in order to become eligible for capitation grants. The government also began to provide increments to the salaries of teachers in recognised schools. Teachers were entitled to receive a salary of not less than £200 in the case of men, and £180 in the case of women, to be paid by the schools. The department would pay State increments based on the length of teachers' approved teaching service.[59]

In June 1924, the Intermediate Education (Amendment) Act was passed which brought about changes in the examination system and the programmes of instruction. Under the new system, the three grades of results examination were abolished to be replaced by two certificate examinations – the intermediate and the leaving certificates. The junior course covered 3 or 4 years and concluded with the intermediate certificate examination at about age 16, and the senior course covered an additional 2 years and led to the leaving certificate examination, which was taken at about age 18.[60]

Speaking in the Dáil on the new secondary programme, Cosgrave exulted in the fact that 'Rigidity has been replaced by freedom. The old programmes, narrow and formal … have been superseded by thoroughly modern and elastic programmes'.[61] A progressive feature of the new programmes was the introduction of 'open courses', whereby the department prescribed the general content for each subject, but allowed schools the freedom to submit for approval the courses and textbooks which they intended to use. In 1912 Pádraic Pearse had identified the practice of using set texts as being 'the direct contrary of the root idea involved in education'.[62]

Cosgrave suggested that some second-level education for all ought to be considered.[63] In the meantime, a number of scholarships were to be awarded on the results of the intermediate certificate examination, to the value of £40 per annum, tenable for 2 years. This would enable the holder to complete the secondary course up to the leaving certificate examination. In 1925 examinations were held in twenty-three counties or county boroughs, which was an increase of four on the 1924 numbers. Some 1,155 candidates sat the examination, but only 230 scholarships were awarded. Proficiency in Irish was essential for the award of a scholarship. The amount offered for the scholarships was generous for the time, but it remained static for the next 30 years or more.[64]

MACNEILL'S 'CLEAR EDUCATIONAL HIGHWAY'

MacNeill was the Southern government's representative on the Boundary Commission which had been set up to partition Ireland. He served on the commission from July 1923 until November 1925. His absences from the Dáil begged the question from O'Connell as to 'whether the Government are really taking this question of education seriously?'[65] Few would dispute that MacNeill's secretary 'could be trusted fully to implement policies, the validity of which he fully accepted'.[66]

When MacNeill outlined the government's education policy in 1925, he claimed that the various branches of the department were now fully coordinated, and that 'Almost at the root of that unification has been the joining together of the inspectorates of the different Departments'.[67] The reality was that as late as 1946, the department of Finance was still urging the Department of Education to unify the three inspectorates.[68] This unification of the inspectorates did not in fact occur until the early 1990s.[69]

He brought glad tidings with the announcement that the much-anticipated Compulsory School Attendance Bill 'will very shortly be presented to you'.[70] One major obstacle to the implementation of the language policy was about to be removed, but others remained, such as the large numbers of untrained teachers and the outdated system of recruitment to teacher training colleges.

Progress had been made with regard to reform of initial teacher training programmes and a new programme was adopted in 1924–25.[71] The department also set up a Committee on Recruitment in 1924 to improve the system of training and the system of recruitment to training colleges, but above all it aimed to determine how the colleges could be supplied with native speakers from the Gaeltacht in order to gaelicise the colleges.[72]

Professor Corcoran made a submission to the committee, in which he supported the establishment of preparatory colleges. He advised that half the entrance scholarships each year should be reserved for native Irish speakers, and that they should be encouraged to compete for the rest. In 1923, in an article entitled 'The Native Speaker as Teacher', he suggested that native speakers should be recruited as teachers, because 'with few exceptions girls who had had a full primary education in Irish are natural teachers'.[73]

Ó Brolcháin gave evidence before the Gaeltacht Commission on 17 April 1925, in which he confirmed that 30 per cent of teachers teaching in Gaeltacht areas were unqualified to teach through the medium of Irish.[74] The department was therefore aware of the urgency of the situation, and in March 1925 the Committee on Recruitment recommended in its interim report, the abolition of the monitorial system, a revision of the pupil–teacher scheme[75] and the establishment of preparatory colleges.

MacNeill proceeded to elaborate on the aim of the department, which was 'to provide a clear educational highway from the most elementary to the most advanced stages of education'.[76] He announced the introduction of a primary leaving certificate examination which would form the means of entrance to post-primary education. This was deemed necessary because of evidence of falling educational standards.[77]

The primary certificate examination was introduced on a voluntary basis in 1928–29. The link between first and second-level education was thereby reinforced.

A further measure, introduced in 1924, strengthened those links when permission was 'given to good primary schools to proceed at the end of the primary stage to give secondary education'.[78]

Primary schools which offered the secondary-school curriculum were known as 'secondary tops'. Some 156 students from these schools were admitted to the secondary certificate examinations in June 1925.[79] The 'secondary tops' were appreciated by parents who could not afford to send their children to fee-paying secondary schools. As late as 1944, there were about 20,800 pupils in the age range 14–16 in primary schools, approximately 4,000 of whom were in 'secondary tops'.[80] MacNeill had no plans to provide free secondary education for all.[81]

He did not in fact provide 'a clear educational highway' either, because 'the path outlined did not indicate, except in the vaguest sense, a structurally integrated education system'.[82] While Cosgrave hailed changes made in secondary education as revolutionary, he said that MacNeill would not take credit for these because he had 'merely put into operation educational reforms that were urged on the British Government year after year by the old Intermediate Board'.[83]

Ernest Blythe, the Minister for Finance (1923–32), was a leading exponent of the language-revival policy through the schools and in the public service. He was the senior cabinet member who assumed responsibility for the Irish language education policy.[84]

In order to encourage secondary schools to use Irish as a medium of instruction, the department recognised three types of secondary school, which were classified and grant-aided according to language usage. These were Grade A, Grade B (which became sub-divided into B1 and B2) and Grade C. Irish was to be the official language in Grade A schools, and all subjects other than English were to be taught through the medium of Irish. Irish was also to be the official language of Grade B schools, and was to be used as a medium of instruction for some subjects. In Grade C schools, Irish was just taught as a school subject. An extra grant of 25 per cent based on capitation was paid to Grade A schools, while Grade B schools got an extra financial incentive depending on the extent of teaching through the medium of Irish.

Incentives were offered to students to use Irish when answering examination papers through the awarding of bonus marks for those who did so in specific subjects. A student who answered papers, other than mathematics or art, through the medium of Irish was given a bonus of 10 per cent, and an extra 5 per cent could be obtained in the mathematics papers.

In the higher education sector, the government established a Committee on University Education in November 1925, but it was mainly through Blythe's direct involvement that legislation and funding were provided to enable UCG to develop higher education in Irish.[85]

Eoin MacNeill was a reluctant Minister who fulfilled his patriotic duty, but it was 'with a sincere sigh of relief that he returned in 1925 to the congenial atmosphere of the university'.[86] He had an aversion to secularised 'State-made' education, and he developed cordial relations between Church and State in the field of education, which was not the case in other countries at this time. He made a number of significant concessions to the schools of the minority churches to assist them in implementing the language policy.

He disapproved of the language policy, but felt honour bound to implement it. He also had a distaste for compulsion, and for that reason was unenthusiastic about introducing a Compulsory School Attendance Bill, but he did his duty and removed one of the biggest obstacles to the revival efforts. The policy was advanced again when measures were taken to reform the system of recruitment to the training colleges, when a new programme was introduced, and when summer courses were continued. MacNeill, who was a founding member of the Gaelic League, had no compunction about allowing preferential treatment to be shown to schools and students who embraced the Irish challenge.

Following the establishment of the Department of Education, he claimed to have united first- and second-level schools under one umbrella, into a coordinated system, by joining the inspectorates together. He further claimed to have provided students with a 'clear educational highway', but there was no evidence to support either claim. Changes to the examination structure had been recommended in 1919, and while the abolition of payment-by-results and the introduction of open courses were welcome, the decision to publish examination results was a retrograde step which had a deleterious effect on secondary education for many decades to follow.

MacNeill was not in a position to offer free secondary education, but he allowed intermediate scholarships, which were few in number, and he permitted the use of 'secondary tops', which proved to be very popular. When there was growing evidence of falling educational standards, he floated the concept of a primary leaving certificate, something which was introduced in 1927–28.

His ministry was undermined by his long absences from the Dáil, as it was obvious from his vague answers to parliamentary questions that he did not have mastery of his brief. At one stage in the Dáil, O'Connell accused him of 'living in the air as it were'. When O'Connell and Professor Thrift requested him to set up an education inquiry, they must have done so more in hope than in expectation that anything would happen.

Eoin MacNeill's ministerial legacy to Irish education consisted of the passing of the Ministers and Secretaries Act, the Intermediate Education (Amendment) Act and the School Attendance Bill, together with a range of policies, no doubt prepared by his dedicated officials, which his successor would bring to fruition.

Notes

1 D. Gwynn, *The Life of John Redmond* (London, 1932), p.484.

2 Eoin MacNeill, 'A plea and a plan for the extension of the movement to preserve and spread the Gaelic language in Ireland' in *Irisleabhar na Gaedhilge* (Dublin, 1893), pp.178–9.

3 In January 1923 pro-Treaty deputies formed a new party, Cumann na nGaedheal, under the leadership of W.T. Cosgrave.

4 Robert Brennan, *Allegiance* (Dublin, 1950), p.153.

5 *Dáil Debates*, vol. 2, col. 548, 4 January 1923.

6 Akenson, *A Mirror to Kathleen's Face*, p.102.

7 John Mescal, *Religion in the Irish System of Education* (Dublin, 1957), p.26.

8 George Seavers, *John Allen Fitzgerald Gregg: Archbishop* (Dublin, 1963), p.126.

9 Finlay Holmes, *The Presbyterian Church in Ireland: A Popular History* (Dublin, 2000), p.287.

10 Bernard Shillman, *A Short History of the Jews in Ireland* (Dublin, 1945), p.126.

11 Mescal, *Religion in the Irish System of Education*, pp.24–5.

12 Kenneth Milne, 'The Protestant churches in independent Ireland' in James P. Mackey and Enda McDonagh (eds) *Religion and Politics in Ireland at the Turn of the Millennium: Essays in Honour of Garret FitzGerald on his Seventy-fifth Birthday* (Dublin, 2003), pp.67–71.

13 H. Kingsmill Moore, *Reminiscences and Reflections from Some Sixty Years of Life in Ireland* (London, 1930), pp.286–94, p.288.

14 Ibid.

15 Report of the Department of Education for the school year 1924-25 and the financial and administrative years 1924–26, p.41.

16 Kingsmill Moore, *Reminiscences and Reflections*, p.293.

17 *Times Educational Supplement*, 1 December 1923, p.526.

18 Coolahan, *Irish Education*, p.47.

19 Parkes, *Kildare Place*, p.140.

20 A. Ó Muimhneacháin, *Dóchas agus duanéis scéal Conradh na Gaeilge 1922–1932* (Cork, 1974), p.18.

21 Terence Brown, *Ireland: A Social and Cultural History 1922-1979* (London, 1981), pp.53–4.

22 Eoin MacNeill, 'Irish education policy' in the *Irish Statesman*, 24 October 1925.

23 *Dáil Debates*, vol. 13, col. 187, 11 November 1925.

24 Ibid., cols 208–9.

25 Ibid., col. 195.

26 NAI *S7801* Ó Neill to Cosgrave, 1925.

27 MacNeill, 'A plea and a plan', p.179.

28 Buafaidh said in *An Claidheamh Soluis*, 29 November 1902, p.623. MacNeill wrote, '*Buafaidh siad I ngéar-chúiseacht ar an bhfear fadó a bhi ag iarraidh cosa maide chur faoi na cearca.*'

29 *Dáil Debates*, vol. 3, cols 1351–2, 31 May 1923.

30 *Dáil Debates*, vol. 8, col. 411, 3 July 1924.

31 Ibid., col. 450.

32 *Dáil Debates*, vol. 13, cols 471–6, 17 November 1925.

33 Ibid., col. 544, 18 November 1925.

34 *Dáil Debates*, vol. 3, col. 1352, 31 May 1923.

35 *Dáil Debates*, vol. 13, cols 205–6, 11 November 1925.

36 Ibid., col. 548, 18 November 1925.

37 Jones, *A Gaelic Experiment*, p.26.

38 *Dáil Debates*, vol. 3, col. 1361, 31 May 1923.

39 *Dáil Debates*, vol. 8, col. 412, 3 July, 1924.

40 *Dáil Debates*, vol. 12, col. 800, 11 June 1925.

41 *Dáil Debates*, vol. 8, cols 417–18, 3 July 1924.

42 Ibid., col. 451.

43 *Dáil Debates*, vol. 1, col. 2552, 1 December 1922; vol. 3, col. 1352, 31 May 1923.

44 *Irish School Weekly*, 6 March 1926, p.300; *Dáil Debates*, vol. 1, col. 2576, 1 December 1922.

45 John Coolahan, 'Labour's education policy fifty-years-a-growing' in the *Education Times*, 26 June 1975; Committee of the Irish Labour Party and Trade Union Congress. Labour's policy on education, September 1925.

46 Parkes, *Kildare Place*, p.133.

47 Graduates of the NUI and TCD elected members to the Dáil until 1937, and to the Senate thereafter.

48 *Dáil Debates*, vol. 8, cols 421–2, 3 July 1924.

49 *Dáil Debates*, vol. 8, cols 449–50, 3 July 1924.

50 *Irish Catholic*, 23 February 1924.

51 Patrick Lynch, 'The social revolution that never was' in *The Irish Struggle*, p.53.

52 Arthur Mitchell, *Labour in Irish Politics 1890-1930, the Irish Labour Movement in an Age of Revolution* (Dublin, 1974), 181.

53 Mary E. Daly, *Social and Economic History of Ireland since 1800* (Dublin, 1981), pp.183–4.

54 Akenson, *A Mirror to Kathleen's Face*, p.33.

55 Report of the Department of Education for the school year 1924-25, p.7.

56 Coolahan, *Irish Education*, p.74.

57 Fr Seán Ó Catháin SJ, 'Education in the new Ireland' in Francis McManus (ed.) *The Year of the Great Test* (Dublin, 1967), pp.107–8.

58 Op. cit., p.17.

59 Report of the Department of Education for the school year 1924-25, pp.52–3.

60 Ibid.

61 *Dáil Debates*, vol. 12, col. 817, 11 June 1925.

62 Pádraic Pearse, *The Murder Machine* (Cork, 1976), p.20.

63 Op. cit., col. 820.

64 Report of the Department of Education for the school year 1924-25, pp.43–53.

65 *Dáil Debates*, vol. 13, col. 194, 11 November 1925.

66 Kenneth Milne, *New Approaches to the Teaching of History* (Dublin, 1979), p.8.

67 *Dáil Debates*, vol. 13, col. 188, 11 November 1925.

68 Ó Buachalla, *Education Policy*, p.252.

69 Coolahan and O'Donovan, *A History*, pp.305–6.

70 *Dáil Debates*, vol. 13, col. 190, 11 November 1925.

71 Department of Education, Clár i gcóir macléinn um na colaistí múinteoireachta 1924-25.

72 Jones, *A Gaelic Experiment*, pp.21–2.

73 *Irish Monthly*, April 1923, p.188.

74 Coimisiún na Gaeltachta report, 1926, p.2.

75 The monitorial system was a nineteenth-century teaching method whereby a senior primary pupil taught a group of his younger peers, he having first received instruction from the teacher.

76 *Dáil Debates*, vol. 13, cols 190–1, 11 November 1925.

77 Ibid., col. 196.

78 Ibid., col. 191.

79 Report of the Department of Education for the school year 1924-25, p.54.

80 Coolahan, *Irish Education*, p.44.

81 *Dáil Debates*, vol. 12, cols 192–3, 11 June 1925.

82 Seán Farren, *The Politics of Irish Education, 1920-1965* (Belfast 1995), p.107.

83 *Dáil Debates*, vol. 12, col. 818, 11 June 1925.

84 *Dáil Debates*, vol. 3, col. 1377, 31 May 1923.

85 Ibid., pp.348–9.

86 John Ryan SJ, 'Eoin MacNeill 1867-1945', in *Studies*, 34 (1945), p.437.

5

John Marcus O'Sullivan (1926-32): 'the policy of raising the standard of education has never been tried'

This intellectual giant had the faith of a child as well and he nurtured it.
The Psalms, the Missal, and the New Testament were of his daily food.[1]

John Marcus O'Sullivan (1881–1948) was Cosgrave's choice of Minister for Education to succeed MacNeill. He may well have selected them for the same reasons, as they shared many of the qualities required for such a sensitive portfolio. Both were academics with deep political convictions, both had a strong connection with the Catholic Church (the new Minister's uncle being Bishop of Kerry), both were opposed to State control of education and both were loyal servants of the State.

O'Sullivan too was a Professor of History at UCD, but unlike MacNeill, he lacked fluency in Irish.[2] This did not inhibit him from pressing forward with schemes to revive the language through the schools. He gave official acceptance to the recommendations of the Second National Programme Conference and he supported aggressive measures to further the language policy.

The transition of power from MacNeill to O'Sullivan was smooth as the latter continued implementing the policy proposals of his predecessor. There was, of course, a noticeable difference in style between the two Ministers, as O'Connell observed in the Dáil in June 1926 when he complimented O'Sullivan for his clear policy objectives.[3]

O'Sullivan was aware of the urgency of dealing with the school accommodation problem as a census of school buildings revealed that 'over one-third of the schools of the country required to be replaced or altered'.[4] He had planned to replace school accommodation for 145,000 students over 4–5 years at a cost of £1.16 million, but the Department of Finance and the Office of Public Works objected to his proposals.[5]

O'Connell suggested 'that the whole capital cost of building the new schools should be advanced from government sources'.[6] However, he considered the ordinary maintenance and upkeep of schools to be the more urgent problem. An inadequate grant was made from the estimates amounting to about £13,000, which would average about £2 10s per school. But conditions in schools remained 'simply deplorable and indescribable', and there was no provision for sweeping and dusting the schools.[7] Schools were 'often the centres of disease and, even death'.[8]

He suggested yet again, that school committees should be set up in each county, with power to strike a local rate to cover the cost of maintenance of school buildings. This had been recommended by the Killanin Committee which examined primary education in 1918.[9] A more astute politician would have recognised that this was unlikely to find favour with the Catholic Clerical Managers. At their annual meeting in May 1926, they passed a resolution that 'the cost of new schools and of the enlargement of school buildings should be borne as hitherto by the Government and Managers and that the work of the Managers might be helped by a loan on easy terms by the central government'.[10]

Speaking in the Senate in 1926, W.B. Yeats made a similar suggestion regarding school building. He said, 'I hold that this should be done by a national loan'.[11] Yeats was more of a realist than O'Connell; he knew there was 'an obvious way out of the difficulty, a way which we cannot take perhaps … and that is to put the care of the school buildings in the hands of local committees'. He recognised that an abandonment of the managerial system would be as unacceptable to the Protestant Church as it was to the Catholic Church.[12]

Despite the Clerical Managers objections to local education authorities, the INTO passed a resolution in 1928 calling for an education authority in each county and county borough to make provision for suitable accommodation and school maintenance. Professor Corcoran issued a gentle warning to the INTO against the establishment of yet another hierarchy of officials. It would also 'be generally taken – even though the INTO did not mean it as such – to be a first move against the managerial system'.[13]

O'Sullivan shared MacNeill's fear of State control in education, although perhaps to a lesser extent. In an address to the Catholic Truth Society[14] he defended the managerial system and opposed State control of schools because he claimed the latter fostered secularisation.[15] Speaking in the Dáil in 1928, he expressed his satisfaction with the status quo. He said, 'I am not complaining that we have not control of the monopoly of education … quite the contrary … our system is a mixture of co-operation, of voluntary effort and state support'.[16]

In 1929 Pope Pius XI's papal encyclical on the Christian Education of Youth, *Divinii Illius Magistri*, appeared. This was generally regarded by Irish Catholic educators and by O'Sullivan as a modern charter on the religious basis of education. This papal encyclical pointed to the differences in educational ideals between strongly Catholic and Christian countries on the one hand and secularised states on the other.[17] It also pointed out the necessity for, and the advantages of, mutual agreement between the State and the Church. Pope Pius XI cited Pope Leo XIII's *Immortale Dei* (1 November 1885), which stated that 'Christ commanded us to give to Caesar the things that are Caesar's and to God the things that are God's'.[18]

O'Sullivan, who had studied at Heidelberg University, was conscious of what he called 'the sterile debates, the bitter warfare … caused by the school question in other countries'. He considered that we were 'lucky in this country that we have a system that satisfies the legitimate demands of the Church and the State in this matter'.[19] Historians generally would agree with this assessment.[20]

COMMISSION ON TECHNICAL EDUCATION

One of the major policy initiatives successfully undertaken by O'Sullivan and the government was the reform of the technical education sector. The government recognised that technical education needed to be upgraded to bring it into line with the trading and industrial needs of the country as plans were afoot for industrial development and the establishment of State-sponsored bodies. In 1926 the department set up the Commission on Technical Education 'to enquire into and advise upon the system of technical education … in relation to the requirements of Trade and Industry'.[21]

The commission had representatives on it from Swedish and Swiss educational bodies, as well as representatives of organised labour and employers, government departments and teachers. Officials from the department accompanied members of the commission on visits to schools and colleges, as well as to the Shannon Power Station and to the first Irish sugar beet factory in Carlow.

The commission presented its report a year later. It found that there was a preponderance of instruction in commerce and domestic economy in the technical schools, with only 23 per cent of instruction being given in the technological area. The work of the schools 'in the more important districts' did not answer 'the local requirements of trade and industry'. It called for radical changes 'to meet the existing and probable requirements of traditional industry'.[22] Technical schools were failing in their duty to provide specialised training for those already in employment.

It made ninety recommendations, one of which suggested that a school leaving certificate should be introduced for all sixth-standard primary school pupils in an effort to improve basic standards of elementary education. It stressed the desirability of making rural science and drawing obligatory subjects in primary schools, and suggested that secondary schools should include science, drawing, manual instruction and domestic economy as compulsory subjects.

The commission put forward the proposal that a system of practical continuation schools and classes should be established for students between 14 and 16 years of age. The programme of these schools would be separate from that of technical schools, which would cater for the 16+ age group. It recommended that attendance at technical schools would be made compulsory in the first 2 years of apprenticeship to skilled trades, for at least 180 days each year. It also called for an Apprenticeship Act.[23]

The Vocational Education Act of 1930 which followed established thirty-eight VECs. These were 'local authorities, supported by local rates'. They provided continuation, apprentice and technical education. Under the Act, continuation education was intended to supplement education provided in primary schools 'to provide practical training for employment in trades and for those in the early stages of employment'.[24]

Technical education was defined under the 1930 Act as 'education pertaining to trades, manufactures, commerce and other industrial pursuits'. There were weaknesses in the Act. One was the lack of provision for general schemes of agricultural education. Responsibility for agricultural education would remain with the Department of Agriculture, a decision that would subsequently lead to much criticism. Another weakness was the failure to provide for reform of teacher training, as recommended by the Commission on Technical Education.[25]

As these schools were under secular control, non-denominational and co-educational, they were bound to cause concern to the Catholic hierarchy, particularly as Pope Pius XI had proscribed co-education in his encyclical *Divinii Illius Magistri* of 1929. On 12 October 1930, O'Sullivan met a delegation from the hierarchy who outlined their concerns regarding the potential dangers for 14–16-year-olds in co-educational settings and night classes in the proposed continuation schools. In response, O'Sullivan advised the VECs to schedule classes in such a way that boys and girls would attend at different times or on different evenings. He hoped that night classes could be avoided altogether. He sent a letter to Bishop David Keane of Limerick on 31 October 1931 giving his assurance that vocational schools would not impinge in any way on the existing national or secondary-school system, but would provide a practical and vocational education. He confirmed that he had given specific instructions to the VECs regarding co-education and night classes.[26]

The bishops accepted O'Sullivan's assurances, and they judged 'it permissible that Catholic pupils in company with non-Catholics should attend'.[27]

The bishops' disquiet over the non-denominational, secular nature of the schools was ameliorated somewhat by the knowledge that priests were eligible for appointment to local VECs, and invariably they were elected as chairmen of VECs. By the mid-1950s, twenty-two out of twenty-seven VECs were headed by priests.[28]

Professor Corcoran was suspicious of the vocational education scheme. He argued before the Commission on Technical Education that the proposed schools should be under the control of the churches.[29] Prior to the passing of the Vocational Education Act, he wrote a series of articles in the *Irish Monthly* warning that without clerical management, continuation schools might promote co-education and neglect religious instruction.[30]

POLICY OF AMALGAMATION

O'Sullivan undertook a policy of amalgamation of small primary schools from 1928 to 1932. In Ireland, 71 per cent of primary schools were two-teacher schools and catered for children ranging from 4 or 5 to 14 years of age.[31] The amalgamation policy was necessary not just for educational and economic reasons, but also for demographic reasons as the population had fallen so sharply in some rural areas as to leave only a handful of pupils in the local primary schools. This problem was exacerbated when the Compulsory School Attendance Act was introduced in 1927. Across the country, it was estimated that an additional 500 teachers would have to be appointed if no changes were made in school organisation.[32] The merger of neighbouring schools was the obvious solution.

In 1928 the department altered the rules for the recognition of primary schools by increasing the minimum size for schools from thirty to thirty-five pupils.[33] In the case of Protestant schools, the department continued to interpret in a liberal way its regulations dealing with the recognition of their primary schools.[34]

However, with regard to the amalgamation policy, overall progress was slow due to demographic decline and to clerical concerns. As early as May 1926, the Catholic bishops passed a resolution stating that 'mixed education (that is co-education) in public schools is very undesirable, especially among the older children'.[35]

The Church's fear of co-education stemmed from the general concern with the decline in morals in Irish society. After the Civil War the bishops' public statements referred to 'the very low level of degeneracy' reached in Ireland.[36] They believed that moral standards were threatened by the new mass media – the cinema, the radio, and above all the English newspapers, whose circulation in Ireland increased during the 1920s.[37] Little wonder then that, in such a climate of suspicion, the amalgamation of small schools was resisted by clergymen.

COMMITTEE ON INSPECTION OF PRIMARY SCHOOLS

It was on foot of an assurance given by O'Sullivan that a Committee on Inspection of Primary Schools would be set up, that the INTO representatives signed the Second National Programme Conference report. In a note appended to the report, they stated that a radical reform of the inspection system was vital to the success of the programme.[38]

O'Sullivan honoured his promise in June 1926, when he appointed a Committee on Inspection of Primary Schools, many members of which had previously served on the Second National Programme Conference. Once again Fr Lambert McKenna SJ was appointed as chairman. There were ten other members on the committee, including representatives of the inspectorate, school managers, teachers and the Christian Brothers. The terms of reference on this occasion were also narrow. Members were asked 'to investigate the present system of inspection in primary schools and of the award of merit-marks to schools and to teachers'.

They were requested also 'to advise as to the desirability of instituting a primary leaving certificate examination or examinations'. A thirty-nine-point questionnaire was distributed to various individuals and heads of institutions, seeking their views on the inspection system and on the proposed primary leaving certificate examination.

It was agreed by the committee that McKenna, who had Jesuit friends in many of the main cities in Europe, should travel abroad for the purpose of securing first-hand evidence 'as to the practical working of foreign inspection systems'.[39] He visited five countries which included trips to twelve cities where he met teachers and inspectors during September and October 1926. The report of the committee contained 'not a single idea of any consequence'. It made minor recommendations regarding inspection and suggested 'more frequent incidental visits and more thorough general inspections'.[40]

However, it did pinpoint the chief defect in the inspectorial system, which appeared 'to be that too little importance was attached to the directive and specifically educational aspect of inspection in comparison with its aspect as a controlling agency'.[41] The INTO continued to express concerns, particularly about the rating system of inspection, in the context of increments of salary as arranged in the 1920 salary agreement, that linked pay to efficiency in teaching.[42]

The report called for the setting up of an appeals board against inspectors' ratings, a recommendation which was implemented soon afterwards. The committee also recommended the introduction of a primary school certificate examination, and it expressed the hope that it would be recognised as qualifying for entrance to post-primary schools. It hoped too that it would be of value to those leaving school and seeking employment. Further weight was given to the views of supporters of the examination when, in October 1927, the Commission on Technical Education made the same recommendation for a primary leaving certificate examination.[43]

A number of inspectorial reforms were introduced in 1928 but they 'provided only a brief respite'[44] because in April 1930 the department pressurised teachers to gain Irish qualifications. It did so by declaring that, effective from 30 June 1932, all teachers in English-speaking districts who were under 30 years of age as of July 1932, would have to obtain a certificate of competence to teach Irish (the 'ordinary certificate') or face the loss of their salary increments. It further stated that as of 30 June 1935, those same teachers had to have the bilingual certificate certifying their competency to teach through the medium of Irish, if they were not to lose their salary increments.[45]

Inevitably tensions were heightened between teachers and inspectors in the implementation of such harsh measures. The regulation was in fact found to be unlawful by the Supreme Court in 1940, and the government was forced to rescind its decision, and to provide back pay to those affected.[46]

Circulars issued by the department in June and July 1931 did little to ease the strained relationship. In June, O'Sullivan broke a promise given almost a decade earlier by three of his predecessors, when his officials issued a directive instructing school inspectors when rating teachers to give close attention to their good will and capacity in relation to the Irish language.[47] Only those teachers who were pressing forward with the introduction of Irish as a teaching medium could expect efficient ratings.[48]

In July the department sent Circular 11/31 on teaching through the medium of Irish, to managers, teachers and inspectors. The circular reiterated that the intention of the school programme was that 'Where a teacher is competent to teach through Irish and where the children can assimilate the instruction so given, the teachers should endeavour to extend the use of Irish as a medium of instruction'. The aim of the programme was to secure the use of Irish as the teaching medium in all schools as soon as possible.[49]

The Cosgrave government pressed forward relentlessly with the language revival policy by announcing that the salaries of Gaeltacht teachers would be raised by as much as 10 per cent.[50] Pressure was applied at second level also. In the past a secondary school could provide either Irish or English as essential subjects to merit recognition. O'Sullivan confirmed in the Dáil in November 1927 that 'A secondary school in which Irish is not taught cannot receive grants'. The regulation required that 'a reasonable proportion of the pupils must receive instruction in Irish'.[51] Students in secondary schools were required to present Irish as an essential subject in the intermediate certificate from 1928 onwards. These policy changes resulted in 99 per cent of intermediate students and 92 per cent of leaving certificate students presenting Irish as a subject in the June 1929 examinations.[52]

Blythe continued to provide funding and accommodation for All-Irish secondary schools. The first three such schools to be built in Dublin were Scoil Mhuire in Marlborough Street, Scoil Bhríde in Earlsfort Terrace, and Coláiste Mhuire in Harcourt Street, later Parnell Square. The number of secondary schools using Irish as a medium of instruction increased from five in 1925–26 to twenty-four in 1930–31, and those where some subjects were taught through Irish rose from ten to sixty-eight.[53]

TEACHER TRAINING

O'Sullivan continued with the policy of gaelicising the training colleges. Irish became an essential subject for all student teachers, so that by 1927 four of the five training colleges then in operation taught the majority of their subjects through the medium of Irish.[54] In the CITC, the teaching of subjects through the medium of Irish was not undertaken. According to the report of the department, however, there was 'a marked improvement from year to year in the students' ability to use Irish fluently'.[55] From 1931 onwards, before a training college graduate received his/her final diploma, they had to pass the bilingual certificate examination attesting to his/her competence to teach through Irish.[56] In 1932 a new programme for the training colleges was devised which gave due emphasis to oral proficiency as well as literary knowledge of the language.

The shortage of students entering the training colleges, and the poor educational standard of those who did, still persisted. O'Sullivan was aware of the extent of the problem.[57] Now that there was compulsory school attendance, more trained teachers were required and O'Sullivan proceeded to establish the preparatory colleges as recommended by the departmental Committee on Recruitment.

The first four of the seven preparatory colleges were established in 1926 in order to supply the training colleges with a number of Irish-speaking candidates. Half the vacancies in each college were to be reserved for candidates who obtained not less than 85 per cent for oral Irish at the entrance test, and 50 per cent of these in turn were reserved for native speakers of Irish who otherwise fulfilled the conditions for entrance.[58] Not only did Gaeltacht candidates get preferential access to these colleges, but they were also guaranteed places in the training colleges on securing the leaving certificate. The preparatory colleges were established and funded by the State, and placed under the control of Catholic religious orders, or in the case of Coláiste Moibhí, under the Church of Ireland authorities.

The preparatory colleges were not greeted with universal approval. O'Connell and the INTO were vehemently opposed to them and to the segregation of boys

and girls aged 14 or 15 years. The nine primary school inspectors specially charged
with the language revival opposed the founding of the colleges, on the grounds
that competent professors would be hard to procure, and that there would not
be an opportunity for the students and the natives to converse meaningfully,
as the promoters of the scheme had claimed. One inspector observed that 'clerical
officials convinced the authorities of the soundness of this bizarre Preparatory
College scheme'.[59]

Critics pointed out that the preparatory colleges could not be considered the
equivalent of academic secondary schools, as no language except Irish or English
was taught in them.[60] The Department of Finance, which was more concerned
with the financial implications of the undertaking, insisted that the preparatory
college course should be reduced from 5 to 4 years, thereby creating difficulties for the teaching of Latin and the introduction of a modern language. It was
also responsible for the introduction of the agreement whereby students had to
promise to teach for 5 years in a primary school and on failing to do so, had to
repay their fees. This resulted in many misfits remaining in the teaching profession.
But this stipulation was merely following precedent as the Ministry for Irish had
introduced a similar condition when awarding scholarships to the preparatory
schools in May 1921.[61]

By 1928 officials in the Department of Finance were complaining about the
huge cost involved in copper-fastening the language policy and in building the
preparatory colleges.[62] The complaint was justified as the department failed to
forecast accurately the cost of establishing the seven residential colleges, and the
cost eventually came to about three times the original estimate.[63] Most of the
preparatory colleges were located in or near Gaeltacht areas, and helped to fill the
shortage in the number of second-level schools there.

Reform of the system of recruitment to the training colleges was long
overdue. Teachers had previously been recruited from primary school pupils
with an aptitude for teaching, in the case of the monitorial system, and from
pupil teachers who attended model schools either as boarders or day pupils.
Monitors and pupil teachers put in a certain number of hours teaching each day,
under the supervision of the principal of the school. Monitors and pupil teachers
were in reality apprentice teachers.[64] They were supplemented by graduates who
passed the Easter examination in subjects not covered by their degree, and who
passed a test in teaching. There were also Junior Assistant Mistresses (JAMs) who
were employed in schools in which the average attendance had increased to fifty
pupils. They were allowed to keep their places by becoming untrained assistants
on passing the Easter examination. Finally, private students were also accepted
into the training colleges.

The department acknowledged the failure of the old recruitment system. In 1924 the monitorial system supplied less than 14 per cent of those gaining places in training at the Easter examination.[65] The pupil teacher scheme supplied 40 per cent of candidates for women's colleges, but the number recruited for men's colleges had fallen to 1 or 2 per cent a year. Consequently, the supply of candidates to the training colleges had to be drawn almost entirely from private students whose general education was often defective and who had not undergone any preliminary test or training in teaching.[66]

The department abandoned the monitorial system and adopted a new pupil teacher scheme, along with the preparatory colleges. The revised pupil teacher scheme enabled the department 'to draw pupil-teachers not merely from day secondary, but also from secondary boarding schools, and to provide them with an education for 2 years in a secondary school'. During the second period of the course, pupil teachers would be required to do practical teaching for not more than 3 hours per week. In 1929 the pupil teacher scheme supplied 28 per cent of the entrants to the training colleges, but from 1930 the preparatory college students and pupil teachers would supply the majority of the entrants to the training colleges.[67]

By the 1930s the new pupil teachers were much better educated on entering training college as a result of reforms introduced, as candidates now needed to have passed the leaving certificate examination. Furthermore, from 1931 the old Easter examination was discontinued and open competition candidates for teaching were recruited on the basis of results attained from the leaving certificate, and some oral examinations undertaken at Easter.

The preparatory colleges were a success. The reports of the department for 1930–31 and 1931–32 confirmed that the work of the four main training colleges was almost entirely through Irish, while the CITC was making steady progress.[68]

FAILURE OF THE IRISH LANGUAGE POLICY

Small one-teacher Protestant schools had particular difficulties implementing the language policy, but O'Sullivan devised a plan to ensure that other subjects would not be neglected in these schools in order to promote Irish. He allowed their teachers to give oral instruction in Irish to all pupils for half an hour daily, and to set some of the pupils to work for half an hour on 'silent reading' of Irish, while they could proceed to teach the full curriculum.[69]

O'Sullivan was concerned at what he regarded as parental apathy in relation to education. He wondered 'How many of them are interested in what is happening their children at school? What interest do they take?'[70] He seemed to be far removed from the harsh realities of Irish life. In May 1930, Deputy Fahy quoted alarming statistics on the malnourishment of Irish children, and he questioned the wisdom of teaching Irish to hungry children.[71]

Hunger and poverty certainly militated against the success of the language policy, but so too did the lack of public commitment to speaking Irish. The report of the Department of Education for 1928–29 acknowledged that it was 'inevitable that a very considerable part of the work done by the schools must fail to bear fruit and failing help from outside it may well be that the revival of the language may prove to be beyond their powers'.[72]

The inspectors had no reason to give a more promising forecast in 1931. They merely reiterated that 'the English-speaking life of the home does much to nullify the work of the schools in creating Irish speakers'.[73] A year later they were forced to concede, that after 10 years of effort, the language policy as carried out in primary schools had failed.[74]

Advocates of the Irish language policy in the department and elsewhere regarded it as a 'matter of patriotism' that teachers should be dedicated to this cause.[75] They tended to blame teachers for the failure of the language policy as they castigated them for their lack of patriotism.[76] In 1931, 38 per cent of teachers still had no formal qualification in Irish, while 30 per cent were qualified to use Irish as a medium of instruction.

Inspectors observed the apathy of native Irish speakers towards the revival policy. In 1930 a divisional inspector reported that 'In the Gaeltacht Irish is not being made the spoken language there'.[77] Witnesses from the Gaeltacht who came before the Second National Programme Conference testified to 'the indifference, in some cases even to the hostility with which Irish in general was regarded by those who spoke it from birth'.[78] Their lack of enthusiasm was understandable when one considers that most school leavers in the Gaeltacht were destined to emigrate to English-speaking countries, and that most of them would never advance past primary school level. The small number who reached the educational standard to gain entry to the preparatory colleges was not sufficient to gain support for the policy. One commentator regarded the policy as 'a wild innumerate dream', adding that 'Not only were there insufficient children … but also the hereditary educational pattern of Gaeltacht people were quite foreign to the proposed crash programme'.[79]

The inspectors erred by excluding oral Irish examinations in secondary schools, when their desired objective was oral competency in the language. In his evidence before the Gaeltacht Commission, Seoirse Mac Niocaill, on behalf of the department's secondary education branch, testified that the department had considered the introduction of oral examinations, but had decided that they were unnecessary, on the grounds that 'you couldn't teach a subject without it being done orally in Irish'.[80] 'It was unfortunate that his views were accepted'[81] as the emphasis quickly shifted to written examinations and written Irish, to the detriment of oral Irish fluency.[82]

The department was slow to respond to the need for a greater supply of Irish textbooks and Irish literature. According to León Ó Broin, who had responsibility for *An Gúm*, the newly formed publication section of the department, 'books in Irish, other than elementary school texts were regarded as economic monstrosities'.[83] Initially the challenge proved too great for *An Gúm*, and the department was forced to suggest to teachers that they should conduct their work without having recourse to books, especially when teaching infants. It added gratuitously. 'All our teachers are over-reliant on books'.[84]

The department succeeded in the school year 1928–29 in publishing two books of terms, one for the teaching of history and geography, and the other for the teaching of grammar and literature. However, the lack of a standardised spelling, grammar and vocabulary for the Irish language continued to hamper progress for the next two decades.[85]

All calls for an inquiry into the language policy were ignored. The many calls for a council of education were completely rejected. O'Sullivan objected to a council of education on principle. He believed that he 'would get much more solid advice from the component parts of such a body, from the managers and teachers'.[86] It is interesting to note that de Valera favoured the introduction of an advisory council of education at this time.[87]

Concerns were being expressed in the Dáil and elsewhere about falling educational standards, which many attributed to the language revival policy in the schools. According to a contributor to *The Bell*, 'The policy of raising the standard of education has never been tried'.[88] However, the teaching profession was defended by O'Connell, who claimed that 'There is no proof, none whatever, rather is the contrary the case, that the standard of education in the other subjects than Irish has suffered, or has fallen in any way by the introduction of compulsory Irish in the schools'.[89] The INTO's 1941 report would prove the exact opposite.

There were complaints in the Dáil that the State was not getting value for the £3¾ million spent on Irish education as only 6 per cent of children completed sixth standard, and 55 per cent of primary schoolchildren failed the entrance examination for technical schools. In 1929, of the 9,827 students who presented for the primary certificate examination, only 5,062 passed. The Minister for Industry and Commerce reported that due to low educational standards, it was proving almost impossible to fix standards of education to be incorporated in the forthcoming Apprenticeship Bill.[90]

John Marcus O'Sullivan may have implemented MacNeill's policies, shared his aversion to State-controlled education and his attachment to the managerial system, but his single minded pursuit of his objectives set him apart from the 'wholly detached' approach of MacNeill.

O'Sullivan was aware of the deplorable condition of school buildings and he had ambitious plans to replace school accommodation, but he allowed the strong arm of the department and the Office of Public Works to stymie his plans. School maintenance grants were completely inadequate and there was also evidence of managerial neglect of schools, but O'Sullivan did not countenance the introduction of LECs, instead he allowed the status quo to continue.

School amalgamations became a matter of some urgency in the wake of the School Attendance Act, but O'Sullivan continued to give favourable treatment to small Protestant schools and to allow the concerns of the Catholic hierarchy over co-education to take precedence over what was best for children's education.

Two reports in 1927 recommended the introduction of the primary certificate examination, and the departmental Committee on Recruitment recommended the establishment of the preparatory colleges, so O'Sullivan was justified in rejecting the INTO's objections to both. But there was no justification for the inordinate pressure he applied to teachers to gain qualifications to teach through the medium of Irish. In 1921–22, O'Kelly, Hayes and Lynch gave the INTO a guarantee that no teacher would be penalised if they were unable 'to take up or fit themselves for the teaching of Irish',[91] but that guarantee was now well and truly broken.

When the department faced the grim reality that the language policy had failed, O'Sullivan blamed it on parental apathy, and his officials blamed it on unpatriotic, unqualified teachers and apathetic native Irish speakers, but the blame lay closer to home, as inspectors were instrumental in ensuring that the emphasis lay on written Irish. The department failed to provide a standardised spelling, grammar and vocabulary for the Irish language. It was also tardy in providing suitable textbooks and reading material in Irish, but suggested unashamedly, that teachers were over-reliant on textbooks in their teaching.

However, the most worrying aspect of the failure of the policy was the detrimental effect it had on general educational standards, the evidence for which was contained in the reports of the Department of Education. Patrick O'Callaghan's comment in 1947 that 'The policy of raising the standard of education has never been tried',[92] had more than a ring of truth to it.

John Marcus O'Sullivan's legacy to Irish education lay in his reform of the system of recruitment to training colleges and in his introduction of the preparatory colleges, despite formidable opposition. His enduring legacy lay in the introduction of the 1930 Vocational Education Act and the vocational schools.

Gaining acceptance of these schools was an impressive achievement considering that Pope Pius XI had proscribed co-education in 1929 and Professor Timothy Corcoran had raised dire warnings about them in 1930, but O'Sullivan's vocational schools were to suffer many traumas in the years ahead.

Notes

1   Professor Mary Macken, 'John Marcus O'Sullivan obit 9 February 1946' in *Studies*, 37 (1948), pp.1–6.

2   O'Connor, 'The teaching of Irish', p.212.

3   *Dáil Debates*, vol. 16, col. 398, 4 June 1926.

4   *Dáil Debates*, vol. 26, col. 350, 24 October 1928.

5   NAI *S20/26.26*.

6   *Dáil Debates*, vol. 26, col. 878, 24 October 1928.

7   *Dáil Debates*, vol. 16, col. 400, 4 June 1926.

8   Op. cit., col. 881.

9   *Dáil Debates*, vol. 16, col. 402, 4 June 1926.

10   *Irish Catholic Directory* entry for 26 May 1926, pp.586–7.

11   *Senate Reports*, vol. 6, col. 520, 26 March, 1926.

12   Ibid., col. 521.

13   *Irish Monthly*, June 1928, p.285.

14   The Catholic Truth Society was originally founded in 1868 in the UK. The Catholic Truth Society of Ireland was founded in 1899 to publish and make available a range of religious materials which previously came from England. In 1928 Veritas Company took over the commercial aspect of The Catholic Truth Society. In 1969 the Communications Centre founded in Booterstown by the Irish Catholic Bishops' Conference merged with the Catholic Truth Society to become the Catholic Communications Institute of Ireland.

15   *Times Educational Supplement*, October 1926, p.446.

16   *Dáil Debates*, vol. 23, cols 2049–52, 24 May 1928.

17   Mescal, *Religion in the Irish System of Education*, pp.57–8.

18   Revd John C. Joy SJ, 'Notes on current educational topics. Papal encyclical' in *Irish Monthly*, November 1930, pp.550–2.

19   *Dáil Debates*, vol. 38, col. 1902, 22 May 1931.

20   J.H. Whyte, *Church and State in Modern Ireland, 1923–70* (Dublin, 1970), p.20.

21   Report of the Commission on Technical Education (Dublin, 1927), p.7.

22   Ibid., p.18.

23   Ibid., pp.145–7.

24   Vocational Education Act, 1930, no. 29 in public statutes of the Oireachtas 1930, p.601.

25   Coolahan, *Irish Education*, p.97.

26   J.M. O'Sullivan, 'Letter from J.M. O'Sullivan TD, Minister for Education, to Dr Keane, Bishop of Limerick on the 1930 Vocational Education Act, 31 October 1930' in Ó Buachalla, *Education Policy*, pp.399–403.

27 Joy, 'Notes on current educational topics', pp.551–2; *Acta et decreta* 1927, 120, 402.1 in Ó Buachalla, *Education Policy*, p.224.

28 Whyte, *Church and State*, p.38.

29 Commission on Technical Education, minutes of evidence 1, pp.11–22.

30 Past Master, 'The vocational education bill' in *Irish Monthly*, 58 (1930), pp.276–80.

31 Report of the Department of Education for the school year 1924-25, pp.24–5.

32 *Times Educational Supplement*, 27 March 1926, p.148.

33 Report of the Department of Education 1927-28, pp.10–12.

34 *Times Educational Supplement*, 24 May 1930, p.230.

35 *Acta et decreta concilii plenarii* ... 1926, p.207; Ó Buachalla, *Education Policy*, p.370.

36 *Irish Catholic Directory*, 3 August 1924, p.589.

37 Revd R.S. Devane SJ, 'Indecent literature : some legal remedies' in *Irish Ecclesiastical Record*, (1928), p.557.

38 Report and programme of the National Programme Conference (1926), p.55.

39 Report of the Committee on Inspection of Primary Schools (1927), p.5.

40 Coolahan and O'Donovan, *A History*, pp.117–9.

41 Report of the Committee on Inspection, p.7.

42 Coolahan and O'Donovan, *A History*, pp.118–9.

43 Report of the Committee on Inspection, pp.16–18; Report of the Commission on Technical Education, p.37.

44 Akenson, *A Mirror to Kathleen's Face*, p.52.

45 Report of the Department of Education for 1928-29, pp.20–1.

46 O'Connell, *History of the INTO*, pp.383–4.

47 *Irish School Weekly*, 28 January 1922, p.77. T.J. O'Connell had predicted that this would happen in January 1922.

48 Report of the Council of Education on the Function and Curriculum of the Primary school (Dublin, 1954), pp.330–4.

49 Department of Education C11/31 circular to managers, teachers, and inspectors on teaching through Irish. NAI *S7801C* Irish language development in the schools.

50 *Irish School Weekly*, 27 June 1931, p.711.

51 *Dáil Debates*, vol. 21, col. 1723, 10 November 1927.

52 Report of the Department of Education for 1928-29, p.166.

53 Report of the Department of Education for 1930-31, p.37.

54 *Dáil Debates*, vol. 21, col. 1176, 10 November 1927.

55 Report of the Department of Education for 1931-32, p.15.

56 Report of the Council of Education on the Function of the Primary school, p.72.

57 *Dáil Debates*, vol. 16, col. 390, 6 June 1926.

58 Report of the Department of Education for 1928-29, pp.13–14.

59 Seamus Fenton, *It All Happened: Reminiscences of Seamus Fenton* (Dublin, 1948), p.269.

60 *Times Educational Supplement*, 23 January 1932, p.30.

61 *Misneach*, 21 May 1921.

62 NAI *S20/4/28* Establishment of training college for national teachers at Galway.

63 Jones, *A Gaelic Experiment*, p.154.

64 O'Connell, *History of the INTO*, pp.393–4.

65 Report of the Department of Education for the school year 1924-25, pp.40–1.

66 Report of the Department of Education for the school years 1925–27 and the financial and administrative year 1926-27, pp.21–2.

67 Report of the Department of Education for 1928-29 pp.12–13.

68 Report of the Department of Education for 1930-31, p.6.; 1931–32, p.15.

69 *Times Educational Supplement*, 24 May 1930, p.230.

70 *Dáil Debates*, vol. 38, col. 1900, 22 May 1931.

71 Ibid., cols 1700–09, 21 May 1931.

72 Ó Catháin, 'Education in the new Ireland', pp.111–12.

73 Report of the Department of Education for 1931-32, p.23.

74 Report of the Department of Education for 1932-33, pp.22–5.

75 Arnold Marsh, 'The revival of the Irish language' in *Year Book of Education* (London, 1949), p.159.

76 Report of the Department of Education for 1932-32 p.20.

77 *Dáil Debates*, vol. 38, cols 1714–15, 21 May 1931.

78 Kingsmill Moore, *Reminiscences and Reflections*, pp.290–1.

79 Oliver MacDonagh, *States of Mind: Two Centuries of Anglo-Irish Conflict 1780-1980* (London, 1983), p.122.

80 Coimisiún na Gaeltachta Report, p.9.

81 Jones, *A Gaelic Experiment*, p.34.

82 Ó Catháin, 'Education in the new Ireland', p.110. There was an oral examination for the primary certificate up until 1943.

83 Ó Broin, *Just Like Yesterday*, p.62.

84 Report of the Department of Education for 1929-30, pp.30–1.

85 Seán Ó Riain, *Pleanáil teanga in Éirinn 1919-1985* (Dublin, 1994), p.74. Change was effected in 1945 with the publication of *Litriú na Gaeilge – An Caighdeán Oifigúil*. It was introduced into all national schools in 1948.

86 *Dáil Debates*, vol. 26, col. 1908, 24 October 1928.

87 *Dáil Debates*, vol. 38, cols 1746–7, 21 May 1931. In 1932 Thomas Derrig, as Minister for Education would continue with the status quo, despite several requests for such a council.

88 Patrick O'Callaghan, 'Irish in schools' in *The Bell*, 14:1, 1947, p.63.

89 *Dáil Reports*, vol. 26, col. 873, 24 October 1928.

90 *Dáil Reports*, vol. 38, cols 1718–21, 21 May 1931.

91 *Irish School Weekly*, 28 January 1922, p.77.

92 Patrick O'Callaghan, 'Irish in schools' in *The Bell*, 14:1, 1947, p.63.

6

Thomas Derrig (1932–39; 1940–48): 'Our system of education approaches the ideal'

> When, if ever, was the Minister prepared to listen to the only people who could give him information – the National Teachers' Organisation? ... The Minister has even refused to attend their annual Congress.[1]

Thomas Derrig (1887–1956) was Minister for Education from 9 March 1932 until 8 September 1939, when Seán T. Ó Ceallaigh[2] took over as Acting Minister for 19 days, to be followed by de Valera who fulfilled the role until June 1940. Derrig then resumed his ministry, which lasted until 1948. He remains the longest serving Minister for Education and he was de Valera's appointment in his first cabinet.[3] Fahy was widely expected to get the education portfolio and teachers had harboured high hopes that he would.[4] A 1916 veteran and a founder member of Fianna Fáil, Derrig was also the ex-headmaster of Ballina Technical School, having 'been sacked for refusing to take the Oath to the Saorstát'.[5]

The newly installed anti-Treaty Fianna Fáil government faced a dilemma: whether to continue with a failed language policy, or whether to set up an inquiry and run the risk of revealing that their major nationalist aspiration was doomed to failure. Derrig and the government decided to pursue the language policy with the utmost zeal, during a period of great austerity.

Prior to the 1932 general election, the Cumann na nGaedheal government cut teachers' salaries by 6 per cent, while the Fianna Fáil party promised not to implement the proposal if elected. Fianna Fáil won the election, but the Minister for Finance, Seán MacEntee, introduced the Economies Bill in March 1933. Its purpose was to reduce the salaries of civil servants, members of the Gárda Síochána, the army and primary teachers. Of the four services affected, the teachers were the most harshly treated, and they had their salaries cut by 10 per cent. This led to a 1-day teachers' strike that year.[6]

In 1934 a further 9 per cent reduction in teachers' salaries was introduced, along with a new pension scheme. Salaries were increased slightly in 1938 and 1942, but the increase did not meet the increased cost of living at the time. Some primary teachers were placed under further financial pressure by the threat from the department that their salary increments would not be paid if they had not acquired an Irish certificate by June 1932 and a bilingual certificate by June 1935. Derrig did not reverse the policy decision taken by the previous government, and consequently the threat continued to hang over teachers until the Supreme Court ruling of 1940 found in their favour.

In 1932 compulsion was applied at second level too when the department withheld capitation grants from schools in respect of students who were not studying Irish, and 2 years later Irish became a compulsory subject for passing the leaving certificate examination. Incentives were offered to Gaeltacht students to apply for places in the preparatory colleges, where the number of places reserved for them was increased from 25 to 40 per cent. In 1933–34, the department offered one of its most popular financial incentives: the £2 *deontas* or grant to Irish-speaking school-going children, aged between 6 and 14 years, from Irish or partially Irish-speaking areas.[7] The scheme was extended in 1945 to 16-year-olds who met the requirements and the *deontas* was increased in value to £5.[8]

De Valera, who was a founding member of the ASTI, took the initiative as Taoiseach to call a conference of the Minister for Education, the secretary of the department and the secondary-school inspectors in July 1937. He wished to re-introduce set texts. In 1925 Cosgrave described the introduction of open courses as 'a complete revolution' because 'rigidity has been replaced by freedom'.[9] This view was not shared by de Valera, who thought that existing programmes were 'too extensive and too vague'.

He wished to see 'a narrowing of the subjects of the programme' on the grounds that 'its range hampered the gaelicisation task'. Inspectors disagreed with his proposed curricular changes, but de Valera succeeded in having set texts re-introduced between 1939 and 1941. One would have expected some discussion on the absence of oral Irish examinations as part of the programmes, especially in light of the fact that an oral Irish examination was a feature of programmes in Northern Ireland since the 1920s.[10] However, no such discussion took place.

REVISED PROGRAMME OF PRIMARY INSTRUCTION

In February 1934, following inconclusive meetings with department officials in 1933, the INTO submitted a document to Derrig which suggested a lightening of the national programme, and which urged that '… rural sciences should be eliminated from all schools and that algebra and geometry' should be confined to larger schools.[12] Derrig, who was dissatisfied with the rate of progress in Irish, offered a lightening of some subjects, and an intensification of the programme in Irish. The INTO strongly objected to this.[13] In September he presented his Revised Programme of Primary Instruction, which included a reversion to an all-Irish programme for infants and the teaching in all other classes of the higher Irish course, as prescribed in the 1926 programme. English was made optional for first class, and in other classes the lower course in English was to be taken. In mathematics, algebra and geometry were made optional in one-teacher and two-teacher schools, three-teacher mixed schools, and in all classes taught by women.[14]

Rural science was made an optional subject, thereby reversing one of the recommendations of the Second National Programme Conference and of the Commission on Technical Education. The decision was criticised in the report of the Commission on Vocational Organisation because Ireland was a predominantly agricultural country, and 'within a few years' rural science 'ceased to be taught in 90% of schools'.[15] These changes had the effect of narrowing the primary school curriculum even more than in 1922 or 1926. Its effects would be long lasting as this curriculum would remain largely unchanged until 1971. Educational standards were lowered in mathematics, and in English there was 'a drop in standard of approximately one year's school work'.[16] English books which were previously used in fourth class were now used in sixth class.

In the 1930s, the language policy came under sustained criticism in the press, among educationalists, and from right across the political divide. James Dillon of the Fine Gael party urged Derrig to set up a commission of inquiry, as he warned him that there was widespread parental dissatisfaction with the policy.[17] Derrig refused to hold an inquiry and dismissed parents' views on the grounds that he, as Minister, was 'in possession of greater knowledge and greater experience of the matter'.[18]

His claim was put to the test in the early 1930s and 1940s. In an effort to re-energise language revival efforts, he attempted to take advantage of a loophole in the 1926 Compulsory School Attendance Act, which stated that a child had to attend a 'national or other suitable school'. However, the Act failed to specify criteria for suitability. It would appear that it was Derrig's intention to force parents who opted for an English language private school education for their children to attend Irish language primary schools instead.

In 1934 he took a test case against parents whose children attended a private school in Enniscorthy, County Wexford, on the grounds that they had contravened the terms of the School Attendance Act. The department stated that Derrig considered the private school to be unsuitable as the Irish language was not taught in it. The District Justice ruled in favour of Derrig by asserting that the School Attendance Act did not specify that Irish was obligatory, but as Irish was the national language, he failed to see how a school could be considered suitable if it did not teach the Irish language. The parents were fined a shilling but were given the right to appeal, which they duly did.[19] Judge Devitt heard the appeal in the Circuit Court and the appeal was allowed, on the grounds that nowhere in the Attendance Act was Irish made compulsory, and the Constitution of the Irish Free State expressly recognised English as an official language equal with Irish.

Undaunted by this defeat, Derrig tried again 8 years later to force parents to cease the practice of sending their children to private schools in Ireland or abroad. This time he attempted to do so by means of the 1942 School Attendance Bill. The Bill passed through both Houses of the Oireachtas, but due to the constitutional issues involved, the President of Ireland, Dr Douglas Hyde, referred the Bill to the Supreme Court. The Bill was found to be repugnant to the constitution, and the matter was not proceeded with.[20]

When faced with criticism of its language policy, the favoured departmental response was to discredit its critics. The Report of the Department of Education for 1934–35[21] maintained that most critics were unfamiliar with the work of the schools, a viewpoint echoed by the government-sponsored *Irish Press* newspaper in November 1944, when it commented that criticism came mostly from 'people who, for one reason or another, have no language but English'.[22] The department also took the precaution of issuing Circular 4/36 in March 1936 to all inspectors and school managers. The circular merely reiterated the contents of Circular 11/31. Derrig could at least take some satisfaction in the knowledge that the language policy reached the zenith of its success during his ministry, when in the early 1940s, 12 per cent of primary schools and 28 per cent of secondary schools in English-speaking areas used Irish as a medium of instruction.[23] However, the problem still persisted that pupils had very little opportunity to converse in Irish outside school.

INTO INQUIRY

In 1935 the Dublin branch of the INTO called on Derrig to set up an inquiry into the language policy. As this was not forthcoming, it initiated its own inquiry into the use of Irish as a teaching medium for children whose home language was English. In 1937 it conducted a survey by means of questionnaires which were distributed to 9,000 primary teachers, of whom 1,347 replied. In 1939 an interim report was produced and a copy was sent to Derrig. The final report was published in 1941.

It confirmed that subjects such as mathematics, history and geography were affected detrimentally by teaching through Irish, and that teaching through Irish placed a mental strain on children. Such was the level of parental dissatisfaction, that some parents requested teachers to provide their children with English primers 'so that they might be given in the home, the instruction in English reading denied them in the schools'. The report called for a return to the use of English as a teaching medium, and for a greater emphasis to be placed on oral Irish. It also called for a raising of the school leaving age.[24]

The department based its response to the report mainly on the solicited views of the inspectorate. O'Neill responded by claiming that the report represented 'the views of middle-aged, somewhat tired and not too linguistically-equipped teachers'. He was critical of the composition of the survey committee, which consisted of five men, as he believed that they lacked experience of teaching infants, and that they were ignorant of the most recent thinking in this area of pedagogy. In fact, the five members were experienced teachers with 'highly efficient' ratings, two of whom were former presidents of the INTO. O'Neill proceeded to blame the teachers who ignored inspectorial advice. He suggested also that compulsion was essential to the success of the policy, and that a lowering of educational standards was inevitable.[25]

Derrig repeated O'Neill's views in the Dáil in June 1942, when he concluded that the INTO report gave 'an entirely unjustifiable and wrong account ... of actual conditions in infant schools'.[26] His public statements, however, differed from his private revelations. In 1943 he presented a memo on the language policy to cabinet in which he admitted that the policy was futile as children reverted to speaking English once they left school.[27] De Valera supported Derrig's rejection of the 'unscientific' report, stating that 'the reports from the inspectors are very much more to be relied upon'.[28] But the fact of the matter was that de Valera had been harbouring doubts about the language policy since the 1930s and in 1943 he requested Dr Johanna Pollak, a Czechoslovakian educationalist who was familiar with the methods used to revive the Czech language, to assess the situation with regard to Irish in the schools in Ireland. She produced an unpublished report in which she concluded that 'the children get an overdose of it (Irish) in the school when they are still too young to benefit from it'.[29]

De Valera had already antagonised teachers by supporting the introduction of the primary certificate examination despite INTO objections to it. He stated bluntly, 'I do not care what teachers are offended by it ... I am less interested in the teachers' method of teaching than I am in the results he achieves'.[30] The government proceeded to make the primary certificate examination compulsory for all sixth class children in 1943. The examination was a written one only in Irish, English and arithmetic, even though it was government policy to revive Irish as a vernacular language.

Tension existed between the government and the INTO for much of the 15 years of Derrig's ministry. Persistent requests by the INTO for a council of education, an Irish language inquiry, the abolition of the primary certificate, and a lifting of a ban on married women teachers which Derrig imposed in 1933 due to a teacher surplus, were all refused. Besides, the government was forced to adopt a series of unpopular measures to ameliorate the effects of the teacher surplus. In 1938 Derrig imposed a retiring age for women earlier than that for men, and the government put a temporary halt to recruitment to both the preparatory and the training colleges. In 1944 the situation demanded that St Patrick's Training College in Drumcondra should be closed temporarily, and this caused much concern to teachers.

The INTO was still smarting under the government's rejection of its 1941 report, but it was the inspectors' report for 1941–42 which exacerbated the situation, when it urged teachers 'to make a more intelligent and profitable use of the official notes' for the teaching of Irish.[31] The teachers found it 'difficult to keep patience with this kind of criticism' considering that the 'famous notes' had been 'studied, copied and annotated and put into practice in every school in the country'.[32]

De Valera also angered the INTO when he delivered an offensive speech at a meeting of Comhdháil Náisiúnta na Gaedhlige[33] in Ennis, County Clare, in October 1944. Referring to the Irish language policy in the schools, he said that 'the Government could not be expected to go into every school or introduce a spying system to ensure that teachers would see that the pupils spoke Irish everywhere'.[34] The INTO responded that the speech was 'hardly likely to encourage "the willing and hearty co-operation of every one" which the Taoiseach asked for'.[35]

The INTO had a long-standing grievance with the department dating from the early 1920s, concerning what they regarded as an invidious rating system of inspection. Teachers were rated 'highly efficient', 'efficient' or 'non-efficient'. About one in every three teachers was rated 'highly efficient' and got a higher salary than their colleagues.[36] Teachers' competency in the Irish language was also bound up with the efficiency rating. However, the biggest bone of contention between the INTO and the government was undoubtedly their pay claim.

There was widespread support for the teachers on this issue, including from the bishops and the Archbishop of Dublin, John Charles McQuaid. McQuaid wrote a letter to the INTO's assistant secretary, assuring him of the support of 'the Clerical

Managers of this city and the Religious Superiors' for 'a salary in keeping with the dignity … of your profession'.[37]

Derrig and the government adopted a firm stance when they rejected the teachers' pay claim and denounced their pending strike as 'a definite challenge to the authority of the State'.[38] De Valera's erstwhile friend McQuaid offered to mediate in the dispute,[39] but the government refused his offer. The Dublin teachers went on strike on 20 March 1946, and the first person to be informed of the result of the ballot to strike was McQuaid. McQuaid tried to persuade de Valera of the justice of the teachers' claim, but the government refused to consider settlement through arbitration.

Teachers were paid 90 per cent of their salaries from a strike fund for the duration of the strike. *The Irish Times* editorial was very critical of Derrig's unyielding approach and of his insistence 'that the strike could only be terminated' by the teachers' 'unconditional surrender'. It commented 'this is rank folly'. The Dublin teachers returned to work on 31 October 1946 at McQuaid's request.

Derrig's decision to make a special payment to those teachers who made their services available during the strike provoked an angry response from teachers and union leaders alike. The chairman of the Dublin branch of the INTO called it 'One of the darkest blots on the pages of the history of the relations between their organisation and the department'.[40]

FULL-SCALE REVIEW OF EDUCATIONAL STRUCTURES

Free second-level education was available in England and Wales from 1944, and in Northern Ireland from 1947. It was now expected that Derrig and the government would make it available countrywide. The president of the INTO remarked, that 'If Ireland is to take its rightful place among the nations after the war, the whole educational structures must be rebuilt' and 'every child must have the benefit of secondary education'.[41]

Following a number of requests from de Valera to Derrig between July and October 1942,[42] Derrig finally submitted his unambitious post-war planning proposals.[43] In December 1944, de Valera wrote to Derrig again, urging him to undertake a thorough examination of the education system including primary, secondary, vocational, agricultural and university education, and to establish how 'the standard of education among the mass of the people' could be raised and how 'to provide improved educational facilities'.

He drew Derrig's attention to 'certain plans that have been published by the British Government and by the Government in the Six Counties' and suggested that 'perhaps these white papers contain ideas which we should examine in order to see if they might be useful to all'.[44]

Derrig's feeble response was to set up a departmental committee in March 1945, which concentrated on the educational needs of 14–16-year-olds. De Valera continued to maintain pressure on Derrig, who reported to him in August that the preparation of a white paper would be premature until the committee had progressed its work.[45] An interim report appeared in August 1946 and the final report was produced in June 1947.

Among its recommendations were that children should leave primary school aged 12 and proceed to 'senior schools' which would offer a free literary and practical education. This restructuring would be linked to a raising of the school leaving age to 15, and later to 16 years. There was an acknowledgement of the narrowness of the primary school curriculum, as the committee recommended that it should be enlarged to include physical education, drawing and nature study as compulsory subjects. It was not to Derrig's credit that the report was never published.[46]

A Plan for Education 1947

The INTO once more took the lead, as it produced its own report entitled 'A Plan for Education', which identified defects in the educational system, and which made important recommendations. It took issue with Derrig's 'ostrich-like attitude of wilful blindness to its defects'.[47] The report stated that Ireland was lagging well behind her neighbours with regard to educational reform.[48]

It highlighted several weaknesses in the education system, and identified the main one as lack of educational opportunity, and the fact that it 'was denied to the majority of our people'.[49] It noted that for most children their formal education ended in the primary school, a fact acknowledged by de Valera in the Dáil in June 1940, when he stated that 'For nine out of every ten Irish people, the primary school is their only centre of learning'.[50] It objected to the fact that secondary and university education, which were denied to most people, were 'financed on a much more generous scale than primary education'.[51]

It pointed to the number and value of scholarships, which were so low as to be negligible, and which were characterised more by parsimony than by generosity. It referred to the lack of co-ordination between primary, secondary, vocational and university education, which resulted in a collection of systems lacking unity or cohesion.[52]

The report recommended the setting up of an advisory council of education and an inquiry into the Irish language policy. It called for a child-centred curriculum which emphasised oral Irish, a much wider subject range, and an end to the rating system of inspection and to the primary certificate. With regard to

second-level education, it called for equality of status between secondary and
vocational schools, by ensuring that the curricula in both types of schools had
more in common.[53] The report insisted that there must be an extension of the
school leaving age to 16 years, 'with provision for further education for those who
wish to avail themselves of it'.[54]

Derrig was dismissive of A Plan for Education, claiming that it was superfluous
in light of the fact that Ireland had not been affected, like other European countries,
by the Second World War. He stated that Church and State worked harmoniously
in partnership together in education, an arrangement which had 'been described
as ideal'.[55]

VOCATIONAL EDUCATION 1930–47

In the wake of the Vocational Education Act, the government prioritised vocational education for funding. By 1936 there were forty-six new vocational schools,
twenty-six extensions to existing schools, and plans for a further forty-eight
vocational schools.[56] But O'Neill had a number of concerns regarding vocational
education in rural areas, which he conveyed to de Valera in a memo in July 1933.
He suggested that these schools were not attaining the required educational
standard in general subjects, and neither was the attention of students being
directed towards an agricultural life.[57]

O'Neill favoured the provision of higher primary schools, involving a junior
and senior cycle, and he recommended that these schools should be provided
in Gaeltacht districts, where the need was greatest. Derrig supported the senior
schools proposition, and in January 1934 the department drew up plans for
twenty-one higher primary schools in Gaeltacht districts to supply a practical
second-level education. Derrig had major plans to create 'senior schools'
throughout the entire country in due course.[58] This plan was treated with
derision by the Department of Finance, and in particular his transport scheme.
It involved 'free school transport by means of free bicycles and waterproof
clothing', to which suggestion the Department of Finance remarked 'bicycles for
pupils three miles from new schools is "fantastic" … Will "disappear" frequently.
Accident riding Dept machine'.[59]

The Department of Finance favoured the provision of additional vocational
schools rather than senior schools. The scheme was not proceeded with, however,
following its rejection by the bishops after their meeting in October 1934.
They rejected it on the grounds that the proposals would lead to an erosion of
clerical management and an extension of State control. They were also concerned

about the possible risk to morals 'for boys and girls from twelve to sixteen years coming long distances without any supervision'.[60]

Consideration was given to the question of raising the school leaving age when an inter-departmental committee was set up in 1934 to examine the issue. Provision had been made in the 1926 School Attendance Act, whereby the school leaving age could be raised to 16 years. The Commission on Technical Education which was chaired by John Ingram, the Chief Inspector in the Technical Instruction Branch (TIB) of the department, had recommended that the school leaving age should be raised to 15 years and later to 16 years.[61] The latest inter-departmental committee which was also chaired by Ingram, reported in 1935 that it could see 'no reason for raising of the school-leaving age on the grounds that young people are too immature for employment at the age of 14 years'.

It considered the fact that 'If the school leaving age were raised, there would be a very strong demand for maintenance grants for the disemployed juveniles'. It was satisfied that juvenile employment in non-agricultural occupations was mainly in 'blind-alley employment as messengers, etc'. It failed to see how education could benefit 'such juveniles'. But it recommended that pilot schemes should be initiated in two or three urban areas under the provisions of Part V of the Vocational Education Act, that juveniles in employment should have to 'attend classes for not more than 180 hours per year', and all unemployed juveniles should be 'required to attend whole-time schools'.[62]

The Commission on Youth Unemployment, which was set up in May 1943 under the chairmanship of McQuaid, recommended that the school leaving age should be raised ultimately to 16 years, but as a first step it should be raised to 15 years. It suggested raising 'the school leaving age area by area, according as local conditions become favourable'. In order to proceed in this direction, it urged 'that arrangements be made to expedite the application of Part V of the Vocational Education Act, 1930' and it pointed out that the situation in the county borough of Dublin required immediate action.[63]

O'Neill gave consideration to this question also in his post-war planning report on education, which he prepared for de Valera in July 1942. In it he proposed that vocational education policy should concentrate on extending full-time attendance to 16 years of age as soon as possible.[64] The department recognised that young people often contributed to the family income when they reached this age, and it therefore considered that a system of family allowances should accompany any introduction of compulsory attendance at school up to 16 years.

It was aware that such a scheme could not be confined to vocational education students but would have to be extended to include all second-level students in other schools. Under the circumstances, it settled for the more modest objective of confining compulsory attendance to urban areas, and expanding the scheme when a suitable opportunity arose.[65] Derrig implemented the recommendations of the inter-departmental committee, when as an experimental arrangement, Part V of the Vocational Education Act was enforced in the county boroughs of Cork in 1938, in Limerick in 1942 and in Waterford in 1947.

OPPOSITION TO CONTINUATION EDUCATION

De Valera stated that he was not convinced that continuation schools were worth the public money spent on them. He suggested that programmes carried out in continuation schools could be conducted more effectively in special rooms allocated for the purpose in national schools.[66] His response was coloured by the Catholic Church's criticism of vocational schools. It was even believed in some quarters that he offered the vocational system to an Irish male religious order which refused the offer.[67] His views replicated those expressed in Bishop Michael Browne's Report of the Commission on Vocational Organisation, which claimed that continuation education 'should and could less expensively be given by properly organised primary or secondary schools'.[68]

Revd Martin Brenan, Professor of Education at St Patrick's College, Maynooth, advocated a similar approach in a controversial article published in the *Irish Ecclesiastical Record*. In so doing he caused offence to vocational teachers when he claimed that there was no 'reference to religion as a formative element in the instruction of these schools'. Just as Corcoran had done in 1930, he objected to co-education, which he considered to be 'a form of naturalism that is not tolerated even in Nazi Germany'.[69]

The general secretary of the Vocational Education Officers' Organisation, Frank McNamara, replied to Brenan's article. He cited a number of bishops and priests who had defended the vocational education system, and drew attention to the significant number of clergymen serving on VECs. He implied that Brenan adopted double standards in relation to vocational education when he accepted 'the excuse for co-education in national schools, but ignores it in reference to the Vocational Schools'.[70]

Prompted by the Irish Technical Education Association (ITEA), a departmental committee was set up in 1942 which reviewed the work of continuation education. It subsequently circulated Memorandum V40 for the guidance of VECs and their employees. It was drafted by J.P. Hackett, the head of the TIB and chairman of the committee. The memorandum allayed fears regarding the concerns raised. The emphasis was now placed on religious instruction, which was to be incorporated into the normal teaching day. Lay teachers were expected to play their part by ensuring that their subject matter was permeated with Christian values. It also placed a greater emphasis on the Irish language 'and other distinctive features of national life'.[71] It concluded by emphasising the role of women in the home and 'advised that the domestic economy programme should be focussed on the home needs and family role of girls'.[72]

The ITEA, having achieved what it wanted on this issue, now turned its attention to securing the introduction of an examination for vocational schools.[73] This had been called for by employers, parents and teachers, mainly to enhance the employment prospects of students. The department was initially opposed to the idea of a national examination, on the grounds that one of the fundamental aims of the Vocational Education Act was to provide structures whereby schools could deliver courses which would reflect local needs.

The ITEA seized the initiative and, following its 1943 congress, urged Derrig to establish a committee to devise a system of examination for day vocational schools. He agreed to this and nominated three inspectors to sit on the committee. The committee devised an examination scheme which became known as the day group certificate, and the first nationwide examination was held in June 1947.[74]

FURTHER PLANS TO REPLACE VOCATIONAL SCHOOLS

Vocational education came under the critical scrutiny of O'Neill again in 1942, when he submitted a memo to de Valera on agricultural education in the schools. He was dissatisfied with the contribution this sector was making towards the promotion of agricultural education, especially at a time when increasing numbers were leaving the land. He proposed replacing vocational schools by restructuring the primary school into junior and senior schools. The junior school would provide the traditional primary education for students up to 12 years of age, while the senior school would provide a 4-year full-time course of a practical and literary type, suited to the needs of an agricultural economy. It was proposed that the schools in question would be under the primary school management system.[75]

O'Neill's dissatisfaction with the curriculum of vocational schools was echoed in the report of the Commission on Vocational Organisation, which condemned the reluctance of VECs to promote the full integration of agricultural education in vocational schools. The criticism was unwarranted as the department of Agriculture had responsibility for agricultural education and it was 'assiduous in arguing that it alone had the right to organise agricultural education'.[76] The commission referred to the fact that the two departments of the State which had most to do with the vocational needs of the country – the Department of Agriculture and the Department of Industry and Commerce – had only indirect and relatively restricted functions in regard to vocational education. It was highly critical of the Department of Education's decision to found a network of expensive vocational schools that reached into every parish and town 'to teach not agriculture, but commerce and domestic economy'.[77]

Like the INTO's A Plan for Education, the commission regretted the lack of co-ordi-nation in the education system, a system where there was no link between primary and vocational schools and overlapping between secondary and vocational schools, and the higher standards of primary schools.[78] As in the INTO document, the commission recommended an expansion of the narrow primary school curriculum.[79]

The government did not welcome the report of the commission, which had been chaired by Bishop Michael Browne, a person not known for his 'eirenic temperament'[80] or for his diplomatic skills. The conclusions of the report were particularly hard hitting. The Department of Education remarked that its 'comments consist mainly of sweeping generalisations and inaccuracies which do not give a correct estimate of the work done in Vocational Schools'.[81] Seán Lemass was Minister for Industry and Commerce, and he took exception to criticisms of his department in the report. Speaking in the Senate, he referred to the 'querulous, nagging, propagandist tone of its observations' and castigated it as 'such a slovenly document'.[82] Commentators did not agree that this comprehensive and very thorough report was 'a slovenly document'.[83]

The departmental committee of 1945–47 posed a further threat to the existence of vocational schools, as its recommendations bore an uncanny resemblance to O'Neill's plans as set out in his memo to de Valera in 1942. The VECs had good reason to be concerned about the committee's recommendation that 'the new system … should be subject to ecclesiastical sanction'.[84]

Hackett, who was the author of Memorandum V40, was also a member of the departmental committee. He felt obliged to issue a personal statement on noting the criticism of the non-religious control of continuation education. He observed that Memorandum V40 had been 'an effort to effect a reconciliation by the denominationalism of continuation education'. In despondent tones, he concluded 'I am now satisfied that no reconciliation is possible and that there is no real future for Continuation education under vocational committees'.[85] Vocational schools were offered a reprieve when disaffected teachers and the Irish public voted Fianna Fáil out of office in the general election of 1948.

Like O'Sullivan, Derrig attempted unsuccessfully to overcome the problem of poor school accommodation. He had been in correspondence with Bishop James Staunton of Ferns, County Wexford, the secretary to the Catholic hierarchy, in May and October 1943, as he tried to get the hierarchy to change the method of raising the local contribution towards school buildings. Staunton did not support his plans.[86]

Following the precedent set by MacNeill and O'Sullivan, Derrig allowed a number of concessions to the Protestant community. Under a plan initiated on 1 July 1934, the department, which was already operating van and boat services for children on islands or in isolated rural areas, expanded the programme to cover Protestant children who lived a considerable distance from a Protestant school.[87] In 1937 a major concession was sanctioned in order to enable Protestant primary schools to employ as JAMs those with qualifications lower than that specified in the rules. It was directed that this concession was not to appear in the published rules.[88] Two years later he sanctioned a scheme for the State subvention of books for all necessitous children.[89]

Thomas Derrig became an authoritarian Minister over his 15 years in office, but as a young Minister he supported radical plans to introduce senior schools into Gaeltacht areas. He was even prepared to replace O'Sullivan's fledgling vocational schools with senior schools under clerical management. The vocational schools were saved, but children were deprived of free second-level education when Derrig's resolve weakened in the face of episcopal opposition.

A decade later he came under pressure from de Valera to produce plans 'to provide improved educational facilities'. Just as in the 1930s, he was prepared to replace vocational schools with senior schools, which would be 'subject to ecclesiastical sanction'. Once again the vocational schools were saved because his party was voted out of office, and yet again Irish children were deprived of a golden educational opportunity.

Derrig's Revised Programme of Primary Instruction was a ruthless attempt to revive the Irish language, done in the knowledge that it would lead to falling standards in all other subjects. In 1943 the primary certificate was made a compulsory examination in the hope of raising educational standards, but oral Irish did not form part of it, even though Derrig and the government wished to revive Irish as a vernacular language.

Thomas Derrig had a fractious relationship with the INTO. He rejected their 1941 report which showed that the language policy was placing a mental strain on children, and that it was educationally regressive and unacceptable to parents. In rejecting this report, Derrig made a serious error of judgment, as research conducted in the 1960s confirmed the accuracy of the 1941 report and the high educational price children paid for the language policy. Derrig's claim that 'our system of education approaches the ideal'[90] because Church and State worked harmoniously in partnership together, was his lame excuse for rejecting the INTO's 1947 report, which was a progressive document providing a blueprint for the reform of Irish education.

He revealed his true feelings about the futility of the language policy in 1943, at which stage he had access to the Pollak report, yet he stubbornly refused to acknowledge the truth in the INTO reports, and refused their call for an education inquiry as he could not admit to the failure of his key educational policy and nationalist aim.

Parents' concerns were completely ignored, because Derrig as Minister believed he knew more about education than they did, and the failure of his court battle did not convince him otherwise. When he felt that his authority and that of the government was being challenged by the Dublin teachers' strike, he insisted on their unconditional surrender. This strike was avoidable because the teachers had a just claim which won them widespread public support and ecclesiastical sanction. His decision to make a special payment to teachers who made their services available during the strike was anathema to the INTO, and undoubtedly contributed to the government's defeat in the 1948 general election.

The only authority he yielded to was that of the bishops. He bowed to their wishes in 1934 and demurred from bringing Bishop Staunton to book in 1943. Thomas Derrig could have left a vital legacy to Irish education if only he had the energy and drive to accept de Valera's invitation 'to provide improved educational facilities'. Had he done so, free second-level education could have been introduced in southern Ireland, as it had been in Northern Ireland, as early as 1947.

Notes

1 *Irish Press*, 19 April 1945. Said by Deputy Morrissey, Fine Gael.

2 He took part in the 1916 Rising and was an associate of de Valera. He was Minister for Finance 1939–45. In 1945 he was elected as Ireland's second President.

3 De Valera was the main driving force behind the founding of Fianna Fáil in 1926. It became the largest political party in the country. He was elected third President of Ireland in 1959, a post he held for two terms until 1973.

4 O'Connell, *History of the INTO*, pp.208–9. Frank Fahy was O'Kelly's assistant since O'Kelly was Minister for Irish in the First Dáil, and he was shadow Minister for Education 1927–32.

5 D.R. O'Connor Lysaght, *The Republic of Ireland: An Hypothesis in Eight Chapters and Two Intermissions* (Cork, 1970), p.133. According to Liam C. Skinner's *Politicians by Accident* (1946), Derrig chose to resign.

6 Op. cit., pp.265–8. This resulted from the Economic War when de Valera withheld land annuities previously paid to the British Government and when the latter, in retaliation, imposed duties on Irish exports of livestock and livestock products.

7 Report of the Department of Education for 1933–34, p.29.

8 Report of the Department of Education for 1945–46, p.9.

9 *Dáil Debates*, vol. 12, col. 817, 11 June 1925.

10 Coolahan, *Irish Education*, p.180.

11 *Belfast Telegraph*, 24 April 1930.

12 Department of Education, Registered File 34809, cited in Coolahan and O'Donovan, *A History*, p. 120.

13 O'Connell, *A History of the INTO*, p. 363.

14 Department of Education Revised Programme of Primary Instruction (Dublin, 1934), p.3.

15 Report of the Commission on Vocational Organisation (Dublin, 1944), pp.332–3. In 1939 the Government appointed the commission under the chairmanship of one of the few bishops identifiably sympathetic to Fianna Fáil, Bishop Browne of Galway. Browne's report was scathing in its criticism of vocational education and of government bureaucracy. The report was presented to government in November 1943 and was published in August 1944.

16 Coolahan, *Irish Education*, p.42.

17 *Times Educational Supplement*, 8 December 1934. Fine Gael was formed in 1933, when Cumann na nGaedheal merged with the Centre Party and the Blueshirts – see Maurice Manning, *The Blueshirts* (Dublin, 2006).

18 *Dáil Debates*, vol. 59, cols 2195–8, 10 December 1935.

19 *Times Educational Supplement*, 17 November 1934.

20 Dr Alfred O'Rahilly, 'The Republic of Ireland' in *The Year Book of 1951* (London, 1951), p.353; *Times Educational Supplement*, 20 April 1943.

21 Report of the Department of Education for 1934-35, p.25.

22 *Irish Press*, 22 November 1944.

23 O'Connell, *History of the INTO*, p.365; Donal McCartney, 'Education and language 1938-51' in Kevin B. Nowlan and T. Desmond Williams (eds) *Ireland in the War Years and After 1939–51* (Dublin, 1969), pp.83–4.

24 INTO Report of the Committee of Inquiry into the Use of Irish as a Teaching Medium to Children whose Home Language is English (Dublin, 1941), p.12, p.24, p.60.

25 NAI *S7801A*.

26 *Dáil Debates*, vol. 87, col. 735, 1 June 1942.

27 NAI DT *S13180A*. Irish Language Policy 1943, 1949 and 1950. Memorandum Position of Irish Language 30 March 1943.

28 *Irish School Weekly*, 6–13 May 1944, p.186.

29 NAI *S7801* Dr Johanna Pollak, 'On teaching Irish', 1943.

30 *Dáil Debates*, vol. 83, col. 1097, 27 May 1941.

31 This was a reference to the *Notes for Teachers – Irish* which the inspectors compiled and which was published by the Department of Education in 1933. It was the forerunner of a number of booklets providing advice to primary teachers and students in training. It was in use until the 1960s, when new teaching methods were introduced.

32 *Irish School Weekly*, 9–14 October 1943, p.342.

33 Comhdháil Náisiúnta na Gaeilge was established as a coordinating body for a number of Irish organisations, including the Gaelic League in 1946. It was a formidable pressure group for the advancement of the gaelicisation policy. It demanded that the government do more to save Irish.

34 *The Irish Times*, 2 October 1944.

35 *Irish School Weekly*, 18–25 November 1944, p.467.

36 The 'highly efficient' rating was a restricted category, so that a teacher might have to wait for another teacher to retire, resign or die before becoming eligible for the grade.

37 *Irish Independent*, 20 March 1944.

38 *Senate Reports*, vol. 31, col. 1047, 21 March 1946.

39 The publication of McQuaid's letter reputedly swayed some teachers to join the strike. His support for the strike caused a rift between himself and the Taoiseach.

40 *The Irish Times*, 20 March 1946.

41 *Irish Weekly Independent*, 15 April 1944.

42 NAI *S12891 'A'*.

43 NAI *S12891 'B'* Submission by Department of Education, 7 December 1944.

44 Ibid., Letter from de Valera to Derrig, 16 December 1944.

45 Ibid., Letter from Derrig to de Valera, 29 August 1945.

46 NAI *S13638*.

47 INTO, A Plan for Education (Dublin, 1947), p.10.

48 Ibid., p.15.

49 Ibid., p.10.

50 *Dáil Debates*, vol. 80, col. 1566, 6 June 1940.

51 A Plan for Education, p.10.

52 Ibid., p.12.

53 Ibid., p.73.

54 Ibid., p.16.

55 *Senate Reports*, vol. 33, col. 1927, 18 June 1947.

56 Coolahan, *Irish Education*, p.97.

57 NAI *S9271*. Educational reconstruction. S. O'Neill, 21 July 1933.

58 Ó Buachalla, *Education Policy*, p.262.

59 NAI *S20/1/34*.

60 NAI *S9271*. Copy of minutes of the meeting of the hierarchy, 9 October 1934, forwarded to O'Neill.

61 The two reports of the INTO in 1941 and 1947 called for the raising of the school leaving age.

62 Report of the Inter-Departmental Committee on the Raising of the School Leaving Age (Dublin, 1935) in Report of the Council of Education on the Function and Curriculum of the Primary school, appendix 10, pp.338–9.

63 Report of the Commission on Youth Unemployment (Dublin, 1951), pp.42–3.

64 NAI *S12891 'A'*. Post-war planning education, 16 July 1942.

65 NAI *S12891 'A'*. Memorandum on vocational education 15 October 1942.

66 *Dáil Debates*, vol. 80, col. 1573, 6 June 1940.

67 Ó Buachalla, *Education Policy*, p.269.

68 Report of the Commission on Vocational Organisation, p.269.

69 Martin Brenan, 'The vocational school' in *Irish Ecclesiastical Record*, 57 (1941) pp.124–7.

70 Frank McNamara, 'Reply to Dr Brenan's articles by the general secretary, VEOO' in

The Vocational Education Bulletin, 22 (1941), pp.416–8. The VEOO (1930–54) preceded the VTA.

71 Department of Education, Organisation of whole-time continuation education.
    Memorandum V.40. (1942), p.22.

72 Coolahan and O'Donovan, *A History*, p.155.

73 ITEA annual congress report 1942, p.67.

74 Op. cit., pp.156–7.

75 NAI *S14392*.

76 Áine Hyland, 'The curriculum of vocational education 1930-1966' in John Logan (ed.)
    Teachers' Union: The TUI and its Forerunners in Irish Education 1899-1994 (Dublin, 1999), p.140.

77 Report of the Commission on Vocational Organisation, p.216.

78 Ibid., p.333.

79 Ibid., p.268.

80 Lee, *Ireland 1912–1985*, p.274; Walsh, *UPSTART*, p.20. 'His flock in Galway called
    him "Cross Michael," a nickname derived … from the way he signed letters and his
    severe demeanour.'

81 NAI *S13552*.

82 *Senate Reports*, vol. 29, col. 1323, 21 February 1945.

83 Dermot Keogh, *Twentieth-Century Ireland: Revolution and State Building* (Dublin, 1994), p.150.

84 NAI *S12891 'B'*. Report of the Departmental Committee on Education Provision,
    June 1947, paragraph 25.

85 NAI *S12891 'B'*. Note on continuation schools with special references to paragraph 31,
    J.P. Hackett, 18 July 1947.

86 NAI *S12891*.

87 Akenson, *A Mirror to Kathleen's Face*, p.118.

88 NAI *S12753 'A'*. Cabinet memo 17 November 1944; Ó Buachalla, *Education Policy*, p.267.

89 McElligott, *Education in Ireland*, p.52.

90 INTO, A Plan for Education, p.10.

7

Richard Mulcahy (1948–51): 'I think the function of the Minister for Education is a very, very narrow one'

At his suggestion the Government established Coimisiún na Gaeltachta. Naturally he was made Chairman.[1]

Richard Mulcahy (1886–1971) is an iconic figure in Irish political history. As Chief-of-Staff of the Irish Republican Army, he played a leading role in the War of Independence, and became Commander-in-Chief of the Irish Free State army following the death of Michael Collins. He took over from W.T. Cosgrave in 1944 but he stepped aside as leader of the Fine Gael party to allow John A. Costello to become Taoiseach in the first Inter-Party government, in deference to those parties whose memories of his role in the civil war made him unacceptable as Taoiseach. William Norton, the 32-year-old leader of the Labour Party, became Tánaiste.[2]

In retirement Mulcahy recalled 'at length' his first impressions on entering the Department of Education. It took him 6 months to realise the nature of the malaise which he found there, a malaise which was aggravated by a 7½-month strike by Dublin teachers at the time. He laid the blame firmly on Derrig's shoulders as 'There was no sense of initiative, vision or power … Derrig was simply a blue bottle on a window there'.[3]

Mulcahy set about honouring commitments he had given to teachers while he was in opposition. First, he arranged for a review of the language policy by a committee of primary school inspectors. The review was not a comprehensive one as it was conducted by just four inspectors who visited twenty-nine schools, rural and urban, in fourteen different counties.[4] This resulted in some modification of the language programme in 1948, and in the introduction of the Revised Programme for Infants.[5] The programme allowed for the teaching of English as an optional subject for infants and first class for half an hour each day, provided the manager of the school approved. Mulcahy then left the future of the language policy to the proposed Council of Education to pass judgment on.

As part of the rapprochement following the bitter strike by Dublin teachers, and following the recent rejection of A Plan for Education, he held a series of meetings in the department with representatives of the INTO, managerial authorities, including Archbishop McQuaid, and department officials. The decision was then taken to drop the 'highly efficient' rating of inspection so that, in future, teachers' salaries would no longer be affected by an inspector's rating. He also changed the basis for calculating staff ratios, from attendance to enrolment numbers.[6] In addition, Mulcahy guaranteed incremental and pension rights to the teachers who had gone on strike.

However, the teachers were somewhat aggrieved with his selective implementation of the Roe Committee's recommendations on their salaries.[7] They could at least take consolation from the progressive methods for infant teaching promoted in the inspectors' booklet, *An Naí Scoil: The Infant School: Notes for Teachers*, published in 1951, which showed an awareness of the importance of child-centred education. The INTO had called for the adoption of such methods in A Plan for Education.

Mulcahy's first ministerial speech was uninspiring. He said, 'I want it to be understood that I think the function of the Minister for Education is a very, very narrow one'.[8] A year later he addressed delegates at the INTO congress in Arklow, County Wicklow, and proceeded to give his famous 'oil-can' speech, in which he visualised his ministerial role as that of peacekeeper and 'fixer' of the education system. He was the one who removed causes of friction between the authorities and the teachers. He went on to explain that 'It was the function of the Minister to watch out for causes of irritation, and having found them, to go around with the oil-can'.[9]

Seán O'Connor, who became assistant secretary in the department in the mid-1950s when there were many changes at senior level, disagreed fundamentally 'with the view that the Minister had no function in the making of policy'. He believed that had these modernising officials been in place in the department in 1949, they would have persuaded Mulcahy to reconsider his attitude 'because he was a man of courage who was not afraid to admit to a change of mind'.[10]

Mulcahy faced a severe shortage of trained primary teachers. The problem was compounded by the rise in the birth rate and by increased enrolments in primary schools. Different solutions were put forward. The Department of Education sought an additional training college, but the Department of Finance, like the INTO, wanted a removal of the ban on married women teaching and the recruitment of graduates for primary teaching. Mulcahy suggested that the preparatory college in Galway, Coláiste Éinde, could be converted into a training college, but the Department of Finance rejected his suggestion. It allowed the recruitment of an extra forty students per year to Carysfort Training College in 1947 and 1948,[11] and an extra twenty students to St Patrick's Training College in 1951.

A COUNCIL OF EDUCATION

A council of education had been requested by the INTO, among others, for 30 years.[12] Throughout most of this period the Catholic Church was opposed to a council, but following the papal encyclical *Quadragesimo Anno* of Pope Pius XI in 1931, Church opposition faded. The encyclical proposed the establishment of vocational groups, corporations or guilds in which workers and employers would collaborate for their mutual benefit.[13] The Commission on Vocational Organisation, which followed strictly along the lines set out in the encyclical, and which quoted copiously from it, recommended the setting up of an advisory council of education in its report of 1943.

After 2 years in office, Mulcahy set up a Council of Education in order to advise on the function and curriculum of the primary school. His terms of reference to the council were limited. It quickly became apparent that his main aim was to preserve the managerial system intact, and to maintain the status quo in the control of Irish education. He wished the council members 'to make clear that whatever the function of the State was, it had no power to interfere ... with the rights of the parents or with the authority of the Church'.[14]

Addressing members of the council in the department, Mulcahy said that 'World circumstances of the last 30 years ... have obviously prevented the natural development of our educational thought but our schools and syllabuses have served our fundamental needs and given good service'. The chairman of the council, Canon Denis O'Keeffe, Professor of Ethics and Politics at UCD, was also happy to maintain the status quo, particularly in relation to the balance of power in the field of education. In his address he stated that 'our education system is superior to anything that I know of anywhere', because of 'an exact appreciation of what is and what is not the legitimate function of the State'.[15]

The council consisted of men and women with experience and standing in the educational world, twenty-six of whom were professional educators, and eleven of whom were clerics of various denominations. It was an unrepresentative council as trade unions were not represented, and neither was there a representative appointed from the inspectorate. It was surprising that no parents' representative was appointed, especially when one considers the great care which was taken to ensure protection for parents' rights in the terms of reference.

The first inter-party government lasted until 1951, when a major controversy erupted over the plans of the Minister for Health, Dr Noel Browne, to introduce a free medical scheme for mothers and children, known as the Mother and Child Scheme. The scheme provoked an angry response from the medical profession and the hierarchy, and had the effect of destabilising the government, which eventually led to its dissolution.

Mulcahy was beginning his second term as Minister in the second inter-party government of 1954 when the Report of the Council of Education was published. The proposals were indeed modest, but the report did recommend an expansion of the primary school curriculum, just as the Commission on Vocational Organisation, the departmental committee of 1945–47, and A Plan for Education had previously done. It urged the inclusion of drawing, nature study and physical education as compulsory subjects in primary school.[16] It endorsed the language policy[17] without having conducted the requisite scientific research in this area, and without making any reference to the survey conducted by the INTO. It was also at odds with the recommendations of the Commission on Youth Unemployment in 1951, which called for an examination of primary education and in particular the teaching of Irish. The report had no influence on the curriculum, but in November 1954 Mulcahy requested the council to proceed to examine the curriculum of secondary schools.

Notes

1   *The Irish Times*, 17 December 1971. Tribute on death of General R. Mulcahy by Ernest Blythe, Minister for Finance, 1923–32.

2   Norton was leader of the Labour Party from 1932 to 1960.

3   Richard Mulcahy, *Richard Mulcahy (1886-1971): A Family Memoir* (Dublin, 1999), p.228.

4   *Irish Press*, 27 May 1948; *Dáil Debates*, vol. 113, cols 1369–70, 14 December 1948; NAI *S7801 'A'*.

5   NAI *S7801 'C'*.

6   *Dáil Debates*, vol. 115, col. 296, 28 April 1949.

7   Report of the Committee on National Teachers' Salaries, 1949.

8   *Dáil Debates*, vol. 110, col. 1089, 4 May 1948.

9   *Irish School Weekly*, 30 April and 7 May 1949, p.200.

10 Seán O'Connor, *A Troubled Sky: Reflections on the Irish Educational Scene 1957-68* (Dublin, 1968), p.5.

11 Report of the Department of Education for 1946-47, p.2.

12 Pádraic Pearse is generally credited with being the first to propose the idea of a council in 1912.

13 Whyte, *Church and State*, p.67.

14 *Dáil Debates*, vol. 110, col. 1093, 4 May 1948; *Department of Education, A Council of Education: Terms of Reference and General Regulations* (Dublin, 1950).

15 *Irish Independent*, 6 May 1950 'Council of education begins its work'.

16 Report of the Council of Education on the Function and Curriculum of the Primary school, p.116, p.120.

17 Ibid., pp.144–6.

8

Seán Moylan (1951–54):
'I do not agree with this idea
of equal opportunities for all'

I do not think there is any interest in education amongst the people in this country.[1]

... that self-righteous most cultured of carpenters.[2]

Seán Moylan (1889–1957) became Minister for Education in the newly elected Fianna Fáil government during a period of economic stagnation with high inflation and rising emigration levels. Bishop Cornelius Lucey of Cork captured the mood of the time when he remarked that 'rural Ireland is stricken and dying. The will to marry and live on the land is almost gone'. He referred to the alarming decline in the Irish population which had been plummeting for over a century, rendering the Irish 'the vanishing Irish'.[3] John A. O'Brien wrote about this phenomenon in his book of essays, *The Vanishing Irish*.[4]

Moylan, who was a self-educated building contractor from a teaching background, was a close friend of de Valera.[5] It was believed that he was appointed Minister primarily because he had built up a relationship of trust with teachers when attempting to bring an end to the Dublin teachers' strike. Like Mulcahy, his educational plans were unambitious, being confined to the provision of more school buildings and a new training college for Catholic women. In outlining his general education policy, Moylan stated that 'it is not my intention to make any drastic changes with regard either to departmental policy or administration'.[6]

He had some liberal views on education, but they rested alongside some very conservative ones. He understood the importance of nurturing a child's interest and of ensuring that the school environment was stimulating for teachers and students.

To this end, he arrived at the innovative idea of allowing teachers a 'free' half-day each week, during which they could select the curriculum of their choice. He was also an ardent supporter of school libraries as a means of encouraging children to read. On the other hand, he rejected the idea that the primary school curriculum should be expanded to include extra subjects. He believed that as 'this curriculum would mark the end of formal education for most children, it must therefore be complete in itself'.[7] De Valera shared similar views.[8]

Moylan showed concern for children with special needs as he allowed a pupil–teacher ratio of 15:1 in schools for the blind in 1952. He also sanctioned the purchase of specialised equipment for these children. Just 5 years previously, the first special school for children with general learning disabilities, St Vincent's House for Mentally Defective Children, was recognised by the State.[9] But Moylan, like so many of his contemporaries in Ireland and elsewhere, did not see the need for widespread remedial education provision for children with general learning disabilities. In his opinion, it was 'a very small problem' in rural schools and was 'of significant proportions only in a city like Dublin'.[10]

Seán Brosnahan, the general secretary of the INTO, was acutely aware of the extent of this problem, and he commented angrily that 'One of the greatest crimes of our system is the callous disregard for subnormal and backward children', many of whom were 'condemned as fool and dunces'.[11] It was the mother of a son with learning disabilities who in June 1955 took the first step towards starting what became known as the Association of Parents and Friends of Mentally Handicapped Children, later called St Michael's House.[12]

Moylan's strong allegiance to vocational education became immediately apparent. Speaking at the opening of a new vocational school in Lucan, he encouraged students to take up the profession of vocational teaching. He expressed sentiments that would be repeated 5 years later by the secretary in the Department of Finance, when he said that 'The teachers they had were excellent and worked as if they had a mission rather than a job'.[13] He invested heavily in vocational education and during his 3-year tenure as Minister, 160 vocational schools were built and numbers attending whole-time courses in vocational schools rose from 18,000 to 20,000 between 1951 and 1954.[14] According to the 1950–51 Report of the department, there was such 'strong demand' for both continuation and technical education that in many centres 'long lists of students were awaiting admission' and enrolments at country VECs 'taxed to the maximum the available accommodation'.[15]

The INTO commented on Moylan's extraordinary zeal for vocational education. Primary teachers alleged that department officials displayed a clear bias in favour of vocational education in its annual report for 1953, which devoted 'whole pages to the names of technical-school prizewinners'.[16]

Secondary education was not as appealing to Moylan. Speaking in the Dáil, he said, 'I do not agree with this idea of equal opportunities for all'.[17] His argument was that, as everyone did not have the ability to benefit from the opportunity offered by free secondary education, he failed to see why it should be freely available to all. Later he questioned whether a secondary-school education could equip students with the necessary skills to improve the economy of the nation.[18] Addressing an audience at the opening of a new vocational school at Banagher in County Offaly, he asked, 'Are we satisfied that 80% of our children should leave the primary school at the age of 14?'

He acknowledged that 'It was not sound economics that we should allow the great majority of these children to degenerate into illiteracy'. Moylan saw the connection between the lack of educational opportunity for 80 per cent of Irish children and the corresponding loss to the Irish economy, but his solution lay solely in 'The provision of adequate vocational education'.[19] His response reflected his own personal preference, but it disregarded parental choice, which was demonstrated by the growing demand for secondary education. The number of secondary schools rose from 278 in 1924–25 to 424 in 1950–51.[20]

The shortage in teacher supply was a problem that Moylan had inherited. Mulcahy had unsuccessfully attempted to procure a new training college, but action was now required as the number of students at primary level was growing and was expected to reach 500,000 by 1960.[21] The Department of Finance's proposal to remove the marriage ban, as a solution to the teacher shortage, was successfully resisted by Moylan and the department, on such grounds as 'the woman cannot with full efficiency serve both home and school', 'two salaries coming into one house causes unfavourable comment', and 'the later months of pregnancy will occasion unhealthy curiosity'.[22]

Moylan disregarded the objections of the INTO when he sanctioned the recruitment of untrained assistants or JAMs. David Kelleher, the general secretary of the INTO, protested against the injustice being perpetuated against children living in areas without secondary schools who were being taught in national schools by untrained teachers. In 1953 the number of untrained teachers was its highest ever level.[23]

The department took a further measure to ameliorate the problem when it allowed teachers who had reached the retirement age of 65 years to postpone retirement for 3 years, with the inspector's approval. Finally, in December 1953, the cabinet agreed that Coláiste Éinde should be converted into a training college, a proposal which had been rejected by the Department of Finance in February 1951. However, when Moylan's secretary contacted McQuaid, he offered him places for additional students at Carysfort Training College, thereby granting a reprieve for Coláiste Éinde and avoiding a confrontation between Moylan and Bishop Browne, who was opposed to the plan from the start.[24]

SCHOOL ACCOMMODATION CRISIS

T.J. O'Connell, as general secretary of the INTO, called once more for the State to take responsibility for the building of schools, and for local authorities to take charge of school maintenance. He did so at the INTO congress of 1945, and moreover he had the courage to do so in the presence of Bishop Browne, who addressed the congress. His suggestion was stoutly rejected by Bishop Browne, who saw it 'as a threat to the managerial system', which he said 'has given Ireland, the most satisfactory state of Catholic school control of any country in Christendom'.[25]

The INTO was prompted to take action, and in 1950 it conducted a survey among its members, and ascertained that there was widespread dissatisfaction with school conditions. For the next 18 years it conducted a vigorous campaign to lobby the support of members of Church and State to bring about an improvement in the situation. The INTO took some comfort from a speech delivered by Moylan at the opening of another vocational school, this time in County Galway. He spoke of the necessity of speeding up the building of primary schools throughout the country. He admitted that the replacement of defective and dilapidated schools was not as swift as it should be, but he was 'Hopeful that it would be possible to make drastic changes for the provision of school buildings'.[26]

It was obvious from his address to the INTO congress in 1952 that he was acutely aware of the seriousness of the problem to be tackled, when he admitted that many schools were 'a national disgrace' and that about 10 per cent of them were 'practically derelict'.[27] In the Dáil he suggested that LECs should be set up for school maintenance purposes and that the local community should contribute more. He expected the children to sweep their schools once a month, thereby bringing 'a saving to the State ... of possibly £100'.[28] A year later the topic came up for discussion in the Dáil, and once again he suggested that 'the children could do a good deal towards keeping the school neat and tidy during the week', only this time he estimated the saving to the State at £100,000.[29]

Matters were brought to a head when Bishop Eugene O'Callaghan of the diocese of Clogher, accused the teachers of trying to take the schools out of the hands of the Church and of giving them over to the State. Speaking at a confirmation service, he accused the INTO of undermining the managerial system and asked, 'Why should a caretaker be required to clean out a school for these lords who are coming in for a few hours?' He feared 'that Civil Servants from Dublin might come down and attempt to take control of a school'. He told managers to assert themselves and 'show that schools belonged to them and the Church'.[30] The INTO objected to the use of the pulpit to launch an attack on the teachers of Ireland, with its 'references which would be laughable if they were not made by a member of the Hierarchy'.

It challenged O'Callaghan to specify when, where and by whom such a policy had been advocated. The Bishop replied that he had been informed by reputable teachers, 'but was now grateful to the INTO for declaring their views'.[31]

In June 1952, Kelleher wrote to Cardinal D'Alton on the vexed question of school maintenance, and he put forward the INTO policy on the matter. D'Alton wrote to Kelleher stating that 'if these proposals were adopted, it would undermine and most likely, ultimately lead to the abolition of the managerial system'. He requested the INTO to cease its campaign and to concentrate on getting a better allocation of State funds, to which the INTO agreed. Two years later D'Alton wrote to Kelleher repeating the concerns of the bishops, that if school maintenance was removed from managers 'that it would circumscribe and endanger the rights of managers'.[32] One thing was certain, preserving the managerial system intact was as important to the bishops in the 1950s as it was to them during the height of the MacPherson controversy.

Seán Moylan was a self-educated Minister who set great store on reading. He favoured school libraries and encouraged teachers to make school life stimulating for children. Yet he adopted a utilitarian view of the value of education. He promoted vocational education determinedly because of its potential benefits to the Irish economy, but he did not enthuse over secondary education, as he did not think it could provide the same function as effectively. Even though an increasing number of parents sought a secondary education for their children, Moylan held firmly to his view that free secondary education for all was unwarranted, as all children could not benefit from it equally. He did not mince his words when he said, 'I do not agree with this idea of equal opportunities for all'.[33]

Several reports called for an expansion of the narrow primary school curriculum, but Moylan disregarded them because it was his view that children required a curriculum that was 'complete in itself' as most of them would leave school at primary level. There were at least three occasions when he ignored the professional advice of the INTO and relied on his own judgment. One was when the general secretary of the INTO complained bitterly about the callous disregard for children with special educational needs, the other was when David Kelleher condemned in the strongest terms his policy of recruitment of untrained teachers, and lastly when he abnegated his responsibilities and left it to the INTO to confront Cardinal D'Alton on the school maintenance issue.

As he approached the end of his political career he had little appetite for altering the status quo or for holding school managers to account. However, Seán Moylan did leave a ministerial legacy when he invested the limited funding available to him in developing vocational education.

Notes

1   *Irish Press*, 5 November 1952. Seán Moylan TD, Minister for Education speaking at the Fianna Fáil árd-fheis.

2   Michael McInerney, *Peadar O'Donnell: Irish Social Rebel* (Dublin 1974), p.102.

3   *Irish Independent*, 28 May 1952.

4   John A. O'Brien (ed.) *The Vanishing Irish: The Enigma of the Modern World* (London, 1954), pp.33–5.

5   Moylan took part in the War of Independence as leader of the Newmarket Battalion and later as officer commanding the Cork No. 2 Brigade. He also took part in the civil war.

6   *Dáil Debates*, vol. 125, col. 1670, 17 July 1951.

7   *The Irish Times*, 18 April 1953, 'Danger of state control of schools'.

8   *Irish Press*, 19 April 1945, 'Taoiseach's Dáil speech on education plan'.

9   Seán Griffin and Michael Shevlin, *Responding to Special Educational Needs: An Irish Perspective* (Dublin, 2007), p.38.

10 *Dáil Debates*, vol. 139, col. 1338, 16 June 1953.

11 *Irish School Weekly*, 15 and 22 March 1952, p.127.

12 Griffin and Shevlin, *Responding to Special Educational Needs*, pp.39–40.

13 *Irish Press*, 10 February 1953. The secretary in the Department of Finance was Dr T.K. Whitaker.

14 Report of the Department of Education for 1951; 1954.

15 Report of the Department of Education for 1950–51, p.23.

16 *Irish School Weekly*, 10–17 October 1953, p.444.

17 *Dáil Debates*, vol. 126, col. 1743, 17 July 1951.

18 *Dáil Debates*, vol. 131, col. 1088, 6 May 1952.

19 *Irish School Weekly*, 10–17 October 1953, p.444.

20 Report of the Department of Education for 1924–25; 1950–51.

21 Akenson, *A Mirror to Kathleen's Face*, p.135.

22 *Dáil Debates*, vol. 126, cols 1741–2, 17 July 1951; NAI *S6369*

23 *Irish School Weekly*, 5–12 December 1953, p.531.

24 Jones, *A Gaelic Experiment*, pp.130–1.

25 *Catholic Herald*, 20 April 1945; Irish newsletter 'Education: Irish dilemma'.

26 *Times Educational Supplement*, 8 February 1952.

27 *Irish Weekly Independent*, 19 April 1952.

28 *Dáil Debates*, vol. 132, cols 241–2, 28 May 1952.

29 *Dáil Debates*, vol. 139, col. 1330, 16 June 1953.

30 *Times Educational Supplement*, 17 June 1952.

31 *Irish Weekly Independent*, 14 June 1952.

32 O'Connell, *History of the INTO*, pp.440–2.

33 *Dáil Debates*, vol. 126, col. 1743, 17 July 1951.

9

Richard Mulcahy (1954-57): 'I was in the Department of Education for two periods of office and I ask myself, what did I do there?'

Richard Mulcahy succeeded Seán Moylan when he became Minister for Education for the second time, after the inter-party government took over power from Fianna Fáil in 1954. Once again Costello served as Taoiseach and Norton as Tánaiste. Two years later the government established a Department of the Gaeltacht. This in turn led to the setting up of the semi-State body Gaeltarra Éireann, whose function it was to attract industries to Gaeltacht areas. There was now a general acceptance of the failure of the language policy. This development was seen as confirmation of government acceptance of that failure, as 'increasing industrial development would hasten the demise of the language by encouraging the spread of English'.[1] Nonetheless, educators and Irish language enthusiasts alike awaited with interest the Report of the Council of Education on the curriculum of the secondary school, which Mulcahy had commissioned in 1954. They had to wait 8 years for its publication.[2]

It was a conservative report with little new to offer. It identified the dominant purpose of the secondary school as being for 'the inculcation of religious ideals and values'.[3] It endorsed the academic curriculum,[4] and it gave its blessing to the language revival policy, without having recourse to empirical research. Free post-primary education, which had been called for by the ASTI in 1923, the Labour Party in 1925, and the departmental committee and the INTO in 1947, was considered by the council to be 'untenable and utopian'.

However, it recommended an extension of the scholarship scheme and improved grants to secondary schools, recommendations which were taken on board by the government.[5] It also favoured continued support for small secondary schools, even though they might not be able to provide 'a full science programme with science laboratories'. It stated that there was no need to formalise existing arrangements for 'vocational guidance', which took 'the form of discussion between teachers and pupils and parents'.[6]

Reaction to the report was generally negative. The commentary in the May edition of *Hibernia* was representative of the overall reaction, when it dismissed the report as an anodyne document which deteriorated 'in places into generalization and platitude'.[7] There was widespread disappointment that it did not recommend the introduction of free second-level education. Many agreed with the editor of *The Irish Times* that the report had 'missed a singular opportunity to give a new direction to the cultural and commercial orientation of Irish secondary education'.[8]

In *A Family Memoir*, Richard Mulcahy admitted that he did not believe in the language policy, but he was caught for a way out. It was at Mulcahy's instigation that the government set up Coimisiún na Gaeltachta in 1925, which he chaired, but by the 1950s he was prepared to recommend the closure of Coláiste Éinde and to support the establishment of Gaeltarra Éireann in the Irish heartland.

Mulcahy has long been ridiculed for his limited view of his role as Minister for Education. He did not see a leadership role for himself in policy making, but he did endeavour to honour his commitments to teachers who were demoralised after the Dublin teachers' strike and following the rejection of A Plan for Education.

Mulcahy was approaching the end of his political career, and according to his son, he was unable 'to adopt new ideas and to accept the necessity for change'. There was much truth in his comment that 'The same could be said of his ageing political colleagues, on both sides of the political divide'.[9]

Notes

1 Jones, *A Gaelic Experiment*, p.139.
2 Report of the Council of Education: the curriculum of the secondary school (Dublin, 1962). The report was completed in 1960 but it took a further 2 years to translate it into Irish.
3 Ibid., p.80.
4 Ibid., p.88.
5 Ibid., p.252.
6 Ibid., pp.82–4.
7 *Hibernia*, May 1962, p.6.
8 *The Irish Times*, 26 April 1962.
9 Mulcahy, *A Family Memoir*, p.230.

10

Jack Lynch (1957–59): 'Vocational schools are being turned into educational dustbins'

As the youngest member of the cabinet in 1957, he seemed to adhere to the old ways of doing things … he showed little Ministerial imagination during his tenure at education. Of course, he could always plead that the lack of finances hampered him initially.[1]

Following the general election of 1957, Fianna Fáil was returned to power having won an impressive electoral victory of sixty-seven seats.[2] This was de Valera's last general election, and he served as Taoiseach for 2 years before becoming President of Ireland. He nominated Jack Lynch (1917–99), a 40-year-old barrister and civil servant, as Minister for Education and the Gaeltacht.[3]

In 1957 unemployment in Ireland peaked at 78,000.[4] The country continued to have a stagnant economy, unlike most other countries in post-war Europe. Emigration reached its highest level in 1956–57, more than at any time since the Famine.[5] The Bishop of Clonfert, William J. Philbin, called it 'the capital sin of our young Irish state'.[6]

When introducing the department's estimates for 1957–58, Lynch was forced to continue the cutbacks first introduced by Mulcahy in 1956–57, which saw capitation grants paid to secondary schools cut by 10 per cent and the annual grant paid to VECs cut by 6 per cent.[7]

In May 1957, Dáil deputies sought action from Lynch on a range of educational issues, including raising the school leaving age. He informed them that raising the school leaving age to 16 would require the employment of between 400 and 450 extra teachers[8] as well as the provision of additional educational facilities. He wanted to do so, but was not in a position to, due to scarce resources and the fact that existing facilities were already under great strain because of increased demand.

The education system was not without its critics. In the spring issue of *Studies*, the Irish quarterly review published by the Jesuits, Fr Seán Ó Catháin produced his final essay in a series on secondary education in Ireland. In it he rejected the department's external examinations as being harmful to education and he urged their replacement by individual school certificates.[9] This suggestion of school-based assessment did not even warrant a reply from Lynch, nor was he presented with a parliamentary question on it.[10]

In March 1958, John O'Meara, Professor of Classical Languages at UCD, launched an attack on the Department of Education, comparing it to a 'stagnant pond' that 'Hardly more than a ripple or two has come to disturb' or was likely to disturb in the future.[11]

O'Meara made several salient points as he called for rationalisation of buildings, equipment and teachers at second level. Students who should have been availing of the 'first class scientific equipment in the vocational schools' were attending the more prestigious secondary schools. He called for urgent action to be taken to break down the prejudice against the vocational schools and for their status to be enhanced. He was echoing a call made over a decade previously by the INTO in A Plan for Education.[12]

The vocational schools operated at a disadvantage as they could only offer a 2-year day vocational (group) certificate examination, which had little or no transfer value to further education. The drop-out rate in vocational schools was very high and some teachers became demoralised at the perception of their schools as 'just dead-end schools for dead-end kids'. Vocational schools attracted under-motivated students. One dispirited vocational teacher commented in 1957 that 'vocational schools are being turned into educational dustbins into which are thrown the boys and girls who can't get into secondary schools'.[13]

In his estimates speech for 1957–58, Lynch commented on the haphazard manner in which students enrolled in one type of post-primary school rather than another. On one point at least he was in agreement with O'Meara and the INTO, when he said, 'There might be too many children of a certain intellectual calibre in one type of school who should be in another'.[14] However, he did not comment on O'Meara's verbal onslaught on his department.

Traditionally, governments had underfunded secondary schools, which were privately owned. O'Meara castigated the department for forcing the school authorities to engage in cost-cutting measures, such as the employment of unqualified members of their religious orders in teaching roles and the abandonment of the teaching of expensive subjects in favour of cheaper ones.[15]

Lynch handled the vexed question of the funding of secondary schools with political adroitness. Referring to the absence of State grants for the building, maintenance and general equipment of secondary schools, he explained that when the State provided a capitation grant it was 'intended indirectly, to assist in meeting … the cost of providing and maintaining schools'. If the State were to subsidise the building of secondary schools, then it would be 'forced to intervene to a much greater degree than at present in matters connected with the establishment of schools, such as their location, the pupils attending'.[16]

For 1958 and for most of 1959, there was almost total silence from Lynch on the subject of secondary education[17] as he awaited the report of the Council of Education. The exception to this was the announcement that the 10 per cent cut which had been taken away from secondary schools was to be restored, and that extra money was to be made available to secondary-school authorities to assist them provide for the inordinate increase in student numbers.[18] The only other announcement of significance made by Lynch came in the spring of 1958, when he confirmed that an oral Irish test would be included in the leaving certificate examination from 1960.

According to T.K. Whitaker, the vocational education system was more flexible 'than the Primary and Secondary systems', and those concerned with it were imbued with an enthusiasm, which gave 'something of a missionary character to the work involved'.[19] Like Moylan, Lynch concentrated his efforts on developing vocational education. In 1958 he announced that the grants to VECs were to be restored, that Bolton Street College of Technology was to be extended, and that a new building was to be provided for the Kevin Street college. Demand for vocational education increased with the continuing decline in the agricultural sector. Consequently, the number of vocational schools grew to 260, with another 537 centres being used for vocational education. Evening and adult education classes were attended by three times as many students as attended the full-time day courses.[20]

One of the main attractions of the vocational education system was its flexibility, a feature which earned favourable comment from Whitaker in his ground-breaking report 'Economic Development'. Charles McCarthy, the general secretary of the Vocational Teachers' Association (VTA), pointed out that courses could 'spring up' as soon as local need arose – courses were run for Aran fishermen in County Galway every year since 1954, for 7–8 weeks during the summer months.[21] Both Whitaker's report and the government's subsequent White Paper on Economic Development,[22] which incorporated much of the former report, acknowledged the part that vocational schools could play in providing agricultural education.

It was evident that the government recognised the importance of vocational education in the economic recovery of the country. A clear change in emphasis in education policy could now be detected from the speeches delivered by Lynch within a year of each other. When he addressed the annual conference of the ASTI in April 1958, he was still emphasising the importance of education as a means of instilling 'a sense of national, cultural and ethical values'.[23] A year later he was informing the VTA congress about 'courses of instruction which were contributing in an increasing way to our economic development'.[24]

When interviewed in January 1969, Lemass was asked to identify the biggest problem which faced the industrial drive of the 1930s and he replied, 'The lack of technical knowledge'.[25] It was the responsibility of each VEC to supply or aid technical education in its own area. The aim of technical education was not only to train students for entry to specific employments, but also to improve the skills of those already in employment.

By 1950 full-time technical education was available only in the large urban centres of Dublin, Cork, Limerick, Waterford and County Clare. The total number enrolled came to 514. Two possible reasons for the limited provision of technical education may have been the high cost of providing technical instruction and the low demand for the type of expertise it supplied. Part-time technical instruction and evening technical courses proved to be popular in areas such as hairdressing, mechanical engineering and radio operation.

However, with the introduction of rural electrification in 1948, there was an increased demand for related courses which were available in technical schools. In 1949 the department reported that demand outstripped supply and that waiting lists were being employed for popular courses. In the same year, technical education got a fillip from the establishment of the Industrial Development Authority (IDA), which was a State industrial agency. Growth in this area continued, and the Department's Report for 1950–51 commented on 'the strong demand' which was in evidence for both continuation and technical education. It reported that at many centres 'long lists of students were awaiting admission'.[26]

Apprenticeship education in technical schools was not properly regulated. The government passed an Apprenticeship Act in 1931 which enabled the Minister for Industry and Commerce to make an order declaring a trade to be a designated trade in an area. Apprenticeship committees were set up, but the Act was very weak as it enabled rather than obliged the committees to make rules requiring employers to train and instruct their apprentices in a specified way. Many trades disregarded the provisions, and in 1951 the Report of the Commission on Youth Unemployment recommended 'that it be mandatory on Apprenticeship Committees to make rules relating to educational qualifications … and the training and instruction to be given to apprentices'.[27]

These recommendations were taken on board by Lynch as Minister for Industry and Commerce. From June 1959 he devoted much of his time to the preparation of a comprehensive scheme for regulating the sector. This led to the 1959 Apprenticeship Act being passed and a national apprenticeship board, An Cheárd Chomhairle, being set up, with power to require all employers to send their apprentices to training courses in technical schools. Vocational education and vocational teachers received a considerable boost in 1960 when An Cheárd Chomhairle stipulated that the day vocational (group) certificate examination should be the entrance qualification for apprenticeship.

The VTA was riding on the crest of a wave in the late 1950s, so much so that its president, L. McGreena, called for higher technological units for each VEC area, on the basis that the routes to higher education should be open to all students, 'whether through Secondary schools to the universities or through Technical schools to Technological Colleges'.[28]

LOW EDUCATIONAL STANDARDS

Lynch was the first Minister to have 'gone through the machinery of compulsory Irish' himself, as the editor of the *Sunday Independent* observed.[29] He was less likely then to repeat the mistakes of his predecessors who identified education with the revival of the Irish language, and who placed an undue burden on teachers. Lynch expressed confidence in the teachers and pointed to the lack of public support for their efforts in reviving the language. He suggested that 'It might be that the public had failed the teachers'.[30] He adopted a moderate stance regarding the teaching of Irish as he believed that Irish was 'never going to replace English, but I would like to see it rank as an equal'.[31]

He and his department were subjected to a barrage of criticism, mainly from the press and the INTO, regarding deteriorating educational standards. It was sparked off by the results of entrance examinations held in a number vocational schools, which showed that 'Some children leaving national schools are almost illiterate ... Some cannot write their own names correctly'.[32]

The finger of blame was immediately pointed at officials in the department, who had been 'experimenting on Irish children for twenty-five years ... with disastrous results' in their efforts to revive Irish. The press completely exonerated the teachers, who had 'cried out in a vain effort to alarm both officials and Ministers against the disasters ahead'.[33]

The president of the INTO, Liam O'Reilly, regarded the allegations by anonymous vocational teachers as 'mischievous, misleading and without foundation'. He said it was a well-established fact that at least 10 per cent of the school children of any country were educationally sub-normal. It was unlikely that their parents would send them to secondary schools. The only alternative for Irish parents was to send them to vocational schools and 'he regretted that the educational facilities necessary for the advancement of these retarded children had not been provided by the authorities'.[34]

The department faced a formidable challenge to its language policy in September 1957 when Fr E.F. O'Doherty, Professor of Psychology at UCD, alleged that Irish educational policy was 'based on the production of a pseudo-bilingualism that was psychologically, emotionally and educationally, bad for children'. According to O'Doherty, experiments showed that monoglots did better in intelligence tests than bilingual or pseudo-bilingual children.[35] In January 1958 he delivered a lecture to Tuairim,[36] in the course of which he attributed the language policy to 'a series of erroneous beliefs held in good faith by honourable men' who remained convinced that it was 'through the schools the Irish language could be restored … without any evidence that it was even possible'.[37]

Lynch and the department remained sceptical about O'Doherty's theories. Lynch believed that 'A person who learned Irish had an advantage over the person who knew only English, in the study of other languages'.[38] However, de Valera who had been harbouring doubts about the school-based language revival policy since the 1930s, set up an inquiry into the language policy in February 1958, known as the Commission on the Restoration of the Irish Language, whose broad terms of reference included activities both inside and outside the school. It had the effect of shielding Lynch from further consideration of the language issue until the inquiry was completed.[39]

THE MINISTER'S REFORMS

The majority of the members of the 1954 Council of Education arrived at a figure of thirty as the optimum class size for primary schools, and they considered that forty should be the maximum number. They noted that 23 per cent of teachers were untrained, and they recommended that they should be trained immediately.[40]

One in five lay teachers in primary schools had not undergone teacher training, and almost one in three religious teachers had no teaching qualification. There was a shortage of 3,000 trained teachers and, with the high rate of attrition from teaching, it was estimated that it would take over three and a half decades to make up the shortfall. In addition, an extra 4,000 teachers would be required to bring class sizes down to 30. However, Lynch was determined that this was 'a target we should endeavour to achieve in the shortest possible time'.[41]

He took a number of significant steps to achieve this goal. At the 1958 ASTI conference, he signalled his willingness to rescind the marriage ban, claiming that it was 'unjustified and intolerable' that those forced out of teaching by the ban were in many cases replaced by unqualified teachers. He believed that 'The employment of so many untrained teachers' was 'educationally indefensible'.[42] In May 1958 he removed the marriage ban.[43] By this action alone an extra 330 teachers had been added to the workforce. Two further ministerial actions contributed greatly towards reducing the pupil–teacher ratio, and one was the decision taken to lower the averages required to appoint an extra teacher. In two-teacher schools, a third teacher could be appointed from 1 July 1959, as the department had lowered the average on rolls and the average attendance required from 100 and 85, respectively, to 90 and 75.[44]

When he introduced the estimates to the Dáil in April 1959, Lynch announced the end of the policy of recruitment of untrained teachers. He specified that JAMs were to be trained on special courses to be provided for them. The courses were conducted between 1967 and 1976.[45] During his speech he revealed that 'In 1958 the department completed the largest ever school building programme in the history of the State'. This would go a long way towards solving the long-standing problem of large classes in Irish schools.[46]

From his maiden speech in the Dáil in 1948, Lynch showed a keen awareness of the suspicion with which inspectors were viewed by teachers. When Liam O'Reilly complained about 'the 79 inspectors who patrol the national schools',[47] and about 'the coercive atmosphere of an obsolete system of inspection'[48] in which teachers 'still suffered from many pin-pricks which should find no place in an enlightened age' due to 'the system of merit marks',[49] Lynch responded appropriately. Within a year he announced the end of the efficiency rating system of inspection, with only a few exceptions, and the end of the Observation Book in which inspectors made their comments. This had the effect of leading to much more harmonious relations between teachers and inspectors.[50]

He brought further comfort to the INTO, which had been strongly opposed to the preparatory colleges since their inception, with the introduction of suitability interviews for all candidates for training colleges. Students from the preparatory colleges would have to compete for places in training colleges with secondary-school candidates. This open competition, coupled with the introduction of an oral Irish test as part of the leaving certificate examination, meant that candidates from secondary schools would have to reach a high level of fluency in the Irish language. This marked the beginning of the end for the preparatory colleges. It also brought succour to Liam O'Reilly, who had stressed 'the urgency of a complete overhaul of the present method for the selection and training of candidates' in the training colleges.[51]

Although Lynch had very little involvement in third-level education, he took a vitally important decision to appoint a Committee on Accommodation Needs of the National University of Ireland (NUI), in response to the overcrowding problems in the universities. He was also party to the decision to transfer UCD from the antiquated buildings it occupied at Earlsfort Terrace to the modern campus at Belfield, County Dublin.

Jack Lynch ushered in a new generation of Ministers for Education who had no links to Ireland's revolutionary past. He was a reforming Minister, but he was also a Minister who avoided engaging in public debate on educational issues. He had three opportunities to do so, one was when Ó Catháin criticised the public examination system, and again when O'Meara excoriated his department and gave a highly critical appraisal of second-level education, and lastly when O'Doherty questioned what he called the government's 'pseudo-bilingual policy'. Had he responded to these criticisms, he might have stimulated public interest in education in a country where Ministers had complained for decades about educational apathy.

He revived the vocational education sector as its importance for the economic recovery of the country was now accepted by the government. He did so at a time when vocational teachers complained that 'vocational schools are being turned into educational dustbins into which are thrown boys and girls who can't get into secondary schools'.[52] The INTO (in A Plan for Education) and O'Meara had called for the raising of the status of vocational schools, but Lynch took few steps in that direction, as vocational schools continued to attract under-motivated students.

Secondary schools were hardly mentioned by Lynch during 1958 and for most of 1959 as he awaited the Report of the Council of Education. This was a much more problematic sector as the schools were privately owned and had a plethora of management bodies. Compared to the vocational sector, secondary schools were grossly underfunded as they only received a capitation grant. Lynch's observation that if the government provided building grants to secondary schools, then it could decide the location of any new schools in the future, was indeed insightful, as time would tell.

There was a reasonable expectation that as a Minister who had first-hand experience of the compulsory Irish policy, that he would take steps to set up an Irish language inquiry. Contrary to expectations, it was left to the Taoiseach to take the initiative to do so. This meant that Lynch was shielded from further consideration of the issue until the inquiry was completed.

Lynch was guided by the recommendations of the Council of Education when he reduced the pupil–teacher ratio, when he discontinued the policy of recruitment of untrained teachers, and when he insisted that all JAMs would have to be trained. He accepted the professional advice of the INTO, and consequently the system of inspection was reformed and suitability interviews were introduced for entry to the training colleges, thereby ending the preferential treatment afforded to preparatory college candidates in the past. The introduction of an oral Irish test for the leaving certificate for all students signalled the beginning of the end for the preparatory colleges.

Jack Lynch was the first Minister to recognise that he had a leading role to play in education policy making, that education policy was not synonymous with the Irish language policy, and that it was essential to rely on professional reports and professional advice in order to advance worthwhile reforms. This was his ministerial legacy to Irish education.

SEÁN LEMASS

The withdrawal of de Valera from the Dáil marked the end of an era. Seán Lemass, who replaced him as Taoiseach, had a different vision for Ireland. De Valera gave expression to his vision in his famous 1943 St Patrick's Day radio broadcast to the Irish at home and abroad. 'That Ireland that we dreamed of' speech portrayed a vision of an arcadian idyll where people would be 'satisfied with frugal comfort', where they 'devoted their leisure to things of the spirit'.[53]

Lemass's vision for Ireland was defined by his pragmatism and his desire to raise the country's economic standing.[54] He was the first Taoiseach to recognise the indispensable role education would play in the long-term economic development of the country.

Notes

1   T. Ryle Dwyer, *Nice Fellow: A Biography of Jack Lynch* (Cork, 2001), p.54.

2   Keogh, *Twentieth-Century Ireland*, p.239.

3   Jack Lynch held the portfolio of Minister for the Gaeltacht for 3 months.

4   John A. Murphy, 'The achievement of Éamon de Valera' in John P. Carroll and John A. Murphy (eds) *De Valera and His Times* (Cork, 1983), p.10.

5   *Irish Press*, 2 May 1957.

6   Revd William Philbin, 'A city on a hill' in *Studies*, 46 (1957), pp.264–5.

7   *Dáil Debates*, vol. 161, col. 703, 2 May 1957.

8   Ibid., col. 701.

9   Revd Seán Ó Catháin, 'Secondary education in Ireland: a new plan' in *Studies*, 46 (1957), pp.60–75.

10 O'Connor, *A Troubled Sky*, pp.19–20.

11 J.J. O'Meara, *Reform in Education* (Dublin, 1958), p.6, p.16.

12 INTO, A Plan for Education, pp.10–11.

13 *Sunday Independent*, 22 December 1957; O'Meara, *Reform in Education*, p.16.

14 *Irish Press*, 2 May 1957.

15 O'Meara, *Reform in Education*, pp.9–10.

16 Jack Lynch, 'Minister's address to convention' in *School and College Year Book* (Dublin, 1959), p.33.

17 Randles, *Post-primary Education*, p.30.

18 *Dáil Debates*, vol. 174, col. 59, 8 April 1959.

19 T.K. Whitaker, *Economic Development* (Dublin, 1958), paragraph 9, chapter 11.

20 Report of the Department of Education for 1959-60, p.118, p.121.

21 Charles McCarthy, 'The quiet revolution' in *Sunday Press*, 18 October 1959.

22 Programme for Economic Expansion (Dublin, 1958).

23 Jack Lynch, 'Minister's address to convention', p.35.

24 Dwyer, *Nice Fellow*, p.66.

25 *Irish Press*, 24 January 1969.

26 Coolahan and O'Donovan, *A History*, p.161.

27 Report of the Commission on Youth Unemployment, p.22, pp.44–5.

28 L. McGreena, Presidential address to the VTA congress, 31 March 1959.

29 *Sunday Independent*, 5 January 1958.

30 *Irish Press*, 2 May 1957.

31 Dwyer, *Nice Fellow*, p.64.

32 *Sunday Independent*, 22 December 1957.

33 *Sunday Independent*, 29 December 1957.

34 *Irish Independent*, 20 January 1958.

35 O'Connor, *A Troubled Sky*, p.22.

36 Tuairim was a research group or 'think tank' of the late 1950s, composed of young academics and researchers seeking solutions to Ireland's social, economic and political problems.

37 E.F. O'Doherty, 'Bilingual school policy' in *Studies*, 67, pp.266–7.

38 *The Irish Times*, 25 October 1957.

39 *Dáil Debates*, vol. 168, col. 1494, 11 June 1958.

40 Report of the council of education on the function and curriculum of the primary school, p.202, p.212.

41 *Dáil Debates*, vol. 161, col. 701, 2 May 1957.

42 Dwyer, *Nice Fellow*, pp.61–2.

43 *Dáil Debates*, vol. 168, col. 1501, 11 June 1958.

44 *Dáil Debates*, vol. 174, col. 57, 8 April 1959.

45 Ibid., col. 58.

46 Ibid., col. 57.

47 *Irish Independent*, 20 January 1958.

48 *The Irish Times*, 20 January 1958.

49 *The Irish Times*, 9 April 1958.

50 *Dáil Debates*, vol. 174, col. 58, 8 April 1959.

51 *The Irish Times*, 9 April 1958.

52 *Sunday Independent*, 22 December 1957.

53 Richard Aldous, *Great Irish Speeches* (London, 2007), pp.92–5.

54 Brian Farrell, *Seán Lemass* (Dublin, 1983), pp.120–1.

11

Patrick J. Hillery (1959–65): 'The Modern Third Estate'

The appointment of Patrick Hillery as Minister for Education in June 1959 was crucial, for under his regime education was transformed from a political albatross, into a subject of continual public interest and continual debate.[1]

Seán Lemass's choice for the education portfolio was a 36-year-old doctor, Dr Patrick Hillery[2] (1923–2008). Hillery was a reluctant Minister. His initial response to Lemass's offer was, 'I can't do a thing like that; I have people booked in for babies', but he accepted when Lemass allowed him to fulfil his commitments to his patients.[3]

He had no previous parliamentary experience and he faced formidable opposition from Noel Browne, who had founded the left-wing National Progressive Democrats party in May 1958. Browne tabled a motion in the Dáil in October 1959, calling for the extension of the statutory school leaving age to at least 15 years. During the process, Browne engaged in a lengthy critique of the education system.[4] Hillery defended it when he replied that 'the picture is very much better than many of our critics would appear to believe'.[5] He then outlined the department's education policy.

He regarded it as one of his main functions as Minister to increase the rate of provision of the necessary facilities for post-primary education. He also intended to broaden the scope of scholarships.[6] The Taoiseach took the unusual action of intervening in the education debate on 28 October 1959[7] as he set out the government's education policy for post-primary education, which was 'to bring about a situation in which all children will continue their schooling until they are at least fifteen years of age … Our immediate policy is to increase the facilities for post-primary education'.[8]

Hillery recognised the key role education would play in the economic development of Ireland. He saw education as the foundation stone 'of all hope for the progress of this country', and therefore he believed that it was imperative 'that the system of education should, as far as possible, fit the pupils to face the modern world by, for example, promoting the study of science.[9]

The Organisation for European Economic Co-operation (OEEC), the international organisation which was set up in 1948, and which was superseded by the OECD in 1961, examined provision for the teaching of science in Irish schools and colleges. The results were disappointing. The OEEC summoned representatives of the department and other interested parties to its headquarters in Paris for what was called 'a confrontation meeting' about 'this gap in our system'.[10] It transpired that only 50 per cent of science teachers in second-level schools were university graduates in science.[11] In March 1960, Professor T.S. Wheeler of UCD told the OEEC seminar on chemistry teaching, that fewer than one in six secondary schools taught chemistry to leaving certificate.

The OEEC reviewers also noted a strong classical bias in the Irish secondary-school curriculum, which was almost entirely linguistic. However, the situation had improved since 1955 when 90 per cent of the boys who sat the leaving certificate examination presented for Latin, and 100 per cent presented for Irish, while only 9 per cent took French, and two students took Spanish, both of whom failed. In the same year, 18 per cent of the boys took physics and 21 per cent chemistry.[12] As late as the academic year 1962–63, only about 30 per cent of the boys and about 14 per cent of the girls taking the leaving certificate examination answered papers in the sciences. Once again Latin proved to be a popular subject, with 80 per cent of the boys taking the leaving certificate examination presenting for Latin, whereas only 21 per cent presented for French.[13] According to Ó Catháin, 'For the majority Latin is a tragic waste of time, of opportunity, of energy'.[14]

Tuairim was highly critical of the secondary-school curriculum. It concluded that, 'It is possible to complete the whole secondary-school course and matriculate without ever having read a complete book'.[15] There was some justification for the claim, as prescribed texts were re-introduced between 1939 and 1941,[16] with the result that English courses in particular assumed 'a predictable pattern of a limited range of set texts, many of which had the status of "dusty classics"'.[17]

Browne alerted Hillery to the inequities in the education system, where 3,126 primary school students competed in 1959 for a mere 635 scholarships. He reminded him that the value of scholarships awarded on the results of the intermediate certificate examination had remained static since 1929. He accused the department of 'creating a class of permanently stratified society'.[18]

Hillery was conscious of the inequalities that existed in the education system, and he promised to increase the number of scholarships, but Tuairim did not believe that scholarships were a panacea for the injustices of the system of selection for post-primary education. As far as they were concerned, increasing the number of scholarships for those capable of benefiting from secondary education implied that some children deserved an academic post-primary education and some did not.[19]

Browne also drew Hillery's attention to Ireland's paltry level of expenditure on education compared to other countries, as he quoted the relevant figures from the World Survey of Education prepared by the United Nations Educational, Scientific and Cultural Organization. In Russia the figure was £7 per head of population, in the USA £5, in Scotland £2.25p, and in England and Northern Ireland £2. The equivalent Irish expenditure was 50p. Hillery pointed out that if vocational education was taken into account, the figure would be 86p.[20] This debate was continued in the press when O'Meara attacked the 'meagre endowment by the State' in education. He cited the UNESCO figures again to bolster his case. This prompted a reply from Hillery's secretary clarifying that the State expenditure per head of population was not 50p as stated by O'Meara, but rather 86p.[21]

REFORMS IN EDUCATION

The 1960s was a decade of optimism. 'There was a certain sense of spring in the air'.[22] The morale of the people rose as the economy had been revived, emigration and unemployment figures had fallen, and industrial production had risen. Hillery had a fair wind to his back – with modernising officials in his department and a Taoiseach whose support and political guidance he could rely on.

Hillery continued with the policy already initiated of lowering average class sizes still further for the employment of additional assistant teachers, and of increasing teacher supply. The INTO kept him regularly informed on the overcrowding problem in Dublin classrooms, which peaked at seventy students per class in the early 1960s. In early 1964, he took decisive action by deploying the department's inspectors to all national schools in Dublin City, with instructions to ensure that, either by rearrangement of classes and classrooms or by the appointment of additional teachers and the provision of prefabricated classrooms, no class in any school would have more than fifty students.[23]

Speaking in the Dáil, he announced the supply of 100 prefabricated classrooms and 100 teachers for Dublin schools. When the survey of all Dublin schools was completed, he intended 'to have one done for the rest of the country'.[24] Official approval was given for the supply of 112 prefabricated classrooms and the appointment of 104 additional teachers in the Dublin area between June and

September 1964.[25] The survey of Dublin schools established that a total of 737 classes had more than fifty pupils. In order to ensure 'that the outrageously large classes should not re-appear with the heavy summer enrolments',[26] the department issued Circular 16/64 to all Dublin schools, instructing that infant classes must be limited in size to fifty from 1 July 1964.[27]

The Minister also announced the lowering of averages in schools with a staff of between five and eleven teachers, where the pupil–teacher ratio was at its worst, for the appointment of fourth up to ninth assistant teachers from 1 October 1964.[28] He had already decreased by ten units the averages necessary for the appointment of a second assistant teacher, with a further decrease of ten units for the average required for the appointment of third, fourth, fifth and sixth assistant teachers from July 1960.[29]

The Minister and the department were also making steady progress in reducing the number of untrained teachers in primary schools. On 1 July 1959 the figure stood at 2,907 untrained teachers, 364 of whom were awaiting entrance to a training college, but in 1963 that number had fallen to 2,275.[30]

Educational reforms, spearheaded by Jack Lynch and implemented by Hillery, brought gains for St Patrick's Training College in particular. The college, which had been closed throughout the year 1944–45 due to the availability of a surplus of teachers, was now expanded due to a teacher shortage. In May 1962, Hillery announced in the Dáil that the Department of Education would finance the building and renovation programme for the college. The reconstruction of the college was completed in September 1966 at a cost of £1,500,000.[31] The department had initiated plans to train an additional 100 teachers annually, and it was committed to increasing this number in the future.[32] Two years later the government was in a position to double the total annual expenditure on education and Hillery informed the Dáil that it was their intention to increase the number of primary school teachers by a further 1,000 by 1970.[33]

Since 1930 the training colleges had been obliged to accept candidates from the preparatory colleges on a preferential basis; however, this situation was no longer tenable as criticism mounted against the colleges. The INTO and in more recent times the Catholic bishops, were opposed to them, as well as senior officials in the department itself, who had regarded the system as a liability from the late 1950s onwards. This was largely due to their unimpressive academic record at this time. The standard achieved by preparatory college students in the leaving certificate was lower than that attained by successful candidates in the open competition for entry to the training colleges.[34] In the late 1950s, just over one-third of students were unlikely to have obtained places in training colleges had they been in competition with other students.[35]

The raison d'être of the preparatory colleges had been removed following two educational reforms implemented by the Minister in 1960. The first one was the introduction of the oral Irish test at leaving certificate level and the second one was the change of policy regarding the teaching of Irish, as outlined in Circular 11/60. The circular which was issued to the primary school authorities in January 1960, stipulated that inspectors would in future attach greater importance to oral than to written Irish when assessing the work of teachers. From now on teachers of junior classes, who had been obliged since the 1920s to teach through the medium of Irish, would be at liberty to change 'the emphasis from teaching through Irish to the teaching of Irish conversation' if they considered that greater progress would be made in oral Irish.[36]

In announcing the closure of the preparatory colleges, Hillery said that 'when the Preparatory Colleges were set up they were necessary but they had their weaknesses', and that in the light of recent reforms, it was appropriate to cease their operation. He intended instead to increase the number of scholarships to secondary schools for Gaeltacht students from eighteen to eighty, and to increase the number of university scholarships from five to fifteen. Coláiste Moibhí was to remain open[37] as he did not believe that the Protestant secondary schools would be able to supply sufficient numbers for the Church of Ireland Training College (CITC). Three of the preparatory colleges were to be used as All-Irish secondary schools.[38]

SPECIAL EDUCATION

Hillery took significant steps in the early 1960s to enhance the area of special education by giving formal recognition to it as a distinctive sector. As a result of a recommendation from two inspectors, Seán de Búrca and Tomás Ó Cuilleanáin,[39] who had been sent on a 4-month study visit to Jordanhill in Glasgow for special education needs training, a new course for teachers in special schools was initiated in St Patrick's Training College, Drumcondra in October 1961.[40] It was a 1-year programme leading to a post-graduate diploma which enabled graduates to qualify as recognised teachers in special schools or special classes, other than for blind and deaf students.[41] A special diploma course was also provided in UCD in the early 1960s in conjunction with St Mary's School for Deaf Girls, Cabra.[42] In 1962 the department authorised a pupil–teacher ratio of 15:1 and provided a grant for specialised equipment for special schools.[43] Within the space of 5 years, the number of special schools grew from twenty-six to forty-five and the number of students increased from 1,950 to 2,800.[44]

The modernisation of the education system was advanced further when the secretary of the department, Dr Torlach Ó Raifeartaigh, visited various schools and colleges in the USA from 4 April 1960 to 10 June 1960. He returned to the department with innovative ideas, many of which were later applied in the Irish education system. He was impressed by students' project work and by the broad range of subjects taught in elementary schools, which was in contrast to the situation prevailing in Ireland. In the USA, the usual subjects were taught in a 'wider connotation', for example history and geography extended 'into the realms of sociology'.[45]

The notion of a 'wider connotation' would form part of the thinking behind the 'new curriculum' introduced into primary schools in 1971, which would also include the concept of project work. Ó Raifeartaigh took note of the 'mechanical aids' in use in American classrooms, 'especially the film and the recording machine' which were widely employed.[46] The department benefited greatly from Ó Raifeartaigh's research, particularly with regard to the comprehensive curriculum for second-level education, which it would implement in Ireland in the late 1960s.[47] In 1960 educational aids were not generally used in this country, but that was soon set to change. Lemass confirmed in July 1964 that 'Research into new teaching methods is in process as is also the provision of modern teaching aids'. He confirmed also that 'consideration is being given to extending the range of subjects taught in primary schools'.[48]

School building came under the scrutiny of the department when a divisional inspector and an architect from the Board of Works visited England and Scotland in May and June 1962. The purpose of their visit was to study school design, classroom size, furniture, play areas, teaching methods, curriculum, the role of head teachers and standards of attainment. They produced an important report based on their research. This report, coupled with the advances made in special education, influenced the shape of education policy for primary education. Subsequently, school buildings were modernised with regard to design and furnishings. Teaching methodologies were reviewed in the light of lessons learned from the techniques and skills applied to special education, and the curriculum now became the focus of a more child-centred approach to teaching children.[49]

Advances were also made in the area of language teaching when Hillery supported a study of the Irish language and language learning in general. A new language laboratory was set up in the Franciscan College, Gormanston, County Meath, under the direction of the distinguished linguist, Fr Colmán Ó hUallacháin. Such was the level of success achieved that within a few years a series of Irish language conversation lessons had been developed by the department for use in primary schools as part of an audio-visual method of teaching Irish. The programme, known as *Buntús Cáinte* or 'rudiments of language' involved new teaching methods and teaching aids, such as film-strip projectors and tape-recorders. This was quite an achievement 'Given the fact that many schools did not have electricity at this time'.[50]

Hillery was well advised when he enhanced the resources available to primary schools by providing grants from November 1963 for the establishment of school reference libraries.[51] They were installed in five counties initially, encompassing 640 primary schools.[52] The initiative was gradually extended to the entire country between 1964 and 1968.[53] Other practical improvements to primary schools included a new scheme which provided funding for painting and decorating.[54] The scheme made State grants available from 1 April 1962 towards the cost of painting primary schools externally every 4 years and for internal decoration every 8 years. Ó Raifeartaigh encouraged school managers to co-operate with the scheme in order to avoid the 'premature reconstruction' of primary schools.[55]

The education correspondent of *The Irish Times* was very critical of the paltry amount being provided by way of grants towards the heating and cleaning of primary schools. He did not attach any blame to the managers of schools or to parents, as many managers had outstanding debts for church building and parents believed that the State should provide the extra contribution.[56] Another commentator blamed the poor condition of some primary schools primarily on 'bureaucratic delays in replacing buildings and the inadequate public budgetary allocation'.[57]

There can be little doubt that the pressure applied by the INTO on school managers and on the government resulted in positive gains in this area. Joint deputations of the Clerical Managers and the INTO representatives met three Ministers for Education in order to resolve the contentious issue of proper school maintenance. They met Mulcahy on 21 June 1955, and Lynch on 24 June 1957 and on 25 June 1958. They were due to meet Hillery on 6 November 1964.[58] Prior to Hillery's meeting with the deputation, he informed the Dáil that he had arranged for 'a complete survey' of all schools with a view to ensuring that they had an adequate water supply.[59]

At that meeting of 6 November, officials of the department informed the joint deputation that while the amount spent on the building programme in 1958–59 was £59,000, the amount had risen to approximately £250,000 for 1963–64. The deputation received improved grants and a new simplified application form. Improvements in this area were clear for all to see in the following years, as the quality and design of new schools reached a high standard, 'especially in the rural areas where the necessity was greatest'.[60] To a large extent, the conditions were now in place for the successful introduction of the child-centred curriculum.

SCHOLARSHIPS

In May 1961, Hillery presented the estimates of his department to the Dáil for 1961–62. He recorded a considerable growth in the number of students in secondary and vocational schools. In 1949–50 there were 47,065 students in 416 secondary schools, and in 1960–61 there were 76,843 students in 526 secondary schools. In the vocational sector, there were 26,322 students following full-time continuation and technical courses, a growth of 1,700 on the previous year.[61]

Hillery was clearly fulfilling the main requirements of the government's education policy by expanding educational facilities. The following July he honoured another commitment which he gave to expand the scholarship scheme. On 4 July he was granted leave in the Dáil to introduce a Bill entitled the Local Authorities (Education Scholarships) (Amendment) Bill, 1961.[62]

The Bill was read a second time on 25 July. Hillery told the Dáil that the proposed Bill was 'a new approach inasmuch as it is now for the first time proposed that the State step in to provide money for scholarships on a general scale'.[63]

The legislation provided for central State funding of approximately £300,000 for the local authority scholarships over a period of 4 years. The contribution from the exchequer was intended to increase the proportion to the funding raised by the local authority with a 5:4 ratio between State and local contributions. In order to benefit talented students whose parents were marginally outside the means test, the Bill provided that a quarter of the scholarships would be awarded without a means test, and that two-thirds of the total scholarship fund should be given for post-primary education, and one-third of the total fund for university education. The proposal got Dáil approval on 2 August 1961.[64]

At this time, secondary teachers had one of their grievances resolved to their satisfaction. From 1 August 1961 secondary teachers on probation would be paid an incremental salary of £200 per annum on top of the salary paid by the school, which was generally £200 per annum. This had been a bone of contention with secondary teachers for some time, as their counterparts in the primary and vocational schools were already being paid a State salary during probation.[65] On 1 December 1961, the government was dissolved for a general election, leading many people to believe that the revised scheme of scholarships and other recent reforms were as politically opportunistic as they were welcome.

THE WASHINGTON CONFERENCE

Officials in the department recognised that they needed to familiarise them-selves with educational developments abroad. This outward-looking approach was replicated in the government's application for Ireland's membership of the European Economic Community. In 1961 Ireland became a member of UNESCO, one of the specialised agencies of the UN. Many advantages would accrue to Irish education from this important development, such as the 'promotion of scientific teaching and research' and 'schemes of exchange of workers and teachers'.[66]

Teachers too developed European contacts by forming the European Association of Teachers, a move welcomed by Hillery as one designed to strengthen links with educational developments on the continent.[67] But it was he himself who opened up the Irish education system, with all its defects, not only to international scrutiny but also to international influences.

Lemass's government was returned to power on 4 October 1961, and Hillery was re-appointed as Minister for Education. Twelve days later the OECD was to hold a major policy conference in Washington, from 16 to 20 October, which was to be its first official event since being restructured and renamed. Prior to the conference, a study group on the economics of education had been set up by the OECD, which brought together 'various economists in the western world, who had a contribution to make to the understanding of education. The Washington conference provided a forum for these economic experts'.[68]

Hillery was not convinced that Ireland could benefit from such a conference, but Seán MacGearailt convinced him 'that the imprimatur of an independent international body was necessary to validate the case for reform of Irish education'.[69] He accepted this wise counsel even though he knew that it would most likely result in an OECD examination of the Irish education system. Ireland was represented at the Washington conference by the senior assistant secretary of the Department of Education, Seán MacGearailt, and John F. McInerney, deputy assistant secretary of the Department of Finance.

The Washington conference agreed an international initiative, the Education Investment and Planning Programme for the establishment of pilot studies on long-term educational needs in developed countries. The Irish representatives were approached with the request that they recommend such a pilot study of Ireland's education system to the Irish Government. They agreed to do so, as did the Austrian officials. Hillery 'sought and got the Government's approval for the setting up, in cooperation with the OECD, of an expert team to survey Irish education and report its findings'.[70]

On 22 June 1962, he announced that the project would be implemented by a national Survey Team under the auspices of the OECD and the Department of Education. He gave the terms of reference for the pilot study to the members of the Dáil on 3 July 1962,[71] and on 29 July he appointed the Survey Team. The team were assisted by a National Steering Committee with Seán MacGearailt as chairman.

In early January 1962, Hillery earned the praise and gratitude of Cardinal D'Alton and David Kelleher, the general secretary of the INTO, for bringing to an end a 10-day strike by teachers in Ballina Primary School. The dispute arose in 1956 when the Bishop of Killala introduced the Marist Order to the seven-teacher school, thereby depriving some teachers of promotional opportunities. It was a celebrated case which even involved the Vatican Secretariat in Rome. The INTO wished to ensure that 'there would be no recurrence of a take-over of a lay school by religious'. Hillery's settlement proposal, which obliged the manager of the Ballina Primary School to pay an annual allowance to a lay teacher on the staff, equivalent to that of the principal 'as long as the school continues to be conducted by the Marist Order', achieved that objective.[72]

COMPREHENSIVE POST-PRIMARY EDUCATION

Speaking in the Dáil, Hillery expressed his dissatisfaction with the inequities in the post-primary education system, and he vowed to produce plans for the expansion of second-level education 'in the near future'.[73] He was under pressure to do so as Tuairim had produced two pamphlets, which had a wide circulation, in which it alleged that the department had 'remained unchanged, indeed stagnant, while rapid and worthwhile progress has been made in other European countries'. It asserted that Irish education had remained static 'because it suited the interests of powerful sections of society – the middle classes, the churches, the politicians – to keep it so'.[74] The department was an administrative body only, which took no responsibility for general education policy, and Tuairim suggested that no one in Ireland accepted that responsibility.

Pressure for educational reform mounted with the publication of the Labour Party policy document entitled 'Challenge and Change in Education', which promised a radical overhaul of the education system. However, Hillery had already set the wheels in motion for the introduction of comprehensive post-primary schools in Ireland. He first mooted the proposal on 7 July 1962 in a memorandum addressed to Lemass.

The proposed schools would offer a comprehensive-type education, for 3 years, for students aged 12–15 years. However, the initiative was strongly opposed by the Department of Finance on cost grounds, but Lemass signalled his approval in August 1962.[75]

Hillery took the next step by requesting Ó Raifeartaigh to set up a departmental committee to advise him regarding appropriate changes that might be made to the post-primary system. Ó Raifeartaigh did so in June 1962 and the committee was chaired by the Deputy Chief Inspector, Dr Maurice Duggan. Hillery realised from the outset that many senior inspectors were resistant to change and remained convinced that change was impossible, because they believed 'that the system was working' and 'that the Department of Finance would not tolerate ... the spending necessary' and 'that the Church would obstruct it'.[76]

The establishment of the Duggan committee was Hillery's line of defence against the negative forces in his department. When he received the Duggan report, he was selective in the recommendations he adopted from it for inclusion in the department's plan. He selected the recommendation for a common post-primary course for all pupils aged 12–15 years, but he excluded the radical recommendation for free post-primary education for all children.

The proposal was submitted to the Department of Finance and was rejected for a second time. Hillery sought Lemass's assistance, and his department prepared a lengthy memorandum which was sent directly to Lemass. In it Hillery observed that private interests had failed to provide second-level education in these areas, and therefore could not reasonably object to State provision through comprehensive schools. He added, 'Once a beginning is made the general application of this system to the whole country would follow slowly with time'.

On Lemass's instructions, the proposal was sent to an ad hoc committee comprising Hillery, Lemass and Jim Ryan, who was Minister for Finance, for consideration. In a written response to Hillery on 14 January, Lemass fully supported his proposal and gave explicit instructions on the best strategy to be adopted to achieve his goal.[77]

PRESS CONFERENCE, 20 MAY 1963

Hillery secured agreement for the scheme by following the procedures laid out by Lemass, only to be told by the latter, 'You'll never get that through the Government'. A deflated Minister asked, 'What will I do then?', to which Lemass responded, 'Announce it'.[78] With Lemass's support, Hillery called a press conference on 20 May 1963 to announce ground-breaking policy changes for second and third-level education. First, he referred to the main weaknesses in the post-primary system. These included the lack of second-level schools in certain areas, and the fact that only two-thirds of children received some post-primary education. However, his concern was for the third who did not receive any at all, those he called 'The Modern Third Estate'.

Another weakness was the lack of co-ordination in the system, as there was no 'connecting link between the secondary and vocational schools'. In an effort to unify both systems, and to break down barriers between vocational and secondary schools, Hillery intended to build comprehensive post-primary schools offering both academic and practical education. He announced that the 2-year course in vocational schools would be extended to 3 years, and that a common intermediate certificate would be introduced into both types of school, putting them on a par academically and socially.[79] In attempting to raise the status of vocational schools by enabling them to offer full post-primary courses, Hillery had defaulted on a promise given by John Marcus O'Sullivan to the Catholic hierarchy in October 1930, that the vocational schools would not offer the full range of post-primary studies.[80]

But the die was cast and Hillery committed the department to increased involvement in education as he planned to 'introduce a new principle into Irish education, namely direct State provision of a post-primary school building'.[81] It was not in fact a new principle as the State had already provided buildings for the seven preparatory colleges in 1926. Even so, this represented a seismic change in education policy. Writing in 1957, one commentator could confidently claim that 'There is no State system of education in Ireland. That would be an anachronism.'[82] In 1963 few if any regarded State involvement in education as anachronistic, and there was widespread approval for Hillery's 'new type of school',[83] the introduction of which was 'influenced by contemporary trends in Britain and in some continental countries which were promoting comprehensive schools'.[84]

Technical education received a much-needed boost when Hillery also announced his intention to establish RTCs in conjunction with the VECs. The RTCs would provide courses for a new public examination, the technical leaving certificate. The VTA had been campaigning for third-level technological institutions for almost two decades. Hillery had referred to this lacuna in March 1960 when he said, 'there is a missing rung in our educational ladder ... as there is no official channel for the ... vocational education student to proceed via the National University to a degree in his own subject'.[85]

The plan for RTCs had been suggested to him by an OECD investigating team who were conducting a survey on the training of technicians in Ireland. He was asked to consider providing higher technical education in centres outside Dublin.[86] It was hoped that the RTCs would help align technical education provision with manpower needs.

Vocational education was an area of immediate growth in September 1963 as the educational requirements prescribed by An Cheárd Chomhairle came into force from that date. The vocational teachers' journal *Gairm* reported that 'Enough applicants to fill three additional schools failed to find accommodation in Dublin city vocational schools'.[87]

The department introduced economy measures whereby many local authorities combined their building programmes by engaging in joint purchasing.[88] Many VECs were in debt and the government passed the Vocational Education (Amendment) Act to provide them with additional money.[89] It became necessary also to include in the educational estimates for 1966–67 special State 'solvency grants' for VECs, which amounted to £946,000.[90]

Three of Hillery's main policy initiatives were brought to fruition after he left office. The first one was the opening of the three comprehensive schools in 1966 at Carraroe, County Galway, Cootehill, County Cavan, County Clare. The common intermediate certificate was introduced the same year and permission to offer the leaving certificate course was granted by Hillery in February 1964. In September 1969, the first five RTCs were opened in Athlone, County Westmeath, Arklow, County Wicklow, Dundalk, County Louth and in Sligo and Waterford.[91] Proposals for the introduction of the technical leaving certificate were not endorsed, following a decision taken by the Review Committee on the leaving certificate in 1967. Instead, the leaving certificate curriculum for secondary schools was broadened to include the appropriate technical subjects.

The media welcomed Hillery's proposals on comprehensive schools, with the *Irish Press* describing them as 'The most far-reaching plans for improving and modernising post-primary education in Ireland',[92] and *The Irish Times* was equally eulogistic about the comprehensive model.[93] There was public approval for Hillery's policy statement, but the teaching unions, the INTO, the ASTI and the VTA issued a joint statement on 25 May, lamenting the fact that there had been no consultation with them prior to the announcement.[94] When questioned in the Dáil about the teachers' statement, Hillery's dismissive response further damaged his relationship with the teaching unions, when he referred to them as 'outside bodies'[95] that he did not need to consult.

A journalist questioned Hillery shortly after his press conference as to whether 'people concerned with education in this country had been consulted about the proposals'. He did not reveal that he had consulted the Catholic bishops informally on the matter, and that their initial reaction was hostile.[96] He added, 'I am launching the plan now and the talking, I am sure, will come afterwards'.[97] A year later, in the course of an interview he explained why he did not consult widely.

He said 'We have about 20 organisations that might be consulted and really, I don't think you would get anything done'.[98]

No one could question Hillery's courage. He took the bold step of making his major policy announcement without the approval of the Catholic hierarchy. He did so on the basis that 'it is easier to get forgiveness than permission'.[99] There was no immediate response from the bishops, but subsequent negotiations with them would prove testing. He intimated that if a proposal to build a comprehensive school for Protestant children was put forward, he would agree to its being built, provided there was a demand for it. The Jewish school authorities welcomed the comprehensive schools. The Chief Rabbi, Dr Isaac Cohen, said he 'felt the steps would increase the opportunity for further education and therefore must be steps in the right direction'.[100]

There were two crises which Hillery had to cope with in the department in 1964, and in such highly charged situations the 'Quiet Education Minister ... showed his steel'.[101] The first crisis involved protracted negotiations with the hierarchy regarding the introduction of comprehensive schools, and the second one was the ASTI pay dispute, which resulted in a 3-week strike. These two areas of conflict were interconnected as the church authorities came out in support of the ASTI, an association whose membership consisted solely of lay teachers.

The INTO and the ASTI had separate conciliation and arbitration panels, which resulted in competing pay claims by primary and secondary teachers. When the primary teachers were granted a generous salary increase in April 1963 to avoid industrial action, the secondary teachers sought a corresponding increase in their salaries in order to maintain a higher salary. The ASTI's claim was rejected by the arbitrator, but the ASTI refused to accept the arbitration findings.[102]

The ASTI believed it could exercise sufficient pressure to force Hillery's hand on the issue, as they threatened to boycott the summer examinations. He refused to capitulate to them. Negotiations between high-ranking department officials and the hierarchy commenced in earnest from 28 June 1963. Details of the new comprehensive scheme were sparse. When Browne questioned Hillery about the rationale behind his educational plans, his pragmatic reply was, 'To do what is possible is my job and not to have the whole matter upset because of some supposed principle or ideal'.[103]

The lack of detail was probably due to the delicate negotiations which were taking place with the hierarchy, who regarded the initiative as 'a revolutionary step'. They were looking for a guarantee that the new comprehensive schools would have a clerical manager who would have the power to appoint teachers and to determine whether the curriculum was in accordance with Catholic teaching. Assurances were sought that the new schools would not adversely affect existing secondary schools. Genuine fears were expressed that the reform of the State-funded vocational education system would threaten the viability of existing secondary schools. However, the necessary assurances were given to assuage any such fears.

In December 1963, Hillery met Cardinal Conway and a deputation from the hierarchy. In order to ensure that the new schools would be denominational, they sought Deeds of Trust. As many secondary schools had crippling debts, Conway also sought financial assistance for them. Clerical school authorities had fought hard since the nineteenth century to avoid State involvement in their secondary schools, but now the hierarchy sought an increase in State involvement. Hillery's recognition of the need for further financial help for secondary schools led to a breakthrough in the negotiations. The standing committee of the hierarchy agreed on 7 January 1964 that individual bishops could hold discussions with the department for the establishment of comprehensive schools.[104]

Two by-elections were due to be held in Kildare and Cork, the results of which would determine the government's ability to retain power without calling a general election.[105] Hillery therefore recommended to Lemass that the government should give building grants for secondary schools. This would also help to win the bishops' support for the introduction of comprehensive schools. Just 9 days later, the new grants for secondary-school buildings were announced by Lemass. A banner headline on the front page of *The Irish Times* the following morning read, 'Scheme of grants for Secondary School Building. Lemass outlines education plans',[106] and the *Irish Independent* gave it prominent coverage also.[107]

The editor called Lemass's statement 'a quite historic announcement' which 'was also almost historic in its brevity'.[108] Now 60 per cent grants were to be provided for the building of secondary schools with a prospective population of 150 students or more, and for the extension of old schools which intended to add an incremental 73 or more students. Approximately half of academic secondary schools had under 150 students.[109] The government won the two by-elections, and on 20 February Hillery announced that the education estimates for 1964–65 would include provision to enable the capitation grants to be increased.[110]

The summer of 1964 was Hillery's summer of discontent, as the negotiations with individual bishops stalled and the ASTI strike threatened the State examinations. The department placed advertisements in the national newspapers to recruit examiners and superintendents. The response to this was such that the department was in a position to hold the examinations and to assess the results. This occurred against a backdrop of obstructionist and intimidatory behaviour engaged in by some teachers and managers, many of whom were resentful of State involvement in post-primary education. Episcopal opposition to the planned comprehensive schools dissolved following a ministerial threat to publish a dossier of complaints against clerical and religious managers who had assisted teachers' efforts to disrupt the examinations.[111]

SECOND-LEVEL CURRICULUM REFORM

According to the government, the First Programme for Economic Expansion of 1958 brought not just economic gains to Ireland but 'a pronounced change of national mentality'.[112] This growth in national pride was also due to the visit to Ireland in June 1963 of John Fitzgerald Kennedy, the first Irish-American President of the United States. It was as if President Kennedy 'personified the wider ambitions of a new Ireland in which anything was possible'.[113]

In the Second Programme for Economic Expansion (part 1), which was published by the government in August, it was indicated that 'special attention' would be given to education and training. Education was now seen as an investment, as the interdependence of education and the economy was recognised.

The aims of Hillery's new scheme for comprehensive education were set out in the Second Programme, as well as a commitment to provide an increasing number of scholarships. More money would be made available for school buildings and equipment, and for the training of additional teachers. The Second Programme (part 11), which was issued in July 1964, indicated that the school leaving age would be raised to 15 years by 1970.[114]

On 11 December 1963, Hillery introduced the education estimates for the school year 1963–64.[115] He pointed out that the in-service courses for secondary teachers, initiated in 1959, had continued to be provided each year since then. In 1963 ten courses had been provided: three in physics, three in chemistry, and one in mathematics, French, German and geography. Leaving certificate courses in physics and chemistry had been revised and draft courses in mathematics and in the other science subjects had been prepared.[116]

In order to attract graduates to the teaching of science, the estimates allowed an additional annual grant of £150 for science graduates. This must be seen in the context of the emerging importance of science, and the worldwide interest in the subject due to the launching of the Russian and American satellites at the end of 1957 and early 1958. As the country lacked a sufficient number of science graduates, short summer courses for the training of science teachers were recognised by the department.

A survey was carried out by the department in late 1960s, and as a result a special fund was established which would provide additional grants towards the furnishing and equipping of laboratories.[117] RTÉ, in collaboration with the secondary inspectorate, initiated educational programmes, so that by 1964 Telefís Scoile was broadcasting programmes for intermediate and leaving certificate physics. Furthermore, evening courses were provided at university for mathematics and science teachers. In order to facilitate the teaching of the new mathematics programme, 4-week courses were provided throughout the country.[118] By 1965, 573 secondary schools were co-operating with the government with regard to the teaching of science.[119]

In 1961 Tuairim had warned that 'a 3–5 year plan for training language teachers would need to be produced right now if we are to obtain full benefit from participation in the Common Market'.[120] The department needed little prompting, as in January 1961 it announced that credit on the incremental salary scales would in future be given to lay teachers for service in certain underdeveloped countries of Africa,[121] and 6 months later schools were notified that recognised teachers of French, German, Italian or Spanish, would get credit for service in schools on the Continent.[122] In August 1964, the department gave grants for teaching aids for modern languages, so that in future it would pay 50 per cent of the expenditure involved in purchasing tape-recorders, tapes or records for the teaching of modern languages by the audio-visual method.[123] A grant for a television set for viewing the new Telefís Scoile programmes was to be extended to schools throughout the country.[124] By 1965 the teaching of modern continental languages had been stimulated by the provision of grants for visual aids in language laboratories and by the provision of special residential courses at the language laboratory at Gormanston for teachers of modern languages. Hillery was pleased to observe, 'Now more boys are studying modern languages'.[125]

In 1964 Lemass confirmed that it was still government policy 'to revive and restore the language'.[126] The government finally received the Report of the Commission on the Restoration of the Irish Language in January 1964, 8 years after it had been set up, and with twenty-seven of the original thirty members still serving. Like the Council of Education reports, this one also came in for criticism, mainly because it lacked the benefit of empirical research. Bishop Lucey of Cork and Ross expressed 'profound disappointment' at the final report of the commission.[127]

Fr John Macnamara from St Patrick's Training College, Drumcondra, who had conducted extensive research on the Irish language policy and bilingualism, accused the commission 'of searching about for statements to support recommendations which it considered favourable to the restoration of the Irish language'.[128]

In the Second Programme for Economic Expansion (part II), an entire chapter was devoted to education. The department's awareness of the importance of educational research was reinforced in the Programme, as it confirmed that

St Patrick's Training College would provide for the establishment of a research
centre on teaching methods and modes of assessment. The Educational Research
Centre (ERC) was established in January 1966.[129] It was also confirmed in the
Programme that the government intended to appoint a number of educational
psychologists to the department, who would devise aptitude tests and intelligence
tests for students. Tuairim remarked that this lacuna was:

> a source of amazement to our continental colleagues that there is no such
> service here, apart from the very successful pilot one run by one psycholo-
> gist, for the boys in the City of Dublin Vocational Education Committee
> (CDVEC) schools.[130]

This was a reference to Thomas McCarthy, the vocational psychologist appointed
by the CDVEC in June 1960 to organise a vocational guidance service in the
Dublin vocational schools. McCarthy proposed that each school should have one
teacher whose recognised duties would include the vocational guidance of the
students, with the help of the visiting vocational psychologist. This system formed
the nucleus for the guidance service later established by the department for
post-primary schools in general.[131]

During the Dáil debate on the estimates for the Taoiseach's department for
1964–65, Lemass referred to the rapid increase in the number of students in secondary
schools. He mentioned the measures taken by the government to cope with the
planned raising of the school leaving age by 1970. The measures included a fourfold
increase in expenditure on scholarships, and on building and extension grants for
secondary schools. He added, 'but as our secondary schools are mostly private institutions, increased initiative on the part of their management is essential'.[132]

But the school authorities had been waiting for a 'direct request to them to
proceed with the necessary development', because 'provision of all compulsory
schooling was the duty of the State'.[133] There was a lack of communication
between the department and the secondary-school authorities. Hillery admitted
that he had 'to take the initiative all the time',[134] while secondary-school
authorities felt far removed from 'the remote Civil Servants who directed and
dictated developments'.[135]

Secondary teachers too felt alienated from the department, particularly in the
wake of a bitter 3-week strike, and many of them believed that the department was
planning a State take-over of their schools. The editor of the secondary teachers'
journal, D. Ó Connaláin, expressed distrust of the department and a belief 'That
it was behind closed doors that decisions were made and reforms of post-primary
education decided'.[136]

At third level, Hillery formally established the Commission on Higher Education in October 1960, with Chief Justice Cearbhall Ó Dálaigh as chairman. Back in September the government approved the appointment of twenty-six members to the commission. Hillery believed that the group was too large to function efficiently and to report in a timely fashion, but the government was anxious to include all influential interest groups and ward off criticism.[137]

The terms of reference for the commission were 'to inquire into, and make recommendation in relation to university, professional, technological, and higher education generally'.[138] These terms ensured that no constraints were placed on the commission in respect of any area of higher education, and the members 'diligently pursued its investigation of the problem until 1967'.[139]

Numbers at universities throughout the world had been rising for over a decade. In Ireland, UCD had 530 students in 1910, but almost nine times that number in 1960. On 23 March 1960, Hillery told the Dáil that 'the quietly expanding flow of students into the universities had suddenly become a torrent'.[140] Eight days later he secured the agreement of the Dáil to the transfer of UCD to the Belfield campus.[141]

Patrick Hillery transformed Irish education when he accepted official advice and exposed the education system to OECD scrutiny and international influence. By so doing, he applied more scientific methods of policy making. Special education policy was now informed by research conducted by his officials in Glasgow, the design for modern school buildings resulted from research conducted in England and Scotland, the seed for comprehensive education was sown following Ó Raifeartaigh's visit to educational institutions in the USA, and RTCs were introduced following a recommendation by the 1964 OECD team.

Educators were concerned about the utilitarian nature of education policy as set out in the Second Programme for Economic Expansion, which emphasised the interdependence of education and the economy. When Hillery referred to investment in education as a gilt-edged investment, he did nothing to alter that perception.

OECD progress reports on the Irish second-level curriculum formed the basis for major curricular reforms, so that science, which had been neglected in the past, was now being taught in 573 secondary schools.[142] Oral Irish formed part of leaving certificate Irish, and modern languages experienced a resurgence. Hillery was pleased to reveal that 'Now more boys are studying modern languages'.[143]

Advances made in developing special education had positive gains for mainstream primary teaching, as the focus shifted to a child-centred approach. Reforms to facilitate this included lowering the pupil–teacher ratio by reducing the averages required for the appointment of assistant teachers, and increasing the supply of teachers. It was also facilitated by the removal of the compulsory Irish policy, which allowed for more progressive methods of teaching to be employed. Grants for school reference libraries and for the modernisation and maintenance of school buildings were essential to the process.

It was through political skill and through following the advice of his political masters that Hillery gained acceptance of comprehensive education. Remarkably, he did so against the wishes of the bishops, but the old order was changing and Cardinal Conway was forced to seek financial assistance for the debt-ridden secondary schools. Permitting building grants to secondary schools softened attitudes, but it was the threat of disclosure of the dossier of complaints that forced the bishops' agreement to comprehensive education. Cabinet approval was also in doubt before Hillery took Lemass' advice to 'Announce it', after which there was no going back.

Hillery 'showed his steel' again during the secondary teachers' 3-week strike, when he refused to capitulate to their salary demands in the face of threats to boycott the State examinations. But he did not have a good working relationship with the teaching unions since he failed to consult them prior to his policy announcement. He explained why with the utmost candour: 'There could be no question of submitting such matters to outside bodies prior to their promulgation'.[144]

Secondary-school authorities complained that they were not consulted either, but they could have united into one strong body to ensure that their voice was heard in the policy-making process.[145] It was because they remained aloof from the government that Hillery could claim that 'the State is coming out as the only body geared to take the initiative'.[146] Lemass reiterated this point in the Dáil in July 1964. Now that the government was providing building grants and increased capitation grants to secondary schools, Lemass felt entitled to call on them to play their part.

Hillery was conscious of the inequities in the education system which affected those he styled 'The Modern Third Estate'. By announcing a common intermediate certificate and later a common leaving certificate, he broke down the social barriers between the vocational and secondary schools, and raised the status of the former. These students now had a bright future, as they could avail of a comprehensive second-level education and then advance to third-level technological colleges. By exposing the Irish education system to international scrutiny and international influence, and by drawing on the expertise of the OECD, Patrick Hillery transformed an education system which was underfunded, undeveloped and uncoordinated for four decades, into a modern vibrant system. This was his great ministerial legacy to Irish education.

Notes

1 D.H. Akenson, Sean Farren and John Coolahan, 'Pre-university education 1921-1984' in J.R. Hill (ed.) *A New History of Ireland VII. Ireland 1921-84* (Oxford, 2003), p.732.

2 Hillery was appointed Ireland's first European Commissioner in 1973. In 1976 he was elected unopposed as Ireland's sixth President. He served two terms as President, until December 1990.

3 John Walsh, *Patrick Hillery: The Official Biography* (Dublin, 2008), p.71.

4 *Dáil Debates*, vol. 177, col. 199, 21 October 1959.

5 Ibid., col. 206.

6 Ibid., col. 292.

7 Sr Eileen Randles, *Post-primary Education in Ireland 1957-1970* (Dublin, 1975), p.41.

8 *Dáil Debates*, vol. 177, cols 470–1, 28 October 1959.

9 Patrick Hillery, 'Address of Dr P.J. Hillery Minister for Education, at the Golden Jubilee Dinner of the ASTI, 31 October 1959' in *School and College Year Book* (1960), p.5.

10 *Dáil Debates*, vol. 180, col. 949, 23 March 1960.

11 Ibid., col. 933; George Lyons, Presidential address to the ASTI congress 1963, in *School and College Year Book* (1964), pp.7–17.

12 O'Meara, *Reform in Education*, p.11.

13 Akenson, *A Mirror to Kathleen's Face*, p.76.

14 Fr Seán Ó Catháin, 'Secondary education in Ireland' in Studies, 45 (1956), pp.54–5; O'Meara, *Reform in Education*, p.12.

15 Tuairim, pamphlet 9, 'Irish education', London research group, 1962, p.7.

16 Coolahan, *Irish Education*, p.80.

17 Coolahan, 'The secondary-school curriculum experiment, 1924-42', p.61.

18 *Dáil Debates*, vol. 177, col. 194, 21 October 1959.

19 Tuairim, pamphlet 9, p.4.

20 *Dáil Debates*, vol. 177, cols 196–203, 21 October 1959.

21 *Sunday Press*, 4 October 1959.

22 Dermot Keogh, *Twentieth-Century Ireland: Revolution and State Building* (Dublin, 2005), p.250.

23 O'Connor, *A Troubled Sky*, pp.84–5.

24 *Dáil Debates*, vol. 208, col. 1566, 14 May 1964.

25 Walsh, *Patrick Hillery*, p.100.

26 O'Connor, *A Troubled Sky*, p.85.

27 Circular 16/64, Department of Education, May 1964.

28 *Dáil Debates*, vol. 208, col. 1566, 14 May 1964.

29 *Dáil Debates*, vol. 182, cols 70–1, 24 May 1960.

30 *Dáil Debates*, vol. 183, col. 422, 28 June 1960; vol. 207, col. 381, 5 February 1964.

31 John Walsh, 'An era of expansion, 1945-75' in James Kelly (ed.) *St Patrick's College, Drumcondra 1875–2000* (Dublin, 2006), pp.170–1.

32 *Dáil Debates*, vol. 195, cols 1376–8, 23 May 1962.

33 *Dáil Debates*, vol. 211, col. 1339, 1 July 1964.

34 O'Connor, *A Troubled Sky*, pp.52–4.

35 Jones, *A Gaelic Experiment*, p.143.

36 Circular 11/60, Department of Education, January 1960; Walsh, *Patrick Hillery*, pp.79–80.

37 Coláiste Moibhí was closed in 1995.

38 *Dáil Reports*, vol. 182, cols 71–2, 24 May 1960.

39 In 1959 Tomás Ó Cuilleanáin was appointed as the first inspector for special education.

40 Coolahan and O'Donovan, *A History*, p.180.

41 Walsh, 'A new era of expansion', p.179.

42 *Dáil Debates*, vol. 210, col. 330, 2 June 1964.

43 Tomás Ó Cuilleanáin, 'Special education in Ireland' in *Oideas*, 1 (1968), pp.5–17.

44 *Dáil Debates*, vol. 210, col. 329, 2 June 1964.

45 T. Ó Raifeartaigh, 'Some impressions of education in the USA' in *Studies*, 50 (1961) pp.57–74, pp.61–5.

46 Ibid., p.66.

47 Ibid., p.62.

48 *Dáil Debates*, vol. 211, col. 1339, 1 July 1964.

49 Coolahan and O'Donovan, *A History*, pp.180–1.

50 Ibid., p.181.

51 Circular 21/63, Department of Education, November 1963.

52 *Dáil Debates*, vol. 208, col. 1567, 14 May 1964.

53 Walsh, *Patrick Hillery*, p.107.

54 *Dáil Debates*, vol. 189, col. 842, 24 May 1961.

55 Circular 22/61, Department of Education, October 1961.

56 *The Irish Times*, 28 January 1964.

57 John Sheehan, 'Education and society in Ireland 1945-70' in J.J. Lee (ed.) *Ireland 1945–70* (Dublin, 1979), p.64. Sheehan, an economics lecturer in UCD, had a special interest in the economics of education.

58 O'Connell, *History of the INTO*, pp.444–7.

59 *Dáil Debates*, vol. 210, col. 331, 2 June 1964.

60 Op. cit., pp.446–7.

61 *Dáil Debates*, vol. 189, col. 844, 24 May 1961.

62 *Dáil Debates*, vol. 191, col. 15, 4 July 1961.

63 Ibid., col. 1684, 25 July 1961.

64 *Dáil Debates*, vol. 191, cols 2423–5, 2 August 1961.

65 O'Connor, *A Troubled Sky*, p.57.

66 *Dáil Debates*, vol. 191, col. 709, 12 July 1961.

67 Randles, *Post-primary Education*, p.77.

68 Ibid., pp.78–9.

69 Walsh, *Patrick Hillery*, p.92.

70 O'Connor, *A Troubled Sky*, p.63.

71 *Dáil Debates*, vol. 196, cols 1303–4, 3 July 1962.

72 O'Connell, *History of the INTO*, pp.93–120.

73 *Dáil Debates*, vol. 195, col. 2185, 6 June 1962.

74 Tuairim, pamphlet 8, 'Educating towards a united Europe', pp.6–7.

75 Walsh, *Patrick Hillery*, p.105.

76 Imelda Bonel-Elliott, 'The role of the Duggan report (1962) in the reform of the Irish education system' in *Administration*, 44:3 (1996), p.46.

77 John Horgan, *Seán Lemass: The Enigmatic Patriot* (Dublin, 1997), p.294.

78 Walsh, *Patrick Hillery*, p.109.

79 Press conference Dr Patrick Hillery TD, Minister for Education, 20 May 1963.

80 Coolahan, *Irish Education*, p.134.

81 Op. cit.

82 Mescal, *Religion in the Irish System of Education*, p.19.

83 *Hibernia*, February 1964. Interview with Dr P. Hillery, Minister for Education by J. Dillon.

84 Coolahan, *Irish Education*, p.134.

85 *Dáil Debates*, vol. 180, col. 949, 23 March 1960.

86 OECD, *Training of Technicians in Ireland* (Paris, 1964), pp.104–6.

87 *Gairm*, 4:4 October 1963, p.3.

88 Randles, *Post-primary Education*, p.73.

89 *Dáil Debates*, vol. 197, col. 146, 30 October 1962.

90 *Dáil Debates*, vol. 225, col. 1877, 30 November 1966.

91 Coolahan, *Irish Education*, p.250.

92 *Irish Press*, 22 May 1963.

93 *The Irish Times*, 21 May 1963.

94 O'Connor, *A Troubled Sky*, p.79.

95 *Dáil Debates*, vol. 203, col. 598, 30 May 1963.

96 Walsh, *Patrick Hillery*, pp.113–4.

97 *Irish Press*, 22 May 1963.

98 *Hibernia*, February 1964, p.26.

99 Walsh, *Patrick Hillery*, p.144.

100 *Irish Press*, 22 May 1963.

101 *Irish Independent*, 17 April 2008. 'Quiet Education Minister who showed his steel' by Prof. John Coolahan, on the death of Patrick J. Hillery.

102 O'Connor, *A Troubled Sky*, pp.86–7.

103 *Dáil Debates*, vol. 203, col. 684, 11 June 1963.

104 Walsh, *Patrick Hillery*, pp.115–6.

105 Randles, *Post-primary Education*, p.145.

106 *The Irish Times*, 14 February 1964.

107 *Irish Independent*, 14 February 1964.

108 Ibid., Editorial 'Grant for schools'.

109 Circular 15/64, Department of Education, April 1964; *Dáil Debates*, vol. 209, col. 1569, 14 May 1964.

110 *Dáil Debates*, vol. 207, cols 1379–80, 20 February 1964.

111 Walsh, *Patrick Hillery*, pp.120–4.

112 Second Programme for Economic Expansion (part 1), August 1963 paragraph 4. The programme was based on T.K. Whitaker's ground-breaking report *Economic Development*.

113 Fanning, *Independent Ireland*, p.203. President Kennedy addressed a joint session of the Oireachtas in which he elevated the role of Ireland in world history.

114 Second Programme for Economic Expansion (part 11), July 1964.

115 *Dáil Debates*, vol. 206, cols 1087–8, 11 December 1963.

116 *Dáil Debates*, vol. 206, col. 1087, 11 December 1963; O'Connor, *A Troubled Sky*, p.83.

117 Randles, *Post-primary Education*, pp.46–7.

118 *Dáil Debates*, vol. 208, col. 1569, 14 May 1964.

119 *Dáil Debates*, vol. 214, col. 716, 18 February 1965.

120 Tuairim, pamphlet 8, p.14.

121 Circular 6/61, Department of Education, January 1961.

122 Circular 17/61, Department of Education, July 1961.

123 Circular 20/64, Department of Education, August 1964.

124 Circular 27/64, Department of Education, 1964.

125 *Dáil Debates*, vol. 214, col. 715, 18 February 1965.

126 *Dáil Debates*, vol. 211, col. 1339, 1 July 1964.

127 *The Irish Times*, 11 January 1964.

128 Fr John Macnamara, 'The Commission on Irish: psychological aspects', in *Studies*, 53 (1964), p.171.

129 Walsh, 'An era of expansion, 1945-75', pp.171–2.

130 Tuairim, pamphlet 8, pp.12–13.

131 Randles, *Post-primary Education*, p.61.

132 *Dáil Debates*, vol. 211, cols 1339–40, 1 July 1964.

133 Randles, *Post-primary Education*, p.155.

134 *Hibernia*, February 1964, p.26.

135 Op. cit., p.148.

136 D. Ó Connaláin, 'Leathanach an eagarthóra' in *School and College Year Book* (1965), p.5.

137 Walsh, *Patrick Hillery*, pp.86–8.

138 Commission on Higher Education 1960-67 presentation and summary of report (Dublin, 1967), p.1.

139 O'Connor, *A Troubled Sky*, p.55.

140 *Dáil Debates*, vol. 180, cols 929–30, 23 March 1960.

141 Ibid., col. 1507, 31 March 1960.

142 *Dáil Debates*, vol. 214, col. 716, 18 February 1965.

143 Ibid., col. 715.

144 *Dáil Debates*, vol. 203, col. 598, 30 May 1963.

145 Randles, *Post-primary Education*, p.155.

146 *Hibernia*, February, p.26.

12

George Colley (1965–66): 'If that is so, why could not His Lordship use the courts to test his point?'

… it is … of paramount importance that we seek out and develop the talents not just of the few who were intellectually gifted but all our children.[1]

Following the general election on 7 April 1965, Fianna Fáil were returned to power with half the Dáil seats and Lemass named the 'youngest cabinet in Europe'.[2] The education portfolio went to George Colley (1925–83), a 40-year-old solicitor who had served briefly as parliamentary secretary to the Minister for Lands. He was an Irish-language enthusiast and a regular contributor to Dáil debates on education since his entry to the Dáil in 1961. He 'had made no secret of the fact that he had hoped one day to become Minister for Education'. On 21 April 1965 that day had come.[3]

It was also the day that the president of the ASTI, Patrick Finnegan, addressed the association's annual convention. He was concerned about the utilitarian bias in education policy as outlined in the Second Programme for Economic Expansion. He questioned how secondary schools could possibly compete, with limited subvention, against State-sponsored comprehensive schools and he suggested that an advisory council should be set up 'which the Department could consult on any proposed changes in curricula or policy'.[4]

Colley set about restoring harmonious relationships with disaffected teachers and school managers by holding official meetings with representatives of all the major teaching organisations and school authorities. When introducing the estimates for education for 1965–66, he stated that rather than attempting to consult a plethora of educational bodies individually, he would set up 'a Central Advisory Committee ... of representatives of all levels of education ... with which he could liaise and get advice at short notice'.[5]

He was a committed supporter of the comprehensive model of post-primary education. In 1964 he expressed the belief that comprehensive schools would 'constitute a considerable weapon in the effort to break down the snob value of the secondary schools' and would help 'to modernise and improve our education system'.[6] He was now in a position to elaborate on his plans for the development of comprehensive education as he had early access to the report of the joint OECD/Irish Survey Team, entitled 'Investment in Education'[7] (IIE). This was widely regarded as a landmark report.

Colley referred to 'the necessity of endeavouring for the future to provide larger schools if all our children are to benefit fully from what is in our teachers' capacity to give them'.[8] He introduced the radical idea of sharing staff and facilities in a locality in order to provide a comprehensive curriculum and to avoid duplication of resources.

Finnegan could take some solace from Colley's reassurance that comprehensive schools were not intended to replace existing post-primary schools. He stated categorically that comprehensive schools 'are not and never were intended to replace ... our secondary or vocational school system'. Comprehensive schools would be large schools, offering a practical and academic education, catering for various aptitudes and abilities, and guaranteeing 'a very wide range of subjects'.[9]

Parents had a strong ally in Colley. In the past he had complained that parents had been deliberately excluded from the education system and were 'regarded as interlopers'.[10] As Minister he would 'consult parents often and after three years of comprehensive education, parents would be advised on suitable courses for their children, depending on their aptitudes'.[11] He appointed four psychologists to the department who would be central to this process of vocational guidance.[12] He made a conscious effort to include parents when he established an advisory council in Dublin to plan educational provision.[13] An advisory council for Cork was also constituted some time later in order to consider the size and location of schools. However, parents did not have an input into government policy planning.[14]

Colley implemented the only recommendation made in the IIE report when he set up a Development Branch in the Department of Education. Seán O'Connor, the assistant secretary in the department, was appointed head of the Development Branch. Colley proceeded to outline the function of this new unit, which was 'to assemble statistics regarding existing facilities ... to plan, consult, stimulate, lay out the stages of programmes ... and to see to the implementing of educational improvements and reforms'.[15]

He unveiled his policy regarding the amalgamation of small one- and two-teacher schools, and he explained the rationale for amalgamation, based on IIE data. He informed the Dáil that in the case of these schools, the educational attainment of children was on average 2 years behind that of children in larger schools. In future the department would not arbitrarily replace old school buildings but would consider the possibility of having these children 'attend a central school'. He guaranteed 'provision by the State of transport for the children concerned'.[16] This would occur when the national survey of post-primary education facilities had been completed.

He defended his policy by referring to the high proportion of untrained teachers in the 730 one-teacher schools in the State. He pointed to the educational loss to children attending smaller schools over those attending larger ones, who had the benefit of one teacher per class and an array of educational facilities. Oliver J. Flanagan, a Fine Gael deputy who was a devout Catholic, asked Colley if he had 'sought the advice of the school managers in this connection, and if the Hierarchy had expressed an opinion on it'. Colley assured him that he had consulted school managers and teachers some time ago, and that they 'concurred in the closing of one-teacher schools'.[17]

At second-level, the ramifications of the policy became clear when Deputy Clinton questioned the department's motives in refusing to grant permission to County Dublin VEC to proceed with the building of a vocational school in Clondalkin. He wondered was it 'because of a shortage of money'. This was a reasonable deduction considering that preliminary permission had already been granted by the department for this building, and considering that there was a £50 million deficit in the country's balance of payments. Colley strongly denied the accusation, and he gave what was to become his stock reply to all such queries regarding proposed building projects, which was that it 'must be considered in conjunction with the result of a survey ... in relation to the existing provision for post-primary education'.[18]

The results of the county surveys were to hand in 1965 and this led to the emergence of a national plan for the provision of post-primary education facilities. Colley was now in a position to refuse or delay sanction for the building of individual schools.[19] Jack Lynch's prediction was now a reality.

The IIE report highlighted two major weaknesses in the educational system. One was the preponderance of small rural primary schools, and the other was the haphazard provision of post-primary education. Colley could set about implementing his policy of amalgamation of small primary schools, having secured the agreement of the INTO and the Catholic hierarchy for his plans. The CEC of the INTO indicated to Colley that it had no objection to the principle of the policy.

According to one commentator, they had taken cognisance of the 'likely positive effect that amalgamation would have on promotional prospects for teachers'.[20] The Catholic hierarchy wrote to Colley and sent a deputation to him regarding the policy, but they did not oppose it.[21]

The interests of one notable opponent of the policy, Bishop Browne, were upheld in the Dáil by Oliver J. Flanagan, who claimed that 'the fact that schools are to be centralised is … the first step towards State control of education'. He believed the government had not secured 'the full approval and consent of the managers of the schools and of the parents'.

Colley informed him that he had been advised on this matter by sixty inspectors who approved of his plan, as did the majority of school managers whom they had consulted. Once again he relied on data from the IIE report to defend government policy, by pointing to the fact that students in large schools outperformed those attending small schools in the scholarship examinations, irrespective of location. He noted also that the progression of pupils in smaller schools was slower than in larger schools and yet, per pupil, these schools were 'more costly to erect and the costliest to maintain'.[22]

BISHOP CHALLENGES MINISTER

> Parents have their rights and I am all for them. Not alone am I Minister for Education: I am a father of seven children.[23]

A public controversy took place between Bishop Browne and Colley over the proposed closure of one- and two-teacher rural primary schools. On 2 September 1965, Browne attacked Colley's policy by rejecting his claim that two-teacher schools were inefficient. He described the decision to abolish them as 'disgusting', considering that school managers had never been consulted.[24] Colley replied to Browne on 11 September, and he described the Bishop's statement as 'distressingly inaccurate and intemperate and by no means representing the unanimous view of the Catholic hierarchy'.

The dispute reached its climax when Browne and Colley both addressed a gathering of the western branch of the Irish Graduates Association. When Colley had finished his address, Browne proceeded to denigrate his proposals for the amalgamation of small schools and then withdrew from the room. In his address, Browne denounced the new policy as 'a catastrophe – a major calamity for our Irish countryside', and asserted that closures of small schools were 'illegal and unconstitutional'. Colley's response was strong and unequivocal and he suggested that 'If that is so, why could not His Lordship use the courts to test his point'. However, he told the meeting that 'Even unsound criticism, if honestly indignant' was better 'than no criticism at all'.[25] He welcomed it because it stimulated interest in a subject which had been greeted with apathy for decades.[26]

Throughout the debacle, Colley kept Lemass informed on the development of his amalgamation plans, and on how he was engaged in a flanking manoeuvre with the Catholic Primate Cardinal Conway. The cardinal had 'agreed in principle with the policy and, in fact, suggested an area in his own diocese where it might be carried out'.[27] Lemass was supportive of his strategy, but he observed that the case for larger central schools had not yet been 'sufficiently publicised' and he urged him to make a series of speeches to promote public understanding of the new policy.[28]

In fact, the department failed to outline the advantages of the policy and how it could benefit parents. Parents were all but excluded from the overall process of closures and amalgamations. When repairs or replacements of schools were being considered, it was customary for an inspector to examine the feasibility of such work, to consult with the manager, and then to make his recommendation to the department. However, 'in some cases parents and groups in the local community considered that they should have been directly consulted'.[29]

It was a public relations fiasco as far as one union leader was concerned. He said, 'the decision about these schools was not explained, put across, 'sold' to the general public'. He believed that it was insufficient for Colley to make fine speeches in the Dáil in defence of his policy as few parents read reports of Dáil proceedings. He suggested to Colley that he 'should have spoken on radio and appeared on television' in order to make his case and to explain 'the reasons for the decision taken and what it involved'.[30]

The IIE report pointed to the gross disparities in pupil–teacher ratios in one- and two-teacher schools and large schools. Considerable numbers of small rural schools had pupil–teacher ratios of less than 20:1, while at the other end of the spectrum, many urban schools had pupil–teacher ratios in excess of 40:1. Schools of fewer than fifty pupils had 21 per cent of all the teachers, whereas they had only 11.5 per cent of all the pupils. On the other hand, the schools of over 200 pupils had 45 per cent of the pupils but only 34 per cent of the teachers. More than half of city pupils were in classes of fifty and over.[31]

According to the Survey Team, the imbalance was a historical legacy as 45 per cent of primary schools dated from the nineteenth century. Over 2,000 of them were without drinking water, flush toilets or chemical closets, and over 22 per cent had been declared obsolete by the Board of Works.[32]

Hillery had already taken measures to supply new schools, and to renovate and maintain existing ones. The IIE report confirmed that the government's policy in the mid-1960s was 'to erect 100 new schools and to complete major improvements on 50 schools each year'.[33] It acknowledged also that 'State grants are now being paid towards the cost of painting schools'. Hillery had made these grants available from April 1962.[34] In November 1964, Hillery met a joint deputation from the INTO and the Clerical Managers of Catholic Schools, prior to which he had arranged 'a complete survey' of all schools to ensure that they had an adequate water supply.[35]

There was no room for complacency with regard to the primary school curriculum either. It was reported that it was 'safe to conclude that the pupil of the smaller school' was 'likely to have a more restricted curriculum available to him or her' than was available in larger schools.[36] Even in schools where the curriculum was not so narrow, teaching equipment was minimal.[37] The progress of some pupils was hampered by the practice, particularly in smaller schools, of delaying the progression of pupils by a year or even more through the primary school. The report drew attention to the fact that by fifth standard, 30 per cent of pupils were delayed for 1 year, and 13 per cent for 2 or more years in 1963.[38]

The department took decisive action on remedying this situation in March 1967, when Donogh O'Malley as Minister sanctioned Circular 10/67, which stated that 'The normal procedure should be that a pupil is promoted to a higher standard at the end of each school year'.[39] In exceptional cases, a child could be held back for one extra year. Research conducted by Dr Thomas Kellaghan, director of the ERC, had indicated that when non-promotion of pupils was carried out on a large scale, 'it had educationally undesirable effects'.[40]

There was one important element in subject teaching which was not established with precision by the Survey Team and that was the allocation of time to different subjects in primary schools. Four months after the publication of the IIE report, the doctoral research of Fr John Macnamara revealed that Irish primary schools devoted 42 per cent of the time available over the first 6 years of primary education to Irish and a mere 22 per cent to English. Consequently, Irish children were on average 17 months behind their English counterparts in written English and 11 months behind in problem arithmetic.[41] The INTO report of 1941 had warned of these dangers, but its report was treated with derision by O'Neill, Derrig and de Valera.[42]

Irish primary school children were already at a disadvantage compared to their English counterparts as the length of the Irish primary school year was shorter than in other Western European countries. Not only that, but for one-third of Irish children their full-time education would terminate in primary schools. One in five of them would be forced to leave the country on the emigrant ship, 'most of them to compete in Britain with people who have received almost twice as much education as they have, in subjects other than Irish'.[43]

Colley and the department refrained from comment. In fact, Colley did not believe that Irish should be placed on an equal footing with continental languages because to him, Irish was unique. He told a gathering of Tuairim in Cork that 'the right to a place in an Irish school is the intrinsic one that it is not French, German, Italian or Spanish but Irish'.[44]

Macnamara's study deserved to be taken seriously by Colley, after all the tests upon which his conclusions were based had been administered by inspectors from his own department, and the statistical analysis had been carried out with the aid of two statistical experts in the Agricultural Institute. Garret FitzGerald, a future spokesman on education and future Taoiseach, called for a radical review of the Irish primary school curriculum because it was 'now demanded by common justice to the children we have condemned to this system'.[45]

The suitability of the narrow primary school curriculum came into question once more following the revelation in the IIE report that of the 17,459 pupils who withdrew from full-time education in 1962–63, 11,000 left without having sat the primary certificate examination. The report urged that 'In view of the apparent seriousness of this phenomenon it would seem to merit full attention'.[46]

COLLEY'S LETTER

In 1959 Noel Browne called for the provision of equality of educational opportunity for all children, as it was 'implied in the undertaking of the democratic Proclamation of the Republic – to cherish all the children of the nation equally'.[47] Colley made the same appeal in January 1966, in his letter to the secondary and vocational school authorities requesting their co-operation in the pooling of post-primary facilities and staff.[48] He reiterated the government's intention to raise the school leaving age, a step which would 'create problems of accommodation and teaching power as well as of curriculum content'. The current situation was untenable because 'the operation of two rigidly separated post-primary systems could no longer be maintained'.[49]

The IIE report provided evidence that Colley was pursuing the correct policy in order to introduce a level of equity into the post-primary education system. It had discovered 'a very marked association between social group and participation in education'.[50] Students aged 15–19 years of age and belonging to socio-economic categories A, B and C (farmers, professionals, senior employers, clerks etc.) were shown to have a four to five times greater chance of participating in post-primary education than those belonging to categories D, E and F (skilled, semi-skilled and unskilled workers).

There were also significant variations in educational participation by geographical area, with participation rates of 13–17-year-olds in second-level education in County Cork at a high of 49 per cent, while in County Donegal this figure fell to 30 per cent. Inequality of educational opportunity was not something unique to Ireland, 'but the stark statistics emphasised the urgency for remedial action'.[51]

School size was problematic at post-primary level also, with 64 per cent of secondary schools having fewer than 150 pupils, and 73 per cent of the day vocational schools having fewer than 150 pupils on the roll. It was noted that in smaller schools fewer than 100 pupils, the pupil–teacher ratio was 13.6:1, and in schools of 300+ pupils, the ratio was 20.9:1.[52] It concluded that 'smaller schools cost per pupil anything from one-third to one-half more than larger schools', and they also provided a narrow curriculum, as low enrolments precluded teachers from specialising in teaching the subjects they had taken to university degree level.[53] O'Meara's criticisms of the secondary education system in 1958 were justified, as the IIE report showed 'that over the system as a whole the provision of subjects is closely linked to size and to fee levels'.[54]

This would partially account for the neglect of modern continental languages in secondary schools where Latin was a popular choice. This was probably due also to its requirement as a university matriculation subject, and its widespread use, prior to the Second Vatican Council, as the medium of Catholic Church services. The Survey Team expressed concern about the standard of science and mathematics in secondary schools. Fortunately by the time the IIE report was published, Hillery had brought about important reforms in both of these areas of the secondary-school curriculum.

This pattern was repeated in vocational schools, where it was found that there were just 'not sufficient graduate teachers of mathematics and science or engineering to sustain the level of activity in these subjects'.[55] In light of the fact that plans were being advanced to introduce a common intermediate certificate for vocational and secondary schools and the continuation course was to be extended to 3 years, with 'an avenue provided to higher levels', it was stressed that 'The efficient utilisation of resources will therefore be all the more necessary'.[56]

The Survey Team assessed manpower requirements for 1970–71. It pointed out that there would be a severe shortage of holders of intermediate and group certificates. It was estimated[57] that there would be a deficit of 76,000 junior certificants, with only 110,000 being likely to be produced during the decade to meet a 'demand' for 186,000.[58] It was expected that there would be 172,600 in second-level education by 1970, which was an increase of some 40,000 over the number in second-level education in 1963–64, an increase which was less than that already predicted by the government.

This shortfall resulted from the Survey Team's anticipation of a slowing down in the growth rate expected in the early and mid-1960s. This expected deceleration was based on a survey of students which showed that any significant increase in participation would have to come mainly from the lower income group. Another factor which prevented fuller participation in second-level education was that many potential students lived at a considerable distance from post-primary centres.[59] Colley's proposals for central schools and free transport would meet some of these difficulties, so too would his announcement of his intention to double the annual expenditure on scholarships.[60]

NIEC SUPPORTS COLLEY'S EDUCATION POLICY

In explaining the comprehensive school idea, Colley said: 'Negatively, it is not anything ideological or political', he saw it simply as a means of providing equality of educational opportunity for all children.[61] His aim was supported in the National Industrial Economic Council's Comments on Investment in Education (NIEC).[62] The NIEC was a governmental body tasked with preparing general reports on principles which ought to be applied for the development of the national economy. Their comments on the IIE report were confined to the economic function of education. The council strongly supported efforts to provide equality of educational opportunity, because inequality was depriving society of the talents of the educationally disadvantaged, and this was affecting the quality of leadership in Ireland.[63]

There was a strong basis for this argument as almost 20 per cent of administrative, managerial and executive posts in Ireland were held by immigrants in 1961, as well as almost 10 per cent of professional and technical posts.[64] Professor Joe Lee recorded that 'Not only managers but researchers had to be imported in droves in the early 1960s to raise the level of socio-economic analysis'.[65]

The NIEC accepted the scheme suggested by the Survey Team, whereby the value of scholarships and grants would vary according to parental income, family size and home location. It called for increased expenditure on education in order to improve the economic state of the country, and it emphasised that this should be done even at the expense of other worthwhile projects.[66] Lemass confirmed that the government would give educational development 'the priority it deserves' in any future allocation of public funds.[67] The NIEC also welcomed the department's new emphasis on larger schools which promised to be more economical and educationally more beneficial than the existing multiplicity of smaller units.[68]

COLLEY URGES CO-OPERATION IN POST-PRIMARY EDUCATION

Following on from Colley's letter to the school authorities, the department produced a report for each county based on the survey undertaken of post-primary facilities in the country. The report supplied statistics about pupil enrolment in each school centre and the facilities provided in each centre, as well as future enrolment and facility requirements. It also offered specific suggestions for co-operation between schools, and set out the criteria on which viability would be judged.[69] These reports were circulated to all school authorities and were discussed on two fronts – at county meetings, where all the educational interests in the county were represented, and at local meetings, where the problems posed for particular areas were discussed in more detail. Colley appointed inspectors from his department who were given responsibility for convening meetings in each county and the department was to be represented at each meeting.[70]

However, the desired co-operation and collaboration which Colley had hoped for never quite materialised, even though the Second Vatican Council's *Declaration on Christian Education* urged at the time that 'every effort should be made to see that suitable coordination is fostered between various Catholic schools and that between these schools and others that kind of collaboration develops'.[71]

Perhaps it was expecting too much from secondary-school authorities, whose schools had functioned for decades in open competition with one another for a small school population, to suddenly pool resources. It was even harder to imagine how secondary and vocational schools would come to a similar arrangement, considering that these schools had 'been estranged by their historical development'.[72] Moreover, vocational schools were preoccupied with the preparation of new courses pending the introduction of the common intermediate certificate, and they were also coping with increased student numbers.

Other obstacles which militated against progress included the 'chain of command' structure in the vocational sector, which meant that the principal of a vocational school had to seek permission from the CEO, who would then consult the VEC, before agreeing to any decision. There were difficulties regarding the distance between the different schools, the question of insurance, timetables, the different rates and methods of payment, the different hours of work in the vocational and secondary schools, and the problematic issues of co-education and of discipline.

The lay teachers associations were less than enthusiastic about sharing teachers. The president of the ASTI, Daniel Buckley, pointed out that lay secondary teachers were 'contracted to teach the pupils of a secondary school in that school', and that 'any change in those conditions' should not be arbitrarily imposed.[73]

As one commentator suggested, the Colley letter promoting voluntary co-operative schemes between second-level schools 'had virtually no effect'.[74] Co-operative ventures did develop in Ballinamore, County Leitrim and in Boyle, County Roscommon.

George Colley's style of leadership was in stark contrast to Hillery's. He held official meetings with disaffected teaching unions and school authorities from the outset, and promised to set up Central Advisory Committees for consultation purposes. He offered reassurance to teachers that comprehensive schools would not replace existing post-primary schools, yet he adopted a very forceful stance when it came to sanctioning new school buildings. Decisions would now be based on the data supplied in the county reports. Colley set a high value on educational planning and on making the maximum use of available resources. He deployed the Development Branch for this purpose in order to make the necessary preparations for the raising of the school leaving age.

He gained acceptance for his contentious policy of amalgamation of one- and two-teacher primary schools from the INTO and the Catholic hierarchy, mainly through judicious use of the IIE report. Ironically, he failed to communicate the merits of amalgamation to parents, although he was a great champion of their rights in education. He spoke at length in the Dáil on the topic instead of using the mass media more effectively. He goaded Bishop Browne to challenge him in the courts on the issue, while at the same time he successfully courted the support of Cardinal Conway for his plans.

Colley continued with curricular reforms commenced by Lynch and Hillery by piloting subjects in preparation for the introduction of the new curriculum at first level, and by revising subject syllabi at second level. However, he paid scant attention to the vitally important research of Fr Macnamara highlighting the disproportionate amount of time being spent on the teaching of Irish and its detrimental effects on children's educational progress.

Despite George Colley's diplomatic letter to school authorities seeking their co-operation and collaboration in the sharing of staff and resources, progress in this area was negligible. But he can be credited with raising an awareness of the importance of comprehensive education. Following the opening of the first three comprehensive schools and the introduction of the common intermediate certificate, the momentum for policy change was gathering. Discussion of the IIE report helped to stimulate greater interest in education and now parents' expectations were raised about the future prospects which awaited their children if they could participate in post-primary education. It was left to Donogh O'Malley to satisfy parents' expectations, as Hillery and Colley had prepared the way for him 'to introduce the policy quantum jump to "free" education'.[75]

Notes

1   *Sunday Press*, 9 January 1966. 'Our future in education today', George Colley TD, Minister for Education.

2   Farrell, *Seán Lemass*, p.122.

3   O'Connor, *A Troubled Sky*, p.94.

4   *The Irish Times*, 22 April 1965.

5   *Dáil Debates*, vol. 216, col. 967, 16 June 1965.

6   *Dáil Debates*, vol. 207, cols 405–6, 5 February 1964.

7   Investment in Education report of the survey team appointed by the Minister for Education in October 1962 (Dublin, 1965).

8   *Dáil Debates*, vol. 216, col. 969, 16 June 1965.

9   Ibid., cols 969– 971.

10 *Dáil Debates*, vol. 207, col. 408, 5 February 1964.

11 *Dáil Debates*, vol. 216, col. 972, 16 June 1965.

12 *Dáil Debates*, vol. 217, col. 1962, 21 July 1965.

13 *Dáil Debates*, vol. 220, col. 1797, 17 February 1966.

14 *Dáil Debates*, vol. 223, col. 1733, 30 June 1966.

15 *Dáil Debates*, vol. 216, cols 977–8, 16 June 1965.

16 Ibid., cols 1968–9.

17 *Dáil Debates*, vol. 218, cols 432–5, 21 October 1965; Maye, *Fine Gael 1923-1987*, p.351. Oliver J. Flanagan was conferred with the Knighthood of St Gregory the Great by Pope Paul I on 21 September 1978.

18 *Dáil Debates*, vol. 218, cols 442–3, 21 October 1965.

19 Randles, *Post-primary Education*, p.182.

20 Horgan, *Seán Lemass*, p.296.

21 John Coolahan, 'Education policy for national schools, 1960–1985' in Mulcahy and O'Sullivan (eds) *Irish Education Policy*, p.41.

22 *Dáil Debates*, vol. 220, cols 1779–83, 15 February 1966.

23 *The Irish Times*, 7 February 1966. George Colley TD, Minister for Education.

24 *The Irish Times*, 13 September 1965.

25 *The Irish Times*, 7 February 1966; *Irish Press*, 7 February 1966.

26 *Dáil Debates*, vol. 220, col. 1199, 17 February 1966.

27 *Sunday Independent*, 16 September 1979, 'George Colley the heir apparent', Bruce Arnold.

28 NAI *96/6/36 S12891E*. Lemass to Colley, 25 September 1965.

29 Coolahan, 'Education policy', p.42.

30 Daniel Buckley, Presidential address to the ASTI in *The Secondary Teacher* 1:6, June 1966.

31 IIE report, p.227, p.234.

32 Coolahan, 'Education policy', p.39; IIE report, pp.225–64.

33 IIE report, p.259.

34 Circular 22/61, Department of Education, October 1961.

35 *Dáil Debates*, vol. 210, col. 331, 2 June 1964.

36 IIE Report, p.247.

37 Thomas Kellaghan and Liam Gorman, 'A survey of teaching aids in Irish primary schools' in *Irish Journal of Education*, 2:1 (1968), pp.32–40.

38 IIE report, p.575. Annexes and appendices ix, table c2.

39 Circular 10/67, Department of Education, October 1967.

40 Thomas Kellaghan, 'The organisation of classes in the primary school' in *Irish Journal of Education*, 1:1 (1967), p.16.

41 John Macnamara, *Bilingualism and Primary Education: A Study of Irish Experience* (Edinburgh, 1966), p.136.

42 Report of the Committee of Inquiry into the Use of Irish as a Teaching Medium to Children whose Home Language is English, p.18.

43 Garret FitzGerald, 'Economic comment. Primary school curriculum' in *The Irish Times*, 4 May 1966.

44 Address by George Colley TD, Minister for Education to the Cork branch of Tuairim, 15 November 1965.

45 FitzGerald, 'Economic comment'. Dr FitzGerald was leader of Fine Gael from 1977. He was Taoiseach twice in less than 18 months between June 1981 and November 1982.

46 IIE report, pp.140–1.

47 *Dáil Debates*, vol. 177, col. 193, 21 October 1959.

48 Letter from Seoirse Ó Colla TD, Minister for Education, to the authorities of secondary and vocational schools, January 1966 in Ó Buachalla, *Education Policy*, appendix 1, pp.393–7.

49 Ibid., pp.393–5.

50 IIE report, p.150.

51 Coolahan, *Irish Education*, p.166.

52 IIE report, p.269, table 10.6.

53 Ibid., pp.270–2.

54 Ibid., p.280.

55 Ibid., p.292.

56 Ibid., p.302.

57 IIE report, p.201, table 8.4.

58 Ibid., p.367.

59 Ibid., paragraph 6.118.

60 *Dáil Debates*, vol. 216, col. 957, 16 June 1965.

61 George Colley, 'Our future in education today' in *Sunday Press*, 9 January 1966.

62 National Industrial Economic Council's comments on investment in education. Report No. 16, 20 May 1966, p.13.

63 Ibid.

64 Garret FitzGerald, 'Investment in education', in *Studies*, 54, winter 1965, p.366.

65 Joseph Lee, 'de Valera's legacy', in *Spectator*, 19 September 1970, p.808.

66 NIEC, report no. 16, p.21.

67 *Dáil Debates*, vol. 223, cols 2194–5, 7 July 1966.

68 Op. cit., pp.25–6.

69 O'Connor, 'Post-primary education now and in the future', pp.9–10.

70 *Dáil Debates*, vol. 222, col. 2214, 25 May 1966.

71 Declaration on Christian Education, paragraph 12, 28 October 1965.

72 *The Irish Times*, 6 June 1966.

73 Presidential address ASTI, Daniel Buckley in *The Secondary Teacher* 1:6, June 1966.

74 John Horgan, 'Education in the Republic of Ireland' in Robert Bell, Gerald Fowler, Ken Little (eds) *Education in Great Britain and Ireland* (London, 1973), p.41.

75 Ó Buachalla, *Education Policy*, p.284.

13

Donogh O'Malley (1966–68):
'This is a dark stain on
the national conscience'

He had a reputation for being a hell-raiser, as being impetuous, and as having little respect for convention which blinded many to his ability and his deep concern for the underdog.[1]

In a cabinet reshuffle in July 1966, Colley was transferred from the Department of Education and his post was filled by Donogh O'Malley (1921–68), a 45-year-old engineer from Limerick. O'Malley first entered the Dáil on 25 June 1954, and 7 years later served in government as parliamentary secretary to the Minister for Finance with responsibility for the Board of Works, before obtaining full ministerial office in 1965 as Minister for Health.

Officials in the department did not know what to expect from the new Minister, who had not displayed much interest in education except to express the view that he favoured free universal education. The appointment of O'Malley, who 'had a reputation as a hell-raiser', was known to have 'terrified that department at the time'.[2]

News of his appointment received front-page coverage in *The Irish Times*. The appointment was referred to as 'The most topical and controversial', and the editor remarked with great prescience that 'Mr. O'Malley will have less respect for tradition in the sense of red tape … and if he rips through the department of Education he will have most of the parents of the country behind him'.[3]

O'Malley was indeed poised to 'rip through' the department. His officials believed that he would adhere to the scheduled raising of the school leaving age to 15 years by 1970, which would involve a measure of free universal education, at least up to the end of compulsory schooling. O'Connor reminded O'Malley that the common intermediate certificate had just been introduced into vocational schools, and that they 'would need some years' experience of the examination, if vocational schools were to be acceptable to parents'. But O'Malley was determined to introduce free post-primary education as soon as possible, and he requested O'Connor prepare such a scheme.

In fact, O'Connor had two schemes prepared – A and B. Scheme A made provision for free schooling and free transport up to the end of second-level education, and scheme B provided for free education and transport up to 15 years, and free education and transport after that, but subject to a means test. O'Malley later confirmed that a means test was not acceptable to Lemass, but that Scheme A was. It is doubtful that he ever consulted the Taoiseach.[4]

O'Malley met Lemass on 7 September 1966 to discuss his proposals for the introduction of some form of free post-primary education.[5] Just before the meeting he addressed a letter to Lemass marked 'Personal – by hand', which he sent around to Lemass's office, together with a copy of a memorandum outlining scheme A and scheme B for the introduction of free post-primary education. He informed Lemass that in a forthcoming speech he would make 'a general reference – without going into details – to some of the matters referred to in this memorandum, should you so approve'. He warned Lemass that Fine Gael was on the verge of publishing educational plans in its policy document 'The Just Society – Education', and he stressed the 'importance of pre-empting the largest opposition party with a policy announcement by the Government'.[6]

Subsequently, Lemass and O'Malley gave different accounts of what transpired at that fateful meeting, with the latter contending that his speech had been amended and approved by Lemass before he delivered it at a weekend seminar of the National Union of Journalists (NUJ) on 10 September in Dun Laoghaire. Addressing the seminar, O'Malley gave an outline of a free post-primary scheme with free school transport up to intermediate certificate level. In so doing, he committed the government to massive expenditure without the knowledge of the cabinet or the approval of the Department of Finance, and without having consulted the churches. He had arranged for his two Assistant Secretaries to brief the teaching unions and the school authorities on the scheme that afternoon. The officials 'were suitably vague, giving no more than an outline of what O'Malley proposed to say'. O'Connor believed that the school authorities were pleased to have been given some advance notice of the proposals.[7]

The secondary teachers were far from pleased, judging from the editorial in *The Secondary Teacher*. The editor took umbrage at the department's failure to observe the ordinary decencies of communication, and he commented that 'Few of the department's efforts at public relations … can have been as exquisitively muffed as was the recent briefing'. He added, 'As an attempt at public relations this was the drollest burlesque'.[8] His annoyance was understandable according to a former president of the ASTI, as 'those who would be expected to implement the scheme were to get their first knowledge of what was intended from Sunday newspapers'.[9]

O'Malley's announcement shocked the managers of private secondary schools. It was they who had provided secondary education with an inadequate government subsidy and borne the burden of capital costs prior to 1964. Cardinal Conway referred to this fact when he quoted statistics from the IIE report, which showed that there were 'more students in secondary schools in Ireland, age 16, than in Great Britain, thanks to the religious'.[10] In fact, managers of secondary schools had to cater for a doubling of enrolments between 1945 and 1963, yet they 'managed to keep fees at an exceedingly modest level and to remit them entirely in many cases'.[11]

To this day commentators, spanning the generations, hold the view that O'Malley embellished the content of his announcement without Lemass's approval.[12] Hillery's biographer considered O'Malley's version of events 'clearly implausible',[13] while Lemass's biographer observed that there was 'evidence to indicate that Lemass had seen and even amended the text in advance'.[14]

According to O'Malley's friend Michael Mills, the *Irish Press* political correspondent, O'Malley told Charles Haughey that he had shown Lemass the speech, and that Lemass had changed it to make it less definite.[15] Kevin Boland, another cabinet colleague, 'understood that Lemass had warned O'Malley that if the government came down against him, he would have to withdraw it'.[16] It should be remembered that Lemass was due to retire within 2 months, and as John Healy, another journalist friend of O'Malley's, commented in his *Irish Times* column under the pseudonym 'Backbencher', 'Lemass was not short of reasons for allowing O'Malley to unveil the plan ... the Government had made the dream of the 1916 martyrs a reality, and henceforth the children of the nation would be cherished equally'.[17]

According to one historian, 'O'Malley's speech was a ploy used often by Lemass to anticipate opposition and get a radical shift in policy approved by acclamation. This pre-empted interminable cabinet discussion and blocking tactics by the Department of Finance'.[18]

O'MALLEY'S SPEECH TO THE NUJ

On 10 September 1966, O'Malley addressed the NUJ on the role of education in the future development of Ireland. He was very much at home with journalists as he spent much of his leisure time in their company or entertaining them.[19] On this occasion, he informed his audience that it was 'rather fortunate that I should be making my maiden speech as Minister for Education before a body of journalists'.[20] He told them that now was the time to invest in education as 'The world of to-day and tomorrow will give scant attention to the uneducated and those lacking any qualification'.

He pinpointed the basic fault in the education system, which was that so many families could not afford to pay 'even part of the cost of the education of their children'. This lack of educational opportunity resulted in a 'terrible loss to the national potential for economic and cultural advancement'. The human cost involved was of greater concern to O'Malley, and the fact that one-third of students completed their education in a primary school and were left to make their way in the world as they competed with the better educated. He regarded this as 'a dark stain on the national conscience'.

He was pleased to be able to announce that from September 1967, the opportunity for free post-primary education would be available to all families. In addition, he intended to make financial provision to assist towards the cost of books and accessories 'to the student on whom it is a hardship to meet all such costs'. Financial assistance would be available also for those pupils who 'because of the location of his home, can have post-primary education available to him only if he enters boarding school'.[21]

The announcement was broadly welcomed by the media, with *The Irish Times* expressing surprise at the breadth of the scheme, and it predicted that it would meet considerable difficulties in its implementation.[22] The *Irish Press* saw the new scheme as a vote of confidence by the government in the Irish people and in their 'unproven children'. It was a vote of confidence also in the system of post-primary education and its teachers, that 'devoted band of teachers' to whom Mr O'Malley specifically referred in his speech.[23]

Patrick Heerin, vice-president of the ASTI, described it as 'something which everyone must welcome'.[24] Senator Seán Brosnahan, general secretary elect of the INTO, said that it was a child's entitlement to 'have the opportunity to develop himself to his full potential ... regardless of his parents' means'.[25]

Charles McCarthy, general secretary of the VTA, thought O'Malley's plan was a necessary step towards the raising of the compulsory school leaving age from 14 to 15 years by 1970. He welcomed it as a 'practical underpinning of plans for the development of education'.

The CHA welcomed the principle of free education as 'something that must come and the sooner the better'.[26] The Catholic bishops also favoured the scheme. In 1944 McQuaid recommended the raising of the school leaving age to 16 years as soon as conditions permitted.[27] Cardinal Conway confirmed in January 1966 that the policy had 'the enthusiastic support of the Church'.[28]

O'Malley lost little time before consulting the hierarchy in the wake of his announcement, having already 'made media capital out of not having consulted McQuaid'.[29] Accompanied by Ó Raifeartaigh and the two assistant secretaries, O'Malley travelled to Maynooth on 4 October to hold discussions with Conway and McQuaid. The meeting was seen as mutually beneficial, and O'Malley agreed to make special financial arrangements 'for the Diocesan Colleges run by the Bishops'.[30] The diocesan colleges and juniorates educated students intended for the priesthood, most of whom were boarders. It was arranged 'that the tuition element of the fee of the pupils in these colleges should be paid under the scheme of free education' from 1968 onwards.[31] No statement was issued afterwards, but all the indications were 'that it took place in the most candid and cooperative spirit'.[32]

O'Malley then turned his attention to the Protestant Church, and he met representatives of the Protestant communities on 13 October. This was a successful meeting also, at which it was agreed that the supplemental grant of £25 per pupil would be given to 75 per cent of Protestant day pupils, which amounted to the same overall ratio as for Catholics. O'Malley 'proposed to channel the grant through a central representative agency' which would distribute the money to the individual schools on the basis of the needs of the pupils. There were 3,600 Protestant day pupils in total and it was decided to give a lump sum of £70,000 per annum in order to provide a grant of £25 for about 75 per cent of that number.[33] The agency in question was the Secondary Education Committee, which was established in 1965 and whose membership consisted of representatives of the Church of Ireland, the Presbyterian Church, the Methodist Church and the Religious Society of Friends.[34]

The reasons for this particular arrangement under the free post-primary education scheme were that the Protestant community was more dispersed and consequently more reliant on boarding schools. In addition, the cost of Protestant schools was higher than that of Catholic schools because of the hidden subsidy provided by religious orders in the latter institutions.[35] Dr Kenneth Milne, the secretary of the Board of Education of the general synod of the Church of Ireland, was agreeable to O'Malley's plan.[36]

Milne was aware that some Protestant parents resented being means tested when their Catholic counterparts were not, and that they believed that the department should have administered the scheme for them. The Secondary Education Committee were obliged 'to defend their action in participating in a scheme which appeared to be unjust to many of their co-religionists'.[37]

OPPOSITION TO THE FREE POST-PRIMARY SCHEME

The opposition parties in government greeted O'Malley's announcement with incredulity. Barry Desmond, a prominent member of the Labour Party's education committee,[38] said that 'Even if he were to implement his general aspirations, they would be a partial implementation of the comprehensive plan of the Labour party' as set out in their policy document Challenge and Change.[39]

Pat Lindsay, the Fine Gael spokesman on Education and Transport and Power, was very sceptical of O'Malley's plan, believing it to be a diversionary tactic in order to deflect attention from the Fine Gael education policy document which was due to be published.[40]

The reaction of the secretary of the Department of Finance, Dr T.K. Whitaker, was predictable. He was so enraged that he immediately forwarded a strongly worded letter of complaint to Lemass.[41] Lemass was obliged to reprimand O'Malley, and he did so by writing a letter to him, dated 12 September, which took the form of a mild rebuke.[42]

In a handwritten reply to Lemass's letter, O'Malley produced 'one of the best letters written by a government minister in twentieth-century Ireland'.[43] He said he believed he had Lemass's agreement to his line of action 'particularly in view of the fact that Fine Gael were planning to announce a comprehensive education policy' that week. He added that the public agreed with Lemass's decision to prioritise education, and he had received an unprecedented number of letters of commendation, particularly from parents. He believed 'that it was essential for a Government from time to time to propound bold new policies' and he apologised if he had misunderstood Lemass's intentions, but he hoped that Lemass would give him his full support in getting his plans approved by the government.[44] O'Malley had skilfully succeeded in providing Lemass with an escape route which enabled 'him to maintain his tacit support for' his endeavour.[45]

Jack Lynch, the Minister for Finance, had been out of the country and on his return he raised the question of O'Malley's announcement with Lemass on 21 September 1966. Lemass saw fit to address another letter of mild rebuke to O'Malley in which he told him that 'any new proposals even in the field of education, must be framed with strict regard to financial possibilities'.[46] He insisted that he should personally approve in advance, any draft answers to Dáil questions on the free education scheme addressed to O'Malley. On 26 September, Lemass wrote to O'Malley confirming that he had vetted his answers to Dáil questions and commented, 'I suggest that your reply should be along these lines'. O'Malley dutifully complied.[47] Lemass kept O'Malley under observation until he 'decided abruptly to retire from the position of Taoiseach'[48] in October 1966. Jack Lynch took over as Taoiseach a month later.

O'Malley's announcement was made without prior consultation with the teachers involved. In his speech he paid a compliment to the teachers, as he proudly proclaimed that 'Above all, I have under my department a devoted band of teachers'. Even so, his hasty action, coupled with a lack of information on various aspects of the scheme, left many teachers anxious about an uncertain future. Séamus Ó Súilleabháin, Professor of Education at St Patrick's College, Maynooth, spelled out the benefits which could result from developing the professional status of teachers, and suggested that recent educational developments failed to take cognisance of this.[49]

When O'Malley met representatives of the ASTI in February 1967, the main item on the agenda for discussion was not the 'free education' scheme but rather the possible rationalisation of second-level schools. It transpired that O'Malley was just as committed to the policy of rationalisation of facilities as Colley ever was. He stated in the Dáil that 'the rationalisation of post-primary educational facilities requires that we insist on reasonably sized units'. He believed that this was a policy that was 'right on educational and economic grounds', and furthermore it was 'in line with that suggested by Investment in Education' and it was also 'supported by the NIEC comments on that Report'.[50]

The authorities of private secondary schools were also concerned about O'Malley's plans for rationalisation. They had just been issued with the results of the county surveys of post-primary educational facilities. The county reports introduced the idea of a 'post-primary centre' which consisted of the following; a large boys' secondary school, and a girls' secondary or a vocational school. All primary schools within a 6-mile radius were assigned to the post-primary centre in the area. Post-primary schools now became 'junior centres' or 'major centres', depending on school size and location. Major centres could accommodate between 320-400 students, and junior centres could accommodate about fifty students.[51] The 'free education' scheme coupled with rationalisation proposals would offer a most serious challenge to the private status of secondary schools.

SENATE OUTBURST

When introducing the estimates for 1966-67, O'Malley informed the Dáil that it was estimated that there would be a 75 per cent take-up of the free education scheme. He was dissatisfied with this, especially as the 25 per cent who would remain outside, would be concentrated almost entirely in Dublin and Cork. He refused to accept this situation and sought the assistance of McQuaid in an effort to persuade other schools to come on board.[52] By February 1967 many representatives of high-fee secondary schools were openly critical of the scheme.

In the course of a debate in the Senate on 9 February, during which his scheme came in for further criticism, O'Malley asserted that the newspapers and parents were fully supportive of his plans, and that he would undoubtedly have the required teachers and schools for September, but he could not guarantee that he would have the co-operation of all secondary-school managers. He vowed that 'no vested interest or group ... will sabotage what every reasonable-minded men consider to be a just scheme ... I shall pull no punches. Christian charity how are you'.[53]

O'Connor considered that O'Malley's verbal attack on secondary-school managers was uncalled for, that it was foolishly undiplomatic and that 'he was never forgiven'.[54] This speech served only to raise O'Malley's stature in the eyes of the media, which lambasted his critics.

A week later O'Malley addressed a public meeting in Clontarf, on the topic 'Free education and after?' The main thrust of his argument was that private secondary schools, by their very nature, were inegalitarian insofar as they had the right to accept or reject any student arbitrarily. He found this objectionable because 'with such a system we would not be cherishing all the children of the nation, not to mention cherishing them equally'.[55] His address had been well prepared and was delivered 'at a critical point in the negotiations between the department and the school authorities'. His forthright approach was effective as it 'enabled O'Malley to save his scheme against a number of alternative schemes put forward by the managerial bodies'.[56]

By 24 February, O'Malley had received a letter from representatives of the Catholic managerial associations pledging the support of the Catholic Managerial Committee for his scheme.[57] McQuaid played an important role in gaining this support by encouraging priests, nuns and brothers running schools in his Dublin archdiocese to participate in it. O'Connor conjectured that he did so because 'he wanted the convent schools to attract to themselves the newcomers to secondary education'.[58]

The relationship between O'Malley and McQuaid was one of mutual self-interest. O'Malley had recently accused the religious authorities of trying to sabotage his scheme and of failing to cherish all the children of the nation equally in their private schools. In October 1967, McQuaid defended the contribution of the religious authorities to Irish education, and he suggested to their critics that they were ignorant of the history of Irish education. He reminded them that had it not been 'for the intelligent preparation and constant self-sacrifice of the Congregations ... the present system of free education could not have been even partially initiated'.[59]

In the spring of 1967, the Dublin evening newspapers published lists of schools which intended to participate in the free education scheme. Many schools felt pressurised into doing so as those who did not 'found a stiff reaction from parents'.[60]

Secondary teachers took exception to this type of coverage, as speculation grew over why some schools would not participate. The annoyance felt by secondary teachers found expression in the editorial of the May 1967 issue of *The Secondary Teacher*, which castigated the department, the media and finally the bishops for their failure to speak out in support of the secondary schools. It concluded that 'it is a fact that the religious orders, have been grievously betrayed by the bishops'.[61]

O'Connor commenced the county meetings to discuss rationalisation proposals, and he described the atmosphere at meetings 'in a few cases' as one 'of outright hostility'. He attributed this to a combination of Colley's co-operation policy, O'Malley's 'free education' scheme and the county meetings themselves, which teachers saw as measures to enable a State take-over of 'all secondary schools'.[62] Secondary teachers were scarcely considered throughout this period of rapid changes, even so they 'gave the scheme a cautious welcome',[63] as indeed did the school authorities, from whom much was required if the scheme was to be a success.

FREE POST-PRIMARY EDUCATION

Pat Lindsay told O'Malley that he did not believe his plan would work. He pointed out to him that 'nowhere in the course of this whole document is there a single reference to the fundamentals of what education is'.[64] Lindsay, who was a former secondary teacher himself,[65] was well placed to challenge O'Malley, but what he failed to realise was that ministers such as O'Malley, Hillery or Colley never espoused a philosophy of education, that their aim was the egalitarian one of 'cherishing all the children of the nation equally'. With this one magnanimous gesture, O'Malley came the closest of the three to achieving, in some measure, this goal. The scheme proved to be a great success, with 92 per cent of day pupils benefiting from it. This amounted to an annual increase of 15,000 students.[66]

The department made special arrangements to assist the school authorities to meet the demand. It increased the building grant to secondary schools from 60 to 70 per cent. The annual amount of capital available was 'very substantially increased'. All funds for educational expansion were channelled through the department, which acted as a central agency for the processing of building grants.[67] The money was made available to school authorities by way of a direct grant of 70 per cent, and the remaining 30 per cent by way of a loan repayable over 15 years. Arrangements were made to make available to school authorities 'where necessary to meet urgent requirements, pre-fabricated classrooms on which the 70 per cent grant was payable'.[68]

Numbers attending vocational schools had also increased but not as spectacularly as in the secondary sector. It cost the government an additional £1,211,040. Nonetheless, O'Malley was happy to reveal that the total number of candidates who presented themselves for the day group certificate examinations was 19,444, as compared with 16,767 in 1966.[69]

Progress in the provision of transportation to schools surpassed O'Malley's expectations. Of the 55,000 children who were eligible, service was provided for 52,000 of them. Less than a year after its initiation, transport was available to all eligible children. The progress made meant that the original estimate of £300,000 was inadequate as the cost for the financial year 1967–68 came to £840,000.[70] The government made up the shortfall.

O'Malley announced plans for three additional comprehensive schools, while a fourth was under construction in Glenties, County Donegal. One of the proposed schools was 'for Protestant pupils at Raphoe'.[71] Nobody could accuse him of discriminating against religious minorities.

The 'free education' scheme generated much controversy, but in the end Church and State co-operated to ensure its successful introduction. McQuaid's contribution was crucial, but so too was Lemass's as he overcame the opposition of the Department of Finance. O'Malley gained media support for his scheme without which Lemass might not have supported it. The scheme had its flaws, having been 'pushed through quickly and with little thought of implementation, which added unnecessarily to its cost'.[72] It also had the 'unintended, inegalitarian and unfortunate side-effect of sidelining vocational education'.[73] However, it provided an opportunity for all children to experience second-level education, and it 'opened up many doors that were previously shut to children born into the wrong families'.[74]

INTO ISSUES ULTIMATUM

O'Malley lauded the government's record in the provision of new school buildings and renovations. He reminded the opposition parties that when they were in coalition governments together, they failed to match Fianna Fáil's outstanding record in this area.[75]

Despite the progress made regarding school maintenance following four joint deputations of representatives of the INTO and the clerical managers to various Ministers, problems still persisted. Matters came to a head in February 1967, when the general secretary of the INTO, on the instructions of the CEC, issued an ultimatum to the secretaries of the clerical managers of Catholic

National Schools, the Department of Education and the office of the Board of Works. It warned that if the Executive received a serious complaint about sub-standard conditions in any national school, it would, having verified the authenticity of the complaint, withdraw the staff from the school concerned after November 1967.[76]

In July 1967, a conference took place with representatives of the department, the clerical managers and the INTO. As a result, a circular was to be sent to managers allowing them to bypass existing procedures governing grants for the repair and maintenance of school buildings. Applications were to be sent directly to the Board of Works for the immediate attention of the architects of the School Building Branch. Grants of two-thirds of the cost involved or more, if necessary, were to be made available.[77]

Despite these reforms, unsatisfactory conditions were reported to the INTO from five national schools in Ardfert, County Kerry. The twelve teachers involved voted to withdraw their services on 16 January 1968. They resumed work 3 weeks later when repairs were satisfactorily completed.[78] School maintenance now became a priority countrywide. O'Malley informed the Dáil in February 1968 of progress made during this period while carefully avoiding any reference to the 3-week work stoppage at Ardfert.[79]

When introducing the estimates of his department for 1967–68, he announced that a third teacher could now be appointed when an average enrolment of eighty pupils had been established, instead of the former requirement of ninety pupils. He intended improving the pupil–teacher ratio 'until the position will be reached, when no teacher will have more than 35 pupils in his class', and he was satisfied that the amalgamation of small schools was 'proceeding in a reasonably smooth manner'. The extension of St Patrick's Training College was completed and he reported that the total number of trained teachers in June 1967 was 585.[80]

The reform of first level education was aided by the introduction of free post-primary education as more students proceeded to second level at age 12+. Teachers were no longer burdened by having to prepare sixth class students for scholarships to post-primary schools,[81] or indeed for the primary certificate examination which O'Malley abolished early in 1968 and replaced by a system of record cards 'showing the progress through the primary school of each individual child'.[82] Furthermore, from the beginning of the school year 1966–67, schools were informed by the department that a pass in the entrance examination for secondary schools would no longer be a condition of recognition of a pupil for the payment of the capitation grant.[83] All the major obstacles to an expansion of the primary school curriculum were now removed.

BUNTÚS GAEILGE

O'Malley offered reassurance to Irish language supporters when delivering his address to the NUJ by saying that he had not 'come to the post of Minister for Education to preside over the obsequies of the national language'. He then elaborated on the new method of teaching Irish, through the *Buntús Gaeilge* or foundation Irish programme, which facilitated rapid language acquisition in a simple way. All one had to do was to learn 900 words and phrases 'and one can converse widely in Irish'.

The *Buntús* method was being followed in 150 primary schools and 50 secondary and vocational schools.[84] In November 1966, further trial courses were being conducted in 200 primary schools, much to O'Malley's satisfaction.[85]

In 1967 the Government Publications Office produced *Buntús Cainte*,[86] the first multi-media, graded course in Irish for beginners, based on books, audio tapes and a radio and television series. It received a very positive public response.[87]

The government's compulsory Irish policy became a contentious issue in September 1966, with a number of Irish authors and other activists going on a 7-day hunger strike to focus attention on the policy.[88] A 'great confrontation' took place between the Language Freedom Movement (LFM) and Irish language enthusiasts. LFM was an organisation established in 1965 with the aim of seeking to abolish the compulsory Irish policy.[89] The movement had arranged a public meeting on the topic in the Mansion House, Dublin, where they were attacked by militant revivalists. The protest was organised mainly by Sinn Féin, but all thirteen language organisations were represented.

The Irish Times reported that nearly 2,000 people 'jammed the hall' and 'Several hundred more waited outside the door, which was kept locked by Gardaí'. Following the intervention of Dónall Ó Móráin, head of Gael Linn,[90] equal speaking rights were allowed to language revival enthusiasts, two of whom were academic clergymen – Fr Colmán Ó hUallacháin and Fr Tomás Ó Fiaich of St Patrick's College, Maynooth, a future Cardinal and Primate of all Ireland.[91]

It was not just militant nationalists, Irish academics or Irish language organisations who wanted to see the language preserved. Within the space of a few years, parents in urban areas took the initiative to set up All-Irish primary schools and pre-schools.

Some progress was also made with regard to special education, particularly when Hillery was Minister. Colley addressed the issue by setting up a Special Committee in October 1965 to report on the problem of 'the retarded or slow learning children in the primary schools'. He did so in the wake of the publication of the Report of the Commission of Inquiry on Mental Handicap by the

Department of Health in March 1965. O'Malley was still awaiting the report of the Special Committee. However, he achieved some success with regard to the education of mentally handicapped children when new primary schools were established for them in Kilkenny, Navan, Drumcar, Waterford City, Ennis, Enniscorthy and Cootehill. At the same time, facilities in Dublin for the education of mentally handicapped children were being extended.[92]

In 1968 O'Malley was responsible for setting up the Kennedy Committee[93] to investigate industrial and reformatory schools, whose origins went back to the pre-industrial era. Industrial schools were introduced into Ireland in 1869, shortly after the reformatory schools, and they catered for neglected, orphaned or abandoned children. The purpose of the schools was to teach these children reading, writing and arithmetic and to prepare them for a trade. Local authorities were reluctant to take on the job of providing industrial schools, so 'the onus fell on various religious orders'.[94] Following a damning report from the Kennedy Committee, the schools were gradually phased out in the 1970s. The years ahead would see the uncovering of startling revelations regarding the treatment of children in these schools.[95]

It was now considered timely to engage in long-term educational projects, and to prepare a green paper on education as a discussion document, to be followed by a white paper. O'Malley was averse to long-term planning and to the preparation of a white paper,[96] but eventually his officials convinced him of its merits and he requested one to be ready for publication in 1967. In December 1966, a steering committee consisting of a small group of inspectors was set up in the department to advise on the primary education aspect of the white paper. The steering committee examined the primary school curriculum and it decided to abandon the old programme and to start from first principles in developing what became known as the 'new curriculum'.[97]

POST-PRIMARY CURRICULUM DEVELOPMENTS

The introduction of free post-primary education resulted in students of mixed ability taking their places in senior cycle courses for the leaving certificate. Some teachers had grave reservations about the merits of open entry for students who were unlikely to benefit from it, particularly in light of the fact that remedial teaching was in its infancy in second-level schools in the late-1960s. Seán Brommell, in his Presidential address to the ASTI congress in 1967, articulated teachers' fears,[98] but O'Malley insisted that there should be no obstacle to entry to senior cycle courses for the leaving certificate.

In January 1967, the department considered that the time had come for a re-appraisal of the leaving certificate courses. A meeting was called for this purpose, which was attended by representatives from the secondary and vocational associations, the department itself, and for the first time, the NUI and TCD. This 'revision of the Leaving Certificate was a logical consequence to the introduction of the new arrangements for the Intermediate examination'.[99] The department, however, was more concerned about the dominant influence of the matriculation requirements of the NUI on the leaving certificate courses offered. In light of the fact that only one in ten progressed to university up until 1968, when student grants became available, it seemed anomalous that second-level courses should be geared towards the matriculation requirements of so few.

The Leaving Certificate Committee met weekly from January to March 1967. By the end of the year, it was in a position to send its report to the schools for consideration. The main point for discussion was whether the leaving certificate subjects should be concentrated in groups of related subjects to avoid specialisation. It was suggested that there should be five groups of subjects – languages, commerce, science, technical studies and social studies – and that a student would have to choose at least three subjects from one of these groups. This suggestion was clearly at odds with the committee's own objective of avoiding specialisation. In any event neither the secondary schools nor the universities found the proposal acceptable and grouping remained optional.[100] O'Malley was blamed for this as he had not kept his promise to consult the teachers' associations when bringing in changes to the curriculum for second-level schools.[101]

However, he consulted successfully with the teachers' associations with regard to changing the marking system for the leaving certificate examination. An agreement was reached that, commencing from 1969, the general categories of honours, pass and failure would be replaced by grades. These grades would be issued for each subject ranging from Grade A to NG (no grade), from 85–100 per cent to under 10 per cent.[102]

O'Malley built on the earlier achievements of Hillery and Colley regarding curriculum development, most notably in the areas of modern languages, science, and the practical subjects traditionally associated with the vocational schools. The number of students studying French in secondary schools had risen from 37,041 in 1960–61 to 60,956 in 1965–66, and the number studying science had risen from 41,643 in 1960–61 to 69,943 in 1965–66.[103] Two years later he raised the grants to schools for a number of practical subjects to assist them in coping with the growth in numbers studying these subjects. The estimated total cost of these grants was £280,000 as against £150,000 for 1966–67.[104]

O'Malley was scarcely 2 weeks in office when he revealed that he planned to review the method of appointment of vocational teachers. Appointments were made by VECs, but canvassing of members of VECs was widespread. The VTA complained to O'Malley about this practice and he undertook to end it. He attended a VEC meeting in Limerick at which he informed members that he was 'seriously perturbed by their past behaviour' with regard to financial practices and appointments' procedures.[105]

In February 1967, he made a ministerial order dissolving the city of Limerick VEC and transferring all duties of the committee to Pádraig Ó Cuilleanáin, a principal officer in the department.[106] In October he nominated MacGearailt to conduct a local inquiry. The findings of the inquiry exposed breaches in the appointments' procedures. Ó Cuilleanáin continued exercising the powers of the committee until 1970, when a new VEC was appointed.

On 7 March 1967, O'Malley secured the agreement of the Irish Vocational Education Association (IVEA), the representative body of the VECs, for new selection boards for VEC appointments. Each board would consist of one member of the VEC, one member of the IVEA, the CEO of the area, and two educationalists appointed by the Minister. A year later, O'Malley informed the Dáil that the new recruitment procedures, which had been adopted on a trial basis, were working satisfactorily.[107]

COMMISSION ON HIGHER EDUCATION
'SPUR HIM ON WITH THAT REPORT'

The universities would not tolerate interference from a politician and the only way I could deal with them would be through a Commission.[108]

The economic condition of the country, together with a lack of public or political interest, meant that university education was neglected for four decades. It was widely regarded as an elite pursuit.[109]

Patrick McGilligan, Minister for Industry and Commerce in the 1920s and UCD academic, suggested in 1948 that university numbers could be reduced by raising the standard of the matriculation examination, thereby saving the Irish taxpayer money.[110]

By the 1960s, government ministers would provide extra university accommodation at Belfield to facilitate the growing demand for university education, and this would be done with the help of the Irish taxpayer. It was now fully accepted that third-level education would play a vital role in the economic development of the country. This was implied in the extensive terms of reference presented by Hillery to the members of the Higher Education Commission, which held its first meeting on 8 November 1966.[111]

This was the first commission since the foundation of the State to examine all aspects of higher education. It took 7 years to complete its report, which 'was a very long time at a period when many educational issues were pressing for resolution'.[112] Impatience was expressed by Dáil deputies at the slow rate of progress.[113] For over 4 years, Dáil questions were raised as to when the commission would report its findings.[114] O'Malley wrote to Lemass, urging him to 'Spur him on with that Report'.[115]

The parliamentary secretary to the Taoiseach and government Chief Whip, Michael Carty, called for the abolition of the commission. He believed that the commissioners had threatened to resign if the Minister made any reference to proposals for university education. His advice to O'Malley would be 'Let them resign and be damned'.[116] The chairman of the commission, Chief Justice Cearbhall Ó Dálaigh, did threaten to resign, but Jack Lynch, the newly installed Taoiseach, was careful to distance himself from Carty's comments,[117] and in December 1966 he intervened and prevented the resignation of Ó Dálaigh.[118]

The report's investigative procedures were meticulous and exhaustive.[119] Written submissions alone amounted to 1.1 million words. Part 1 Presentation and Summary consisted of 25,000 words and the report proper came in two volumes, comprising 400,000 words, spread over thirty-two chapters, with each chapter grouped into seven divisions.[120]

The report was a damning indictment of a higher education system which had developed piecemeal into a complex of separate units. This led to unnecessary duplication in some areas, while other areas of higher education were unprovided for. It should be remembered that in 1960 higher education had only recently become the responsibility of the Department of Education.[121] Irish universities had been funded by the Department of Finance and it was not until the mid-1950s that funding was transferred to the Department of Education.[122] There had been no tradition of policy making for higher education in the department, and the vast majority of its administrative staff dealing with higher education were not university graduates and had no direct experience of higher education.[123]

There was no overall planning authority and planning by individual institutions was minimalist. This was evident in the overcrowding in universities, especially in UCD where numbers had trebled from the 1920s to the 1940s. Professor Michael Tierney, president of UCD and Eoin MacNeill's son-in-law,[124] wrote an article in 1944 describing the Dickensian state of the university building at Earlsfort Terrace, which was ill-equipped to cope with burgeoning numbers.[125]

The commissioners noted that 'Sectional interests play too large a part, and antagonisms between individual institutions have been apparent'.[126]

Relations between UCD and TCD were frosty and the reasons for this were mainly historical. The Universities Act of 1908 established the NUI with three non-denominational, co-educational constituent colleges at Dublin, Cork and Galway, while Trinity retained its privileged position, which it had held since its foundation in 1592, as the sole college of the University of Dublin.[127] In reality, the NUI catered primarily for Catholic students and TCD remained predominantly a Protestant university.

The main bone of contention within the commission related to the perception of TCD as being less than fully integrated into the life and culture of independent Ireland. Professor Tierney gave expression to this view, which was shared by few on the commission. He said, 'Close down Trinity College, I look on TCD as a foreign body'.[128]

The provost of TCD, Dr A.J. McConnell, Professor Theo Moody and Basil Chubb representing TCD presented a picture of the status of the college as an asset 'to the intellectual and cultural life of the country and affirmed that it had a proper place in the structure of Irish higher education'.[129]

The Catholic Church ban on Catholic students attending TCD, first introduced in 1875 and reinforced in February 1944 by McQuaid, was a major handicap to the full integration of the college into the mainstream of Irish higher education. McQuaid decreed that 'No Catholic may enter the Protestant University of Trinity without the previous permission of the Ordinary of the Diocese', and any Catholic who disobeyed this law was 'guilty of mortal sin' and was 'unworthy to receive the Sacraments'.[130]

The two Catholic prelates on the commission, Bishop Philbin and Cardinal Conway, strongly upheld the Church's position on the ban. The Trinity representatives regretfully accepted the regulation while regarding it as 'a national tragedy'. The commission ruled out the possibility of a merger between UCD and TCD as a single-based university. It did, however, recommend more co-operation and co-ordination between the two universities, and suggested the setting up of a statutory 'Council of Irish Universities' for mutual planning purposes. It recommended that an intermediary planning and budgetary agency between the State and the individual institutions should be established, such as a 'commission for higher education'.[131]

The commission considered that the standard of entry to the NUI colleges that applied up to 1966-67 was too low for university entrance. Approximately two and a half to three times as many candidates took honours papers and the failure rate in the first arts examination, especially in the colleges of the NUI, sometimes approached 40 per cent.[132] The commission recommended that student entry standards should be raised.

The report referred not only to the problem of inadequate staffing in the universities but also to the 'unsatisfactory' nature of academic appointments in the NUI.[133] The chief offender in this was UCD, which made appointments without any reference to the Senate of the NUI.[134] It should be noted that the Chancellor of the NUI from 1921 until 1975 was de Valera, who owed this honour to the effective canvassing skills of Professor Corcoran.[135]

Another contentious area examined by the commission was the future structure of the existing university institutions. UCD argued strongly for the dissolution of the NUI, while UCC and particularly UCG, favoured its retention. The commission ruled in favour of the dissolution of the NUI with the constituent colleges being established as independent universities. Maynooth College would have the choice of independent status or of forging new links with the reconstituted UCD.

The commission recommended an improvement of staff-student ratios to 12:1. In order to encourage greater participation in third-level education, it called for a comprehensive scheme of educational grants, a grant towards a national association of students and improved student facilities.[136]

The commissioners' views on the role of a university as 'a place for the study and communication of basic knowledge' found few supporters. They argued that the responsibility for the provision of technological education should not rest with the university. They believed that the functions of institutions of higher education, especially universities, as centres of learning, scholarship and liberal education, should not be allowed to become overwhelmed by the claims made upon them to provide the country with the requirements of skilled manpower.[137] It was this 'distinction between basic and applied learning, separating the latter from the proper role of a university' which 'was seen by many as a basic error, indicating a wrong direction for the future of university studies'.[138]

In order to maintain academic standards, which were at risk under existing conditions, the commissioners proposed a new type of third-level institution – the New Colleges. The New Colleges would provide forms of higher education, lower in standard and with a different emphasis, from that of the university and would become centres of intellectual and cultural life in their regions. It was recommended that they would be established in Dublin and Limerick, while others were envisaged for the south-east and north-west.[139] Many educationalists had concerns about the proposed New Colleges, which planned to offer 'something other than university education', as their courses in the humanistic, scientific and commercial field would 'have a stronger vocational bias than would be appropriate to university courses'.[140]

Since 1902 the INTO had called for stronger links between the training colleges and the universities,[141] but now the commissioners were recommending the restructuring of the teacher training colleges, so that the current staff in their educational departments would become the education departments of the New Colleges. The course for national teachers would be extended to 3 years and would lead to the award of a degree from the New Colleges.

However, the commissioners served educationalists well by objecting to the obvious neglect of educational studies in universities. They stated that 'the study of education should not be regarded as the "poor relation" of university studies'.[142] They regarded educational research as being 'the hallmark of a university',[143] but in Irish universities it was 'neither well organised nor well supported'.[144] They attributed this to 'insufficiency of staff, equipment and accommodation'.[145]

The urgency of the problem was reflected in the fact that various universities left the chair of education vacant for long periods. The chair was left vacant in TCD from 1916 to 1922, in UCD from 1950 to 1966, in Maynooth College it was vacant at various times, and in UCC from 1962 to 1969.[146] Understaffed education departments of the universities were being stretched to breaking point in the decade 1959–69, and the calls of the Commission on Higher Education for action to be taken resulted in the chairs of education being refilled by the late 1960s.[147]

The commissioners proposal for New Colleges was to a large extent upstaged by Hillery's announcement of plans to establish RTCs, and by O'Malley's decision to appoint a steering committee on Technical Education in September 1966 to advise, inter alia, on building arrangements for the RTCs. The commissioners recommended the setting up of a Technological Authority with the responsibility of ensuring that advanced technological education, training and research would be provided in relation to the needs of Irish industry.[148] Neither the New Colleges nor the concept of a Technological Authority gained the unanimous support of the commissioners, and neither did they meet government requirements.[149]

THE STEERING COMMITTEE ON TECHNICAL EDUCATION

The Commission on Higher Education presented a summary of its recommendations to O'Malley on 24 February 1967, and he set up a departmental committee to examine its proposals. The departmental committee paid particular attention to technical education because of the massive shortfall in skilled manpower, as highlighted in the recent IIE report. They believed that a Technological Institute of high prestige, on a par with the universities, was what was called for. Counties such as Limerick and Waterford were considered to be suitable for such an institute as they had the student population and they had called for universities in the past.

Such an institute could also provide for training for teachers of technical subjects. Metalwork teachers were reliant on the occasional courses run by the department in selected vocational schools for their training. Woodwork teachers were trained for 1 or 2 years on special courses in woodwork conducted at a centre in County Wexford.

There was also a shortfall in provision for the training of teachers of physical education (PE). Schools were continuously demanding qualified PE teachers, but the department could not meet the demand. The departmental committee proposed to provide 'A College offering courses of training to teachers of these varied specialisations' within a single institute.

They approached O'Malley with their plan, which proposed his native city of Limerick as a suitable location for an institute. O'Malley accepted their proposal and he successfully managed to convince the university lobby group known as the Limerick University Project Committee[150] (LUPC) to accept the idea of a technological institute in lieu of the full university which they sought. Hillery had ear-marked Limerick for a regional technical college in 1963 and that plan was now dropped.[151] Instead Limerick was to get a National Institute of Higher Education (NIHE).

The Steering Committee on Technical Education was launched by O'Malley in September 1966. It presented an interim report in January 1967, but the final report was not published until April, in order to take into account the report of the Commission on Higher Education. The steering committee was appointed to advise on technical education generally, and in particular on building arrangements for the RTCs. Their task was a challenging one as the design consortium had been nominated for the construction of the colleges and were awaiting their planning brief. The long-term mandate of the colleges, as foreseen by the steering committee, was quite broad. It was to 'educate for trade and industry over … occupations ranging from craft to professional level … in engineering and science … commercial, linguistic and other specialities'.[152]

The steering committee displayed originality in their inclusion of linguistics in the spectrum of courses to be offered – this option was unheard of in 1967.[153] They also showed foresight in allowing flexibility regarding course provision.[154] They recommended the building of eight RTCs immediately, and that priority should be given to Cork, Waterford, Limerick and Galway, since these centres, along with Dublin, would absorb almost three-quarters of the student population. A smaller college was proposed for Letterkenny on a site large enough to allow for later expansion. In the Dáil, O'Malley announced the government's decision to locate RTCs at Cork, Limerick, Galway, Waterford, Carlow, Dundalk, Athlone, Sligo and Letterkenny at a cost of £7 million.[155] The decision to build a regional technical college in Limerick was of course later reversed in favour of the NIHE.

The steering committee provided for a wide range of courses to be conducted in the RTCs, including senior cycle post-primary apprentice and technician courses, and various types of adult education. The provision of leaving certificate courses was seen as a means of ensuring the economic viability of the colleges until such time as they were well established. After a few years their work did in fact become 'mainly tertiary education'.[156] An area of disagreement between the Commission on Higher Education and the steering committee was in regard to entry standards and levels of academic attainment proposed for the New Colleges. In general, the steering committee endorsed the government's plans for RTCs 'and largely ignored consideration of how they might mesh with the Commission's Colleges'.[157]

There was one area where the commission and the steering committee made a somewhat similar recommendation, and this was in regard to the validation and certification of technical courses and the granting of academic awards. The steering committee called for the establishment of a NCEA on the lines of the British Council for National Academic Awards, while the commission called for a Technological Authority. However, the steering committee's proposal:

> pointed more firmly towards a binary third-level framework on British lines, while the Commission's Report saw the universities and the New Colleges fitting into a university model, with less emphasis on technical and techno-logical education.[158]

The NCEA was set up on an ad hoc basis in 1972. Two further recommendations of the steering committee were rejected. One was for the establishment of regional education councils. The second one was that an outside consultancy or research organisation should initiate surveys to forecast the demand for places at RTCs, and the demand for courses on offer. As one commentator remarked, 'One would have expected these two valid questions to have been asked ... before the decision was taken to set up the RTCs'.[159]

The steering committee had envisaged close co-operation taking place between the RTCs and a new training authority called An Chomhairle Oiliúna (AnCO). The Industrial Training Act, 1967 (Act No. 5 of 1967) repealed the Apprenticeship Act of 1959 under which An Chéard Chomhairle had been established, and gave AnCO wide powers to make legally enforceable rules covering all aspects of the recruitment and training of apprentices. AnCO took over and expanded the functions of An Céard Chomhairle. It was expected that rules would be more vigorously enforced than they were under An Cheárd Chomhairle.

O'Malley appreciated the 'very thorough Report' prepared by the steering committee.[160] The report of the Commissioners on Higher Education on the other hand, was to suffer two serious setbacks. The first one was the rejection by the government of its proposal for New Colleges, and the second one was O'Malley's announcement on 19 April 1967 that it was the government's intention to establish a single multi-denominational university in Dublin. It would contain two colleges, based on the existing institutions, UCD and TCD. This was more popularly known as 'the merger proposals'.

THE NEW UNIVERSITY OF DUBLIN

It was particularly galling for the Commissioners of Higher Education, who had worked laboriously on their brief for 7 years, to learn that one of their main recommendations had been rejected by the government just as they had presented a summary of their report. O'Malley admitted that the decision to adopt the merger plan had been taken in December 1966, just as Fine Gael had published its education policy.[161]

Cearbhall Ó Dálaigh was of the opinion that it had been O'Malley's objective to ensure that the views of the commission did not have any public airing until his own particular proposal had been launched. Ó Dálaigh believed that his whole purpose had been to get a glimpse of the commission's final recommendations to see if they afforded him any support for what he had already decided to do.[162]

In his briefing to journalists, O'Malley revealed that he had informed the authorities of each college 'only that morning' of his merger plans. He had 'neither sought nor obtained' from the Catholic hierarchy any agreement that the ban on Catholic students attending TCD would be removed. He admitted 'that he had not worked out the constitutional structure of the new university'.[163] As in the past, the print media supported O'Malley.[164] Journalists depicted him as a strong, decisive Minister who was determined to put an end to what he described as 'a most insidious form of partition on our own doorstep'.

It was clear from his statement of April 1967 that O'Malley believed that the commissioners 'were caught in the web of history' in their rejection of any form of merger of the two universities.[165] He ignored the fact that two of the commissioners, Bishop Philbin and Cardinal Conway, 'maintained an uncompromising stand on the ban issue'.[166] Indeed, historical precedent alone should have suggested to him that the removal of the ban, which his merger proposals would necessitate, would not have been welcomed by the Catholic Church. In 1958, when O'Meara suggested such a merger, it was condemned by Cardinal D'Alton as meaning 'a union of incompatibles'.[167]

Cardinal Conway gave the first public comment on O'Malley's proposal on 22 April 1967, which displayed a new flexibility on the Church's part. He said that the plan 'contained a number of good ideas' and 'could make a positive step towards a rationalisation of the situation in all its aspects'.[168] The hierarchy, after its first meeting since the announcement of the plan, issued a non-committal communiqué, which at least expressed no objection in principle to a merger of the two colleges.[169] It is interesting to note also, that in June 1966, even before the report of the commission was published, the Catholic hierarchy opened up St Patrick's College, Maynooth as a centre of higher studies to 'involve nuns, brothers and laity'.[170] A further indication of a softening in attitude on the Catholic Church's part regarding the ban, was detected by Moody who noted that 'There are now far more Catholics at Trinity College than ever before'.[171]

This change in attitude may also have been brought about by the reassurance offered by O'Malley in his statement of 18 April, that 'In the future University of Dublin there will be provision for both Catholic and Protestant Schools of Divinity or Theology'.[172] The Catholic Church was also obliged to take into consideration the increasing demand by Catholic students for entry to TCD.

O'Malley was not prepared to concede to the wishes of UCD by granting the college the status of a separate university.[173] Moody had a better understanding of UCD's predicament, which he expressed in his reply to J.P. MacHale, the secretary-bursar of the college, who put forward UCD's case for a single college. Moody recognised that UCD had 'long outgrown the system under which, for the past sixty years, it had been a Constituent College of the National University of Ireland'.[174]

He contended that UCD would find 'participation in a new University of Dublin of the same federal type' unacceptable, but he disagreed that the only alternative was the unitary University of Dublin advocated by the governing body of UCD. Such a solution, according to Moody, would have ruinous consequences for the smaller university.[175]

O'Malley tried to impress upon TCD that the proposed merger would end Trinity's isolation and bring it into the mainstream of higher education and of Irish life.[176] Moody believed that the removal of the ban would contribute to the 'settlement of a question that has so deeply complicated the problem of university education in Dublin'.[177]

Many and varied were the challenges that faced the provost of TCD, Dr A.J. McConnell, the 'brisk Ulsterman from Ballymena' and 'the first post-Treaty graduate to hold that office'.[178] He would have to overcome years of 'official hostility on the part of UCD towards TCD'.[179] He would have to solve the problem of underfunding and seek a solution to the century-old ban on Catholic students entering Trinity College. All of this he would have to achieve to realise his ambition to 'bring Trinity College into the mainstream of higher education in this country'.[180]

In his statement of 18 April, O'Malley set out his reasons for proposing the merger. In Dublin there were two separate and differently constituted universities 'each ploughing its own furrow with virtually no provision for sharing scarce resources'.[181] He questioned why the State should be expected to pay UCD £160,000 and TCD £86,000 annually towards the support of two distinct veterinary faculties. The merger would lead to educational gains in the areas of staff–student ratios and in the vital area of educational research, areas in which there was a good deal of leeway to be made up.

The merger would ease the financial burden on the State. O'Malley was displeased with TCD, which sought a State grant of £2½ million for 1967–68 and succeeding years, mainly because of a decision taken by the College authorities, without the prior sanction of the government, to raise the intake of students from 3,000 to 4,000. Not only that, but over 1,200 of these students were non-Irish. He had no objection to a reasonable number of foreign students entering TCD, but he believed that they should be evenly distributed throughout the colleges in general.[182]

The main reason why O'Malley desired a merger was to cater for a projected rise in university numbers. The Commission on Higher Education had forecast that there would be 26,000 students in higher education in 1975, of whom 23,000 would be attending university. O'Malley believed that the number was likely to be as high as 27,000.[183] He considered that the problem could be solved by replacing foreign students with Irish ones. He was convinced 'that a debate on the merger would bring about the ending of the ban on Catholics entering Trinity, as indeed it did'.[184]

Prompted by the realisation that if the universities could not 'agree on a plan of association' then 'the Government could impose its will on them',[185] the academic staff of both institutions abandoned hostilities to combine in opposition to the merger plan. In 1968 the government set up the Higher Education Authority (HEA) on an ad hoc basis as a planning and budgetary authority.[186] It was under the aegis of the HEA that negotiations were conducted between UCD and TCD. McConnell gave his full support to these new contacts with UCD. The two universities agreed to a plan for the division of faculties to avoid, where possible, duplication of facilities and expensive equipment.[187] However, fate intervened with the untimely death of Donogh O'Malley on 10 March 1968.

McConnell had the unique ability to reach out to Catholic academics, members of the hierarchy, and indeed the government. He built up a good relationship with de Valera in the 1940s, as a fellow mathematician, and with Lemass in the 1960s. Lemass won government approval for a grant towards the building of a new library for Trinity.[188] McConnell attributed the ending of the college's isolation from Irish society to his friendship with Monsignor Patrick Browne, president of UCG, who advised him to apply for a grant in 1952 as the Fianna Fáil government could be persuaded to help Trinity.

He did so and for the next 22 years of his provostship, Trinity was to receive £750,000 from the government.[189] A further positive development occurred in June 1970, when it was announced that the bishops were seeking approval from Rome for the repeal of the statute prohibiting the attendance, without special permission, of Catholic students at Trinity. The reason for this change of policy was stated to be 'the substantial agreement on basic issues that has been reached between the NUI and TCD'. However, according to Cardinal Conway, it marked 'the conclusion of a process of re-thinking' which had been going on among the bishops since 1965.[190] This begs the question as to why he and Bishop Philbin strongly supported the ban when they were commissioners for higher education in the late 1960s.

The removal of the ban necessitated the appointment of a Catholic chaplain to TCD, so McConnell requested a meeting with McQuaid to discuss his choice of nominee for the position. McQuaid, who had enforced the ban so rigorously in 1944, now told McConnell that lifting the ban 'was something he had been looking forward to for many years'. The provost had served his college well. The removal of the ban was his reward, a fact which he himself acknowledged.[191] He succeeded in bringing TCD into the mainstream of higher education in Ireland.

The introduction of free post-primary education was Donogh O'Malley's enduring legacy to Irish education and it earned him iconic status. Forty years on, the editor of the *Irish Independent* (20 June 2007) attributed Ireland's economic success to its educated workforce and to the vision of Donogh O'Malley.

It was achieved through political adroitness and the employment of unorthodox methods. It would hardly have been achieved without the support of Lemass, of parents and the media. Pragmatism and self-interest played a role too. It was understandably a popular scheme with parents, and Lemass, who was about to retire, wished to leave his own legacy by 'cherishing all the children of the nation equally'. Pragmatism was at the heart of O'Malley's decision to ask for McQuaid's co-operation and it was at the heart of McQuaid's decision to do so.

Secondary teachers were less concerned about 'free education' than they were about county meetings to discuss rationalisations proposals, which they saw as an attempt by the State to take over their schools. O'Malley offered no comfort to them when he laid bare his intention to insist on reasonably sized units. School authorities felt under siege as the building grant scheme, rationalisation talks and the 'free education' scheme eroded their independence and status. He offered no succour to them either.

O'Malley retained continuity when he took steps to prepare for the introduction of child-centred education by introducing reforms such as the abolition of the primary certificate and removing the necessity for scholarships to post-primary schools. He also built on the earlier achievements of Hillery and Colley in curricular development at second level. He took the crucially important decision to set up the Kennedy Committee to investigate industrial and reformatory schools, and he reformed the recruitment procedures of the VECs.

The long-awaited Report of the Commission on Higher Education tested his patience, particularly as events had overtaken the report. Hillery had announced plans for the introduction of RTCs which undermined the commission's proposals for New Colleges, and O'Malley set up the Steering Committee on Technical Education which endorsed plans for the RTCs but largely ignored how they might mesh with the New Colleges. He added insult to injury by announcing merger proposals which the commission opposed, and by revealing that this decision had been taken as far back as December 1966.

He attempted to pull off another political masterstroke with the merger proposals, but he had no master plan. He bargained on media and public support, and on the hierarchy lifting the ban. He had not bargained on UCD and TCD representatives negotiating and co-operating under the aegis of the HEA to avoid the merger, and in so doing contributing to the hierarchy's decision to lift the ban.

In 20 months Donogh O'Malley made Irish education a talking point in Irish households as he fulfilled the wishes of parents by opening up second-level education to their children for the first time. He succeeded where Thomas Derrig had failed exactly 20 years ago. Not only that, but he provided the blueprint for the RTCs, which would in time open up higher technological education to vast numbers of students. This was an extraordinary ministerial legacy to Irish education.

Notes

1 O'Connor, *A Troubled Sky*, p. 136.
2 *Sunday Independent*, 29 April 1979. Jacqui Dunne interview with Kathleen Lemass.
3 *The Irish Times*, 7 July 1966. Editorial 'Handsome is … on Donogh O'Malley'.
4 O'Connor, *A Troubled Sky*, pp. 141–2.
5 NAI *DT 96/6/356, S12891E* Donogh O'Malley Minister for Education; Horgan, *Seán Lemass*, p. 298.
6 Ibid., O'Malley to Lemass, 7 September 1966.
7 O'Connor, *A Troubled Sky*, p. 144.
8 Thomas O'Dea, editorial in *The Secondary Teacher* 1: 7 September 1966, p. 5.
9 Louis O'Flaherty, 'The introduction of free post-primary education in Ireland' in *The Secondary Teacher*, 16:4 (1987), p. 9.
10 Cardinal Conway, 'On threshold of a new educational era' in *The Irish Times*, 27 January 1966.
11 Sheehan, 'Education and society in Ireland', p. 65.
12 Horgan, *Seán Lemass: The Enigmatic Patriot*, p. 299.

13 Walsh, 'The politics of educational expansion', p.2.

14 Farrell, *Seán Lemass*, p.107.

15 *Irish Press*, 31 January 1969.

16 Horgan, *Seán Lemass: The Enigmatic Patriot*, p.299.

17 *The Irish Times*, 17 September 1966.

18 Keogh, *Twentieth-Century Ireland*, p.284.

19 Michael Mills, *Hurler on the Ditch: Memoir of a Journalist who became Ireland's First Ombudsman* (Dublin, 2005), pp.40–1.

20 Speech by Donogh O'Malley, in Browne, *Unfulfilled Promise*, p.183.

21 Ibid., pp.186–9.

22 *The Irish Times*, 12 September 1966.

23 *Irish Press*, 12 September 1966. Editorial 'Investment in people'.

24 Ibid.

25 *The Irish Times*, 12 September 1966.

26 *Irish Press*, 12 September 1966. The CHA was founded in 1879. It consisted of headmasters of Catholic boys' secondary schools managed by priests.

27 Ó Buachalla, *Education Policy*, p.232. Memo from the Department of Education to the cabinet October 1947.

28 *The Irish Times*, 27 January 1966.

29 John Cooney, *John Charles McQuaid: Ruler of Catholic Ireland* (Dublin, 1999), p.385.

30 Randles, *Post-primary Education*, p.246.

31 *Dáil Debates*, vol. 232, col. 477, 6 February 1968.

32 *Irish Catholic Directory 1967*. Entry for October 1966, p.790.

33 *Dáil Debates*, vol. 225, cols 1886–7, 30 November 1966.

34 Kenneth Milne, 'A Church of Ireland view', in *Studies*, autumn 1968, p.262.

35 O'Flaherty, 'The introduction of free post-primary education', p.14.

36 Kenneth Milne, 'Minority problems', in *Hibernia*, January 1967, p.7.

37 O'Flaherty, 'The introduction of free post-primary education', p.14.

38 Barry Desmond was a member of the steering committee of the 1962 OECD Survey Team.

39 *The Irish Times*, 12 September 1966.

40 *Dáil Debates*, vol. 225, col. 1896, 30 November 1966.

41 NAI *DT 96/6/36 S12891E* Education developments 1966-67, 12 September 1966.

42 Ibid.

43 Diarmaid Ferriter (ed.) *What If? Alternative Views of Twentieth-Century Ireland* (Dublin, 2006) pp.140–1.

44 Ibid., Letter from O'Malley to Lemass, 14 September 1966.

45 Browne, *Unfulfilled Promise*, p.83.

46 Ferriter, *What If?*, p.141. Letter from Lemass to O'Malley, 22 September 1966.

47 NAI, *DT S12891E*

48 Keogh, *Twentieth-Century Ireland*, p.299.

49 Bro. S.V. Ó Súilleabháin, CFC, 'Quality in education' in *Hibernia*, January 1967, p.7.

50 *Dáil Debates*, vol. 225, cols 1891–3, 30 November 1966.

51   Randles, *Post-primary Education*, pp.238–9.

52   O'Connor, *A Troubled Sky*, p.155.

53   *Senate Reports*, vol. 62, cols 1089–90, 9 February 1967.

54   Op. cit., p.155.

55   Address by Donogh O'Malley, '*Free Education and After*', Clontarf, 16 February 1967, pp.5–6.

56   Ó Buachalla, *Education Policy*, p.287.

57   Randles, *Post-primary Education*, pp.265–6.

58   O'Connor, *A Troubled Sky*, p.152.

59   *Irish Catholic Directory 1968*, entry for 13 October 1967, pp.840–1.

60   *Evening Herald*, 2 May 1967.

61   *The Secondary Teacher*, 2:5 May 1967. Editorial.

62   O'Connor, *A Troubled Sky*, p.159.

63   O'Flaherty, 'The introduction of free post-primary education', p.12.

64   Browne, *Unfulfilled Promise*, pp.85–6.

65   Lindsay taught classics at the Royal School, Cavan and later at schools in Dublin. He became a Senior Counsel in 1954. He was appointed Master of the High Court 1975–84.

66   *Dáil Debates*, vol. 232, col. 464, 6 February 1968.

67   Randles, *Post-primary Education*, p.277.

68   *Dáil Debates*, vol. 232, cols 464–5, 6 February 1968.

69   Ibid., cols 469–70.

70   Ibid., col. 468.

71   Ibid., col. 475.

72   Browne, *Unfulfilled Promise*, p.89.

73   Garvin, *Preventing the Future*, p.201.

74   J.J. Lee, *Ireland 1912-1985: Politics and Society* (Cambridge, 1989), p.362.

75   *Dáil Debates*, vol. 226, col. 102, 6 December 1966.

76   O'Connell, *History of the INTO*, p.447.

77   *Dáil Debates*, vol. 232, col. 461, 6 February 1968.

78   Op. cit., pp.448–9.

79   *Dáil Debates*, vol. 232, cols 461–2, 6 February 1968.

80   Ibid., col. 460.

81   *Dáil Debates*, vol. 225, col. 1890, 30 November 1966.

82   *Dáil Debates*, vol. 232, col. 463, 6 February 1968. The INTO advocated the use of record cards. O'Connell, *A History of the INTO*, p. 433.

83   Circular M50/66, Department of Education, 1966.

84   Speech by Donogh O'Malley, pp.190–2.

85   *Dáil Debates*, vol. 225, col. 1881, 30 November 1966.

86   It contains a series of graduated lessons, based on the linguistic research in Ó hUallachain's *Buntús Gaeilge*.

87   Adrian Kelly, *Compulsory Irish: Language and Education in Ireland 1870s-1970s* (Dublin, 2002), p.33, p.58.

88   Ferriter, *The Transformation of Ireland*, p.600.

89 *The Irish Times*, 14 September 1965.

90 Gael Linn was founded in 1953 to promote the Irish language and culture nationwide. Its activities have included the production of newsreels, films, and records in Irish, the provision of language courses, and sponsorship of educational activities at all levels of the system.

91 *The Irish Times*, 22 September 1966. 'L.E.M. concedes voice to its opponents'.

92 *Dáil Debates*, vol. 232, cols 462–3, 6 February 1968.

93 Ibid., col. 473.

94 Coolahan, *Irish Education*, p. 191.

95 Mary Raftery and Eoin O'Sullivan, *Suffer the Little Children: The Inside Story of Ireland's Industrial Schools* (Dublin, 1999).

96 O'Connor, *A Troubled Sky*, pp. 192–3.

97 Coolahan, 'Education policy', pp. 48–9.

98 Presidential address Seán Brommell, ASTI, April 1967.

99 Randles, *Post-primary Education*, p. 260.

100 Ibid., pp. 279–82.

101 O'Connor, *A Troubled Sky*, pp. 189–91.

102 Press conference Brian Lenihan TD, Minister for Education, 17 May 1968.

103 *Dáil Debates*, vol. 225, col. 1882, 30 November 1966.

104 *Dáil Debates*, vol. 232, cols 465–6, 6 February 1968.

105 Browne, *Unfulfilled Promise*, p. 80; City of Limerick VEC Minutes, 29 July 1966.

106 Donogh O'Malley Ministerial order 27 February 1967.

107 *Dáil Debates*, vol. 232, col. 469, 6 February 1968.

108 Walsh, *Patrick Hillery*, p. 85. Ó Raifeartaigh's advice to Hillery.

109 John Coolahan, 'Higher education in Ireland 1908-1984' in J.R. Hill (ed.) *A New History of Ireland 1921-84*, p. 763.

110 Garvin, *Preventing the Future*, p. 169, p. 309.

111 Report of the Commission on Higher Education 1960-67, I:1 1967, p. xxviii.

112 Coolahan, 'Higher education in Ireland', p. 1.

113 Tony White, *Investing in People: Higher Education in Ireland from 1960 to 2000* (Dublin, 2001), p. 43.

114 *Dáil Debates*, vol. 217, col. 567, 6 July 1965; vol. 220, cols 681–2, 2 February 1966; vol. 221, col. 1282, 9 March 1966.

115 Ferriter, *The Transformation of Ireland*, p. 598; NAI, *DT 97/6/272*, 19 July 1966.

116 *Dáil Debates*, vol. 225, cols 2019–20, 30 November 1966.

117 White, *Investing in People*, p. 45.

118 Report of the Commission on Higher Education, minutes of the commission, vol. x, p. 2098.

119 Higher education in Ireland: comments on the report of the Commission on Higher Education 1960-67 in *The Irish Journal of Education*, 11:1 (1968) pp. 3–31, p. 3.

120 Ibid., pp. 3–6.

121 White, *Investing in People*, p. 41.

122 *Dáil Debates*, vol. 254, col. 1490, 15 June 1971.

123 *Dáil Debates*, vol. 200, col. 37, 10 March 1963.

124 Professor Michael Tierney was nominated as president of UCD in 1947.

125 Senator Michael Tierney, 'Universities: English and Irish' in *Irish Ecclesiastical Record* (1944), pp.153–4.

126 Commission on Higher Education 1960-67, 1, presentation and summary of report, 1967, pp.22–3.

127 Susan M. Parkes, *A Guide to the Sources for the History of Irish Education 1780–1922* (Dublin, 2010), p.85.

128 Minutes of the Commission, vol. xi, p.119.

129 Presentation and summary of report, p.49.

130 *Irish Catholic Directory and Almanac 1945*. Entry for 20 February 1944, pp.674–5.

131 Presentation and summary of report, p.53–5.

132 Horgan, 'Education in the Republic of Ireland', p.39.

133 Presentation and summary of report, pp.22–3.

134 Coolahan, 'Higher education in Ireland', p.775.

135 Jones, *A Gaelic Experiment*, p.15.

136 John Coolahan, 'The Commission on Higher Education, 1967, and third-level policy in contemporary Ireland' in *Irish Educational Studies*, 9:1 (1990), p.7.

137 Report of the Commission on Higher Education, pp.143–4, p.184.

138 Coolahan, 'Commission on Higher Education', p.8.

139 Op. cit., p.127.

140 George Lodge, 'The new colleges – the Commission on Higher Education' in *The Secondary Teacher*, 2:8 October 1967, pp.8–12, p.8.

141 John Coolahan, 'The fortunes of education as a subject of study and research in Ireland' in *Irish Educational Studies*, 4:1 (1984), p.13.

142 Report of the Commission on Higher Education, p.220, p.211.

143 Presentation and summary of report, pp.22–3.

144 Op. cit., p.235.

145 Presentation and summary of report, pp.22–3.

146 Coolahan, 'The fortunes of education', p.16.

147 Ibid., pp.22–3.

148 Coolahan, 'Higher education in Ireland', p.781.

149 Report of the Commission on Higher Education, p.864, p.899, p.908, p.932, p.937; White, *Investing in People*, pp.46–7.

150 The campaign for a university in Limerick began when the LUPC was founded in September 1959 as a project of the Mayor of Limerick, Ted Russell. It was supported by Mr Justice Dermot Kinlen, a High Court judge, later first State Inspector General of Prisons and Places of Detention.

151 O'Connor, *A Troubled Sky*, pp.174–6.

152 Steering Committee on Technical Education. Report to the Minister on Regional Technical Colleges 1967, p.11.

153 Dr Con Power, 'The RTCs and economic development' in *Irish Education Decision Maker*, No. 4, autumn 1991, p.10.

154 Steering Committee on Technical Education, p.11.

155 *Dáil Debates*, vol. 232, col. 470, 6 February 1968.

156 Coolahan and O'Donovan, *A History*, p.222.

157 Coolahan, 'Higher education in Ireland', p.782.

158 Ibid.

159 Randles, *Post-primary Education*, p.273.

160 *Dáil Debates*, vol. 232, col. 472, 6 February 1968.

161 *The Irish Times*, 19 April 1967.

162 Commission minutes, pp.2333–5, 5 May 1967, manuscript library TCD, file no. 7130.

163 *The Irish Times*, 19 April 1967. 'TCD and UCD to be united. O'Malley announces wedding plans'.

164 *The Irish Times*, 19 April 1967. Editorial 'Mixed marriage'.

165 Statement of the Minister, 18 April 1967, p.117; *Dáil Debates*, vol. 227, col. 2187, 20 April 1967.

166 Coolahan, 'The Commission on Higher Education', p.6.

167 *Irish Weekly Independent*, 3 April 1958; *Irish Weekly Independent*, 26 June 1958. Ruairí Quinn, Minister for Education and Skills, described the proposal to merge TCD and UCD contained in a recent HEA commissioned report on higher education by international experts, as 'neither feasible nor desirable'. See *Irish Times* and *Irish Independent*, 26 September 2012.

168 *The Irish Times*, 22 April 1967.

169 Whyte, *Church and State*, p.342.

170 Coolahan, 'The Commission on Higher Education', p.7.

171 T.W. Moody, FTCD, 'University education in Dublin' in *Studies*, 57, summer 1967, p.177.

172 Statement of the Minister, 18 April 1967, p.121; *Dáil Debates*, vol. 227, col. 2192, 20 April 1967.

173 *The Irish Times*, 19 April 1967. 'TCD and UCD to be united'.

174 Moody, 'University education in Dublin', p.173.

175 Ibid.

176 *The Irish Times*, 19 April 1967.

177 Moody, 'University education in Dublin', p.178.

178 White, Minority report, p.155.

179 Op. cit., p.173.

180 *Irish Press*, 14 August 1985.

181 Statement of the Minister, 18 April 1967, p.113.

182 Ibid., pp.114–5; *Dáil Debates*, vol. 227, cols 2182–4, 20 April 1967.

183 Ibid., p.119; col. 2190.

184 James Downey, *Lenihan: His Life and Loyalties* (Dublin, 1998), p.62.

185 Moody, 'University education in Dublin', p.174.

186 Coolahan, *Irish Education*, p.244.

187 *Irish Press*, 14 August 1985.

188 Ibid.

189 *Irish Press*, 12 August 1985.

190 *The Irish Times*, 26 June 1970; Whyte, *Church and State*, p.343.

191 Ibid.

14

Brian Lenihan (1968-69): 'This was more than a strike of the teachers: it was a revolt of the schools'

Dick Walsh in his book *The Party* describes Lenihan as:

> ... at once 'bombastic and self-deprecating'. Bombastic, perhaps, about how the new men in the party would change the world: certainly self-deprecating and self-mocking and concealing his great intelligence.[1]

Following O'Malley's sudden death, the Taoiseach, Jack Lynch, became Acting Minister from 11 to 23 March 1968. He then appointed Brian Lenihan (1930–95), a 38-year-old barrister, as Minister for Education on 27 March 1968. Lenihan had parliamentary experience having been appointed parliamentary secretary to the Minister for Lands and the Minister for Justice in 1961 by Lemass, following 4 years in the Senate, and 3 years later Lemass appointed him Minister for Justice.[2]

In the course of an interview, Lenihan declared that his first major task was the preparation of a White Paper on education which would deal with career guidance. He intended to have a comprehensive survey undertaken of manpower requirements related directly to education in Ireland. Lenihan wished students to know where there was a shortage and a surplus when they came to making career choices. He then commented, to the dismay of educators, that 'education has never been adequately geared to the requirements of the economy'.

He acknowledged the achievements of his predecessors over the past decade, and confirmed that there were approximately 1,000 extra primary school teachers than there had been in the system in 1957, although there had been no increase in the number of pupils. The pupil–teacher ratio of 35:1 still remained government policy.[3]

Lenihan proceeded with the development of the new curriculum for primary schools, and was strongly supported by his assistant secretary, Seán O'Connor, who said, 'We have buried without regret the primary certificate exam. Let us bury again, without regret, the present national school curriculum'.[4]

In October representatives of the managerial bodies and the Colleges of Education were invited into the department to give their views on the draft curriculum. It received a positive response, and from then on Lenihan promoted it whenever an opportunity to do so presented itself. He addressed the INTO congress in April 1969 and referred to the draft curriculum. He also took the unprecedented step of informing parents about general educational changes when he issued a booklet entitled 'Ár nDaltaí Uile – All Our Children', which was distributed to every household in the country. In it he described the rapid pace of change underway in Irish schools as being akin to 'an educational revolution'.[5]

For the first time, the government took steps to conduct research in the area of educational disadvantage. The experimental Rutland Street Project on the education of socially disadvantaged children was carried out in the Rutland Street area of Dublin from 1969 to 1974 under the auspices of the department and the Dutch philanthropic body, the Van Leer Foundation, in the Hague. The director of the project was Séamas Holland, a former inspector of special education, and the research director was Dr Thomas Kellaghan.

In 1969 a pre-school was established, which was attached to the Rutland Street primary school. A specially designed curriculum was the main feature of this project, together with the involvement of parents in the pre-school. Three social workers were assigned to the staff. A novel feature of the project was that parents could avail of a teacher visiting service, whereby children could be taught in their own homes. Advice was dispensed to parents as to how they might assist their children, and they were encouraged to attend the pre-school to participate in the educational process.[6]

INDUSTRIAL AND REFORMATORY SCHOOLS

The history of the industrial and reformatory school system represents one of the darkest chapters in the history of Irish education. Corporal punishment of children was commonplace in Ireland, especially in schools. With regard to industrial and reformatory schools, specific rules governing punishment existed from 1868. Under the rules, corporal punishment was to be used only as a last resort. A new set of rules was issued by the department in 1933, which repeated this directive.

In 1946 the department issued a circular which stated that punishment 'should be confined as far as possible to forfeiture of rewards and privileges obtained by good conduct'. Details of serious misbehaviours and resultant punishment were supposed to be entered into a punishment book. However, 'the Department's rules were not taken even remotely seriously by the religious orders running the schools' and 'the Department itself paid equally little attention to them'.[7] Punishment books were rarely properly kept and no record remains of inspectors ever seeking them.

Derrig had set up a Commission of Inquiry into the Reformatory and Industrial School System in May 1934, which reported in August 1936. It made fifty-one main recommendations. It found that the system of medical attendance and inspection was unsatisfactory, and that the standard of primary education was 'reasonably satisfactory' according to the inspectors' reports, but that primary teachers were untrained. Many other concerns were expressed, including one regarding the inadequate provision for 'mentally defective children' and children 'suffering from physical defects'. It recommended that new institutions under the control of the Department of Education should be established to cater for these children.

There was no reference in this report to the excessive use of corporal punishment. Two mild suggestions were made, that the school diet should be more varied and that the enforcement of 'Silence at meals and in workrooms ... should be abolished' on the grounds that it was 'a harsh and unnecessary measure'.[8]

Matters were brought to a head in 1946, however, when a case of excessive use of corporal punishment by the Christian Brothers in Glin Industrial School in County Limerick was brought into the public domain. An Independent member of Limerick City's borough council, Martin McGuire, took up the case of one detainee, Gerard Fogarty, with Derrig. Derrig replied to McGuire's letter stating that full enquiries into the circumstances of the case had been conducted and appropriate action had been taken. Fogarty was granted a discharge from the Industrial School at Derrig's request. However, McGuire pursued the matter further and requested an inquiry from Derrig on 12 April 1946 into the running of all industrial schools, a request which was refused on the grounds that it would serve no useful purpose.

Furthermore, McGuire contacted James Shiels, the manager of the Theatre Royal in Dublin, on 5 July 1946, as Shiels had strong links with Fr Edward Flanagan of 'Boys Town', Omaha in the USA. It was said that Fr Flanagan's knowledge of this case made him even more determined to continue the campaign to highlight the excessive use of corporal punishment on children in Ireland's industrial and reformatory schools. He referred to it briefly in one of his public statements, made in October 1946, which was covered by the Irish newspapers. Not one journalist investigated the story at the time, despite the damning documentary evidence to hand.

In 1951 Moylan derided comments by 'the late Fr Flanagan' on Irish industrial schools during his recent visit to Ireland. Flanagan 'had built up a great name for himself in America with regard to boys' homes', but this did not deter Moylan from accusing him of lying to American journalists 'on the subject of the cruelty exercised towards boys in industrial schools in this country'. According to Moylan, Flanagan was relying on hearsay as he had not visited the industrial schools to witness first-hand what was taking place in them. He had done so and he knew one outstanding school. He was prepared to 'challenge any country in the world to produce better'.[9]

Moylan's granddaughter in her recent biography, *Seán Moylan Rebel Leader*, drew a connection between attitudes current at the time and her grandfather's reaction to charges of excessive corporal punishment, particularly in relation to Artane Industrial School, which he regularly visited. She gave as an example the reaction of deputies to a parliamentary question which was raised in April 1954 by Peadar Cowen. It concerned a boy who sustained a broken arm following a beating in Artane Industrial School, which resulted in his hospitalisation. In raising the question in the Dáil, Cowan expressed himself 'satisfied that it was an isolated instance'. Moylan concurred, and added that it was 'in one sense what might be called an accident'. Moylan did not believe that Christian Brothers were capable of such violent acts of cruelty. As far as he was concerned, this was 'an isolated incident: it can only happen again as an accident'.[10]

It was unthinkable, according to Moylan, and indeed to a succession of Ministers for Education, that religious orders could countenance such levels of violence and abuse of children in their care. Mulcahy did not see the need to follow up on the Artane Industrial School query, raised 2 months previously in the Dáil, and neither did Moylan raise the issue from the opposition benches.[11]

The department received a subsequent complaint about conditions in Artane Industrial School in 1962. It was submitted by the chaplain, Fr Moore, and it was peremptorily dismissed by the department. The Inspector of Reformatory and Industrial schools compiled a report on Artane and stated that complaints 'are not infrequent, but from experience, I would say, that the majority are exaggerated and some even untrue.'[12] In 1968 Lenihan paid a visit to Artane Industrial School, a visit which has now become part of folklore. Just as he was about to leave the school, a 15-year-old boy approached him and divulged that the Christian Brothers were beating them every day of the week. Lenihan turned to his driver and pleaded with him in unparliamentary language to remove him from the place.[13] Soon afterwards, the detainees in Artane were to get out too when the school was closed in 1969 following a fire at the premises.

In 1967 O'Malley had set up the Kennedy Committee, so named after its chair-person, District Justice Eileen Kennedy of the Dublin Children's Court, to examine the industrial and reformatory school system. The Kennedy Committee was viewed with some suspicion by the department, and it was only after the direct intervention of Lenihan that they were given a proper secretariat. The department proved unwilling or unable to supply details of all complaints received against these schools over the previous 5 years. It took a year for the department to respond to District Justice Kennedy's request for information, but the details which were supplied were very sparse, and merely took the form of a summary of five complaints, each of which the department dismissed out of hand.[14]

On 28 February 1968, the Kennedy Committee visited Daingean Reformatory School. The manager was well known to the department, and he was highly respected by its officials. Two doctors on the committee questioned the manager as to what arrangements were in place for discipline in the school, and he openly admitted to the punishment of boys while they were stripped naked.

What ensued was disclosed on 13 May 1999 by Micheál Martin as Minister for Education. According to records in his department, District Justice Kennedy had written to the Department of Education on the matter and 'as a result of significant disputes' had got an assurance that Daingean Reformatory School would be closed. Martin revealed the contents of a letter from the secretary of the Department of Justice to the secretary of the Department of Education at this time. It revealed that the Report omitted any reference to the flogging of children while naked because 'to make reference … to this particular method of punishment in Daingean would be likely to lead to a disclosure of the situation and in this way, to cause a great public scandal'.[15]

On 11 May 1999, Taoiseach Bertie Ahern made an unprecedented public statement in the wake of a three-part documentary television programme *States of Fear*, which 'explored in shocking detail the industrial school system in Ireland' and which caused public outrage. In it he apologised 'On behalf of the State and of all citizens of the State … to the victims of childhood abuse for our collective failure to intervene, to detect their pain, to come to their rescue'. An inquiry was set up under the Commission to Inquire into Childhood Abuse Act which was passed by the Oireachtas in 2000. Judge Mary Laffoy, a High Court judge, was appointed to chair the commission.[16]

'POST-PRIMARY EDUCATION NOW AND IN THE FUTURE'

His Grace is not pleased.[17]

O'Connor wrote a controversial article entitled 'Post-primary education Now and in the Future', which was published in the autumn 1968 edition of *Studies*.

When McQuaid investigated the matter, he discovered that the new editor 'had not only commissioned the article' but that he was allowing leading Catholic and Protestant educationalists to respond to it. He summoned the Provincial of the Jesuits to establish whether he intended to proceed with the publication of O'Connor's article. It was a brief encounter in which the Provincial replied in the affirmative, at which stage 'The Archbishop then courteously sent the Provincial on his way'.[18]

The article won few supporters. Milne and the Protestant Education Committee accepted government policy on rationalisation of post-primary facilities, and concurred with O'Connor's view that free education did not equate to equality of educational opportunity. Milne's main concern was with the proposal in the report of the Tribunal on Teachers' Salaries, which called for the abolition of school salaries as a means of equalising teachers' salaries at all levels. The difficulty posed for Protestant schools was 'not so much competition with other schools for staff, but rather competition with other countries'.[19]

The Teaching Brothers Association (TBA) also referred to the Teachers' Salaries Tribunal in their reply, and the government's proposed plan to pay the full teacher's salary. They noted that teachers in comprehensive schools in remote areas could be offered 'extra emoluments' by the State, whereas it was 'recommended that the secondary-school managers be forbidden to do so'.[20]

The general secretary of the VTA welcomed O'Connor's contribution and found it a refreshing change that an influential higher civil servant would express his own personal views. He supported O'Connor's call for an expansive curriculum and for the rationalisation of facilities. He suggested that teachers should be offered assurances regarding their job security, especially as there was a shortage of teachers.[21]

O'Connor's article had the unintended effect of bringing the Joint Managerial Body[22] (JMB) and the ASTI closer together. They joined forces in opposition to the policy of rationalisation and the reduction of some secondary schools to junior centre status.[23] During Lenihan's tenure as Minister, thirty small vocational and secondary schools had either been closed or amalgamated with larger schools.

The TBA rejected O'Connor's call for co-operation with local vocational schools for logistical reasons. While agreeing on the need for a comprehensive curriculum, they opposed O'Connor's plan to establish a number of large central schools. They scorned his proposal to close down small schools and to deprive other schools of their senior cycle.

They told O'Connor that his reference to the grouping of subjects at leaving certificate level, as if it were a fait accompli, had no basis in fact. In 1968, when Lenihan formally announced the introduction of subject groupings on a voluntary basis from 1969, and on a compulsory basis from 1972, the ASTI objected to it. They viewed the proposal to group subjects as an attempt to bolster the rationalisation proposals. Lenihan withdrew the proposal for compulsory grouping at leaving certificate level in 1972. The ASTI had now become a powerful pressure group.[24]

O'Connor's article was seen by many of the religious authorities 'as a denigration of the Religious who conducted 485 secondary schools in the country'.[25] The TBA were at a loss to understand why he did not entertain 'any worries in relation to an exactly similar position that exists for non-Catholics or laymen' in their secondary schools.[26] No doubt this was true in relation to school management structures, but O'Connor had an axe to grind regarding the issue of co-education, which religious orders were generally opposed to and which led to a preponderance of small schools. However, he took heart from the fact that in a number of dioceses, co-education was 'now acceptable in practice'.

O'Connor referred to the 1,986 unfilled teaching positions in the country, and he attributed the majority of the vacancies to the fact that 'the religious authorities were not able to staff them with their own people'. Religious vocations had fallen during this period, and O'Connor alleged that the religious could not afford to employ lay teachers as they could not fulfil the obligation to pay school salaries of £300 to £400 each to them.[27] The TBA accused him of naivety in suggesting that only a small number of vacancies resulted from lack of availability of teachers of specific subjects, when the reality was that there was 'a serious shortage of such specialist teachers'.

The TBA took exception to O'Connor's claim that the financial contribution of the State to secondary schools since 1964 had the effect of freezing the layman out of the decision-making process, and of giving a monopoly to the religious in school management. He claimed that 'The lay secondary teacher remains always the hired man. His responsibility ends at the classroom door … he is never part of the decision making'. He wanted the religious to share power in education. He said, 'I want them in as partners, not always as masters'.[28] Two secondary teachers responded to O'Connor's article, and both of them supported the religious orders.[29]

The TBA challenged O'Connor on the issue of power-sharing in private secondary schools and accused him of suggesting that there was 'something not quite right in members of Religious Orders managing the schools they have themselves built'. They did not accept O'Connor's reassurance that 'No one wants to push the religious out of education', because they had evidence to the contrary.

Their claim that the department's 'approach to management' amounted to 'nationalisation by stealth'[30] reflected the level of fear and suspicion felt by secondary-school authorities towards the department at the time. It was in this atmosphere that discussions on the report of the Tribunal on Teachers' Salaries took place.

THE RYAN TRIBUNAL

In December 1967, O'Malley set up the Tribunal on Teachers' Salaries, or the Ryan Tribunal as it was called, because it was under the chairmanship of Professor Louden Ryan of TCD. It was requested to recommend a common basic scale of salary for teachers in first- and second-level schools, and to recommend what appropriate additions might be made to the basic scale in respect of qualifications, length of training and nature of duties.[31]

The tribunal held its first meeting in January 1968, but O'Malley required the report to be furnished by Easter. The tribunal reported within 5 month, but some commentators believed that much more time was required 'in view of the complexity of the issues' involved. It was placed at an added disadvantage having been established in the year free post-primary education and transport were introduced. This was hardly 'the most propitious year to expect a generous salary settlement, satisfactory to all teachers'.[32]

In 1965 the managers of secondary schools had agreed in principle to a proposal from Colley that the State should be responsible for the full salary of secondary teachers, provided certain contractual safeguards were preserved.[33] It had long been decided by the department to introduce a common basic salary for all teachers, with extra remuneration for qualifications and the exercise of extra responsibilities. It was up to the tribunal to recommend the appropriate figures. The department also favoured the introduction of a common scheme of conciliation and arbitration for all teachers, but O'Malley had already given a guarantee to the ASTI that if they were dissatisfied with this, they could revert to their own conciliation procedures.[34]

Bolstered by this guarantee, the ASTI co-operated with the other teaching unions during the tribunal hearings to bring about a positive outcome, proving that they were not averse to a common salary scale. But a series of blunders by the tribunal and the Departments of Education and Finance eventually led to the three teaching unions engaging in individual industrial action, but the most protracted action was conducted by the ASTI.

The tribunal neglected to invite the Council of Managers of Catholic Secondary Schools[35] (CMCSS) to participate in the hearings. The CMCSS was quick to point out that the managerial bodies were 'legally the employers of the secondary teachers'. They had to insist on their right 'to appear before the Tribunal' and when they did appear they 'explicitly reserved' their 'right of being heard again'. The CMCSS had their request ignored, and the tribunal made its recommendations without consulting them.[36]

The evidence of the representatives from the Departments of Finance and Education before the tribunal was no doubt affected by the pattern of industrial disputes then current. The Department of Finance's representative in his evidence strongly opposed a substantial pay increase for teachers, and the representative of the Department of Education gave evidence opposing the arguments put forward by the teaching unions. The tribunal was swayed by the departments' arguments, and it ignored the O'Malley guarantee to the ASTI. The report became available on 24 May 1968, and it recommended a common basic salary for all teachers, with the maximum salary to be reached in 17 years. It recommended extra allowances to be payable to all teachers for university qualifications, both pass and honours.[37] Existing secondary teachers could choose to remain with their current arrangements if they so wished, but all future teachers would have to be recruited on the basis of the common scale.

Secondary teachers fared very badly under these recommendations as it transpired 'that the maxima of the common basic scale, fell short of the existing maxima of secondary teachers'. In addition, the ASTI had been seeking arbitration on an existing salary claim since 1966, and it had argued for a reduction in the incremental span to 12 years. Consequently, the ASTI's response to the report was one of dismay and astonishment 'that any salary tribunal should … produce a report recommending a reduction in earnings, for a whole sector of the teaching profession'.[38] The VTA also rejected the salary figures proposed by the tribunal.

ASTI THREATENS STRIKE

The Cork branch of the ASTI called for a special convention. The Central Executive Council of the ASTI warned Lenihan in June 1968 that if the tribunal's report was accepted by him, it would result in 'immediate action' being taken. This was followed by a special convention on 30 July 1968 at which the ASTI came up with their own unified incremental scale for secondary teachers. If Lenihan rejected this, it was decided that a referendum would be held for strike action and also that a strike fund would be established.

On 23 September, the ASTI submitted their new pay claim to the conciliation council, and on 4 October Lenihan invited them to meet him, when he argued that the salary scales should be viewed in conjunction with allowances for qualifications and posts of responsibility. However, he disregarded the fact that not all secondary teachers fell into either of these categories. A fortnight later, Lenihan announced that there would be a common basic salary scale for all teachers, along with a common conciliation and arbitration board for teachers from all three branches of the teaching profession.

The INTO and the VTA found these proposals acceptable, but the ASTI voted to reject them in October. On 23 November, the ASTI passed a resolution demanding the processing of its September pay claim through the existing negotiations procedures. They felt entitled to do so based on a verbal assurance given by O'Malley that they could revert back to their own conciliation scheme. An action committee was to be appointed and 'in the event of an unsatisfactory outcome in Arbitration … a strike ballot would be held with a strike proposed for 1 February 1969'.

The department held talks with the JMB in June and July 1968, at which it urged that all posts of responsibility be given to lay staff as a recompense for the loss of the 12½ percent on standard salary, which it was intended to drop. It even suggested that as the State proposed to pay the full salary of secondary teachers, that the managers should pay the State £200 for every teacher on the staff. However, the department's representative 'was told bluntly that we were no longer prepared to finance the schools out of our own pockets' and negotiations were adjourned sine die.[39]

The CHA was disenchanted with the department, especially in the wake of O'Connor's article. At their meeting of 23 October 1968, they reconsidered their agreement in principle to Colley's proposition to them in 1965, and decided that 'the financial relations between the State and the schools be negotiated … before any final agreement … is reached on the payment by the State of the total salary'. All the other managerial bodies endorsed this resolution at the invitation of the CHA.[40] The decision was communicated both to Lenihan and to the ASTI, along with a welcome assurance to the latter that the CHA would stand full force behind them in their claim for an adequate salary.

The CHA's letter was not well received by the department. It prompted the secretary of the department, Seán MacGearailt, to convene a meeting between the Minister and the CHA on 7 November. Tensions ran high at this meeting. The CHA consistently complained about the department's rationalisation proposals, and they declared their distrust 'of the intentions and motives of the Department', to which Lenihan replied, 'The State has no intention of taking over your schools'.

Lenihan took umbrage when the CHA informed him that in the event of the dispute escalating between the department and the ASTI, they would support their staff. Lenihan called for a further meeting with the CHA, which took place on 14 November, at which he requested their assistance in having the department's salary proposals distributed by school managers to individual teachers. They declined to do so as it would have assisted department officials, who wanted to pay secondary teachers according to their individual replies to the proposals. This would have resulted in 'the State being total paymaster and they refused to give any active assistance'.

On 28 November, MacGearailt wrote to Cardinal Conway clearly outlining the department's position as total paymaster of secondary teachers' salaries. He explained that in the new plans 'extra payment for other than normal school work can be paid by school managers, but must be clearly identified as such'.

The CHA also took steps to clarify their position on the issue and on the same day they held a meeting at which they renewed their support for the ASTI's claim 'for a just and adequate salary' and re-affirmed their strong opposition to the State as total paymaster 'until such time as the independent nature of our schools is recognised by an act of the Oireachtas'.[41]

The CHA had just produced the grenade, but it was the CMCSS which threw it. On 6 December, the CMCSS wrongly claimed in a statement published in the newspapers, that only '97 senior cycle schools (or centres) in the country would be educating pupils to Leaving Certificate level in place of the 500 schools now providing this educational opportunity'.

Lenihan issued a statement in which he defended his rationalisation policy. He stated that the need for rationalisation was self-evident as numbers in post-primary education now exceeded 180,000, and a narrow academic curriculum was no longer adequate to cater for diverse abilities. He said it was unfortunate that some religious authorities interpreted 'the Department's actions as an effort to take over their schools'. He explained how confusion may have arisen, as the CMCSS made no distinction between centres and schools when in fact 'one hundred centres could involve five hundred schools'.

In his statement, Lenihan took exception to their resolution passed at a meeting on 28 November which required the department to negotiate with 'the ASTI and the Managerial associations for an equitable and adequate salary'. He pointed out that he had 'an obligation to national teachers and vocational teachers as well as to secondary teachers'.

Lenihan also dealt with the reference by the CMCSS to the necessity for an Act of the Oireachtas, a suggestion he found 'incomprehensible' in light of the 'excellent manner in which Church/State relations in regard to education operate in this country'. He then acknowledged 'the tremendous contribution which the religious orders have made to Irish Education'.[42]

On 18 October, Lenihan made new salary proposals to all teachers, but they were rejected by the secondary teachers, who were holding out for their own conciliation and arbitration.[43] Lenihan proceeded to draft a common scheme of conciliation and arbitration, but he overlooked the fact that he was legally bound to serve 6 months' notice of his intention to terminate the separate scheme.[44] By Christmas 1968, a strike by secondary teachers seemed almost inevitable. The ASTI had not taken industrial action in almost half a century and on that occasion their target was their employers – the CHA, who were now their strongest allies.[45]

Lenihan met with the CMCSS on 9 January 1969 and suggested to them that the allowances for posts of responsibility offered 'scope for manoeuvre in favour of lay secondary teachers' and he urged the religious to be generous in their allocation of these posts. The CMCSS wished to avoid industrial action and they invited Lenihan and the ASTI to a meeting on 16 January. Lenihan agreed that the ASTI claim could be heard at conciliation, but in the event of it going to arbitration, representatives of the other teaching unions would have to be invited as 'witnesses'.

ASTI STRIKE

Conciliation meetings continued and on 24 January Lenihan made a new offer in a last bid to avert a strike. The money which had been intended for extra allowances for principals and vice-principals was to be shared out among teachers from the tenth point of the salary scale upwards, as a special functions allowance. This extra allowance would not be eligible for any future percentage increase in salary.[46] The ASTI rejected the offer on 29 January, and declared a strike on 1 February 1969. The JMB closed all their schools at the request of the ASTI, and in a goodwill gesture, agreed to pay school salaries during the strike. As one observer commented regarding the managerial response, 'This was more than a strike of the teachers: it was a revolt of the schools'.[47]

As white collar workers' strikes were such a rarity, the ASTI strike alarmed 'The bishops in particular', who 'approached the Minister for Education to try to find a solution'.[48] The bishops also approached the ASTI, and their representatives met with representatives of the Episcopal Commission on 12 February. The following day a meeting took place between Lenihan and MacGearailt with the ASTI, at which a range of proposals was discussed. Some of these formed the basis of the settlement proposals.

The ASTI strike lasted 3 weeks before an agreement was finally reached, and teachers returned to work on 24 February. Under the terms of the agreement, the maximum salary for all teachers would be reached in 16 rather than 17 years. Allowances for university qualifications were to be raised and there was to be a re-adjustment in the amount payable for the special functions allowance, ranging from £100 to £300. A standard sum of £400 per annum basic salary was to be paid to each teacher by the schools. The capitation grants to the schools were to be increased to cover this sum for each registered teacher. But surprisingly, the really contentious issue of providing an acceptable conciliation and arbitration scheme for secondary teachers was left unresolved.[49] In March 1969, an agreement on terms acceptable to the ASTI was signed by Lenihan, the JMB and the ASTI, and 'There was an uneasy peace for a time'.[50]

Shortly afterwards, Lenihan experienced more strikes, this time by the vocational and primary school teachers, who were aggrieved at the terms given to the secondary teachers. They claimed that the special functions allowance broke the principle of the common basic salary recommended by the Ryan Tribunal. The VTA held a 2-day strike on 27 and 28 May 1969, as well as a mass rally in Limerick on 27 May. The INTO conducted a series of strikes in selected schools from 27 May to 3 June 1969. When Lenihan gave the ASTI 6 months' notice of his intention to terminate their separate conciliation and arbitration scheme, they immediately rejected this suggestion. This move was probably inevitable due to economic considerations, and the fact that the other teaching unions supported it, but perhaps a more diplomatic approach might have produced a different outcome.

THE 'GENTLE REVOLUTION'

> Besieged at a meeting in Trinity, he escaped through a lavatory window. 'That's Brian for you' people said when they saw in the papers, the picture of him clambering through a window.

Irish student protests in 1968–69 were generally regarded as 'pale copies of events in France and in the U.S.'[51] or 'a UCD version of the "Days of May" revolt that had broken out in so many universities around the world'.[52] What became known as the 'Gentle Revolution' in UCD was a far cry from what actually took place, according to one participant, the journalist Kevin Myers, who commented 'gentle it was, revolution it was not'.[53]

A radical group called Students for Democratic Action occupied the administrative offices of UCD and a more moderate element organised mass meetings in November 1968. One of the student leaders was Ruairi Quinn,[54] a Labour Party activist.

Over 100 students occupied the buildings in the School of Architecture. This was accompanied by mass meetings attended by up to 2,000 students as well as staff members. Quinn recalled that they were supported by Senator Garret FitzGerald, who was a staff member. He believed they were successful insofar as the School of Architecture was restructured satisfactorily the following year.[55] FitzGerald persuaded the Academic Council to refrain from taking any disciplinary measures against the students.[56] The final 2 days of the winter term were to be devoted to a discussion on the role of the university and Lenihan appointed the Students Representative Council to the university's governing body.[57]

Lenihan continued with the policy of providing equality of educational opportunity by introducing the Local Authorities (Higher Education Grants) Bill (No. 24 of 1968; 15 July, 1968). The higher education grants scheme 'was to be the final step in the free education scheme initiated by Donogh O'Malley' and the Local Authorities (Higher Education Grants) Bill 'was to become a memorial gesture to Donogh O'Malley'.[58] When introducing the Bill in the Dáil, it was clear that Lenihan was concerned to open up higher level education to those who were previously excluded through lack of financial resources. He was guided by a sense of social justice.[59]

From now on higher education grants would be distributed on a national basis. In the past each county council had 'to find scholarship money from local funds', and some could only afford to give a very small number of scholarships. Lenihan realised that Irish students needed higher education in order to withstand competition from students in other European countries, and he warned that 'We must think in terms of our entry into the EEC'.[60]

A year later he could claim that as a result of the passing of the Local Authorities (Higher Education Grants) Act, 1968, the number of students benefiting under the scheme was 1,150 compared to the 275 who benefited previously from local authority scholarship awards.[61]

HEA ADVISES LENIHAN

Lenihan was a strong supporter of the proposed merger of TCD and UCD. In January 1969, a year after the establishment of the HEA on an ad hoc basis, he lauded the Authority and supported its role which was 'to further the development of higher education and to co-ordinate public expenditure thereon'. The achievement of co-ordination was the primary reason why the government decided on the rationalisation of higher education facilities in Dublin.[62]

Lenihan did not proceed with the merger himself. He passed the matter over to the HEA to adjudicate upon. The HEA recommended that the two universities in Dublin should be linked by a statutory Conjoint Board and that certain faculties should be developed in one institution only, with special joint arrangements for medicine and engineering. It supported the government's intention to establish UCG and UCC as independent universities.

He sought the HEA's advice on three other educational issues. The first one concerned the setting up of a body to award a national qualification for technicians and technologists, the second was on the nature of a third-level educational institution for Limerick, and the third one was on the possibility of university linkage for the teacher training colleges. The HEA reported in March 1969. With regard to the question of an awards body, it was satisfied that there was an established demand for further and more advanced technological and other specialised third-level courses. It was satisfied also that there should be formal recognition on a national basis for such courses, and 'saw the solution in the establishment of a Council for National Awards, with powers to grant certificates, diplomas and degrees'.[63] The HEA recommended the establishment of a 'pioneering' institute of higher education in Limerick on polytechnic lines.[64]

The HEA report copper-fastened what was known as the 'binary system' within Irish higher education. It did so by referring to the 'university' and 'non-university' sectors and to 'the distinctive parts to be played by each'. The opening of the first RTCs in September 1969 highlighted the need for a body such as the NCEA, which was an accrediting and awarding body for the non-university institutions. It was set up on an ad hoc basis in 1972 and its establishment marked the introduction of a full binary system of higher education.

Lenihan had been placed under pressure by the LUPC to grant a university to Limerick. He reassured the mayor of that city 'that what Limerick was getting would be better than any university'.[65] He compared it 'with European Colleges and the MIT in America'.[66] Finally, the LUPC gave a guarded welcome to the HEA proposals.

LENIHAN'S 'UNRELIABLE COMMITMENT'

We are going to affiliate teacher training Colleges with the universities.[67]

The Commission on Higher Education had proposed the establishment of a new type of educational institution, known as the New Colleges, which student teachers would attend, and where they would be awarded a pass degree for 3-year courses and a diploma for shorter courses.[68] However, the INTO and the representatives of the teacher training colleges continued to lobby the government during the late 1960s for the introduction of a university degree for student teachers.

The departmental committee of senior officials, set up at O'Malley's request in 1967 to prepare a response to the recommendations of the Commission on Higher Education, favoured the INTO and training colleges' stance in this matter. Lenihan informed the INTO and the training college representatives in 1968 that he intended to affiliate the teacher training colleges with the universities, but 'This proved to be an unreliable commitment'.[69]

The HEA published its Report on Teacher Education in July 1970, and it suggested that the training colleges should be reconstituted as colleges of education. It recommended that the training course for all primary teachers should be extended to 3 years and should lead to the award of a primary degree, but it did not recommend that degrees should be awarded by the universities. Instead it argued that the new NCEA should be the awarding body for the degrees.

The president of St Patrick's Training College, Fr Donal Cregan, was highly critical of the HEA's report. He contended that the general principles expounded in it were set at nought with the recommendation for a non-university qualification. His suspicions were aroused by this and he 'speculated that the HEA sought to include student teachers within the remit of the new Council for National Awards in order to confer greater academic status on the awards given by the Council'.

He also suspected that the government wished to retain complete control of primary education, and were therefore not prepared to devolve greater responsibility for primary teacher education to the universities.[70]

During Brian Lenihan's brief ministry, he succeeded in gaining government support for pioneering research on educational disadvantage, which resulted in the influential Rutland Street Project. He advanced the development of the new primary school curriculum, and he ensured that parents were kept informed of educational changes, something which was unheard of in the past.

However, Lenihan displayed poor judgment when he permitted his straight-talking assistant secretary to air his personal but contentious views on post-primary education in *Studies*. He did so at a time when relations were fraught between the department and the religious authorities and the ASTI, and just as delicate negotiations were about to take place at the Ryan Tribunal. When the negotiations faltered and a 3-week strike ensued, unsurprisingly the religious authorities supported the teachers. The flawed March Agreement which followed led to industrial action by the two other teaching unions, and as soon as Lenihan notified the ASTI of his intention to terminate their separate conciliation and arbitration scheme, the Agreement unravelled.

Lenihan continued with the policy of rationalisation and he closed or amalgamated thirty small vocational or secondary schools. But it was when he announced the introduction of compulsory subject grouping without ASTI approval, that he was to feel the full force of their anger, as they regarded it as an attempt to bolster rationalisation proposals. He was forced into an embarrassing climb down by the ASTI, which was now a powerful pressure group.

Lenihan erred when he committed himself to affiliating teacher training colleges with universities, which was something the INTO had sought since the early twentieth century and which the training colleges had looked forward to.

The decision was not his to take once he handed the matter over to the HEA to adjudicate upon. The Minister was then left with a credibility problem once he failed to deliver on his commitment.

He was motivated by a sense of social justice when he introduced the first ever higher education grants scheme. He was also conscious of the need to prepare students for the challenges that lay ahead once Ireland joined the EEC. This he did by providing access to university education to an increased number of students. The higher education grants scheme and the Rutland Street Project represent Brian Lenihan's ministerial legacy to Irish education.

Notes

1   Downey, *Lenihan: His Life and Loyalties*, p.41.
2   As Minister for Justice he repealed Ireland's notorious censorship laws.
3   *Sunday Press*, 31 March 1968. 'My curriculum for success', Kevin Marron interview with Brian Lenihan TD, Minister for Education.
4   Seán O'Connor, 'Post-primary education now and in the future' in *Studies*, 57, autumn 1968. Reprinted in *A Studies Symposium*, pp.9–25, p.16.
5   *Rialtas na hÉireann. Ár nDáiltaí Uile – All Our Children*, 1969.
6   Séamas Holland, *Rutland Street* (London/The Hague, 1979), p.99.
7   Raftery and O'Sullivan, *Suffer the Little Children*, p.205.
8   Report of the Commission of Inquiry into the Reformatory and Industrial School System 1934-1936, pp.49–54.
9   *Dáil Debates*, vol. 126, cols 1744–5, 17 July 1951.
10 *Dáil Debates*, vol. 145, cols 947–51, 23 April 1954.
11 Aideen Carroll, *Seán Moylan Rebel Leader* (Cork, 2010), pp.256–9.
12 Raftery and O'Sullivan, *Suffer the Little Children*, p.226.
13 *The Irish Times*, 23 September 1999. 'Artane boys faced the music and straps' by Patsy McGarry.
14 *Dáil Debates*, vol. 504, cols 1181–2, 13 May 1999.
15 *Dáil Debates*, vol. 504, cols 1181–2, 13 May 1999.
16 Keogh, *Twentieth-Century Ireland*, p.434, p.440.
17 Cooney, *John Charles McQuaid*, p.397.
18 Ibid.
19 Milne, 'A church view', pp.267–8.
20 The executive of the TBA, 'Teaching Brothers' in *Studies*, 1968, p.279.
21 Charles McCarthy, 'Vocational teachers' in *Studies*, 1968, pp.271–3.
22 The JMB comprised all the managerial bodies, Catholic, Protestant and lay, involved in secondary education.
23 David Barry, 'The involvement and impact of a professional interest group' in Mulcahy and O'Sullivan (eds) *Irish Education Policy Process and Substance*, p.143.
24 Ibid., p.145.

25 Randles, *Post-primary Education*, p.292.

26 The executive of the TBA, 'Teaching brothers', p.282.

27 O'Connor, 'Post-primary education now and in the future', pp.23–4.

28 Ibid., p.25.

29 Denis Buckley, 'Secondary teacher' in *Studies*, 1968, pp.363–4; Veronica O'Brien, 'Secondary
    Teacher', p.295.

30 The executive of the TBA, 'Teaching brothers', pp.282–3.

31 Tribunal on teachers' salaries report presented to the Minister for Education, p.5;
    John Coolahan, *The ASTI and Post-primary Education in Ireland, 1909-1984* (Dublin, 1984),
    pp.249–50.

32 Ibid., p.273.

33 Ibid., p.280.

34 Ibid., p.276.

35 The CMCSS comprised of the managerial bodies of Catholic secondary schools, and the
    educational bodies of the hierarchy and the religious superiors.

36 *The Irish Times*, 6 December 1968. 'Managers challenge the schools policy'.

37 Tribunal on teachers' salaries, paragraph 18.

38 ASTI press statement 24 May 1968.

39 Coolahan, *The ASTI*, pp.279–80.

40 *The Irish Times*, 6 December 1968. 'Managers challenge the schools policy'.

41 Coolahan, *The ASTI*, p.281.

42 *The Irish Times*, 10 December 1968. 'Lenihan answers criticism of Department'.

43 Randles, *Post-primary Education*, p.296.

44 Coolahan, *The ASTI*, p.281.

45 John Coolahan, 'The ASTI and the secondary teachers strike of 1920' in *Saothar*, 10 (1984), p.52.

46 Randles, *Post-primary Education*, p.296.

47 Charles McCarthy, *The Decade of Upheaval: Irish Trade Unions in the Nineteen Sixties*
    (Dublin, 1973), p.211.

48 Ibid., pp.212–3.

49 Coolahan, *The ASTI*, p.285.

50 Randles, *Post-primary Education*, p.296.

51 Downey, *Lenihan: His Life and Loyalties*, p.63.

52 Garret FitzGerald, *All in a Life, Garret FitzGerald, An Autobiography* (Dublin, 1992), p.82.

53 Ferriter, *The Transformation of Ireland*, p.599.

54 Ruairi Quinn was leader of the Labour party 1997-2002. Currently holding office as
    Minister for Education and Skills. (2011–).

55 Ruairi Quinn, *Straight Left: A Journey in Politics* (Dublin, 2005), pp.65–6.

56 FitzGerald, *All in a Life*, pp.82–3.

57 Quinn, *Straight Left*, p.66.

58 Randles, *Post-primary Education*, p.283.

59 *Dáil Debates*, vol. 235, col. 556, 5 June 1968.

60 *Sunday Press*, 31 March 1968.

61 *Irish Press*, 21 January 1969.

62 *Irish Press*, 21 January 1969. 'Big changes underway in education'.

63 Tony White, *Investing in People: Higher Education in Ireland from 1960–2000* (Dublin, 2001), p.69.

64 Coolahan, 'Higher education in Ireland', p.784.

65 *The Irish Times*, 18 December 1968. 'One and a half million pound investment in Limerick's third-level institution'.

66 *The Irish Times*, 23 April 1969.

67 *Dáil Debates*, vol. 235, col. 558, 5 June 1968. Brian Lenihan, Minister for Education.

68 Report of the Commission on Higher Education 1960-67, summary, p.95.

69 Walsh, 'An era of expansion', p.180.

70 Ibid.

15

Pádraig Faulkner (1969–73): 'The grand design of the community schools, the National Blueprint, was as dead as a pork chop'

I would miss my time working in the Gaeltacht but I was happy to change to a vibrant Department that I felt would have some immediate relevance to the development of the Irish nation.[1]

Brian Faulkner (1928–2012), a 41-year-old primary teacher from County Louth, had 3 years of parliamentary experience, 2 years as parliamentary secretary to the Minister for Lands and the Gaeltacht and 1 year as Minister for Lands, before being appointed Minister for Education on 2 July 1969 by Taoiseach Jack Lynch. Later he would describe his 4-year period in office as 'one of the most exciting periods in the history of education'.[2]

He continued with plans for educational reform initiated by his predecessors. He supported the Rutland Street Project, but he also recognised that it was not just children from deprived backgrounds who were educationally disadvantaged. He included physically handicapped and emotionally disturbed children, as well as children from the Traveller community in this category.

Following publication of the Report of the Commission on Itinerancy, the department set up an internal committee to plan policy for the education of itinerants. Its report was published in 1970[3] and it adopted a policy of integrating these children into mainstream primary schools at their appropriate age level. Faulkner believed 'that the children of the Traveller community and the children of the settled community should learn about each other's way of life' and he regretted that 'in one instance, because of a large number of Travellers' children in one Dublin area it was necessary to build a school solely for them'.[4]

He took a personal interest in the education of mentally handicapped children as he lived close to St Mary's, a home for mentally handicapped children which was established by the St John of God Brothers.[5] A qualified primary school teacher from the local primary school offered to teach there and applied to the department to do so. The department had no objection, but it refused to pay her salary. As her local deputy, Faulkner had 'battled with the department to have her recognised and was subsequently successful'. As Minister, he 'continued to pursue a campaign on the children's behalf'.[6]

The Reformatory and Industrial Schools Systems Report, or the Kennedy Report as it was more commonly known, was published in 1970,[7] and 'it was without doubt one of the most damning indictments of the operation of any State system ever'.[8] Faulkner regarded it as 'an excellent report, highlighting as it did the serious deficiencies in the service'.[9]

It was indeed a comprehensive report, as the committee visited all the industrial and reformatory schools in the State. It sought information from forty-five organisations and consulted 113 publications. In addition, committee members examined the child care systems in operation in Northern Ireland, England, Scotland, Wales, Sweden, Denmark, the Netherlands and Austria.[10] The committee's report was unequivocal, as it described the industrial school system as being 'haphazard and amateurish', displaying 'a lack of awareness of the needs of the child in care'.

It was critical of the lowly status accorded to those working in industrial schools by some religious congregations, where there was 'a tendency to staff the schools, in part at least with those who were no longer required in other work'.[11] The department's system of inspection of industrial schools was described as being 'totally ineffective' as it did not honour its statutory obligations. The financial provisions made by the State were considered to be 'totally inadequate', although it acknowledged that the increase of £8 5s per child per week would certainly 'ease the financial difficulties of those running the schools'.[12]

The report recommended the abolition of the institutional system of residential care, to be replaced by group homes which would approximate as closely as possible to the normal family unit. It found 'the present Reformatory system completely inadequate' and recommended that St Conleth's Reformatory, Daingean 'should be closed at the earliest possible opportunity', and that the Remand Home and Place of Detention at Marlborough House, Glasnevin, Dublin 'should be closed forthwith and replaced by a more suitable building with trained child care staff'. It noted that aftercare was practically non-existent, and commented that it should form an integral part of the child care system.

It suggested also that administrative responsibility for child care should be transferred to the Department of Health. It recommended that an independent advisory body with statutory powers should be established to ensure that the highest standards of child care were maintained.[13]

Faulkner took many of these recommendations on board and put plans in place for a replacement building for St Conleth's to be constructed at Oberstown, County Dublin. Plans were already in train to replace Marlborough House with St Laurence's Training Centre at Finglas, Dublin.[14] In the education estimates for 1971–72 Faulkner proposed that the money for reformatory and industrial schools should be increased by 40 per cent. New group home units were provided and many children now attended local schools. Parents were encouraged to visit their children when Faulkner introduced a scheme of free travel for them from September 1971, and some children were allowed home at weekends.

Schools with modern facilities were established, and special in-service training courses for staff were organised. At the same time, 'a screening system to ensure that only genuinely caring people would get places' was also introduced. The first such training course was provided in Kilkenny in July 1971. Three decades later, Faulkner was horrified to learn that one of the first graduates of the training course was a child abuser. He commented that he 'was living in an age of innocence when nobody believed that people in authority, be they religious or lay, could commit such heinous crimes'.[15]

Faulkner pursued the policy of amalgamation of small primary schools. When he took the decision to amalgamate a one-teacher Gaeltacht school in Dún Chaoin in County Kerry with a much larger Gaeltacht school in Ballyferriter, it caused outrage among some Irish language enthusiasts, and it had political consequences. Dick Burke of the Fine Gael party later reversed the decision, much to Faulkner's bewilderment.[16] Like his predecessors, Faulkner stood accused of failing to consult the local people adequately with regard to amalgamations. He 'delegated public debate on schools to hard-headed officials of the Department' and 'Local sensibilities were largely ignored'.[17]

Faulkner introduced the new curriculum into primary schools in 1971. He was aware of the obstacles to its successful implementation, such as the many small schools that existed and a pupil–teacher ratio which remained high in too many schools.[18] He accepted that implementation of the programme in schools generally would take 'about five or six years'.[19]

More teachers were being trained in 1970 than ever before, and 'mature students' up to the age of 28 were now accepted into the training colleges.[20] During the 5-year period from 1963 to 1968, enrolments in primary schools in Dublin city increased by almost 10 per cent, while the number of teachers increased by

18 per cent.[21] Faulkner made provision for the availability of proper equipment and requisites for the new primary school programme.[22]

He suggested that bodies like parents' committees could advance the new curriculum by supplying incidental aid to schools. He also supported the bishops' proposal 'for the formation of managers, teachers, parents associations for primary schools', but this was to be 'without prejudice to their respective functions'. He had no wish to change the managerial system because he believed it had 'served the country well'.[23]

On the other hand, he had ambitious plans for the provision of in-service education, and with this in mind he established Teachers Centres in 1972. He had intended that all teachers between 25 and 60 years would have formal entitlement to in-service education courses every fifth or seventh year.[24] His plans were thwarted, however, due to the oil crisis of 1973, when oil supply was interrupted because of the Arab–Israeli war. Nonetheless the Teachers Centres continued to provide a stimulating educational environment for teachers.

When it came to discussion of the vexed question of lengthening the 2-year teacher training course to 3 years and associating it with university studies, Faulkner was non-committal. In light of the recommendations of the HEA report and of the feedback he received from the parties involved, he concluded that 'This was a subject that would require deep consideration'.[25]

He directed his attention to developing higher level technical and technological education. In order to boost numbers at the RTCs in the early years, he permitted the colleges to provide the leaving certificate course for a period of 5 years only, after which they would become purely third-level institutions.[26] He ensured that students attending RTCs would benefit from a significantly increased number of scholarships, as the higher education grants scheme did not apply to the courses being run by the colleges. By 1971 the department had prepared a scheme for VEC scholarships to RTCs, which was open to all holders of the leaving certificate. The value of the scholarships was equated with the value of higher education grants, with the same means test applying, the only difference being that the VEC scholarships were competitively based.

Approximately 300 VEC scholarships were awarded in 1971–72 and 1972–73, at a cost of £164,056 and £207,699, respectively.[27] In 1972 the department spent £490,000 on RTCs alone, as Faulkner rated them highly.[28] By way of contrast, he appeared to starve the universities of necessary funding in the early 1970s. The editor of *The Irish Times* alerted his readers to the fact that the government only provided £15 million of the minimum of £24 million which the HEA had argued was essential to come to grips with the chronic university accommodation problems that persisted.[29] The universities were so pre-occupied with 'merger' talks that they allowed this oversight to go unchecked.

In February 1972, he established an ad hoc NCEA, whose main function was to grant awards to non-university third-level students. This was a key part of government policy and it became a matter of some urgency as the NIHE in Limerick (NIHEL) had sought permission to commence its courses 18 months before its planned opening in September 1971. However, Faulkner postponed the opening of the NIHEL until 1972 for a number of reasons. First, there was no NCEA in existence in 1971, and second, he had been advised by the HEA that it would not be possible to provide and equip laboratory workshops in time for commencement in 1971. Of equal importance was the fact that detailed plans were not ready in time for a visit by a party from the World Bank, a body which would help finance the project.[30] He also steered legislation through the Oireachtas establishing the HEA on a statutory footing.

THE RYAN TRIBUNAL

Faulkner inherited an unresolved industrial dispute with the ASTI over the terms of the Ryan Tribunal and the subsequent March 1969 agreement, the terms of which he strongly disapproved of. In order to bring clarity to the situation, he invited Professor Ryan to examine the March agreement with the ASTI to see whether it was in contravention of his original scheme. Ryan reported that 'The Tribunal's recommendations had been breached by the settlement made with the ASTI'.[31]

Ryan recommended that a scheme should be devised whereby the special functions allowances would be eroded in favour of his original recommendation of posts of responsibility. Faulkner accepted these recommendations, but they were unacceptable to the ASTI. He proceeded to outline his plan for dismantling the March agreement on 16 September 1969, so that secondary teachers would be assimilated into the new scheme on a gradual basis. The balance of the eleventh round would not be applied to secondary teachers above the tenth point of the common salary scale unless they decided to abandon their special functions allowances. Future secondary teachers would automatically be related to the new scheme.[32]

On 26 September, the ASTI lodged claim 47 to conciliation seeking the balance of the national wage round, but the department and Faulkner adhered to the 16 September proposals. Following separate talks between the department and the ASTI negotiators, and between the JMB and the department, the latter produced an amended scheme. It now decided that existing holders of special functions allowances who also got posts of responsibility, might hold both together. The ASTI and its CEC rejected this offer and threatened strike action within 21 days until claim 47 was met. In a further act of defiance, the CEC included claim 43, which sought allowances for non-graduate teachers.

There was growing discontent among the VTA who had submitted a claim for allowances of £100–£300, which the secondary teachers already had from the tenth point of their scale, in addition to the allowances for posts of responsibility awarded by the Ryan Tribunal. It held a national strike from 11 to 17 February, when it agreed to conciliation talks. These talks took place in the Labour Court on 23 February.

The CHA came to Faulkner's rescue when they informed the ASTI that secondary teachers could not rely on their support if they proceeded with their planned strike action. Full strike action was not called for, but the CEC voted in favour of 1-day strikes on a fortnightly basis, and this prompted Faulkner to request the JMB to urge the ASTI to join the conciliation and arbitration scheme. As a result of the JMB's intervention, a meeting took place between the ASTI, Faulkner and the JMB. It was a heated one in which the ASTI found itself isolated, with the department insisting on common conciliation and arbitration and the JMB pledging to support students rather than teachers in the event of a strike. Dissension then arose among some members of the ASTI who were not supportive of the way the CEC was proceeding, and the planned 1-day strikes were deferred.

The ASTI held a special convention on 7 March at which it was decided that it would not be a party to common conciliation and arbitration. Strike action was ruled out, but the Standing Committee was empowered to take claims 43 and 47 directly to Faulkner, along with a claim for the twelfth round. The committee also took part in discussions at the Labour Court and agreed to put to its annual convention the proposal that, in the event of the eleventh round being paid to all secondary teachers, the ASTI, the JMB and the department would review the March agreement for the purpose of setting up posts of responsibility which were not automatically linked to years of service.

At the ASTI annual convention on 1 April 1970, it was revealed that the Labour Court talks were obstructed by the Department of Finance's failure to make a definite pay offer, and by the view of the Labour Court chairman that special functions allowances were in reality personal salary. The convention did not decide on any new moves to solve the salary problem. Faulkner looked to the CMCSS for assistance in restructuring a scheme of posts of responsibility and it agreed to do so. The department revealed the contents of the rough draft scheme on posts of responsibility to the ASTI's Standing Committee, which it rejected on the basis that seniority had not been specified as being requisite for such posts, and because managers would have to approve of all such appointments.

In May, Faulkner issued Circular M56/70 to managers of secondary schools, which stated that any teacher appointed after 1 June should not be appointed with reference 'to the present arrangements whereby allowances for special functions are payable on seniority bases'.[33] The ASTI decided on 13 June that members appointed as examiners at the intermediate and leaving certificate examinations would withdraw their services unless Faulkner withdrew the circular. He refused to do so and the ASTI carried out its threat. The department succeeded in getting the leaving certificate papers corrected but failed in their efforts to get the intermediate papers corrected. On 2 July, Faulkner appealed to the president of the ASTI to call off the ban, stating that in return schools would not re-open until 22 September. The ASTI agreed to the request, but when Faulkner made a slightly improved pay offer on 3 July, the Standing Committee rejected it.

The ASTI now threatened strike action from 2 February 1971 failing a resolution of their dispute by 15 December 1970. On 13 November, the JMB issued a memorandum to the department and to the ASTI stating that it believed that the July proposals from the department left 'a genuine grievance among the younger teachers, those who had a solid expectancy from the March Agreement of the £100–£300 allowances'.[34] It produced its own generous proposals to resolve the pay issue, which the department rejected.

On 18 November, a tripartite meeting, chaired by O'Connor took place between representatives of the department, the ASTI and the JMB, which ended resulted in a walk-out by the ASTI. Faulkner met with the ASTI negotiators again in December 1970 and urged them to join an ad hoc form of common conciliation. The ASTI rejected the department's suggestion and renewed its threat of strike action from 2 February 1971. A further pay offer was made by way of a compensatory gesture to those teachers who stood to lose out through the replacement of the March 1969 agreement by the July 1970 proposals.

The ASTI was divided on the offer and on 19 January 1971 it held a ballot in which 73 per cent rejected the offer.[35] Finally, talks took place on 28 January between the ASTI, the VTA, the INTO and the department with the chairman of the Labour Court. A further derisory offer was made on 29 January which involved minor improvements.

On the same day, Cardinal Conway sent a telegram of good wishes to the ASTI, in which he expressed his desire to see the three teaching unions coming together and working on the common basic scale and common conciliation and arbitration. On 30 January, the ASTI had a vote on the latest offer, which was rejected by a majority of one, while a vote to defer the strike was carried by forty-seven to twenty-seven. A further ballot which was to take place on 9 February, would decide whether the secondary teachers would go on strike on 16 February 1971.

The CHA drew up a press release on 1 February stating that in the event of a strike they would feel obliged to close their schools. Faulkner was well aware that future events might well hinge on whether the schools of the religious orders would close in the event of a strike. He requested McQuaid's assistance to get the chairman of the CHA to cancel their press statement. McQuaid undertook to organise it himself and notices were retrieved.

When the ASTI balloted on 9 February for strike action to commence on 16 February, the head of the Conference of Convent Secondary Schools announced that convent schools would remain open during the strike. Some Protestant schools also intended to stay open. Due to the level of public concern, top officials in the Irish Congress of Trade Unions (ICTU) appealed to the Standing Committee to postpone their strike for 2 weeks to enable them to resolve the dispute issues. The ASTI was affiliated to the ICTU in early January 1969, and they agreed to do so. However, their decision to defer the strike was communicated to the media before it was relayed to the membership of the ASTI, who had been preparing for a strike the following morning. Irate members occupied the headquarters of the ASTI on 16 February, and 200 of them picketed the ICTU talks with the ASTI negotiators.

After 4 days of difficult talks, new proposals were put forward which failed to impress the majority of the Standing Committee members, 'but they had no confidence that a strike would achieve the Agreement of 1969 or better'.[36] A meeting with representatives of the INTO, the VTA and the department on 22 February brought further disappointment for the ASTI. Modest improvements in the salary scale and its incremental range, as well as improvements in qualification allowances, were secured, but at a high cost. The ASTI had to accept the establishment of a common basic salary scale for all teachers and a common scheme of conciliation and arbitration. The 'secret' May 1964 CHA/ASTI salary agreement[37] was to be replaced, but school managers would still pay a fixed salary of £400 to secondary teachers to reflect their employer status. Non-graduate secondary teachers would not have parity restored.

The ASTI endured a further defeat when they had to accept the introduction of posts of responsibility instead of their preferred choice of special functions allowances. The offer led to disagreement among ASTI members, with the younger members calling for its rejection, while the older members reluctantly accepted that they would not get a better offer. The offer was accepted by a narrow margin on 26 February 1971.

COMMUNITY SCHOOLS

The department's policy of increasing co-operation between vocational and secondary schools ran into difficulties in many areas, since the VECs were precluded by law from contributing towards the cost of management of shared resources. In an effort to help foster co-operation, Faulkner introduced the Vocational Education (Amendment) Act or the Joint Management Bill as it was more popularly known, on 5 August 1970.

The legislation removed one obstacle but calls for co-operation and common enrolment fell mainly on deaf ears. Faulkner's solution to the problem was that 'rather than building separate secondary and vocational schools or rebuilding two or three small schools' he 'would now build one large Community school'.[38] The solution was not original. O'Connor was the first to refer to the community school idea in his article in *Studies* in autumn 1968, and the editor, Fr Peter Troddyn, commented prophetically that 'we are now to dismantle a system which has served us well'.[39]

Faulkner was fortunate that finance for the proposed community schools was forthcoming from a World Bank loan. He was unfortunate in the timing and manner of the announcement, coming as it did during a tense period in the pay negotiations in November 1970.[40] It was also a period of political turmoil. Two government Ministers were sacked during the summer for their alleged involvement in an attempt to import guns for the use of the IRA in Northern Ireland. They were subsequently acquitted following the 'Arms Trial' in October 1970.[41]

As with most major policy decisions taken by the department, the protocol was for the Minister to discuss the details first with the Catholic hierarchy and the other Church leaders, and then with lay and religious school authorities. The reason for this was that 'Each group of management bodies Catholic and Protestant' was 'subject to a superior group of Church leaders or bishops'.[42] When Cardinal Conway requested information on the proposed community schools from Faulkner, he sent him a written reply explaining what was involved in a document entitled 'Community Schools'. The Cardinal forwarded copies of the document to the superiors of Catholic schools for comment. An *Irish Times* correspondent managed to secure a copy of the document, which was published in the paper on 12 November 1970 before Faulkner had an opportunity of discussing its contents with the various parties involved.[43]

Four days later, the Development Branch summoned eight local meetings of appropriate interests to discuss 'the proposed community school'. The ASTI declined the invitation and sought clarification of the title 'community school', while Cardinal Conway requested more time to consider the document. The meetings were postponed on 23 October.[44] The document proposed that community schools could be formed by the amalgamation of existing secondary and vocational schools and that in the case of city areas, they could be built as an alternative to separate secondary and vocational schools. The schools would have increased facilities including halls, gymnasia and swimming pools, and would be available after school hours for the benefit of the community in general. Community school facilities would also serve the adult educational needs of the community.

The proposed boards of management of community schools would consist of representatives of secondary-school managers and of the local VECs. The document stated that 'it might prove possible to include representatives of parents or industrial/commercial interests', but this would be for the parties involved to decide. There would be an independent chairman, who might be a bishop of the diocese or other agreed chairman. There was no reference to teacher representation on the board. The site and buildings would be vested in trustees nominated by the parties involved.[45]

Troddyn saw the proposals as an attempted State take-over of secondary schools, and 'to an extent the VECs, would lose control of their schools too'.[46] The optimum size of a community school was set at between 400 and 800 pupils. He concluded that as the vast majority of post-primary schools fell below the 400-pupil target, 'both the vocational school system and the secondary-schools system … would in the short or the long term, be superseded'.[47] Two Irish journalists who had spent a year researching comprehensive education in Ireland agreed with this analysis.[48]

Faulkner underestimated the effect that the contents of the leaked document, along with the quietly introduced Joint Management Bill, would have on school owners and teachers. This was evident from his comment in the Dáil on 18 November 1970 that he 'was somewhat surprised at the emotional manner in which the document was dealt with'.[49] The ASTI issued a press statement on 12 November deploring the total lack of consultation and the absence of requested clarification of a matter 'that so utterly affects the contractual position of our members'.[50]

The VECs were strongly opposed to what they regarded as a take-over of their schools, and they set about bringing pressure to bear on their Dáil representatives to defend their interests.[51] Faulkner recognised that 'both the religious communities and the VECs were opposed to the community schools' concept because of their fears in respect of ownership and management'.[52] However, in his proposed composition for boards of management, he gave a greater weighting to the representatives of the Catholic Church at the expense of the VECs. He also neglected to consult with leaders of the minority churches on the community school document. All this occurred at a time when Church leaders 'sought to give expression to ideas of ecumenism which had been fostered by the Second Vatican Council'.[53]

The deteriorating situation in Northern Ireland, rooted as it was in sectarianism, encouraged a greater spirit of ecumenism in certain quarters. It was against this backdrop that a group of nineteen men, representing several churches and religious groups in the south, petitioned the President, Eamon de Valera, to use his influence to protect the non-denominational vocational system, which they considered to be under threat by the planned community school proposals.[54] The President replied 'that he had no role in political questions'.[55]

The department was determined to pursue its policy on community schools. Tomás Ó Floinn, the assistant secretary of the department, informed the Post-Primary Teachers Association (Religious) Conference in April 1971 'that there can be no going back' as the government and the department were committed to the development of comprehensive education.[56]

Ó Floinn produced the following international comparisons for 1965–66, indicating those engaged in predominantly technical studies at post-primary level per 100 engaged in predominantly academic studies: Ireland: 31, Finland: 670, Austria: 520; Netherlands: 440, England/Wales: 240; France: 120, Germany: 260.

In Ireland, most students gravitated towards the secondary schools following the introduction of free post-primary education, where there was a 35 per cent increase in numbers by 1970, whereas vocational schools had a 27 per cent increase.[57] However, this trend was changing. Ó Floinn produced statistics which showed that of the 12,224 increase in numbers in post-primary education in the current year, 6,374 could be attributed to vocational schools. Of the 11,160 increase in 1969–70, only 1,125 occurred in those schools. Commentators attributed this trend to the parsimonious attitude of the department to secondary schools with regard to funding. Consequently, secondary-school owners ceased to increase their facilities. They were 'also deterred by the prospect of a State take-over being imminent in the guise of Community Schools'.[58]

Rumours circulated about background talks which were allegedly taking place between Faulkner and the hierarchy on the community school proposals. It was reported that 'The Church was opposed to the idea and there was much acrimonious debate'. According to *The Irish Times* education correspondent, 'the Minister travelled at least twice to Armagh to meet Cardinal Conway, with his officials'.[59] According to another journalist, after months of hard wrangling with the Catholic hierarchy, the department proposed to the IVEA that four of the six members of the boards of management of community schools should be nominated by the local bishop. The VTA reacted angrily and its top-level representatives travelled to Armagh on 10 May for talks with Cardinal Conway.

Weight was added to the rumours when, after several months of silence, the Cardinal spoke out in favour of the new proposals.[60] He made a statement in which he commented on *The Irish Times* report and explained his position. He said, 'What is important to remember is that the Catholic school authorities cannot be expected to consent to arrangements which would legally de-Catholicise their schools'.[61]

MINISTER CLARIFIES PROPOSALS

Faulkner responded on 13 May by providing a document outlining details of further additions to the original Community School document. The controversial proposal that four of the six members of the new schools boards of management would be nominated by the local bishops did not materialise. It was the school authorities who would nominate them as outlined in the original document. According to the proposals, two parents' representatives would sit on the six-member school board of management, all members of the board would be drawn from the local community, an academic advisory body with teacher representatives would assist in the running of the school, and three school trustees would be nominated by the local bishop, one of them to be taken from a list drawn up by the local VEC.

The latest proposals were widely condemned. An eminent educational historian believed that the board of management structure now proposed was 'far from the type of "Community" management appropriate to the new type of school'. He could take no comfort from subsequent statements made by Faulkner in which he confirmed that he viewed 'the schools simply as providing a wider subject range for post-primary pupils on an economic basis'.[62] He consistently argued the case for community schools mainly on the grounds of economic expediency,[63] without any reference to community use of their resources or to the adult education facilities they would provide.[64]

In the wake of the publication of his new proposals, Faulkner was asked whether it was not unusual that proposals agreed between the department and the Catholic hierarchy should now be published before the other parties involved had consented to them. He responded that he 'had consultations with all the relevant bodies', and that it was following the consultation process that he made his proposals. He explained why the secondary-school authorities could nominate four members to the board of management and the VECs could nominate only two. It was because 'about three-quarters of post-primary pupils attend secondary schools' and 'only one quarter attend vocational schools'.

He believed that Protestants were not discriminated against regarding these proposals. He accepted that some Protestant children attended vocational schools, but overall it was impressed upon him that what the Protestant Church authorities wanted was Protestant schools at both primary and post-primary level. He pointed out that the areas chosen for community schools were all Catholic areas.[65]

The VTA denounced Faulkner's proposals on the management of community schools and called for teacher representation on their boards of management.[66] Delegates to the IVEA annual congress rejected the proposals. A report of the sub-committee described the structure of the boards of management as being 'one that because of its overwhelming sectarian bias' was 'bound to be totally unacceptable'.[67] It was also explicitly confirmed at the congress that Faulkner's initial proposal, both to the VTA at a meeting on 23 April and to the IVEA on 3 May, 'was that the Bishop or ordinary of the diocese would nominate 4 members of the new board of management', a fact subsequently denied by O'Connor.[68]

The ASTI was opposed to the proposals and called for teacher representation on boards of management of community schools. The Standing Committee appointed representatives to five local meetings to be held on community schools, to commence on 14 June 1971.[69] The department was keen on proceeding quickly with establishing the new schools as there were from fifteen to thirty school centres in question and in many cases building projects were being held up pending the outcome of the top-level discussions.[70] During the summer of 1971, these meetings took place and were attended by representatives of the department, school management, teachers and parents, and at each of the meetings the community school proposals were rejected.[71]

Even while the meetings were in progress, criticism of the community school proposals was reported daily in the press from religious authorities of all denominations. The main objections which opposition deputies had to the proposals were that they were sectarian and that they favoured the majority religion. Faulkner and some of his Fianna Fáil colleagues 'stoutly denied sectarianism – and seemed to be totally unaware that some of their statements made to rebut charges of sectarianism were in themselves sectarian'.[72]

Fine Gael issued a press statement on community schools on 20 January 1972 in which it called for 'genuine' community schools to be run by a board of management chosen by the school owners, the parents and the teachers'.[73] Ten days later Cardinal Conway issued his statement on community schools, in which he stressed that the Catholic school authorities had 'no desire to "take-over" a single vocational school' and that it was the Department of Education which was 'insisting that Catholic secondary schools and vocational schools should merge together'. Faulkner confirmed the truth of this statement in the Dáil in February 1972.[74]

One commentator in particular was astonished that the Catholic hierarchy 'conceded so much' when 'they allowed the Government to amalgamate Catholic schools with non-denominational vocational schools'. The drop in religious vocations together with the growth in the ecumenical spirit may have been contributing factors.[75]

The self-styled 'political neophyte' in the Dáil,[76] Garret FitzGerald, Fine Gael spokesman on education, recorded the sequence of events which occurred since the community school document was first leaked. He queried why Faulkner had consulted with only one Church and why he had given a disproportionate amount of time to the concerns of the Catholic Church. The latter part of this criticism was groundless as intensive lobbying had taken place between November 1970 and May 1971 by the minority churches. Reports of the Secondary Education Committee for 1971, 1972 and 1973 indicated that the Protestant churches had an input into the development of the policy for community schools.[77]

He proceeded to list the number of meetings Faulkner had with the various parties involved and the dates on which they took place. He concluded that the

VTA, the IVEA, Protestants and the ASTI were 'under consulted', and parents were not consulted at all.[78]

He accused Faulkner of being 'unconsciously sectarian' and he warned him of the damaging effects this could have on North–South relations because it provided 'concrete evidence of an attitude of mind down here that Protestants can be swept to one side and ignored'.[79]

As it transpired, a deputation made up of various Protestant denominations and led by Dr George Otto Simms, Church of Ireland Archbishop of Dublin, met with Faulkner to request two community schools and he 'was glad to agree' to this.[80]

Opposition to the community schools was ubiquitous according to Faulkner's own account of events. The education correspondent of one newspaper reported that 'the grand design of the community schools, the National Blueprint was as dead as a pork chop'.[81] Community schools were introduced into Tallaght and Blanchardstown in Dublin in 1972, and their management structures were in line with the proposals announced on 13 May 1971.

Faulkner allowed some modification of the plans – a clause providing for a check on the 'faith and morals' of teachers in community schools was dropped. The trustees in whom the school property was vested were to be appointed by the Minister and not, as originally proposed, by the Catholic bishop. However, a dispute over the wording of the Deeds of Trust for the community schools was set to continue until 1981.[82] Faulkner attributed the introduction of the community schools to the assistance he received from McQuaid. As McQuaid was not a member of the hierarchy's Education Committee, and as Tallaght and Blanchardstown were located in his archdiocese, he was at liberty to discuss these two projects with McQuaid and to gain his support, 'which was crucial at that time'.[83]

In his memoir, Pádraig Faulkner said that he was 'happy to be appointed to a vibrant Department' and this enthusiasm shone through as he introduced the new primary curriculum. He recognised that its full implementation would take five to six years, when more favourable conditions prevailed. For his part he took measures to provide extra teachers and to reduce the pupil–teacher ratio. However, when it came to school amalgamations, he stood accused of delegating the task to hard-nosed officials who did not pay sufficient attention to local sensibilities.

Faulkner had great respect for the hierarchy, and he could not see the need to replace the managerial system with more democratic structures. He did not envisage a power-sharing role for parents in school management, but he supported parents' committees on the lines suggested by the hierarchy.

It was surprising that he did not take immediate action to fulfil the long-held aspiration of his former union, the INTO, for university degrees for primary

teachers. But he did a great service to the teaching profession with the establishment of Teachers Centres, and by developing an awareness of the importance of
in-service education. He supported the Rutland Street Project, developed Traveller
education and implemented the main recommendations of the Kennedy Report.

Faulkner's handling of the community school debacle lacked precision and
sensitivity. The optimum size of a community school was set at between 400 and
800 students, which meant that 235 schools would have to be amalgamated, yet he
could not understand why the leaked document was received in such an 'emotional
manner'. He erred by consulting just one Church leader on the document and by
giving a greater weighting to representatives of the Catholic Church on boards
of management, but he could not see how this could be interpreted as a sectarian
gesture. When the suggestion was put to him during the height of the crisis, that a
White Paper was called for, he failed to see the necessity for one. He informed the
Dáil that there was 'nothing of such a complicated nature in our policy that would
demand an elaborate White Paper in order to explain it'.[84]

Faulkner resolved the secondary teachers' long-standing pay dispute and secured
his objectives. It took him 3 years to do so, but he could not have achieved it
without the support of Archbishop McQuaid, the Catholic managerial bodies and
the ICTU. The ASTI was out on a limb in the dispute, and was led by those who
clearly misread the situation. The end result for them was a humiliating defeat, but
they did come to public prominence as a force to be reckoned with.

Pádraig Faulkner's ministerial legacy to Irish education lies in the important
role he played in developing the binary system of higher education. He did so
by placing the HEA on a statutory footing, by setting up the ad hoc NCEA,
and also by recognising the vital role RTCs would play in the future development
of technical and technological education. He invested very heavily in this sector,
quite possibly at the expense of the cash-starved universities.

Notes

1 Pádraig Faulkner, *As I Saw It. Reviewing over 30 years of Fianna Fáil and Irish Politics*
   (Dublin, 2005), p.61.
2 Ibid., p.62.
3 'Education facilities for the children of itinerants' in *Oideas*, 5, 1970.
4 Faulkner, *As I Saw It*, pp.71–2.
5 *Dáil Debates*, vol. 245, col. 1978, 23 April 1970.
6 Op. cit., p.72.
7 The Reformatory and Industrial Schools System Report (Dublin, 1970).
8 Raftery and O'Sullivan, *Suffer the Little Children*, p.378.
9 Faulkner, *As I Saw It*, p.68.

10 The Kennedy Report, p.4.

11 Ibid., p.15.

12 Ibid., pp.28–9.

13 Ibid., pp.6–7.

14 *Dáil Debates*, vol. 245, col. 1977, 23 April 1970.

15 Faulkner, *As I Saw It*, pp.69–71.

16 Ibid., pp.63–4.

17 Randles, *Post-primary Education*, p.299.

18 *Dáil Debates*, vol. 256, cols 939–40, 3 November 1971.

19 Ibid., col. 943.

20 Coolahan, 'Educational policy', p.32.

21 *Dáil Debates*, vol. 245, col. 1980, 23 April 1970.

22 Ibid, col. 1312, 15 April 1970.

23 Ibid., cols 1970–1.

24 *Dáil Debates*, vol. 258, col. 2010, 17 February 1972.

25 Ibid., col. 2009, 17 February 1972.

26 *Dáil Debates*, vol. 268, col. 557, 24 October 1973.

27 Ibid., col. 389; col. 558.

28 *Dáil Debates*, vol. 258, col. 2016, 17 February, 1972.

29 *The Irish Times*, 29 April 1970.

30 *The Irish Times*, 26 May 1971; White, *Investing in People*, p.73.

31 *The Irish Times*, 18 June 1969.

32 Coolahan, *The ASTI*, pp.288–9. Special function allowances were in effect long-service allowances.

33 Ibid., pp.293–4.

34 Ibid., p.255.

35 Ibid., p.298.

36 Coolahan, *The ASTI*, pp.301–7. The ASTI disaffiliated from the Irish Trades Union Congress in 1927.

37 Ibid., p.246. When the salary agreement became public in the autumn, it aggravated pay parity talks, and new claims were lodged; John Cunningham, *Unlikely Radicals: Irish Post-primary Teachers and the ASTI 1909–2009* (Cork, 2009), pp.125–9.

38 Faulkner, *As I Saw It*, p.74.

39 Revd P.M. Troddyn SJ, 'State and church in secondary education' in *A Studies Symposium*, p.2.

40 Coolahan, *The ASTI*, p.338.

41 Eamonn Sweeney, *Down Down Deeper and Down: Ireland in the 70s and 80s* (Dublin, 2010), pp.8–9.

42 Ó Buachalla, *Education Policy*, p.166.

43 Faulkner, *As I Saw It*, pp.74–5.

44 Coolahan, *The ASTI*, p.338.

45 *Dáil Debates*, vol. 249, cols 1613–14, 18 November 1970.

46 Troddyn, 'Editorial', p.339.

47 Ibid., p.384, p.351.

48 *The Irish Times*, 12 November 1970. 'Far reaching post-primary reorganisation outlined.
    Keystone of evolution towards comprehensives' by Brendan Spelman and Michael J. Doherty.

49 *Dáil Debates*, vol. 249, col. 1615, 18 November 1970; Troddyn, 'Editorial', p.339.

50 ASTI press statement, 12 November 1970.

51 Akenson, *A Mirror to Kathleen's Face*, p.152.

52 Faulkner, *As I Saw It*, p.75.

53 Louis O'Flaherty, *Management and Control in Irish Education the Post-primary Experience*
    (Dublin, 1992), p.52.

54 'A formal petition by a group of clergymen to President de Valera in 1970' in Ó Buachalla,
    Education Policy, p.398.

55 Ibid., p.220.

56 *The Irish Times*, 4 May 1971. 'Education review' by John Horgan and Michael Heney (eds).

57 Troddyn, 'The community school document', p.348.

58 *The Irish Times*, 4 May 1971.

59 *The Irish Times*, 28 April 1978. 'A final make or break explosion' by Christina Murphy.

60 *The Irish Times*, 11 May 1971.

61 *The Irish Times*, 12 May 1971.

62 John Coolahan, 'Community schools an examination' in *Public Affairs/Léargas*,
    June–July 1971, 3:9, p.7.

63 *The Irish Times*, 11 May 1971.

64 Op. cit., p.9.

65 *The Irish Times*, 15 May 1971.

66 *The Irish Times*, 27 May 1971.

67 *The Irish Times*, 2 June, 1971. Editorial 'Think again'.

68 Ibid., 'Schools plan denounced by IVEA, community proposals "political lunacy"'
    by Michael Heney.

69 Coolahan, *The ASTI*, p.339.

70 *The Irish Times*, 11 May 1971.

71 O'Flaherty, *Management and Control*, p.54.

72 *The Irish Times*, 18 June 1971. 'In the Dáil. Has school kite flown long enough' by John Healy.

73 O'Flaherty, *Management and Control*, pp.54–5.

74 *Dáil Debates*, vol. 258, col. 2014, 17 February 1972.

75 Whyte, *Church and State*, p.383, p.395.

76 FitzGerald, *All in a Life*, p.87.

77 O'Flaherty, *Management and Control*, p.51; *Dáil Debates*, vol. 258, col. 2066, 17 February 1972.

78 *Dáil Debates*, vol. 258, col. 2065, 17 February 1972.

79 Ibid., col. 2068.

80 Faulkner, *As I Saw It*, p.77.

81 Ibid., p.75.

82 Whyte, *Church and State*, p.392.

83 Faulkner, *As I Saw It*, pp.75–6.

84 *Dáil Debates*, vol. 259, col. 875, 2 March 1972.

16

Richard Burke (1973–76): 'The Minister broke the top rung of the ladder'

The conservative educational policies of the Minister for Education, Richard Burke, did little to enhance the liberal image of the Government.[1]

The new Fine Gael/Labour coalition government brought an end to Fianna Fáil's 16 years in power and introduced Ireland to its 'Government of all the Talents', so named because of the number of academics who formed its cabinet. The Tánaiste was Brendan Corish, leader of the Labour Party since 1960, and the Taoiseach was Fine Gael leader Liam Cosgrave, son of W.T. Cosgrave. The latter appointed Dick Burke, a 41-year-old secondary teacher and barrister, as Minister for Education. From 1969 he was Cosgrave's Chief Whip in opposition and his trusted ally.[2] In 1970 he ended his membership of the ASTI, an association that once honoured him for the rigorous role he played in its 'affairs and controversies'.[3]

Burke reversed Faulkner's decision to close the one-teacher, All-Irish school at Dún Chaoin. He accused Faulkner of 'a lack of sensitivity' and 'ruthlessness', claiming that 'Scoil Dún fell victim to an attitude that was almost Cromwellian in its relentlessness'.[4] Burke's action came in the wake of 'a national campaign of protest about Irish language and Gaeltacht issues',[5] and it proved quite popular.[6]

Addressing the INTO congress in Wexford in 1973, O'Connor, now secretary of the department, held that one of the greatest obstacles to the implementation of the new curriculum was that of overcrowded classrooms. He said that it was 'impossible to reconcile a new curriculum … with classes of over fifty pupils'.[7]

Burke was also in attendance, and he told delegates that the government had announced a capital allocation of £5 million for primary school building, the highest amount ever provided in any single year.[8] Speaking in the Dáil, he referred to the results of an INTO survey which covered 333 schools in Dublin city and county and which gave an overall pupil–teacher ratio of 44:1. There were, however, 1,021 classes with more than forty-five pupils, which was 33 per cent of the total. He drew attention to the circular regarding the raised pupil–teacher ratio that was effective from the commencement of the school year 1973–74, which announced that the enrolment in any one class should not exceed forty-five pupils. At the same time he acknowledged that further improvements in the pupil–teacher ratio were called for.[9]

Burke took the unusual step of allowing O'Connor to announce policy initiatives on the establishment of boards of management and for the planned regionalisation of education. 'The desirability of public servants speaking on matters proper to the domain of the politician' was later questioned by the editor of the *Irish Press*[10] and it was repeated in a pamphlet published anonymously under the title *Have the Snakes Come Back?*[11] The latter was a vitriolic attack on the department, the Minister and his officials by an extremist group, but it alarmed the editor of the *Education Times*, who considered it 'fundamentally and subversively anti-democratic'. Burke simply ignored it.[12]

In June 1973, O'Connor put forward proposals for the involvement of parents in the management of primary schools. He did so at a general meeting of the Catholic Primary School Managers' Association (CPSMA). He said he recognised that the Church had to ensure that religion was not neglected or obscured, but he asked 'would it not be politic to share responsibility?' He told them 'that they were fast becoming "the autocrats at the breakfast table"', and that the 'laicisation' of schools was an inescapable reality 'which was going to come anyway by sheer force of numbers'.[13]

O'Connor was probably referring to a recent report prepared by a working party set up by the Education Commissions of the Conference of Major Religious Superiors (CMRS) and the Catholic hierarchy, on the Future Involvement of Religious in Education (FIRE). The FIRE report was leaked to the *Education Times* in May 1973, and it forecast a 28 per cent decline in the proportion of religious to lay teachers in Irish schools by 1975.[14] The report also advocated a policy of 'retrenchment' and of carefully phased withdrawal by the religious into a smaller number of schools.[15]

Burke informed the Dáil that 'the immediate reaction to the proposals when they were aired was favourable'. He implied that the principle of shared management could have been achieved much earlier had it not been for the timidity of his predecessors.[16] In his assessment, he disregarded the influence of the Second Vatican Council of 1962, which saw a role for lay involvement in education, and also the subsequent approval of the Irish Catholic hierarchy 'of some broad principles for the formation of management, teacher parent associations for primary schools'.[17]

It should be pointed out that Burke's success in this area had much to do with the incentives offered by way of improved capitation grants for primary pupils in schools with boards of management, together with the proposed composition of such boards, which favoured school authorities.

When the INTO president, Seán Carew, addressed the INTO congress in 1975, he expressed concern that the election of parents to management committees could lead to these committees becoming 'a stamping ground for aspiring demagogues'. In response, Yvonne McGrath of the Parent School Movement said that if teachers were opposed to the proposal, they were looking 'backward not forward', and that Carew's comments were at odds with the 'attitude of younger teachers'. A spokesman for the National Council of Parents Associations said that his comments were 'so outdated' that no one could possibly treat them seriously.[18]

REGIONALISATION OF EDUCATION

O'Connor was the driving force behind plans for the regionalisation of education. Independently of the Duggan Committee, he had prepared his own plans in 1967 in which he envisaged that many of the Minister's functions with respect to primary and secondary schools would be devolved to regional councils.[19] In his speech to the CPSMA, he announced the introduction of county and regional educational authorities. These new bodies would look after every facet of education locally, with the exception of the universities. Such far-reaching proposals inevitably came up against strong resistance.[20]

In July 1973, Burke issued an official discussion document which involved the introduction of county and regional structures for educational administration.[21] In these plans primary and private secondary schools were not included under the county committees.[22] However, the services to be provided by the proposed intermediate bodies, such as school transport, and specialist services would impact directly on the private church-linked schools. Not only that, but both the primary- and secondary-school teachers and managers were being invited to nominate people to the new bodies, and the churches were invited by Burke to join discussions on regionalisation.

The first such meeting took place on 3 October with representatives of the wide range of interests involved, when it was established that the voluntary schools would come under the proposed educational authorities.[23] Burke agreed that the document on regionalisation was vague, but he said that this was to encourage consultation and debate. The morning session of the meeting progressed well, but according to a memorandum of the proceedings prepared by Fr John Hughes SJ on behalf of the Secretariat of Catholic Secondary Schools, the atmosphere changed in the afternoon as O'Connor indicated that if schools remained out of the scheme, their grants would be frozen.

A working party of seventeen members was then set up, and it held its first meeting on 19 October and a second meeting on 9 November, as Burke hoped that a consensus might be reached before Christmas. By the third meeting, major differences had emerged between the parties on the proposed constitution of county committees. There was disagreement also over the representation of regional authorities on boards of management of schools.[24] At the same time, the education representatives from the Catholic and Protestant churches held their own meetings to promote their mutual interests. The Catholic Church already had its Educational Policy Group, which comprised representatives of the Catholic hierarchy, the CMRS, and the working party who compiled the FIRE report, as well as two members of the TBA.

By January 1974, the Church bodies, with the support of the Protestant managerial organisations, had set down eight minimum conditions for consideration of regionalisation and they looked for 'effective statutory guarantees'. On 11 January, they issued a public statement along these lines, 'which amounted to "Not an Inch"', as it meant in effect the full copper-fastening of the private schools separate from the schools under the proposed regional authorities'.[25] The talks were not resumed.

As one commentator pointed out, it 'would be unfair to blame the Churches for the collapse of the talks, because the vocational sector, which would be absorbed into the new structure, was not enamoured of the proposals either'.[26]

At the final meeting of the committee on regionalisation, a document submitted by the IVEA stated that they would vigorously oppose regionalisation based on a plurality of counties. The Association, together with the Teachers Union of Ireland (TUI) and the Chief Executive Officers' Association, later drew up a response which put forward the idea of county committees to service post-primary schools and RTCs.[27]

Regionalisation of education failed as Burke 'wanted to ensure that the essential rights of the voluntary and public systems' were 'safeguarded'.[28] The government itself did not promote the idea with any great enthusiasm as it was pre-occupied with the challenges it faced following the oil crisis, which peaked between 1973 and 1975. A worldwide economic slump ensued and despite the optimism that accompanied Ireland's entry into the EEC, the country saw its inflation rate soar to 17 per cent in 1974, and to 21 per cent by 1975.[29]

Burke tried to introduce a number of reforms. He disregarded a report of the previous government by setting up a working party to produce a new draft constitution for an independent examination board. It reported on 21 January 1974, but the final recommendation for membership of the proposed Examination

Board was submitted in March 1976.[30] The report was shelved, but there was now an awareness of the excessive workload of inspectors and a realisation that their involvement in the administration of examinations was not integral to their work.

He then set about implementing the recommendations in the HEA Report on Teacher Education. It recommended that in-service education should be provided on a more extensive basis and that a professional body, An Foras Oideachais, should be established to regulate the teaching profession at first and second levels. Due to financial constraints, Burke was forced to reduce the government's contribution for special in-service courses from £77,000 for the year April to December 1974 to a paltry £12,000 for 1975.[31] However, he set up a small ad hoc planning committee to make the necessary arrangements for the constitution of An Foras Oideachais in October 1973.[32]

By 1973 tension between the teaching unions had subsided as they worked together on the planning committee for a Teaching Council. The committee reported within 6 months. It recommended comprehensive functions for the council, whose title was now changed to the Council of Teaching. The council would act as a teacher registration body for all teachers, a validating authority on teacher pre-service and in-service courses, an advisory agency on teacher supply, and a disciplinary agency for breaches of professional ethics among teachers. It would also engage in educational research and publish reports.

Each of the teaching unions could nominate five members to the thirty-five member council.[33] The teaching unions, with the exception of the TUI, welcomed the report. However, the department had no desire to give such wide-ranging powers to the teachers and the report itself had gone further in its range of recommendations than Burke had intended.[34] This report too remained dormant.

Burke had one notable success to his credit and this was in the area of teacher education. The Commission on Higher Education and the HEA had both recommended non-university degrees for trainee primary teachers. But in 1973 at the annual congress of the INTO, Burke announced that the course of training for primary teachers was to be extended to one of 3 years' duration, as from 1974.[35] At his request the NUI investigated the possibility of awarding a B.Ed degree to primary teachers.

Following successful negotiations between the university authorities and the representatives of the Colleges of Education, a university validated B.Ed degree was established. It was eventually agreed that the 3-year B.Ed degree could be conferred with honours. A special arrangement was made with TCD whereby B.Ed degrees would be made available to student teachers in three colleges in Dublin, namely the Church of Ireland College of Education, Rathmines, the Christian Brothers' Marino Institute of Education and the Froebel College in

Sion Hill. A fourth year of study would be required for an honours degree, in line with Trinity's undergraduate tradition.[36]

He informed the INTO delegates that he was confident that they would have a sufficient number of teachers to modify the effects of the blank year of 1976, when there would be no teachers graduating from the colleges. The number of teachers accepted for training in 1973 was the highest on record, so too was the number of non-graduate entrants, while the number of graduates entering in 1975 was more than double that for 1972.[37]

When it came to the introduction of multi-denominational education, Burke was determined that 'The National School system' which 'had been undisturbed for over 100 years' should remain that way.[38] Addressing the annual general meeting of the CPSMA in June 1974, he said he was prepared to support denominational education, and he considered that the most effective way to do this 'might be to establish a Deed of Trust with each school so that existing rights of ownership and control would be unassailable'.[39] Until the 1970s, practically all primary schools were denominational. Their denominational nature was officially recognised in the Rules for National Schools, 1965.[40]

The Dalkey School Project

Many Catholic parents sent their children to Protestant primary schools. Their reasons for doing so ranged from the smaller class sizes on offer to the fact that these schools were more middle class than similar Catholic schools.[41] Others did so because they 'felt that the ethos of such schools was less monolithic than that of Catholic schools'.[42]

The demand for multi-denominational education first arose in the village of Dalkey in south County Dublin. Catholic parents sent their children to the local Church of Ireland primary school, which had grown to a five-teacher school by 1974. At this stage some of the parents called for the school to be recognised as a multi-denominational one. Following unsuccessful discussions between the parent–teacher association of the school and the patron, parents formed an association in 1975 called the Dalkey School Project (DSP) to set up their own school.

The challenges which the DSP had to overcome were formidable, the most urgent one being the outlay, which necessitated major fundraising. The State-paid teachers' salaries, most of the capital costs and 'theoretically the bulk of the running costs, although in practice inflation … swung the actual payment of running costs heavily on the side of local rather than State payment'.[43]

The DSP wanted to set up a multi-denominational school on democratic principles, and it was in this spirit that it held a seminar in July 1975. Mr T.C.G. O'Mahony began by suggesting that all participants should 'put a Christian label' on themselves as this would 'allay the concern of many of us as to what this is all about'. His views were similar to those expressed in the pamphlet *Is Integrated Schooling the Answer? Education and the Irish Child* by the authors of *Have the Snakes Come Back?* when he suggested that there were very many active communists in the country who were trying to take over schools.

Barry Desmond, of the coalition government,[44] was a founding member of the DSP. He spoke at the seminar of the necessity for 'a multi-denominational system of education in the country'. He alleged that 'Our current system did not have a fundamental democratic base built into it'. Michael Johnston, secretary of the DSP, and other members, were keen to impress upon people that they had no wish to bring an end to the denominational system; that what they wanted was choice for parents, and that choice did not exist in 1975.[45]

A survey conducted by the DSP showed that a majority of families favoured the multi-denominational principle. Fr Seyers, the Education Secretary to Archbishop Ryan of Dublin, questioned 'the scientific validity of the survey'. A Dalkey resident, Mrs Treasa Ó Raghallaigh, was also sceptical about the survey and she predicted that if the DSP succeeded in starting a multi-denominational school, that it would quickly become a 'neutral' school, 'a school for atheists and humanists'.[46]

The DSP received a boost when Jack Lynch, the Fianna Fáil opposition leader, initially called for a 'phasing out' of denominational education[47] but later modified his stance by calling for integrated education, and for a multi-denominational school on a pilot basis.[48] The first indication that Lynch favoured the integrated approach came in 1974, when he spoke in Blessington, County Wicklow in support of Basil McIvor's proposed experiment with integrated education in the North of Ireland.[49]

Burke gave the impression of being hostile to integrated education. He maintained that there were already enough primary schools in the Dalkey area, and that there was no need for another school. Johnston pointed out that many classes in these schools were overcrowded.[50] In April 1975, residents in Marley Grange, in Rathfarnham, Dublin, formed The Marley Grange and District School Committee in order to establish a multi-denominational school. It held discussions with the various religious interests. However, the Catholic curate had already obtained outline planning permission for a denominational school in the area and was currently seeking full planning permission.[51]

Burke left himself open to the charge of being deliberately obstructive in the case of Marley Grange as he failed to have a site earmarked for the new multi-denominational school, even when a local site had been offered to him by the planning authorities.[52] His lofty attitude to the right of parents to an integrated education for their children was criticised in the *Education Times*, which pointed out that parents had not asked for the creation of an integrated system 'but merely of an option'.[53]

A year later Burke appeared to confirm the accuracy of the criticisms made against him when he implied that those who were campaigning for multi-denominational education were denigrating denominational education.[54]

It is interesting to compare Burke's response to parents' demands with that of Fr Sayers, who said 'that if a sufficient number of people in the area favoured such a school he would see nothing wrong with them having a school'.[55] The Catholic Church had learned much from the Second Vatican Council, not least religious tolerance and understanding. Nowhere is this more evident than in their acceptance of the principle of multi-denominational education 'contrary to what might have been expected from earlier form'.[56]

THE COMMUNITY SCHOOLS AND THE DEEDS OF TRUST

Despite having committed himself to genuine consultation with all the interested parties,[57] it was noted that during Burke's ministry 'debate on the community school issue became more muted'.[58] Burke did not lack enthusiasm for the community school ideal. There were now twelve community schools in operation, with plans for more. He saw the development as a further step towards correcting the academic/technical imbalance and he appreciated the potential of community schools as centres for adult education.[59]

In May 1974, the department circulated the Draft Deeds of Trust for community schools. According to the document, the Instruments of Management now proposed that the board of management of community schools should consist of six nominated members: two nominated by the religious authorities participating, two nominated by the VECs, and two to be elected by the parents and to be known as 'nominees'. It transpired that the procedures for electing the parent 'nominees' represented 'a slight diminution of the influence of the religious orders involved, compared to the 1971 proposals'.[60] This was to be expected as there was no religious presence in the areas where the first two community schools were established, but there was one vocational school in each area.

The religious authorities were now prepared to share managerial responsibilities through the establishment of boards of management, but there was no guarantee that teachers would be included on these boards.[61] It was believed that a broadly based board of management would 'provide the advantage of access to business expertise in the management of school finances' and would 'strengthen the school's position with regard to the exercise of bargaining power in negotiations'.[62]

Boards of management could also ensure the continuity of Catholic education in the hands of lay teachers if the religious had to withdraw from a school.

In the wake of the leaked FIRE report, the ASTI held a special convention to discuss the functions of any board of management that might be set up. Some delegates viewed the introduction of boards with suspicion, but they were also concerned at the prospect of teacher redundancies. Br Declan Duffy of the TBA[63] thought that this was a possibility in the event of school closures due to inadequate funding from the department and the loss of the private subsidy should it be discontinued.[64] He could see the potential of boards of management for guarding against lay teacher redundancies. It was the fear of redundancy which prompted the CEC of the ASTI to set up a sub-committee on 3 January 1975 to negotiate a redundancy policy with the JMB and the department on a stated ten-point plan.[65]

Having avoided the issue of the composition of boards of management in the past, Burke now invited the authorities of secondary schools to appoint boards of management on which parents could be represented. He did so during his address to the annual convention of the ASTI in 1975. He envisaged that the majority of members of each board would be nominated by the school authorities and that two parents (one a mother) of pupils attending the school and one teacher from the teaching staff of the school would comprise the board. The principal would act as secretary of the board.[66] He impressed upon the delegates that he was not proposing to either interfere with or relieve secondary-school authorities of their duty regarding the maintenance and conduct of their schools; he was simply 'suggesting that they might reach out for help and encouragement'.[67] His speech allayed the fears of both the school authorities and of secondary teachers.

The Secondary Teacher carried a special feature on boards of management in 1975, and the contribution of Fr John Hughes SJ, director of the Secretariat of Secondary Schools, who was writing in a personal capacity, excited the interest of the ASTI. In his article he expressed the opinion that 'the full-time teaching staff should have representation on the board'.[68]

Among the points made in the ASTI report of January 1976 in favour of boards of management, was the fact that the INTO and the TUI had already accepted in principle the establishment of boards, and that boards would entrench local opposition to the closure of small schools.[69] However, the CMRS issued their Articles of Management for Religious Run Catholic Secondary Schools, which proved completely unacceptable to the ASTI.[70] The Articles proposed a board of management consisting of ten members: six to be nominated by the trustees of the school, two elected parents, one full-time teacher from the staff of the school, and one to be nominated by the nine other members. The ASTI had called for equal representation on boards of management, and they now suspected 'that the religious authorities wanted a device to continue control with a token democratic structure'.[71]

REFORMS

The Fine Gael party gave a pre-election promise to drop Irish as a compulsory subject for the award of certificates at intermediate and leaving certificate level. Burke honoured this promise in April 1973 when he announced the end of compulsory Irish. But the change was much less radical than at first appeared, as Irish remained an essential subject if schools were to be 'recognised' – pupils did not have to offer Irish as an examination subject, but their schools would not earn grants unless the pupils followed the appropriate curriculum, which included Irish. The bonus points incentive for answering various examination papers through Irish was to continue and an honours award in Irish at leaving certificate was to count as a double subject for the purposes of student grants at third level.[72]

In 1970 Faulkner set up a ministerial committee to review the intermediate certificate examination, known as the ICE committee. It produced its final report in 1975. The committee was very critical of the intermediate certificate examination and recommended more school-based assessment procedures and more varied assessment techniques. It also recommended the establishment of the Public Examinations Evaluation Project (PEEP), a recommendation which Burke accepted. The project was initiated in the autumn of 1973 to explore new modes of syllabus design and assessment, using mathematics and history as exemplar subjects. An appraisal had already been carried out on the leaving certificate curriculum in 1970 by researchers Madaus and Macnamara which was critical of this examination because of 'its over-reliance on the reproduction of factual data'.[73]

The PEEP presented its report in 1981 and it urged the use of more varied modes of examination, with greater teacher involvement in syllabus design and assessment.[74] Minor changes resulted from these projects, but no major reforms were achieved. However, there was a realisation that the public examinations were not meeting the needs of a diverse student population, where in 1973, 13,000 students left school before completing the intermediate certificate and 2,000 failed the leaving certificate examination.[75]

Burke took a particular interest in the provision of a guidance and counselling service for second-level students. There were 200 guidance teachers in approximately 200 second-level schools, but he released eighty teachers to attend a year-long in-service training course in this area. His goal was to provide a nationwide service. He stated in the Dáil that in schools with more than 250 students, the post of guidance teacher would be a post outside the normal quota of teaching posts for the school.[76]

HIGHER EDUCATION

Higher education had been thrown into turmoil with the O'Malley merger proposals of 1967. The HEA restored stability to the sector in the early 1970s after it gave its approval to the binary system of higher education, and when it accepted the UCD/TCD joint proposals. It also supported the government's intention to establish UCG and UCC as independent universities.

Burke faced a daunting task in relation to university reorganisation, the future of higher education in Dublin and the statutory arrangements to be made for the NIHEL and the NCEA.[77] On 16 December 1974, proposals were announced in relation to higher education, which sent shock waves through the sector as they contained plans to replace the binary system of higher education with a comprehensive system.

There were to be two universities in Dublin, a reduced NUI comprising UCC and UCG, and St Patrick's College, Maynooth was to have the option of becoming a constituent college of any of the three universities. A conjoint board was to be established to co-ordinate the two Dublin universities, and to set out the envisaged redistribution of university faculties in the city. The proposals included the establishment of a Conference of Irish Universities and provided for the statutory recognition of theology as a university discipline.

The degree awarding powers of the fledgling NCEA were to be withdrawn, and it was to be restructured as the Council for Technological Education, which could plan and co-ordinate courses, and validate and award non-degree third-level qualifications in the two NIHEs. The National Institute for Higher Education planned for Dublin (NIHED) was to become a recognised college of one of the Dublin universities or become a degree-awarding institution. NIHEL was to become a recognised college of either UCC or UCG, with the same scope for evolution to constituent college or autonomous status. The RTCs were to continue to be funded through the VECs by the department, but in consultation with the Council for Technological Education.[78]

The aim of the policy was to concentrate higher level institutions within a framework of three universities. Other third-level institutions would be linked to one or other of these universities for all degree and post-graduate work. The overall role of the HEA was to be expanded as the key overseeing body of the third-level institutions.[79] The chairman of the HEA lost no time in confirming that it had 'no part whatsoever in the drawing up of the Minister's proposals'.[80] The status of the NCEA was to be reduced as it was losing its degree awarding powers. It was later confirmed that the validation of all NCEA awards would be fully honoured and safeguarded.[81]

The December 1974 proposals stirred a hornet's nest. Burke was accused of attempting Russian-style government by the president of UCC, Dr Donal McCarthy. He called it 'an attempt to govern by Ministerial ukase'.[82]

Dr F.S.L. Lyons, provost of TCD, regarded the sections of the announcement that related to Trinity as 'quite unacceptable'.[83] Later he claimed that the general effect of the proposals would be to cut the college off from direct contact with the main areas of agricultural, technological and commercial development in the country, in the years ahead.[84] The Irish Federation of University Teachers (IFUT) objected to the proposals as it feared they would threaten university autonomy. The Union of Students in Ireland (USI) questioned the competence of the universities to validate some of the courses provided in VEC colleges.

Burke responded to criticisms by stating that he had received advice from the HEA and had consulted almost every authority in the State over 18 months. He made the point that if UCC and UCG had been granted independent status Ireland would have five universities, while countries such as Holland and Denmark had only two universities each.[85]

Third-level institutions outside the universities were vehemently opposed to Burke's plans. In a statement from the principals and staff of the eight RTCs, they expressed the view that the technical colleges were being sacrificed while the universities were being appeased. The constitution of the planned replacement council for the NCEA, the Council for Technological Education, was criticised for being seriously damaging to applied science and technology.[86]

Initially the chairman of the planning board of the NIHEL, Dr Edward Walsh, welcomed the proposals.[87] However, the board issued a statement within weeks criticising the proposed designation of NIHEL as a recognised college of the NUI. The board was anxious to have the institute established from the outset as a constituent college of the NUI, or alternatively as an autonomous degree awarding institution.[88] Walsh had ambitious plans for his flagship institute.[89]

Prior to the setting up of the RTCs, non-university education in technological disciplines was concentrated mainly within the colleges of the CDVEC together with some third-level VEC colleges in Cork and Limerick. In Dublin, third-level courses were conducted primarily in the Colleges of Technology at Bolton Street and Kevin Street, and in the College of Commerce, Rathmines. There were over 2,000 full-time third-level students in these colleges and this resulted in the CDVEC being confronted with an accommodation problem. A planning committee of the CDVEC submitted a report to the department, in which it proposed to bring together higher technician, technological, higher commercial and management developments from the three colleges, into one campus at Ballymun, Dublin.[90] This was later referred to as the Ballymun Project.

In February 1969, Lenihan referred the Ballymun proposals to the HEA. The CDVEC submitted its proposals to the HEA in June of that year and in 1970 the HEA decided to adopt the Ballymun Project.[91] Third-level activity in Rathmines and Bolton Street was now to be transferred to Ballymun. However, the CDVEC were far from satisfied with the proposed governing structure for the Ballymun Project which, while containing VEC representation, would be independent of the CDVEC and financed by the HEA.[92]

No decision had been taken on the Ballymun Project 4 years after the publication of the HEA report. According to one commentator, much of the blame for the lack of progress in higher technical education provision in Dublin was due to a decision taken by the CDVEC itself. With the exception of two of its colleges – those of Bolton Street and Cathal Brugha Street – the CDVEC colleges shunned the NCEA from the outset. He commented that 'Had the Dublin Colleges sought degree recognition from the ad hoc NCEA … it is possible that the decisions announced on 16 December 1974 might have been substantially different'.[93]

The Ballymun Project was brought to fruition when the government set up the NIHED in 1975. In June of that year the governing body held its first meeting. It took a further 5 years before the institute was ready to admit its 300 students.

Plans were put in place in the late 1960s to locate a College of Education, specialising initially in physical education, on the same campus as the NIHEL. The college opened on an adjoining campus in 1971, known as the National College of Physical Education (NCPE).[94] In 1975 the first cohort of students from NCPE was due to graduate, but the department could not find a university with the necessary expertise to fulfil the degree awarding functions. Consequently, Burke met with the NCEA on 18 February 1975 and empowered it to award degrees to the successful NCPE students. Burke stated that the power to award degrees would remain with the NCEA until such time as the universities were prepared to undertake this function. He had to suffer further indignity when he was forced to reverse the policy decision to change the name of the NCEA to the Council for Technological Education, on 21 March, based on advice received.[95]

In the summer of 1975, the future prospects for the newly revived NCEA were placed in danger. The threat emerged when, in a strategic move, TCD made another alliance, this time with the CDVEC for the awarding of engineering degrees. Trinity had been concerned at government plans to grant it a faculty of engineering science without the requisite capital investment. This alliance would allow Trinity 'to claw back some of the engineering function which the Minister's proposals' seemed 'to cast into limbo'. The move was seen as one that could retard the development of the NCEA, especially as it had 'put forward its own proposals for developing a validating procedure in which the Council would work in partnership with the universities'.[96]

The NCEA was awaiting an official response from Burke, but the latest alliance seemed certain to undermine its chances of success. A joint partnership agreement between TCD and the CDVEC was published in April 1976, and the first conferring of degrees on students from the two VEC colleges took place in December. By then the Marino Institute of Education and Froebel College of Education had made a formal application for an association with TCD, a move which Burke favoured.[97]

Plans for the graduation in 1976 of the NIHEL's first intake of students were put in train well in advance of the event. A governing board was put in place and the institute made a formal application to the NUI for recognised college status.[98] Burke had to nominate the university to be tasked with the 'chore' of evaluating the institute's degree programmes for validation purposes.[99] UCC was mandated to do so and this was followed by a number of protests against the government decision. On 4 November 1975, the NIHEL students organised a week of protest against alleged government silence on the question of degrees to be awarded to them.[100] The governing body of the institute issued a press release advising the government that the recognised college relationship with the NUI was unworkable.

However, worse was to follow when a report by the NUI, which recommended that only some of the institute's courses should be recognised for full degree status, was leaked to the press.[101] Burke remained steadfast and having met a deputation of TDs and students, he insisted that degrees at the NIHEL would be awarded by the NUI. In March 1976, the Senate of the NUI declared the institute a recognised college and validated some of its degree programmes. No provision was made for honours degrees.[102] Burke was then obliged to issue an ultimatum to the institute on foot of complaints received that it was not complying with the requirements of UCC in furnishing documents as requested. The governing body agreed to compliance.

Then it was the students' turn to vent their frustration. The final-year students refused to complete their matriculation forms, and in a dramatic gesture burnt the forms outside the NUI offices in Dublin. This was followed by a 1-day strike.[103] Eventually the students complied with NUI requirements so that they could graduate. In the meantime, Burke transferred responsibility for the supervision and validation of the NIHEL programmes to UCG in an effort to lessen tensions between the institute and the NUI.[104]

In the Dáil, Faulkner, who had set up the NCEA, urged that it should be left to award degrees to the NIHEs and RTCs.[105] Michael O'Kennedy from the Fianna Fáil party wondered whether the World Bank would have afforded Ireland a loan for the NCPE and the NIHEs, had it promoted this new policy. He believed that the advancement of technical education in Ireland depended on third-level institutes such as the NIHEL, but he said 'the Minister broke the top rung of the ladder'.[106]

Burke's decision to grant interim degree-awarding powers to the NCEA was to backfire on him in June 1976. It was also to cause a great deal of stress for four students sitting their final examination in Hotel and Catering Management in Galway RTC. On 15 July 1975, the NCEA had granted degree recognition to this course, but almost a year later the students who had sat the examination did not know by whom their degree would be awarded. The confusion arose when the department invited UCG to become involved in consideration of the programme in the expectation that it would confer the degrees. This did not materialise and to add to the confusion, the NCEA awarded a diploma to the four students, who refused to accept the award at their conferring.[107]

Burke resigned in November 1976 and left office on 1 December to take up a position as Ireland's European Commissioner, and his successor Peter Barry (1928–), who served as Minister from 2 December 1976 to 14 July 1977, allowed the NCEA to award degrees to the four successful students on 7 March 1977.[108] Before departing for Europe, Burke succeeded in setting up the NIHED and in appointing Dr Daniel O'Hare as its first director in October 1976.[109] In November he set up a working party on higher education in Dublin to make proposals regarding the apportionment of academic activities between the NIHED and the CDVEC colleges. The working party reported to Barry in December 1976.[110]

Burke had little to show with regard to restructuring the university sector. TCD and UCD worked well together to bring about rationalisation within the faculties of dentistry, pharmacy and veterinary medicine. TCD's worst fears were not realised as it only lost its veterinary medicine faculty.[111] The government's December 1974 proposals were not given legislative form. In fact, the government made a major alteration to the policy when Burke announced in August 1976 that UCC, UCG and St Patrick's College, Maynooth were to become separate universities, and that the NUI was to be dissolved.[112] There was to be scope for associated and recognised colleges to be linked to the universities.

A working party chaired by Burke was set up on 21 September 1976 to take on the task of preparing the necessary legislation to give effect to comprehensive higher education. But time ran out for the government as it lost the general election in June 1977.

Dick Burke left an important legacy to Irish education when he gained the required funding for the continuation of the crucially important Rutland Street Project. His legacy included the replacement of the 144-year-old managerial system with the more democratic board of management structure, together with the introduction of the 3-year B.Ed degree programme for primary teachers, to be linked to the universities. The INTO had sought this for over seven decades, and it raised the status of primary teaching.

Burke earned his conservative reputation by his strong defence of denominational education, and his staunch criticism of multi-denominational education and
its proponents. In one instance he left himself open to the charge of obstruc-
tionism having failed to have a site ear-marked for a multi-denominational school.
His attempt at implementing plans for the regionalisation of education was
lukewarm at best, and hardly likely to succeed as he tried to appease all sides.

At second level he brought an end to compulsory Irish for State examinations,
but in reality it represented a slight modification of the existing rules. With regard
to the Draft Deeds of Trust for community schools, he merely presided over their
publication and in so doing avoided potential confrontation with his former ASTI
colleagues. However, he brought some hope to secondary-school authorities and
secondary teachers with regard to the composition of boards of management when
he assured them that there would be no government interference. He did so also
by expanding the guidance and counselling provision and by committing to the
expansion of the service nationwide.

His attempt to set up an Examination Board, while unsuccessful, served to
highlight the excessive workload of the inspectorate. The two critical reports he
received on the State examinations, whose recommendations he could not afford
to implement, nonetheless brought into sharp focus the need for change in the
areas of syllabus design and assessment if the department was to meet the requirements of students at risk of early school leaving.

Dick Burke threw higher education into a tailspin when he tried to introduce a
comprehensive higher education system. His assertion that he had consulted all the
parties involved over 18 months is hardly credible, as they all objected to his plans
when they were published. A more likely explanation would be the enthusiasm
which his academic cabinet colleagues who helped draw up the scheme, had for
the policy. But the policy itself was flawed because by stripping the NCEA of its
degree awarding powers and by handing them over to the universities, a message
was conveyed that a university degree was in some way superior to one awarded
by the NCEA. It quickly became apparent that the universities neither had the
desire nor the expertise to validate technical degree programmes. Students paid
the price for the failure of this policy, and so too did the NCEA, which was left in
a weakened position following 2 years in which it was the subject of controversy.

Notes

1 Barry Desmond, *Finally and in Conclusion* (Dublin, 2000), p.146.
2 Mulchay was replaced by James Dillon as party leader in 1959. Six years later Liam
    Cosgrove replaced Dillon.
3 *Education Times*, 19 September 1974.

4 *Dáil Debates*, vol. 268, cols 381–2, 23 October 1973.

5 Coolahan and O'Donovan, *A History*, p. 187.

6 *Education Times*, 19 September 1974. Cosgrave replaced James Dillon as party leader in 1965.

7 Presidential address of Mr Seán O'Connor, delivered at Wexford congress 1973 in *An Múinteoir Náisiúnta*, 1:17 (1973), p. 18.

8 Ibid., Address by Minister for Education Richard Burke TD, pp. 19–20.

9 *Dáil Debates*, vol. 268, cols 377–8, 23 October 1973.

10 *Irish Press*, 2 April 1975.

11 Vera Verba (ed.), *Have the Snakes Come Back? Education and the Irish Child by a Group of Catholic Parents* (1976), pp. 1–72, p. 36.

12 *Education Times*, 3:23, 5 June 1975. 'Snake bite'.

13 *Irish Independent*, 13 June 1973. 'Revolutionary blueprint for Irish schools' by John Walshe.

14 *Education Times*, 13 December 1973.

15 *Education Times*, 14 January 1974.

16 *Dáil Debates*, vol. 268, col. 376, 23 October 1973.

17 Catholic Bishops' Pastoral Letter, 1969. Cited in Coolahan, 'Educational policy', p. 53.

18 *Irish Press*, 2 April 1975. 'Warning by INTO clash over school role of parents'.

19 O'Connor, *A Troubled Sky*, p. 157.

20 *Irish Independent*, 13 June 1973.

21 Department of Education. Regionalisation draft for discussion, 25 July 1973.

22 *Education Times*, 1:13 August 1975, p. 18.

23 *Dáil Debates*, vol. 268, col. 407, 23 October 1973.

24 Walshe, *A New Partnership*, pp. 52–3.

25 John Coolahan, 'Regionalisation of education: a recurrent concern' in Barney O'Reilly (ed.) *Administrative Reform in Irish Education*. Proceedings of the John Marcus O'Sullivan memorial lectures 1988, p. 9.

26 Op. cit., p. 56.

27 IVEA, 'Reorganisation of educational structures'. Annual report of congress (Bantry), appendix v, 1975. The VTA was formed in 1955 and renamed the TUI in 1973.

28 *Education Times*, 26 January 1974, p. 16.

29 Sweeney, *Down Down Deeper and Down*, p. 56.

30 NAI *Box 2006/120/69*; Coolahan and O'Donovan, *A History*, p. 204.

31 *Dáil Debates*, vol. 282, col. 1134, 19 June 1975.

32 *Dáil Debates*, vol. 268, cols 384–5, 23 October 1973.

33 Report of An Chomhairle Mhúinteoireachta (Teaching Council) 1974; Coolahan, *The ASTI*, p. 346.

34 Coolahan, *The ASTI*, p. 346; Interview with Seán O'Connor, July 1984.

35 *Dáil Debates*, vol. 268, col. 380, 23 October 1973.

36 Coolahan, 'Education policy', p. 35.

37 *Dáil Debates*, vol. 268, col. 381, 23 October 1973.

38 Áine Hyland, 'The multi-denominational experience in the national school system of Ireland' in *Irish Educational Studies*, 8:1 (1989), p. 98.

39 *The Irish Times*, 19 June 1974. 'National school system will stay' by John Armstrong.

40 Rules for National Schools, 1965, p.8.

41 Whyte, *Church and State*, pp.372–3.

42 Hyland, 'The multi-denominational experience', p.96.

43 Ibid., pp.98–9.

44 Barry Desmond was a member of the steering committee set up in 1962 to assist the
    OECD Survey Team.

45 *Education Times*, 3 July 1975, p.6. 'Dalkey School Project hold seminar voices for
    integrated education'.

46 *Evening Herald*, 18 February 1976. 'A school for all religions'.

47 Jack Lynch, 'Interdenominational education favoured by leader of the opposition party'
    in *Petrus Holy Year 1975* (Wexford, 1975), p.11.

48 *Sunday Press*, 6 July 1975; *Education Times*, 10 July 1975.

49 *Sunday Press*, 6 July 1975.

50 *Evening Herald*, 18 February 1976. 'Barry and Dick don't see eye to eye'.

51 *The Irish Times*, 31 December 1975. 'Marley group sends its proposals to religious'.

52 *The Irish Times*, 28 July 1976. Jotter.

53 *Education Times*, 19 September 1974, p.7.

54 *The Irish Times*, 29 September 1975. 'Burke attacks parents who want
    multi-denominational education'.

55 *Evening Herald*, 18 February 1976.

56 Whyte, *Church and State*, p.394.

57 *Dáil Debates*, vol. 274, col. 2290, 25 July 1974.

58 O'Flaherty, *Management and Control*, p.58.

59 *Dáil Debates*, vol. 268, col. 391, 23 October 1973.

60 O'Flaherty, *Management and Control*, p.59.

61 *Education Times*, 13 September 1973. 'Key recommendations'.

62 O'Flaherty, *Management and Control*, p.94.

63 Br Duffy would play a leadership role in a number of religious management associations in
    the years ahead.

64 Br Declan Duffy, 'Religious-run secondary schools – a change in management'
    in *The Secondary Teacher*, 4:1, Autumn 1974, p.7.

65 O'Flaherty, *Management and Control*, pp.95–8.

66 'Special feature Boards of Management' in *The Secondary Teacher*, autumn 1975, p.21.

67 Richard Burke's address to the ASTI convention 1975 in *The Secondary Teacher*, 5:1 1975, p.21.

68 Fr John Hughes SJ, 'Opinion' in *The Secondary Teacher*, autumn 1975, p.24.

69 'Draft proposals on Boards of Management' in *ASTIR*, January 1976, p.4.

70 'Articles of Management for Religious run Catholic secondary schools' in *ASTIR*,
    February 1977, p.4. *ASTIR* is the ASTI journal.

71 O'Flaherty, *Management and Control*, p.100.

72 *The Irish Times*, 5 April 1973.

73 George Madaus and John Macnamara, *Public Examinations: A Study of the Leaving Certificate*

(Dublin 1970).

74 John Heywood, Séamus McGuinness and Daniel Murphy, Final report of the public examinations evaluation project 1981.

75 The Irish Times, 14 January 1976.'John Armstrong looks back at some major developments during 1973'.

76 Dáil Debates, vol. 268, cols 393–4, 23 October 1973.

77 White, Investing in People, p.113.

78 Press release of Minister Richard Burke on new government proposals, 16 December 1974.

79 Coolahan, 'Higher education in Ireland', p.786.

80 The Irish Times, 18 December 1974.

81 Ibid.

82 The Irish Times, 21 December 1974.'UCC head accuses Burke of Russian-style rule' David Musgrave.

83 The Irish Times, 17 December 1974.

84 The Irish Times, 14 March 1975.

85 The Irish Times, 23 December 1974. 'University staffs criticise proposals. Not worked out said IFUT', 'Public favouring plans more says Burke'.

86 Irish Independent, 19 December 1974.

87 The Irish Times, 17 December 1974.

88 Irish Press, 27 January 1975.

89 Education Times, 18 October 1973.

90 HEA report on Ballymun Project, p.68, cited in White, Investing in People, pp.90–1.

91 HEA report on Ballymun Project, p.1.

92 Ibid., pp.61–4.

93 White, Investing in People, p.91.

94 The NCPE was renamed Thomond College of Education in 1976.

95 White, Investing in People, pp.120–1.

96 Education Times, 12 June 1975. Editorial 'Breaking ranks'.

97 The Irish Times, 9 June 1975.

98 Irish Independent, 28 September 1975.

99 The Irish Times, 29 October 1975.

100 Limerick Leader, 5 November 1975.

101 White, Investing in People, pp.124–5.

102 The Irish Times, 12 March 1976.

103 Sunday Independent, 4 April 1976; The Irish Times, 6 April 1976.

104 Irish Press, 14 May 1976; The Irish Times, 14 August 1976.

105 Dáil Debates, vol. 288, cols 155–6, 17 February 1976.

106 Dáil Debates, vol. 290, cols 145–6, 27 April 1976.

107 Irish Press, 16 November 1976.

108 White, Investing in People, pp.125–6.

109 Irish Independent, 8 October 1976

110 The Irish Times, 26 November 1976.

111 Whyte, Investing in People, p.126.

112 Irish Press, 2 August 1976.

17

John P. Wilson (1977–81): 'A landmark settlement and a significant victory for the teachers'

Mr Wilson was a member of the ASTI and a past President of their Association. A witty orator and a classics scholar, he was a popular T.D. and advocated strongly Republican sentiments throughout his time in Leinster House.[1]

The coalition 'government of all the talents' suffered heavy losses in the June 1977 general election. After 4 years in office it had failed to agree a national wage agreement, with the result that strikes became a regular feature of Irish working life.[2] The Fianna Fáil party won the election having made 'extravagant commitments, which severely damaged the economy for a period of at least fifteen years'.[3]

John Wilson (1923–2007), a secondary teacher and lecturer from County Cavan, was appointed Minister for Education by the Taoiseach, Jack Lynch, on 15 July 1977. He had been the opposition frontbench spokesman on Education and the Arts from 1973 to 1977, having been first elected to the Dáil in 1973. An urgent problem which Wilson faced was the high pupil–teacher ratio which still persisted in primary schools. A target of 35:1 had been set in the Third Programme for Economic Expansion of 1969, but 10 years on there were still 2,144 classes with forty or more pupils, which constituted about 18 per cent of the total pupil enrolment.

More worrying was the fact that the largest numbers were concentrated in the infants' classes and first class. In 1978 pupils in infants and first class comprised 47,603 of the 73,965 pupils in classes of forty to forty-four pupils, and made up 9,341 of the 19,693 in classes of forty-five or more pupils.[4] In Ireland in the 1970s, remedial teaching was undeveloped and the number of teachers employed in this specialised area came to no more than 342 for the year 1977–78, but this figure was set to rise steadily in subsequent years.[5]

Wilson took steps to reduce the pupil–teacher ratio by devising a scheme of Special Trainee Graduate Teachers in 1977.[6] It was a scheme whereby graduates would be employed in primary schools having first passed a suitability interview and then having successfully completed a year-long teacher training programme. The Colleges of Education were critical of such a scheme, and so too was the INTO. This resulted in 218 special trainee teachers completing the once-off course. Some inroads were made into reducing the pupil–teacher ratio, with the number of pupils in classes of forty or more having fallen from 44 to 13 per cent in the decade between 1970–71 and 1980–81. The annual pupil–teacher ratio had been reduced from 34.5 to 30.4:1.

During the same decade, the number of teachers had increased by 28 per cent, but the number of pupils had only risen by 9 per cent.[7] According to the statistics produced in the long-awaited White Paper on Educational Development, 1980, numbers in primary schools grew from 488,200 in 1965–66 to 529,600 in 1975–76. It projected a continued increase in numbers for the next decade, but these projections were to prove inaccurate due to a decline in the birth rate in the early 1980s.[8]

Ireland's weak economy affected education. The White Paper listed eleven specialist committees whose reports lay dormant due to educational cutbacks. The withdrawal of very substantial investment in in-service education angered the INTO to such an extent that it refused to hold any more in-service courses for a number of years. The government's response was to set up a Committee on In-service Education in June 1980. It produced its report in 1984, which recommended a national council for the co-ordination of a comprehensive plan for in-service education for teachers. No action was taken on foot of that report.[9]

The new curriculum was intended to be the subject of ongoing review, an intention which was signalled in the introduction to the *Teacher's Handbook*. Wilson paid lip-service to this aspiration as he replied to a parliamentary question that 'Reviewing and evaluating the primary school curriculum is an ongoing process'. He referred to the review and evaluation work being done by the Curriculum Development Unit which was established in the department in 1976, and added that he had 'no immediate proposals for a major review of the primary school curriculum'.[10]

In August 1977, Wilson gave an assurance that a multi-denominational school in Dalkey would go ahead. He stated that his party was committed to such projects when they were viable and when people wanted them.[11] In 1978 he funded the DSP, but he was not prepared to consider 'extending the special consideration given to parents who are establishing All-Irish national schools, in the matter of assistance towards the purchase of sites'.[12]

When Burke introduced boards of management into national schools, the INTO agreed to their introduction for a 3-year period only, following which there would be a review of their operation. As no review was forthcoming, the INTO members withdrew from participation on boards. In 1978 the department tried to secure agreement on re-negotiations for boards, but by February 1979 there was little progress to report.[13]

In October it was revealed at the annual meeting of the CPSMA that the bishops were determined 'not to yield to the demands of the INTO which had boycotted boards of management for over a year, for equal representation on boards'.[14] It took another year before an agreement was reached. Under the new arrangements, the churches agreed to reduce the patron's nominees from '6 to 4 in the larger schools and from 4 to 3 in the schools with 6 or less teachers ... the place usually held by the teachers' representative on the selection board for assistant teachers was now given to an independent assessor, nominated by the patron'.[15] The newly restructured boards of management became operational from October 1981. In reality the boards had limited powers, and their main function appeared to be that of fundraising.

'WE ARE LIVING WAY BEYOND OUR MEANS'

Educational development and reform was not a government priority as the political and economic climate favoured neither. In the late 1970s a National Understanding was reached between union leaders and the government, which brought industrial peace. However, rising inflation and a further oil crisis destabilised the government. There was a political heave against Jack Lynch, who was forced to resign on 5 December 1979, and he was replaced as Taoiseach by Charles Haughey.[16] Haughey made a famous televised address to the nation in January 1980, warning the Irish people that 'as a nation we are living way beyond our means'.[17]

He did not take the necessary financial measures to control inflation, especially in the area of public pay. One celebrated case was the teachers' pay award of October 1980 'which was generally regarded as a landmark settlement and a significant victory for the teachers'.[18] This occurred following the publication of the interim report of the review body which recommended salary and allowances which fell far short of teachers' expectations. The three teaching unions adopted a united and firm line in protracted negotiations with Wilson and his officials. Haughey instructed Wilson to concede a pay rise larger than the initial arbitration award.[19] The arbitration board resigned in protest, having been undermined by the Minister's decision to conciliate the unions, but they agreed to postpone the announcement of their resignation at Wilson's request.[20]

The INTO grew increasingly impatient with Wilson as they awaited the White Paper on education. The general secretary, Gerry Quigley, claimed that Wilson never wanted a White Paper but only agreed to one following 'the strong pressure from trade unions'.[21] Wilson defended his position by stating that the White Paper would stimulate wide-ranging, constructive discussion.[22] This did not occur due to its over-concentration on past achievements, but it made one important recommendation, which was for the provision of a Curriculum Council, and this was set up in 1984.

Officials in the department did valuable work in the area of curriculum reform, especially from the time that Ireland joined the EEC in January 1973. They were spurred on to do so when the EEC offered support from the ESF for pre-employment courses which incorporated work experience. They devised programmes which qualified for European funding, although initially it was only students from vocational, comprehensive and community schools who could benefit from this opportunity.

The pre-employment programme proved highly popular with students, who saw it as a more practical 'job relevant' alternative to the established leaving certificate with its academic orientation. In fact, the number of participants on it doubled between 1977 and 1983.[23] The programme comprised three elements: vocational studies, work experience and general studies.

BOARDS OF MANAGEMENT FOR SECONDARY SCHOOLS

Proposals for the introduction of boards of management for secondary schools, first mooted in the FIRE report of 1973, had been further developed by the CMRS in February 1976. As already noted, the CMRS proposed a board of ten members: six to be nominated by the trustees, two by elected parents, one elected full-time teacher and one additional person to be chosen by the nine other members. These proposals were anathema to the ASTI, which described them as a 'democratic sham'.[24]

In February 1977, the ASTI commenced negotiations with the CMRS on proposals for boards of management. There could now be two teachers on a board instead of one, but union representation was not conceded. When the ASTI rejected the proposals, the general secretary of the Secretariat of Catholic Schools, Fr John Hughes, resigned and was replaced by Br Declan Duffy. The ASTI president, Derek Nolan, conveyed the depth of anger felt by his members when he said that the 'attitude of the CMRS is not only regrettable but downright dangerous'.[25]

Later Nolan reminded ASTI members that there was no agreed machinery for redeployment of secondary teachers, and that there was no scheme of compensation whatsoever for them.[26] In February 1978, when talks resumed between the ASTI and the CMRS and representatives of the Episcopal Commission regarding boards of management, it was agreed that redundancy should also form part of the discussions. The negotiations would continue for several more years, with the ASTI periodically threatening to take industrial action or to withdraw from participation in the State examinations.

Eventually tripartite negotiations got underway between the ASTI, the CMCSS[27] and the department on a national scheme to cater for redundancy. The negotiations included discussion on boards of management, parent–teacher meetings and teacher redeployment in the event of redundancy. A final draft of a redeployment scheme, as part of a wider negotiated package, was agreed by the CMCSS and the ASTI negotiators on 11 July 1984. They also agreed on Draft Articles of Management for Catholic Secondary Schools, which proposed that eight-member management boards be set up, to comprise four nominees of the trustees, two elected parents and two elected teachers. With regard to parent–teacher meetings, it was agreed in the negotiated document that meetings would be held within normal school hours and would not exceed five half-day meetings in the school year.[28]

The CEC of the ASTI held a ballot of members on two of the proposals, namely on parent–teacher meetings and on boards of management, on 24 September 1985. Both proposals were passed and boards of management were now accepted by ASTI members 12 years after they had first been suggested in the FIRE report. The main reason for this acceptance was the belief that they could help prevent the danger of redundancy of lay teachers, a fear which it has been alleged 'was exploited by the CMCSS'.[29] The redeployment scheme for lay teachers in secondary schools took a further 3 years to finalise, and in 1988 it was introduced in conjunction with a voluntary redundancy scheme.

DEEDS OF TRUST FOR COMMUNITY SCHOOLS

Wilson was engaged in efforts to bring about the signing of the Deeds of Trust for community schools for the 4 years of his ministry.[30] His task was not made any easier by the banner headline 'Bishops Win School Power', which appeared on the front page of the *Irish Independent* of 18 April 1978. Its education correspondent reported that a department spokesperson had confirmed that Wilson would be signing the Deeds of Trust for Tallaght Community School shortly, and that he felt that he had a moral obligation to honour a document which had been 'negotiated under the previous administration'.[31] The ASTI and TUI were aggrieved at the lack of consultation on this matter, which was in breach of a promise Wilson had given them. He immediately confirmed that if he could get agreement, he would ensure that future community schools would include provision for teacher representation, and that there might be a subsequent revision of the deed applicable to existing schools.[32]

Wilson, who was a former president of the ASTI, made a meaningful gesture to the teachers' union when he extended an invitation to them to have direct discussions regarding the provisions of the Deeds of Trust for community schools. At this juncture, the presidents of the ASTI and the TUI issued statements critical of the Deeds of Trust as they currently stood.[33] The County Dublin VEC had strong objections to the Deeds and refused to sign them for seven schools in the county area. They wanted teachers included on boards of management and they questioned the constitutionality of reserving teaching posts in schools for the religious.[34]

Some of the Catholic religious authorities were just as forthright in their criticisms of the handling of the whole issue. Br Duffy declared that he had no intention of continuing as chairman of Tallaght Community School if it became evident that the religious were not wanted. The education correspondent of *The Irish Times* believed that there was shrewd politics being played on all sides.[35]

The CMRS issued their statement on 18 April expressing concern about the future prospects of lay teachers who might face redundancy in the future. They emphasised the fact that they agreed to join the community schools on invitation from the department in 1972, but pointed out that they were not invited to consultations on the Deeds of Trust. The ASTI was dissatisfied with the provision for reserved places for religious in community schools, but the CMRS implied in their statement that if religious places could not be reserved, then the future involvement of the religious as teachers in community schools could not be guaranteed.[36]

The ASTI representatives met with Wilson on 10 May 1978. They requested two teacher representatives on the proposed management boards for community schools, and that all boards should be similarly constituted. They used the threat of industrial action to impress upon him their fear of possible redundancies should religious orders withdraw their members from existing secondary schools and re-deploy them to reserved places in community schools.[37]

But Wilson had a trump card which he allowed his officials to play for him. They did so when they warned the ASTI that if the religious were to withdraw from community schools, either because of a refusal to grant reserved places or for any other reason, then there would be 'Enormous pressure on the Minister ... to avail himself of the provisions under the Vocational Education Act to provide schools under the VEC'.[38]

It was Burke who, as Minister in 1974, drew the attention of the VECs to Section 21 of the Vocational Education Act, 1930 which provided that 'A VEC may from time to time appoint such and so many sub-committees as it thinks proper for the exercise and performance of any of its powers, duties'.[39]

Section 21 allowed VECs to establish management boards for vocational schools, and from 1978 some VECs used Section 21 to establish what they termed community colleges rather than vocational schools. These were second-level schools which were 'similar in conception to community schools but which had a different management structure', and which were entirely under the aegis of the VECs and the department.[40] By the mid-1970s, VECs became concerned at what they viewed as an erosion of their traditional role in providing non-denominational vocational schools in favour of the new community schools. They therefore set up community colleges, but in reality many of them were renamed vocational schools, as the word 'vocational' did not have public acceptability among parents who had middle-class aspirations for their children. In order to lend status to the community colleges, representatives of the Catholic bishops were invited to participate in them in April 1979.[41]

It was at this stage that secret talks commenced between representatives of the Catholic Archdiocese of Dublin and the County Dublin VEC. The latter had refused to sign any Deeds of Trust until they had reached an agreement with the department as to the future allocation of schools in their area between those that would operate under the proposed Deeds of Trust and those that would come under Section 21 of the Vocational Education Act. Following several meetings, agreed proposals for community colleges for the Dublin Archdiocese emerged.[42] This arrangement was repeated elsewhere, when Bray VEC and County Cork VEC held separate talks with their respective local Church authorities with a view to setting up community colleges in their areas.

Progress was made following a decision taken at the TUI conference in November 1979 to withdraw the union's objections to the signing of the Deeds of Trust. The IVEA was now forced to take action, and on 1 October 1980 it entered into talks with the Episcopal Commission and the CMRS. It requested that the VECs suspend discussions with educational interests other than the department, and to delay signing the Deeds of Trust. However, the publication of the White Paper in December caused alarm in the ranks of the IVEA when it discovered that over seventy community schools had been planned for.

The White Paper stated that Section 21 schools could be established but 'local preference' had to be considered. Wilson met the IVEA to assuage fears and to give guarantees that no obstacles would be placed in the way of the development of the vocational sector, that the IVEA would be fully consulted regarding any future

development of schools and in the matter of 'local preference', and that the department would take cognisance of the views of locally elected representatives. These
assurances were sufficient to enable the IVEA to give its consent to the signing of
the Deeds of Trust. This was done on 23 February 1981, and the way was now clear
for the various VECs to make their own local arrangements for the provision of
community colleges.

On 17 January 1979, representatives of the ASTI met with representatives of
the CMRS and of the Episcopal Commission on Education, and they reached an
agreement on a revised board of management structure for community schools.
Boards would consist of ten members, comprising three representatives of the
VEC, three representatives of the religious, two parents and two teachers, and the
principal as a non-voting member.

The ASTI also reached an agreement with the CMRS and the department
on the question of the appointment of teachers of religion. The department and
the CMRS proposed that the model for the appointment of teachers of religion
adopted by the vocational schools should also be applied to the community
schools. There, the teachers of religion had a second subject, and teachers could be
moved 'sideways' if the religious authorities were not satisfied with the teaching of
religion. Wilson gave a commitment to the ASTI that if a catechetics teacher did
not have a second subject, provision would be made to qualify him or her for this.
The solution arrived at was sufficient for the ASTI to accept the operation of the
Deeds of Trust, and this was agreed to at a meeting of the CEC on 26 May 1979.[43]

The ASTI now came under pressure from department officials who informed its
officers that if consensus could not be reached within 1 week on the 1979 revised
draft Deeds of Trust, the schools which were about to open in September would
be administered under Section 21 of the Vocational Education Act. This spurred
the ASTI to action and following its special convention in April 1979, it sought
legal opinion on reserved places for religious, but it was informed that there was
nothing discriminatory or unconstitutional in this, provided the religious authorities had contributed to the building costs.

The department was growing impatient at the slow rate of progress and in a bold
political manoeuvre, it encouraged the parties involved in the Birr Community
School in County Offaly to sign the Deeds of Trust while the two principal
Church negotiators were abroad.[44] The department was hopeful that once the
Deeds of Trust had been signed in any school, the Catholic authorities would agree
to participate in the schools which were due to open in September. However,
the Catholic authorities were not so easily persuaded and two of the schools
operated with ad hoc boards, and with department inspectors as acting principals,
until matters were finally resolved. The Secondary Education Committee, which

represented the four main Protestant churches, remained silent on this issue for over 7 years, but on 9 October it issued a press statement welcoming the concept of community schools but declining the opportunity for involvement in them.[45]

On 24 March 1981, the first Deeds of Trust were signed for a community school in the Dublin area. It occasioned the following comment from the assistant secretary of the department that it was 'the light at the end of a long, dark tunnel'.[46] It took place a month after the IVEA had given its consent to the signing of Deeds of Trust for existing community schools. One commentator remarked that the outcome was a victory for the Catholic bishops because they 'could claim that they were Catholic schools and could demand and get reserved places, conditions safeguarding religion and paid Catholic chaplains for at most a 5 per cent contribution to the initial building costs'.[47]

The Secondary Education Committee did not get involved in the negotiations on the management structures of community colleges either. A concession was in fact made to minority religions in the drawing up of the Instrument of Management for Community Colleges, which was agreed between the County Dublin VEC and the Catholic Archdiocese of Dublin. Community colleges would have a ten-member board,[48] but an additional clause stated that 'Minority religious representation on boards of management will be considered by the VEC where requests … are received'.[49]

HIGHER EDUCATION

In July 1977, the Fianna Fáil government restored degree-awarding powers to the NCEA, and in March 1978 Wilson indicated that it was government policy that the NCEA should be the body responsible for the awarding of degrees, diplomas and certificates for the non-university sector. He insisted that the National College of Art and Design (NCAD), which had been an integral part of the department since 1971, and which had reached an agreement with regard to the awarding of its degrees with TCD, should submit its degrees to the NCEA. He could impose his will on the NCAD as he had appointed its board. He was less successful with the CDVEC, which by 1978 had decided not to submit any more courses to the NCEA for validation.

Both Burke and Wilson intended that the NIHED would absorb all of the third-level work of the CDVEC. Wilson confirmed this in the Dáil on 7 December 1978.[50] The committee tried to secure its position by strengthening its links with TCD, but progress was so sluggish that it decided to use its own resources by merging its six higher education colleges into a unified institution called the Dublin Institute of Technology (DIT). The committee made an order establishing the DIT to take effect on 1 September 1978. It was now in a position to offer a serious challenge to the NIHED.

Wilson was considered by many to have had an aversion to the CDVEC. He had met with the committee on one occasion in the first 3 years of his ministry. Not only that, but when the draft NCEA Bill was published in November 1978, it made no reference to the DIT or its constituent colleges. Wilson was forced to address the question of the Dublin colleges when it was put to him in the Dáil in April 1979 that 'he had made it quite clear that the NCEA would validate all third-level courses on offer by colleges under the CDVEC'. He was then asked, 'if an institute is designated must it have all its courses validated by the NCEA?', to which he replied, 'There is nothing in the Bill to prevent courses being validated otherwise'.[51]

It certainly looked as if the CDVEC had won a victory over Wilson, although it would also appear that the NCEA Bill was flawed, especially when compared with the original bill which set up the council on an ad hoc basis. The ad hoc council could consider submissions from third-level institutions in general, but the NCEA Act applied only to those colleges in the Act or designated by the Minister. Consequently, the NCEA did not have the monopoly the Minister wished for and the 'statute which was meant to copper-fasten the binary system in effect ensured that such a system could never be watertight'.[52]

In March 1977, O'Hare took up the position as director of the NIHED, and by December the governing body produced a detailed plan for the future of the institute. It avoided any reference to the transfer of existing third-level courses from the CDVEC as it probably anticipated that the committee would refuse any such transfer. This is exactly what happened in November 1978, yet Wilson informed the Dáil that he intended to continue with the transfer of courses. He then set up a body to arrange for the transfer to take place, but the CDVEC/DIT refused to co-operate.[53] The governing body came to Wilson's rescue by not insisting on the transfer of courses and by proceeding with their plans on that basis. Wilson followed suit and dropped his proposals.

The vocational sector in general and the RTCs in particular, received invaluable financial support through the ESF, a source of funding from which universities were precluded. The first students were admitted to the RTCs for the scheme for middle-level technician in the autumn of 1975. They received a training allowance of £8.30 per week, and no means test was applied. The EEC regulations stipulated, however, that the funding was for training and not for education. In Ireland, the line between training and education became blurred, and for this reason the courses received the minimum of publicity. An Economic and Social Research

Institute (ESRI) study[54] of the finance of third-level education conducted by A.C. Barlow in 1981, made no reference to the fact that courses at RTCs had been 'subvented handsomely by the fund over the previous six years', because this fact remained undocumented. Officials at the department also 'obligingly preserved the NCEA from any serious contact with, or knowledge of, the financial arrangements reached with Brussels'.[55]

The HEA-commissioned report by Clancy and Benson on higher education in Dublin, recommended the provision of at least four RTCs for Dublin to meet the needs of a growing population. One of its authors conducted a national survey of participation in higher education, and it was clear from his findings that 'Dublin and its neighbours were among the counties at the bottom of the League Table for rates of admission'.[56] The White Paper revealed plans for the provision of four new RTCs for the greater Dublin area, plans which never materialised due to the serious crisis in the public finances in the early 1980s.[57]

The White Paper was a very forthright document which declared that 'the Government was determined that its own priorities would be paramount in the allocation of funds'. One commentator detected 'signs of impatience with the HEA's status as an independent agency between the government and the higher education institutions'.[58] The White Paper concluded by saying that the Minister for Education would direct the attention of the HEA to the need for ensuring that funds made available by the government for particular projects should be appropriated accordingly.[59] The implied suggestion of misappropriation, or at least misdirection of State funds, was offensive to the HEA.

Ironically, the HEA could point to a good track record in planning and projecting insofar as its own institutions were concerned, which was in contrast to the miscalculations in the department's own projections in the White Paper. The White Paper laid considerable emphasis on the importance of subjects such as science, technology and business studies, so that one could reasonably expect development in these areas in the future, yet this was not reflected in the projections for the RTCs. It expected growth in the four RTCs proposed for Dublin but forecast that the other nine RTCs would increase by a mere 1,000 students in 10 years.[60]

The HEA made a valuable contribution to the department's policy of developing technological education. During the decade 1974–83, the growth in student numbers in HEA-funded institutions equalled that in the non-university sector, with the largest increase in student numbers being recorded in the faculties of engineering, science and commerce. Initially the Department of Industry and Commerce did not lend its support to this policy, so that the impetus had to come from the Department of Education, which was the more vibrant department in the 1960s.

The education sector was relieved of some of its burden with the establishment of the Industrial Training Authority or AnCO[61] in 1967, whose main function was the provision of trained manpower. The IDA played a vital role in bridging industrial and education policy, but it took some time for this to evolve. The first sign of change came in 1978 with the establishment of the Manpower Consultative Committee (MCC) by the Department of Labour. Its terms of reference were to advise the government on the role of manpower policy in meeting economic and social objectives. It commenced by identifying occupational shortages, and these were in the areas of engineering and computer personnel – areas generally supplied by university graduates. There were also lacunae in areas serviced by AnCO.

An important step was taken in early 1979 when the MCC met with the HEA and requested it consult with all higher education institutions in an effort to meet urgent needs in areas where shortages had been identified. This led to a sharp increase in the output of graduates in electronics, mechanical engineering and computer science. Between 1978 and 1983, engineering graduates increased by 40 per cent and computer science graduates increased tenfold in the same period.

The funding from the MCC programme greatly benefited universities such as UCG and TCD. The UCG Engineering Department doubled in size between 1979 and 1983, while engineering numbers in TCD increased by 45 per cent in the same period.[62] The HEA was a body which had served Wilson well. The statistics speak for themselves. In March 1981 there were 2,382 full-time undergraduate students in commerce and business studies and 2,891 in engineering. Ten years later the comparative figures were 4,291 and 4,373. The university sector was mirroring what was happening in the non-university sector and was playing an equally important role in meeting the country's economic and industrial needs.

John Wilson served in office for 4 years and he continued developing policies already in place to reduce the pupil–teacher ratio, and he devised a short-lived Special Trainee Graduate Teachers scheme to increase the number of teachers. In contrast to Dick Burke, he accepted parents' rights to multi-denominational schools, which he supported.

He was not a very active Minister. Pressure had to be applied by the INTO over 3 years before he produced a White Paper. He found excuses to avoid reviewing the primary curriculum, which was supposed to be kept under ongoing review. One would have expected him to rally support to pressurise the Department of Finance to reverse or reduce its swingeing cuts to the in-service budget. But his inaction led to the INTO boycotting in-service education provision for years. Further pressure had to be exercised by the INTO to force him to review the board of management structures, which should have occurred in 1978 on foot of a commitment given to the INTO 3 years previously. This resulted in the withdrawal of INTO representation on boards of management for over a year. Sustained pressure from the three teaching unions in the 1980 pay negotiations led to a spectacular victory for the teachers and humiliation for Wilson and the government, who had established a dangerous precedent.

Wilson's White Paper revealed 'signs of impatience' with the HEA's status, and it implied that the HEA had misappropriated or misdirected funds. The HEA was in fact an efficient body, unlike the Department of Education at the time, whose projections in the White Paper were inaccurate. Ironically, Wilson owed a debt of gratitude to the HEA, which was largely responsible for bringing the universities closer to the business, scientific and industrial life of the country.

Wilson's handling of the contentious issue of higher education provision for Dublin was less than sure-footed. He declared the NCEA as the body responsible for the conferring of awards to the non-university sector, even though the NCEA Bill did not give a monopoly to the NCEA in this area. He lost face when the CDVEC, a body he met only once in 3 years, decided not to submit any more courses for validation to the NCEA. He did not recognise the threat offered by the restructured CDVEC/DIT to the NIHED as he proceeded with plans to ensure that the latter would absorb all the third-level work of the former, which of course the CDVEC/DIT refused to accept. The NIHED saved the Minister's blushes by not insisting on compliance.

Wilson was well served by his hard-working officials, who capitalised on Ireland's membership of the EEC to avail of the ESF to provide popular pre-employment courses as an alternative to the academic leaving certificate. Financial assistance from Europe would help transform Irish education in the years ahead, particularly in the higher education sector.

Wilson's ministerial legacy lay in his skilful handling of the community schools Deeds of Trust negotiations, which brought a resolution to an issue which had been 'on ice' since 1973.

Notes

1 Taoiseach pays tribute to John Wilson – RTÉ news, 9 July 2007.
2 *The Irish Times*, 15 May 1976.
3 FitzGerald, *All in a Life*, p.321.
4 *Dáil Debates*, vol. 315, col. 1827, 10 July 1979.
5 Coolahan, 'Education policy', p.37.
6 *Dáil Debates*, vol. 311, cols 1681–2, 21 February 1979.
7 Op. cit., pp.37–8.
8 White Paper on Educational Development (Dublin 1980), pp.4–5.

9   Coolahan, 'Education Policy', p.52.

10 *Dáil Debates*, vol. 304, cols 1055–6, 8 March 1978.

11 *The Irish Times*, 19 August 1977. 'Go ahead given to controversial Dublin school'
    by Christina Murphy.

12 *Dáil Debates*, vol. 310, cols 1052–3, 7 December 1978.

13 *Dáil Debates*, vol. 311, col. 1688, 21 February 1979.

14 *Irish Independent*, 8 October 1979.

15 Coolahan, 'Education policy', p.57.

16 In the late 1960s Lynch dismissed Haughey for not subscribing to government policy on
    Northern Ireland. In May 1970, Haughey was charged before the courts with conspiring to
    import arms illegally; a jury later acquitted him of all charges. In 1975, under party pressure,
    Lynch invited Haughey back to his front bench and in 1977, he appointed him Minister for
    Health.

17 *The Irish Times*, 10 January 1980.

18 Coolahan, *The ASTI*, p.373.

19 Collins, *The Haughey File*, p.42.

20 Cunningham, *Unlikely Radicals*, p.211.

21 *The Irish Times*, 11 April 1980.

22 White Paper on Educational Development, Foreword by John Wilson TD,
    Minister for Education, December 1980, p.iv.

23 Coolahan and O'Donovan, *A History*, pp.226–7.

24 *Times Education Supplement*, 14 October 1977. 'Who governs? Row angers union'
    by John Walshe.

25 Speech by Derek Nolan, president of the ASTI, delivered at the Gresham Hotel in *ASTIR*,
    October 1977.

26 Derek Nolan, 'Redundancy is a real threat to teachers' in *ASTIR*, November 1977, p.1.

27 The CMCSS was a more representative, broadly based body than the CMRS or the JMB.

28 Draft document on home/school links 20 July 1984, cited in Coolahan, *The ASTI*, pp.365–7.

29 O'Flaherty, *Management and Control*, p.110.

30 *Dáil Debates*, vol. 306, col. 933, 11 May 1978.

31 *Irish Independent*, 18 April 1978.

32 *Irish Independent*, 20 April 1978.

33 *Irish Press*, 21 April 1978.

34 *The Irish Times*, 27 April 1978. 'Report of the meeting of the Dublin county VEC'.

35 *The Irish Times*, 28 April 1978.

36 O'Flaherty, *Management and Control*, p.67.

37 *The Irish Times*, 28 April 1978.

38 Op. cit., p.68.

39 Vocational Education Act, 1930, Section 21 (i).

40 Coolahan, *Irish Education*, pp.220–1.

41 O'Flaherty, *Management and Control*, p.77. In 1996 a failed High Court action against the
    State claimed that payment of chaplains was unconstitutional. An appeal to the Supreme

Court was dismissed in 1998. See Ivana Bacik, *Kicking and Screaming Dragging Ireland into the 21st Century* (Dublin, 2004).

42 Ibid., pp.75–9.
43 Barry, 'The involvement and impact of a professional interest group', p.153.
44 O'Flaherty, *Management and Control*, pp.70–1.
45 Press statement 9 October 1979 in *Journal of the General Synod of the Church of Ireland* 1980, p.170.
46 *The Irish Times*, 25 March 1981.
47 O'Flaherty, *Management and Control*, p.73. In 1996 a failed High Court action against the State claimed that payment of chaplains was unconstitutional. An appeal to the Supreme Court was dismissed in 1998.
48 Three members to be nominated by the appropriate religious authority, three by the VEC, two parents to be elected by parents of pupils in the school, two members to be elected by the whole-time teaching staff, and one member to be nominated by a minority religious group/s if so requested.
49 Op cit., pp.81–90. Model agreement for community colleges. Instrument of management.
50 *Dáil Debates*, vol. 310, col. 1052, 7 December 1978.
51 *Dáil Debates*, vol. 313, cols 997–1001, 3 April 1979.
52 White, *Investing in People*, p.148.
53 *Irish Independent*, 19 January 1979.
54 Coolahan, *Irish Education*, pp.290–1.
55 White, *Investing in People*, p.163; A.C. Barlow, *The Financing of Third Level Education* (Dublin, 1981), pp.10–20, p.16.
56 White, *Investing in People*, p.170; Patrick Clancy and Charles Benson, *Higher Education in Dublin: A Study of Some Emerging Needs* (Dublin, 1979); Patrick Clancy, *Participation Survey*, p.36.
57 White paper on Educational Development, pp.70–84.
58 Coolahan, 'Higher education in Ireland', pp.787–8.
59 White, *Investing in People*, p.70.
60 Anthony White, 'Higher technological education in the 1970s' in *Irish Educational Studies*, 1 (1981), pp.319–20.
61 An Chomhairle Oiliúna. The Apprenticeship Act of 1959 which set up An Chéard Chomhairle – The Apprenticeship Board, was repealed by the 1967 Industrial Training Act, which set up AnCO.
62 White, *Investing in People*, pp.187–8.

18

John Boland (1981-82): 'A majority of the general public agreed with him'

He was elected to Dublin County Council in 1967 at the young age of 23 …
He had the distinction of being the youngest ever Chairman of Dublin
County Council and the youngest elected Senator.[1]

A general election was looming in 1981 as inflation neared 20 per cent and
unemployment peaked at over 100,000.[2] The Stardust night club fire disaster of
14 February obliged Charles Haughey to cancel his pre-election Ard-Fheis as the
night club lay in his constituency.[3] The election was also marred by the tragic
events in Northern Ireland, where the renewal of the 1980 Maze Republican
prisoners' hunger strike for political status led to two deaths. Two more hunger
strikers died within hours of the dissolution of the Dáil on 21 May, and six more
died before polling day on 11 June.[4] Two of the hunger strikers were elected to the
Dáil and Fianna Fáil lost the election. A coalition government of Fine Gael and
Labour came to power with Garret FitzGerald who replaced Cosgrave as leader in
1977, as Taoiseach, and Michael O'Leary as Tánaiste.[5]

FitzGerald's appointment of John Boland (1944–2000), a 37-year-old Dublin
university graduate and sales representative, as Minister for Education in July 1981
raised a few eyebrows. While Boland had some parliamentary experience, having
been spokesman on Health and Social Welfare in FitzGerald's 1977 cabinet,
he had 'no familiarity with the conduct of this office and it was thought that his
somewhat caustic style would not be connotative of the diplomacy which the
post was considered to demand'.[6] But FitzGerald appointed him for his political
acumen, his 'ability to see around corners' which he believed outweighed his puta-
tively pugnacious manner.[7]

Boland appointed two educational advisors to the department. One was Dr John Harris, principal of Newpark Comprehensive School in Dublin, and Gerry Cronin, education advisor with the County Dublin VEC. The Union of Professional and Technical Civil Servants objected to what they regarded as political appointments, and they requested Boland not to proceed with his plans.[8] Boland ignored the request and his decision was later vindicated when Dr Harris was retained as an advisor by two subsequent Ministers for Education.

The coalition included in its Programme for Government a commitment to set up an independent board to deal with both curriculum and examinations. Boland made a speech in the Senate on 29 October outlining his plans for this board.[9] It proved a great source of irritation to him when his successor expressed relief in her *Cabinet Diaries*[10] at obtaining his agreement, as the then Minister for Public Service, to staffing and other arrangements for the Curriculum and Examinations Board.[11]

It was at first level that he made the most far-reaching policy changes. In introducing the supplementary estimates in December 1981, he said he had secured government approval for the recruitment of 300 extra teachers to reduce the pupil–teacher ratio in primary schools. This was the exact number of teachers who were unemployed at the time. He did so despite the fact that an embargo had been placed on additional recruitment to the public sector.[12]

Boland decided to raise the age of entry to primary schools to 4½ years. The minimum school entry age was set at 6 years under the School Attendance Act, 1926, and since 1934 the minimum age at which children could be enrolled was on or after their fourth birthday. He was in no doubt as to the educational merit of his proposal, and he had reason to believe 'that a majority of the general public agreed with him'.[13] In August 1981, he issued a circular changing the age of entry with intended effect from 1 October 1981. The INTO were not consulted on the matter, and this caused resentment and suspicion. The general view was that the decision was influenced by the Department of Finance's concern to cut back on educational expenditure.

Wilson was convinced that this was the case. He quoted from an official document from the Minister for Finance which confirmed that 'Raising the age of entry to primary schools to the compulsory age of six could save an estimated £19 million a year on teacher salaries alone when fully operational'.[14]

Boland responded to his critics by referring to the situation which prevailed in many other countries, where children were enrolled in formal schooling at a later age, so that the tradition in Ireland was quite exceptional. He neglected to mention that these countries had pre-school facilities which were lacking in Ireland. The INTO put up a strong defence for maintaining the status quo on educational and social grounds, and because many of its members would be rendered unemployed.

This issue led to 'A full-scale confrontation … between the INTO and the Minister', one in which 'The opposition party, Fianna Fáil, supported the teachers'.[15]

Boland's handling of the sensitive issue of corporal punishment in schools was the cause of further controversy. His 'snap decision' to abolish corporal punishment with effect from 1 February 1982, and his failure to negotiate alternative disciplinary strategies with the teaching unions and the school authorities, was condemned.[16] The teaching unions 'were unhappy at the alleged abrupt and overbearing manner in which this was done'.[17] Boland agreed to set up an 'informal working committee representing teachers, managers, and inspectors to examine the problem of disruptive pupils and make recommendations'.[18] The report of the committee was published in 1985. He was successful in his endeavours, and an important amendment to the Rules for National Schools was made in 1982, when Rule 130, dealing with school discipline, was amended to reflect the abolition of corporal punishment. Circular C9/82 incorporated this change and introduced more humane methods of discipline into first- and second-level schools.

He was the first Minister for Education to exhibit a keen awareness of the importance of introducing computers into second-level schools as a preparation for entry into the information society. He recognised that the world was experiencing a 'technological revolution' and that students needed to be equipped to meet that challenge. He regretted that primary schools would not benefit from this initiative, but he hoped to rectify this situation during his ministry.[19]

He confirmed that the six colleges of the CDVEC now had official recognition 'as being, collectively, the Dublin Institute of Technology'.[20] He also took steps to ensure that adequate finance was allocated for a new RTC for the greater Dublin area. Boland had plans to develop a national adult education policy, and he set up a commission on adult education with a view to the production of a development plan.[21] He was disappointed when his successor did not act on the report of the commission by Ivor Kenny.[22]

John Boland was a Minister who lacked experience but not confidence. Appointing advisors to the Department of Education was a far-seeing move which came in for criticism at the time. Raising the school entry age without consultation with the INTO or parents because it was common practice in other countries, was not plausible and left him open to the charge that the policy was motivated by financial considerations. Abolishing corporal punishment was his ministerial legacy to Irish education, but he should have consulted the teaching unions and discussed alternative disciplinary strategies before taking his 'snap decision' rather than after it.

Following the collapse of the coalition government in the wake of harsh budget proposals, and the subsequent general election in February 1982,[23] Fianna Fáil took over the reins of power for a further 9 months. During this period from March 1982 to December 1982, there were two heaves against Haughey, and three different Fianna Fáil Ministers for Education. These were Martin O'Donoghue, the Taoiseach who was Acting Minister for 21 days, and Gerard Brady. In December 1982, the coalition government was returned to power following the November general election, and it was set to provide stable government for the next 5 years. Garret FitzGerald was elected Taoiseach and the 32-year-old Dick Spring, the newly installed leader of the Labour Party, was nominated as Tánaiste.[24]

Notes

1 Brian Maye, *Fine Gael 1923-1987: A General History with Biographical Sketches of Leading Members* (Dublin, 1993), p.379.

2 *Magill*, January 1981.

3 Quinn, *Straight Left*, p.156.

4 Sweeney, *Down Down Deeper and Down*, pp.221–5.

5 In 1977 O'Leary was defeated by Frank Cluskey for leadership of the Labour Party, but in February 1982, the latter lost his seat and O'Leary was elected leader.

6 Maye, *Fine Gael 1923-1987*, p.379.

7 FitzGerald, *All in a Life*, p.362.

8 *The Irish Times*, 22 August 1981.

9 Speech by John Boland TD, Minister for Education, in Seanad Éireann to the motion 'That Seanad Éireann welcomes the government's intention to establish an independent CEB', 29 October 1981.

10 Gemma Hussey, *At the Cutting Edge, Cabinet Diaries, 1982-85* (Dublin, 1990).

11 *Sunday Business Post*, John Boland, 'A Minister's life is not for people who worry so much', 22 April 1990.

12 *Dáil Debates*, vols 331–2, cols 1008–09, 3 December 1981.

13 Maye, *Fine Gael 1923-1987*, p.380.

14 *Dáil Debates*, vols 331–2, col. 1019, 3 December 1981.

15 Coolahan, 'Education policy', p.45.

16 *The Irish Times*, 1 February 1982 'Teachers directed on school discipline'.

17 Op. cit.

18 *The Irish Times*, 1 February 1982.

19 *Dáil Debates*, vols 331–2, cols 1010–11, 3 December 1981.

20 Ibid., col. 1006.

21 Ibid., cols 1011–12.

22 *Sunday Business Post*, 22 April 1990.

23 This election is now firmly embedded in popular mythology as the election caused by the coalition government's decision to impose VAT on children's shoes, announced in the budget by Minister for Finance John Bruton.

24 O'Leary had left the Labour Party over disputes regarding the question of coalition. He joined Fine Gael.

19

Gemma Hussey (1982–86): 'We asked for bread, the bread of resources for our schools and she has offered us a stone, the stone of regionalisation'

She was thinking, making tough decisions. I wouldn't at all agree with everything she did, but she was confronting the right issues.[1]

Gemma Hussey was appointed spokesperson on Women's Affairs in 1981 by Garret FitzGerald although she was not yet an elected member of the Dáil. She was, however, leader of the Senate until February 1982, when a general election was held, following which she was elected to the Dáil. FitzGerald nominated her as Fine Gael spokesperson on the Arts, Culture and Broadcasting from June to December 1982, at which stage Fine Gael were back in power as partners in a coalition government with Labour. He then appointed her as Minister for Education, the first woman ever to occupy this office.

The poor state of the country's finances made educational cutbacks an urgent necessity for the new Minister. Within days of taking office she announced the introduction of charges for the previously free school transport system. This was a bold step to take and one which would make her very unpopular.[2]

It caused a political furore, but she persevered with her scheme although the government decided to exclude the children of social welfare recipients from it.[3] Even though she knew the risks involved in upsetting what she called 'The large, wealthy and articulate interest groups',[4] she announced cutbacks in teacher allocations in post-primary schools. The teaching unions mounted a massive campaign to force her to back down on the cuts, but she did not waiver.[5]

She could take satisfaction from the achievement of many of her policy initiatives, not least being the establishment of an Interim Curriculum and Examinations Board (CEB) in January 1984. She laid down specific terms of reference, which called on the board to 'make recommendations regarding a … unified assessment system for the junior cycle of second-level schooling to replace the present Intermediate and Group Certificate examinations'.

She wished to ensure 'that all pupils will have available to them some certification of their achievement, on reaching the end of the period of compulsory school attendance'.[6] The terms of reference spanned both primary and post-primary education and included a review of curricula and modes of assessment at both levels.[7] The Interim Board would have 2 years to complete its brief, after which it would be replaced by a statutory board. The Interim Board would not have responsibility for conducting the public examinations, but the statutory board would.

Hussey nominated Dr Edward Walsh as chairperson and Eileen Doyle was elected vice-chairperson by the board. The ASTI were dissatisfied at the composition of the CEB and complained directly to FitzGerald about their under-representation on the board. When the JMB issued a statement which was critical of board members and the Minister, she could not understand 'the destructiveness of all the interest groups' who were 'being invited right into decision making on a legal, permanent basis'.[8]

The inspectorate was concerned about plans to hand over responsibility for the public examinations to the CEB when statutorily established. This would have the effect of diminishing their 'exclusive control' of 'these central features of the education system'.[9] However, an inspector was appointed to the Interim CEB and inspectors acted on its sub-committees.

The Interim Board was in existence from January 1984 to September 1987, and during this period published a total of thirteen consultative documents, discussion papers and reports, as well as regular newsletters. Its September 1984 publication, *Issues and Structures in Education*,[10] was a consultative document and public meetings were held to discuss it. Hussey recorded that she 'was delighted to accept the CEB's first document, which they got out in double quick time'.[11]

The outcomes of the consultations became the proposals contained in the report entitled 'In Our Schools', which was published in March 1986. This was expected to be the final report of the Interim Board and a starting point for the statutory board. Legislation was prepared in 1986 for that purpose, at which stage Hussey was no longer Minister.

PROGRAMME FOR ACTION IN EDUCATION

> Never before have such detailed consultations been held with a wide range
> of educational interests.[12]

Hussey adopted a consultative approach to education policy making. This was
the strategy she adopted in relation to the Programme for Action 'which gave
substance to the very brief statement of commitments given in the Programme for
Government'.[13] She believed that there was 'a greater level of confidence in a system
where its direction has been clearly signposted'.[14] This led to her decision to publish
annual progress reports on the success or otherwise of policy implementation.

This was highly significant at the time, as the culture in the Department of
Education was one which encouraged secrecy and confidentiality.[15] This openness
of approach was welcomed by educators,[16] but her special advisor recalled how 'in
some of the consultations the working groups met with scepticism or suspicion
from the parties consulted'.[17]

The report itself was greeted with suspicion. Hussey recalled a 2-hour-long
meeting she had with the CMRS, at which she was pushed very hard for a 'clear
statement of values'.[18] Prior to the official publication of the report, the *Irish
Independent* published a leaked copy in what Hussey described as 'a massive leak of
Cabinet documentation'.[19] The education correspondent referred to the report as a
blueprint for a radical shake-up of our entire education system. Deprived students
in primary schools were to be given priority in future government spending
policies, and cash-saving measures were planned for third-level institutions.

In the early 1980s, research suggested that the Irish education system was
inequitable and was not meeting the needs of a large number of students. This was
borne out in 1980 by statistics on school leavers at second level, which showed that
one in five of those who left the school system without any qualifications ended
up unemployed a year later. The position had deteriorated by 1983 'with a massive
44.6% of the unqualified who left school last year jobless this year'.[20]

It was against this backdrop that the Programme for Action was framed.
However, the education correspondent reminded Hussey that her spending cuts
were 'in areas which hit the deprived probably more so than other sections of the
community'.[21] Pádraig Faulkner recalled that she had stated in the Programme
that she would be discriminating positively in favour of the educationally
disadvantaged.[22] He implied that this commitment would not be honoured
because it was given at a 'time when the number of remedial teachers was being
cut back'. Hussey replied that 'there had been no reduction in remedial teachers,
nor indeed in primary teachers'.[23]

In the Programme she acknowledged that the biggest challenge facing the country was the increased demand for third-level college places which would arise in the decade ahead and which would necessitate substantial funding.[24] It was proposed in the Programme to reduce 4-year degree courses to 3 years, and to promote evening degree courses and modular degree programmes. There was also a proposal to employ consultants to carry out a study identifying unit costs on a per-student and per-graduate basis.[25] These proposals were not implemented, but she got FitzGerald's support for increased funding for higher education.[26]

When introducing the estimates for education in 1984, Hussey pointed out that in 1983 some 26.1 per cent of the student body were in receipt of a grant or a scholarship, but for 1984 this had risen to 35.6 per cent. One in three students at third level had their fees paid for them, and most of them received a maintenance allowance. She herself had secured about £37 million from the ESF in March 1984. She recorded in her diary that 'The result of this would be that all the RTC students would have their fees waived and would get grants depending on how far they lived from the college'. She wondered, 'why no education minister came over and did this before now?'[27] As one commentator mused, 'She clearly had never learnt of the coup that had been achieved less than a decade previously'.[28]

In July 1984, Hussey announced the introduction of a new EEC aided Vocational Preparation and Training Programme (VPTP) as an alternative to the leaving certificate, to commence in September 1984, and which would be open to secondary-school students for the first time.[29] Some 19,000 students would receive a maintenance allowance of £30 per month for the 10-month course. But it was third-level students who stood to gain most. She announced that an expanded range of courses would be covered by the middle-level technician programme in RTCs and other VEC colleges, which would be aided by the ESF. The department was set to receive £18.6 million in EEC aid for 1984 and a doubling of that amount was expected for 1985.[30] Little wonder then that in 1984 the student intake into RTCs, colleges of technology and the NIHE colleges was greater than that into the universities, although the total number of students in universities was still greater because of the longer average duration of courses.[31]

The ESF did not extend to the university sector, and the HEA warned Hussey that the rise in university fees was a cause for concern. It argued that lack of funding prevented the initiation of courses which would meet the needs of the economy. Shortages of equipment had reached a critical level as there had been a reduction in expenditure of £9.46 million for the past 3 years. A complaint had also been made by the government-sponsored National Board for Science and Technology that its direct funding role to the universities had been eroded due to financial constraints. Consequently, universities lacked sufficiently strong links with industry.[32]

The IFUT in its response to the Programme referred to the fact that Ireland shared bottom place with Greece in the EEC tables with regard to government funding of research and development. The union contended that by neglecting fundamental research, a country would be condemning its own industry to obsolescence.[33]

It was budgetary concerns too which forced the government to impose a public sector embargo which only permitted one in three vacancies to be filled in third-level institutions. This resulted in a student staff ratio of 17:1 as student numbers had risen greatly. A total of 100 new academic posts would have been justified over the period, but the net increase amounted to only 22. Hussey was aware of the urgency of the situation and was engaged in preparing a discussion document on the options for third-level education.[34]

THE AGES OF LEARNING

On 25 June 1984, she issued her discussion paper 'The Ages of Learning' on the age of entry into the educational system, the age of transfer at subsequent levels, and the restructuring of the post-primary sector. It got cabinet approval in May 1985, following some hard bargaining with officials in the Department of Finance. In October the department sent a circular to all primary schools stating that no child should be retained in infants beyond the 30 June that followed his reaching the age of 6½ nor should he be admitted to first standard unless he had reached the age of 6 years by 1 September.[35]

When 'The Ages of Learning' was published, it received a positive reaction from the print media. Hussey was gratified by this reception and in particular the response to her plans for the 6-year post-primary cycle and transition year.[36] Boland, who had been critical of the Minister, nonetheless praised her efforts in this regard.[37]

The idea of a transition year was not new. In the 1970s, Burke had authorised a Transition Year Programme for students in the senior cycle of a small number of post-primary schools on a pilot basis. In 1985 Hussey permitted more schools to offer a Transition Year, and she requested the CEB to publish guidelines for such a programme, which it did in January 1986. Shortly afterwards the government reversed this decision to permit a 6-year senior cycle.[38]

Hussey issued another circular. This one was sent to second-level schools warning post-primary school authorities that it was unlawful to discriminate on sex or marital status when it came to selecting candidates for appointment. The circular drew attention to the code of practice as laid down by the Employment Equality Agency. A separate code of practice was being prepared for inclusion in the rules governing primary schools. The circular stipulated that when interviews were being conducted, that questions should only refer to the requirements of the job, and it recommended that interview boards should not be composed entirely of members of one sex.[39] The circular had been issued in the wake of a dismissal of a County Wexford secondary teacher, Eileen Flynn, in 1982. Her dismissal was upheld 3 years later in the High Court by Mr Justice Declan Costello.[40] A department spokesman denied that there was any connection between the circular and the controversial Flynn case.

NATIONAL PARENTS' COUNCIL

Article 42 of the 1937 Constitution guaranteed the educational rights of parents. Yet for the first four decades following Independence, parents played a peripheral role in the education of their children. In 1975 Burke invited them to join boards of management, but in the 1980s Hussey recognised that 'The education process' was 'a co-operative venture' and that it was crucial that parents should participate in educational planning. With this in mind, preliminary meetings were arranged by the department with the existing national body of parents to discuss the establishment of a National Parents' Council[41] (NPC). In 1985 Hussey provided funds to facilitate the establishment of such a council, and she designated a range of issues on which the department would formally consult with the NPC.[42]

Storm clouds gathered on the industrial relations front. In August 1985, a report that the Public Service Arbitrator was to award a further 10 per cent on top of the general public service increase to teachers was leaked to RTÉ. A week later Boland, as Minister for the Public Service, issued government-sanctioned guidelines for a pay freeze for 12 months with no special awards. The ASTI threatened to strike in Wicklow and North Dublin, the constituencies of Hussey and Boland, respectively. Later in a speech delivered in her own constituency, Hussey offended teachers by questioning the morality of pursuing their pay claims 'which would require severe cuts in services to find them'[43] and which would be at the expense of less well-off workers. 'The speech enraged teachers and was generally seen as a diplomatic blunder.'[44]

The following morning, during the course of a radio interview, she used the word 'morality' again when discussing teachers' demands for £170 million more in pay on top of the public service increases that they had already received.[45] In response to a question, she replied that the government did not have the money to pay the 10 per cent. The teachers responded immediately by threatening 1-day strikes. All this occurred before the arrival of the official report of the Public Service Arbitrator. In September the teaching unions announced the establishment of a 'Teachers United' campaign, and a series of 1-day strikes was organised to start on 6 November. A month later some 20,000 teachers drawn from the ASTI, the TUI and the INTO protested in Croke Park.

Hussey felt herself under siege as cabinet support dwindled.[46] Nonetheless, on 14 November she launched the Green Paper, Partners in Education Serving Community Needs,[47] which proposed the regionalisation of education and the establishment of thirteen Local Education Committees (LECs). The last attempt to introduce regionalisation had foundered and the prospects for the success of this one were slight. On this occasion, primary schools were to be excluded from the responsibilities of the LECs, possibly because they were operating so well under the new boards of management.[48] The Green Paper was badly received.[49]

Mary O'Rourke, the Fianna Fáil spokesperson on Education, viewed the regionalisation proposals as an attempt to bypass the Fianna Fáil controlled VECs by abolishing them. She favoured the 'county' as opposed to the 'regional' unit for any decentralisation of education decision-making. The Catholic Secondary School Parents Association expressed their alarm that such far-reaching proposals should be put forward 'At a time of conflict with teachers' unions and when educational cuts are eating into the proper provision of ordinary classes'.[50]

The CMCSS complained that Catholic schools had 'asked for bread, the bread of resources for our schools, and she has offered us a stone, the stone of regionalisation'.[51] Hussey 'couldn't believe her eyes' when she read this response.[52] The CMCSS turned down her invitation to talks, stating that it would only do so when action was taken to redress the cuts in secondary education.[53] The CMRS, the CMCSS and the Episcopal Commission prepared a joint response questioning the merit of proposals for regionalisation at a time when the Department of Health was 'frantically attempting to restore some order to a (regionalised) health service which had gone out of control'.[54]

The Protestant sector was concerned about the suggestion in the Green Paper that LEC representatives would sit on the boards of management of all schools. The Secondary School Council of Governors responded that it could 'not imagine that the government would contemplate, against the expressed will of the Church of Ireland, the Methodist Church and the Presbyterian Church, imposing Roman Catholics on Protestant schools'.[55] The IVEA dismissed the proposed regional structures as 'hopelessly large' and alleged that their purpose was to strengthen 'centralised control of all post-primary education'.[56]

Undaunted, Hussey informed her audience at the Fourth John Marcus O'Sullivan Memorial Lecture that she planned to go back to the government in the early summer with recommendations arising from the discussions and submissions on the Green Paper. She hoped that the necessary legislation would be enacted before the end of the year. It was to be a vain hope.

TEACHING UNIONS INVITED TO TALKS

The government issued an invitation to the three teaching unions to talks, which commenced in January 1986. A new political party, the Progressive Democrats, which was spearheaded by disaffected Fianna Fáil members Desmond O'Malley and Mary Harney, was overtaking Fine Gael in the opinion polls, and there was therefore pressure on the government to resolve the dispute speedily. Hussey and Boland met with the General Secretaries of the INTO, ASTI and the TUI for discussions. The negotiations were conducted mainly by Boland, but when they eventually ended in a walk-out by the unions, Hussey suffered the backlash as 'the dispute had become personalised in Mrs. Hussey, against whom the teachers' unions waged an unrelenting campaign'.[57]

Just as the teachers' pay dispute reached its climax, she 'was hit by another torpedo' with regard to the cabinet decision to close Carysfort College. There had been considerable overcapacity in the teacher training system, and it was estimated that by the end of the 1980s the remaining Colleges of Education would have four times as many places as would be required.[58] In addition to falling births, cutbacks in public spending for education resulted in the drive to reduce primary school class sizes being severely curtailed. Fewer teachers left the teaching profession at this time, and the number of retirements had declined remarkably. All of these factors, coupled with the department's failure in the area of manpower planning for primary teaching, led to the dramatic fall in the demand for teachers.[59]

While Hussey was still engaged in private discussions with the college authorities and preparing to make the official announcement, O'Rourke, announced the closure of Carysfort 'in the Dáil to an apparently horrified world'.[60] The editor of *The Irish Times* admonished Hussey for her method of communicating to those involved, the news of the closure 'of this college with its proud tradition'. He said, 'It seems to have been precipitate and insensitive. Surely the Sisters of Mercy deserved to be treated with more dignity after a century of achievement'.[61]

Hussey made one desperate bid to prevail upon the teaching unions to return to the pay talks, and to call off their planned strike. She did so in the Dáil in a style reminiscent of Derrig's appeal to the Dublin primary school teachers prior to their strike in 1946. She said, 'I am asking them to put the country first for the sake of its children and to avoid … causing major disruption to the education system'.

O'Rourke moved an amendment calling on the government to accept in principle the report of the independent arbitrator, and to enter into immediate negotiations with the teaching unions. She accused Hussey of being 'visibly hostile to teachers' and of uniting 'managements, teachers, parents and pupils in a determined bid to oppose her proposals at every level'. She derided her plea to teachers as being 'laced' with 'unctuous verbiage'.[62]

The Taoiseach reshuffled his cabinet on 13 February 1986, and moved Hussey from the Department of Education. He did so in order to safeguard her political future as she occupied a marginal seat in County Wicklow. He had intended to create a special Department of European Affairs for her, but the Labour Minister for Health, Barry Desmond, refused to move from the Department of Health. Hussey was left with the Ministry of Social Welfare, an appointment generally regarded as a demotion for her.[63] She considered herself to have been 'the victim of expediency'.[64] Patrick Cooney (1931–) was appointed Minister for Education on seniority grounds, even though FitzGerald considered him to be 'of a conservative bent' and lacking Hussey's 'commitment to educational reform'.[65]

There was a breakthrough in the teachers' pay talks on 19 February following a cordial meeting between Cooney and representatives of the teaching unions. As a gesture of goodwill towards Cooney and towards parents, the unions agreed not to boycott the leaving certificate oral Irish and music examinations at Easter. *The Irish Times* reported that Cooney and Enda Kenny,[66] the Minister of State at the Department of Education, had 'an exchange of views' with the union leaders at their meeting, which one union source described as 'the first element of decent relations between teachers and the Department of Education in six months'. Cooney issued a statement expressing gratitude for their goodwill gesture.

It seemed certain that in view of their 'courteous' meeting with Cooney, that the unions would delay strike action until the first week in March to give the Minister 'an extra weeks' breathing space'. At this stage teachers felt that they had 'already secured a moral victory in effectively toppling the former Minister for Education, Mrs. Hussey'.[67] A round of regional strikes took place in March 1986, but the beginning of a resolution surfaced on 16 April against a background of student strikes and protest marches by parents and the NPC.[68]

Ruairí Quinn as Minister for Labour and Cooney were charged with negotiating a resolution to the bitter pay dispute. In Quinn's account of events, the three teaching unions succeeded in mounting a very effective campaign. Negotiations continued for the best part of 3 weeks, and on the eve of May Day the two Ministers and their senior officials stayed up all night in the department, awaiting a response from the trade union side. It arrived a few days later 'by way of a phone call to Ruairí Quinn at 3.30 in the morning' seeking urgent approval for a salary rise slightly above what had been agreed at the cabinet table, but one which would not have a knock-on effect on other public service claims. Quinn contacted Cooney, and without consulting the cabinet or Fitzgerald, both men agreed to the deal.[69]

Cooney served as Minister for Education from 14 February 1986 to 10 March 1987. Settling the bitter, long-running teachers' pay dispute marked his major achievement as Minister. He displayed little enthusiasm for proceeding with plans to put the CEB on a statutory footing, or for implementing the Green Paper proposals.

Hussey, like her European counterparts was concerned about teacher education – 'teacher development, including pre-service and inservice education' or what she called the 'professionalism of education'.[70] In 1984 the 'OECD Ministers for Education' issued a 'statement of priority', calling for 'The recruitment, working conditions and training of teachers ... to be re-examined'.[71] She invited the OECD to report on the Irish education system, with special reference to teacher education.[72]

Gemma Hussey's ministerial legacy to Irish education is significant. She provided a blueprint for the overhaul of the education system in her Programme for Action and conducted detailed consultations on it. She introduced a partnership approach to policy making by bringing the educational partners together in the CEB, and by taking parents into the education decision-making process through the NPC. She published progress reports and introduced new accountability measures into a department that had made a virtue out of secrecy and confidentiality. She secured a massive amount of funding from the ESF, which benefited second-level students and third-level technological students. Finally, she invited the OECD to report on the education system, thereby ensuring that Irish education would be subject to European scrutiny and comparison, and in so doing she set an example that others would follow.

Gemma Hussey had an unshakeable belief in the correctness of her opinion that the teachers' pay claim was immoral. Her 'morality speech' was a diplomatic blunder which led to 1-day strikes and a protest by 20,000 teachers in Croke Park. Launching her Green Paper during the dispute was another mistake, as she had little hope of gaining the co-operation of those she needed to introduce her reforms. A promising ministerial career in education was ended in order to save her political career.

Notes

1   *The Irish Times*, 10 September 1968. 'How O'Malley launched free schooling', Christina Murphy interview with Seán O'Connor, retired secretary of the Department of Education.

2   *The Irish Times*, 4 February 1999. 'Who'd be in politics?', Eileen Battersby interview with Gemma Hussey, former Minister for Education.

3   Maye, *Fine Gael 1923-1987*, p.370.

4   Hussey, *At the Cutting Edge*, p.23, 5 January 1983.

5   *The Irish Times*, 14 February 1986. 'Hussey's image clouded an energetic ministry' by Christina Murphy.

6   Áine Hyland and Kenneth Milne (eds), *Irish Educational Documents* 11 (Dublin, 1992), p.291.

7   Áine Hyland, 'The interim Curriculum and Examinations Board 1984-1987: a retrospective view' in Gerry McNamara, Kevin Williams and Donald Herron (eds) *Achievement and Aspiration: Curricular Initiatives in Irish Post-primary Education in the 1980s* (Dublin, 1990), p.3.

8   Hussey, *At the Cutting Edge*, p.85, 10 January 1984, 17 January 1984.

9   Coolahan and O'Donovan, *A History*, p.208.

10 It proposed some school-based assessment and the 1986 document favoured phasing out the junior cycle examination.

11 Op. cit., p.121, 11 September 1984.

12 Programme for Action in Education (Dublin, 1984), Foreword by Gemma Hussey, Minister for Education, January 1984.

13 The fourth annual John Marcus O'Sullivan memorial lecture by Mrs Gemma Hussey TD, Minister for Education (Kerry, 1986), pp.1–39, p.10.

14 Ibid., p.36.

15 Coolahan and O'Donovan, *A History*, p.211, p.197.

16 Coolahan, 'Education policy for national schools', pp.71–2.

17 John Harris, 'The policy-making role of the Department of Education' in Mulcahy and O'Sullivan (eds) *Irish Education Policy*, pp.7–25, p.17.

18 Hussey, *At the Cutting Edge*, p.98, 8 March 1984.

19 Ibid., p.71, 3 December 1983.

20 *Irish Independent*, 2 December 1983. 'Education plan: a move to boost early schooling' by John Walshe.

21 Ibid.

22 Programme for Action, p.1.

23 *The Irish Times*, 25 May 1984. '8% Rise in estimate for Department of Education this year'.

24 Programme for Action, p.28.

25 Ibid., p.40.

26 Fitzgerald, *All in a Life*, p.452.

27 Hussey, *At the Cutting Edge*, p.101.

28 White, *Investing in People*, p.164. See John P. Wilson, footnote 54.

29 Coolahan and O'Donovan, *A History*, p.227.

30 *Irish Independent*, 31 July 1984. 'Pupils to get £300 to stay in school' by John Walshe.

31 *The Irish Times*, 25 May 1984.

32 *Irish Independent*, 30 July 1984. 'Hussey warned on fees crisis' by John Walshe.

33 *Programme for Action in Education 1984 to '87, the IFUT Response* (Dublin, 1984), p.11.

34 Op. cit.

35 Circular 27/85, Department of Education, October 1985.

36 Hussey, *At the Cutting Edge*, p.158, 18 May 1985.

37 Boland, 'A Minister's life is not for people who worry so much'.

38 Hyland and Milne, *Irish Educational Documents* 11, p.305.

39 *Irish Independent*, 25 July 1984. 'Schools warned over discrimination' by John Walshe.

40 *The Irish Times*, 9 February 1985. Eileen Flynn had a relationship with a married man. She was dismissed from her job because her lifestyle was not considered to be in keeping with the ethos and mores of the school that she had worked in.

41 *The Irish Times*, 25 May 1984.

42 Circular 7/85, Department of Education.

43 Hussey, *At the Cutting Edge*, p.137.

44 *The Irish Times*, 14 November 1985.

45 Hussey, *At the Cutting Edge*, p.170, 21 August 1985.

46 Ibid., p.178, 5 November 1985.

47 *Partners in Education Serving Community Needs* (Dublin, 1985).

48 Coolahan, 'Education policy for national schools', p.47.

49 Hussey, *At the Cutting Edge*, p.179, 13 November 1985.

50 *The Irish Times*, 13 November 1985. 'Hussey plans under attack' by Christina Murphy.

51 *The Irish Times*, 14 November 1985.

52 Hussey, *At the Cutting Edge*, p.179, 13 November 1985. On 15 November 1985, Hussey
    recorded the historic Anglo-Irish agreement signed by Garret FitzGerald and Margaret
    Thatcher, which was the forerunner to the Good Friday Agreement of April 1998.

53 Br Declan Duffy, Letter from CMCSS to Department of Education, 2 December 1985.

54 Episcopal Commission for Education/Education Commission of the CMRS/CMCSS,
    Response on local education structures, 10 March 1986.

55 Secondary School Council of Governors, Partners in education, submission to the Minister
    for Education, February 1986.

56 IVEA, The VEC response, 26 February 1986.

57 *The Irish Times*, 14 February 1986.

58 FitzGerald, *All in a Life*, p.621.

59 *The Irish Times*, 6 February 1986. 'Carysfort a victim of falling rolls' by Christina Murphy.

60 Hussey, *At the Cutting Edge*, pp.194–5, 4 February 1986.

61 *The Irish Times*, 6 February 1986. Editorial 'End of a boom'.

62 *The Irish Times*, 6 February 1986. 'Hussey urges teachers to put country first'.

63 *The Irish Times*, 14 February 1986. 'Desmond defiant in reshuffle as Hussey leaves education'
    by John Cooney, political correspondent.

64 Hussey, *At the Cutting Edge*, p.197, 14 February 1986.

65 FitzGerald, *All in a Life*, p.624.

66 Enda Kenny has been Taoiseach since 2011. He has led the Fine Gael party since 2002.
He is the longest-serving TD currently in Dáil Éireann.

67 *The Irish Times*, 20 February 1986. 'Teachers likely to defer strikes after new talks'
    by Christina Murphy.

68 See Cunningham, *Unlikely Radicals*, p.222 for detailed account.

69 Quinn, *Straight Left*, p.231.

70 The fourth annual John Marcus O'Sullivan memorial lecture by Mrs Gemma Hussey, p.65.

71 OECD, 'OECD Ministers discuss education in modern society', Paris, 1985, cited in
    John Coolahan, *Teacher Education in the Nineties: Towards a New Coherence* (Limerick, 1991),
    p.15.

72 John Coolahan, 'Education for the 1990s' in John Quinn (ed.) *The Open Mind Guest
    Lectures, 1989-1998* (Dublin, 1999), p.5.

20

Mary O'Rourke (1987–91): 'Curriculum reform was one of my main priorities'

All those present must have been encouraged by the Minister's positive approach to problems and difficulties, and openness to fresh ideas. She had spoken throughout like a true educator.[1]

Following the February 1987 general election, the Progressive Democrats party won fourteen seats, and Fianna Fáil and Fine Gael tied on eighty-two seats each.[2] Haughey was elected Taoiseach on the casting vote of the Ceann Chomhairle. Mary O'Rourke (1937–), a former secondary teacher, was appointed Minister for Education on 11 March 1987. She was first elected to the Dáil in November 1982, having previously been elected to the Senate in 1981 and 1982. Now she was about to make history as she and her brother Brian Lenihan, a former Minister for Education, became the first ever brother and sister to serve together in an Irish cabinet.[3]

Haughey, who had presided over a failed economy in 1982, now recognised the urgency of coming to grips with the enormous national debt.[4] He succeeded in getting the trade unions, employers and farmers to agree to a new pay deal. This consensus deal, known as the Programme for National Recovery, was reached on 9 October 1987 and was set to run for 3 years. It was based on a 1986 report, entitled 'Strategy for Development', which was produced by the National Economic and Social Council (NESC).[5] All subsequent social partnership agreements were preceded by a NESC strategy report.[6]

The agreement enabled the government to publish the book of estimates for 1988 which contained spending cuts amounting to £485 million. To introduce such austerity measures would require the co-operation of the main opposition party, and Alan Dukes,[7] the new leader of Fine Gael, agreed to co-operate. In a speech delivered to the Tallaght Chamber of Commerce, he stated 'that for as long as the minority Fianna Fáil government implemented Fine Gael economic and fiscal policies, they could rely on Fine Gael support in the Dáil'. This pledge of support was known as the Tallaght Strategy,[8] and it provided the government with the political stability necessary to bring the country's finances under control.

In November 1987, the government faced a crisis following a cabinet decision to introduce educational cutbacks. O'Rourke had to issue Circular 20/87[9] which aimed at reducing the number of primary teachers and at increasing the pupil–teacher ratio. This drew an angry response from the INTO and from parents, which found expression in well-organised street demonstrations. O'Rourke sought the backing of education correspondents in the print media to assist her in avoiding cutbacks she knew to be educationally unsound but which she was obliged to support as a cabinet member. The editor of *The Irish Times* agreed to do so.[10]

She offered a Quota Review Committee to soften the effects of the cuts on schools in disadvantaged areas and in special schools. This was rejected by the INTO and by parents' representatives. Following a weekend of protests in O'Rourke's constituency and elsewhere, one of which necessitated the assistance of the gardaí to restore order, O'Rourke indicated a willingness to expand the scope of the Quota Review Committee to include the 1,000 schools most affected by the cuts. *The Irish Times* editorial advised the protestors that 'it would be short-sighted to turn their backs on this latest offer'.[11]

On 24 November, the government was defeated in the Dáil on a Fine Gael private member's motion which called for a rejection of the educational cutbacks. O'Rourke suffered the wrath of her cabinet colleagues for 'Leaking the announcement of this Committee ... but after some recriminations at cabinet, it was decided to adopt it, as a basis for a deal with Fine Gael on their Dáil motion'.[12] She suspended Circular 20/87,[13] and on 11 December Haughey promised to maintain the quality of Irish primary schools. A joint Review Group of the government and the INTO was then established.[14]

CURRICULUM REFORM

When I became Minister for Education, curriculum reform was one of my main priorities.[15]

The Interim CEB was replaced by a new advisory body to the department, called the National Council for Curriculum and Assessment (NCCA). This was a significant policy decision as it ensured 'that decision making on curricular issues, and responsibility for the public examinations remained firmly under the Department of Education's control'.[16]

O'Rourke then announced the setting up of the Primary Curriculum Review Body in October 1987, within weeks of the disbandment of the CEB. Some members of the CEB felt 'disappointment that this *Review* was to be carried out by a separate body'.[17] No doubt this disappointment was ameliorated somewhat by the fact that the NCCA had the same chairperson and the same vice-chairperson as the CEB, and that the permanent executive was also the same. They could take comfort also from the appointment of Albert Ó Ceallaigh, former CEO of the CEB, as Chief Executive of the NCCA and as secretary of the Primary Curriculum Review Body.

The council was instructed by the department to prioritise plans for the implementation of a unified system of assessment and certification at junior cycle, for a new programme called the junior certificate. In 1988 O'Rourke was in a position to announce the introduction of the junior certificate examination from September 1989. The junior certificate would supersede the intermediate and group certificate examinations from 1992.[18] The NCCA had direct responsibility for primary curriculum development, but by 1988 two separate review bodies had been established, one to examine the primary curriculum and the other to examine the primary education system in general. The latter arose from the recent conflict over the pupil–teacher ratio. Concern was now being expressed that 'consistency and cohesion of approach may be put in jeopardy'.[19]

It should be pointed out that the Primary Education Review Body (PERB), which was set up in February 1988, had access to the Report of the Review Body for over 7 months prior to the publication of its own report in December 1990. This no doubt would have ensured a consistency of approach by the two bodies.

The rationale for reviewing the curriculum was set out by Moya Quinlan, the chairperson of the Review Body. She referred to the major social, economic and cultural changes which had taken place in Ireland. The expansion in the pupil population, the new developments in educational thinking, and the educational benefits which resulted from Ireland's entry into the EEC, meant that changes to the curriculum were urgently required.[20]

Among the recommendations of the Review Body was a call for a reduction in class size, initially in the junior classes, and 'a national programme of inservice training for teachers'.[21] The report urged that 'concise statistical abstracts of important features of the education system be issued regularly and promptly'. But the key recommendation was for a major overhaul of an outdated curriculum.[22]

O'Rourke had access to the PERB report from 1989 and she acted on some of its recommendations. It urged that 'the pupil–teacher ratio be reduced immediately to 25.0:1'.[23] It suggested also that additional remedial teachers should be appointed, and O'Rourke sanctioned additional remedial posts in January 1990, bringing the total number to 890. It also recommended that new criteria should be set down, and rigidly adhered to, in the allocation of all remedial teaching posts. In early 1989 the department issued guidelines on remedial teaching.

In 1984 schools for inclusion in the Schemes of Assistance to Schools in Designated Areas of Disadvantage were selected following consultation with the department's inspectorate. O'Rourke accepted the report of a working party representative of the department, the INTO and management, which established criteria for the identification of schools which were to be designated as disadvantaged. The criteria included the number of families in local authority housing, the number with medical cards, the rate of unemployment and the judgment of the local inspector. The government permitted a threefold increase in funding for the schemes during 1990. However, the PERB report pointed out that the schemes applied predominantly to urban areas, although there was serious disadvantage in evidence in rural areas where the percentage of families who lived on social welfare was high. As many of the schools in such areas would be too small to be included in the existing additional teacher scheme, it suggested that extra financial assistance should be considered for them.

The PERB report referred to studies carried out in Rutland Street from 1969 to 74 and in Connemara in the 1980s, which demonstrated the effectiveness of early intervention in disadvantaged areas and the value of good home/school relations. They recommended the 'feasibility of applying the experience gained from the pilot projects to other areas to be investigated'.[24] Many schools in disadvantaged areas had already forged strong links with parents, local groups and voluntary organisations, well before the official launch of the Home School Community Liaison Scheme (HSCLS) by O'Rourke in November 1990. The national coordinator of the scheme, Dr Concepta Conaty, had been implementing the scheme as principal of a Dublin primary school for the previous 10 years.[25] The scheme included fifty-five primary schools in designated areas of disadvantage, and by 1991 it was extended to thirteen second-level schools with designated status. Six years later, an OECD study made specific mention of Ireland's HSCLS as 'a good example of innovative central government initiatives'.[26]

SPECIAL EDUCATION

The PERB report considered special education provision and it referred to the fact that developments in this area derived primarily from recommendations in the Report of the Commission of Inquiry on Mental Handicap in 1965.

The commission came down mainly in favour of special schools and it did not question the value of segregated provision or the distinct delineation of children with different levels of learning disability. It saw a place for special classes for children with mild general learning disabilities in mainstream schools. The commission also 'accepted the prevailing medical model of service provision'.

While progress was made in education provision for children with special educational needs, less than half of those requiring special education had recourse to it. This was due to a lack of a comprehensive educational psychological service. Responsibility for assessments remained with the Department of Health, but it could do little in the circumstances.[27] O'Rourke was aware of this deficiency. She told an OECD review group on 30 November 1989 that 'current psychological services to primary schools were clinically based but what was needed was school-based services, mediated through the teachers'.[28] The psychological service of the department was mainly involved in the provision of services to post-primary schools, but O'Rourke spearheaded two pilot schemes to provide comprehensive psychological services in the West Tallaght/Clondalkin area and in South Tipperary. The PERB recommended that 'a structured psychological service for primary schools' should be established.[29]

The child-centred curriculum made the ordinary primary school a much more suitable place for children with special educational needs, and a department circular in 1977 'proposed that children with a mild general learning disability could be accommodated in special classes in an ordinary school'. The White Paper confirmed that integration of children with special education needs into mainstream classes was the government's official policy. In 1987 O'Rourke, in common with other Ministers for Education of the European Community, subscribed to a declaration to pursue a policy of integration, but she expressed reservations about the practicability of this policy in certain circumstances.[30] The PERB claimed that 'in many instances partial integration may be the only feasible option'.[31]

The Irish special education policy was being increasingly influenced by European and international developments. The 1989 United Nations Convention on the Rights of the Child explicitly incorporated the rights of children with disabilities to an appropriate high-quality education suited to their needs. The Irish Government signed up to this commitment in 1992.[32] O'Rourke took an important step in the early 1990s to honour her 1987 declaration when she accepted the recommendation of the PERB by establishing the Special Education Review Committee. This was set up to examine how the existing system could be resourced in order that the policy of integration could be effectively implemented.

The PERB report also dealt with the education of children of Traveller families. Progress in this area was barely perceptible over three decades. In 1963 the Report of the commission on Itinerancy stated that 'It is clear that almost no itinerant children attend school'.[33] Government policy on Traveller children's education remained one of 'flexible integration'. In 1968 the first special school for Traveller children was established in Ballyfermot. It subsequently closed, but four others were opened in the following years.[34] The Traveller community was slow to respond to these provisions and attendance at special classes or in mainstream rural classes continued to be very poor.

By the mid-1980s, the department recognised the need for greater provision of pre-school facilities for Traveller children. It funded eighteen pre-schools in 1984, and by May 1991 it had funded forty-seven in total. In addition, further pre-schools were financed either by local authorities or by voluntary organisations such as Barnardos, the St Vincent de Paul Society and Traveller Support Groups.[35] Schools were permitted to appoint a Traveller resource teacher if an average of fifteen Traveller children was attained in two consecutive quarters.

But it was the decision taken in 1980 to establish a visiting teacher service which marked the turning point in the development of the education of Traveller children. By the early 1990s, nine primary teachers were appointed as visiting teachers under the management of a department inspector. The visiting teachers exemplified 'the very best of the home school community liaison approach'.[36] They also co-operated with the inspectorate in conducting detailed surveys of education provision for these children. Their work was greatly facilitated by the growth of pre-schools, which were attended by 563 Traveller children in 1988.[37] The PERB recommended the expansion of the visiting teacher service.[38] In 1992 the post of National Education Officer for Travellers was instituted and in 1993 thirty-one new Special Teachers for Travellers were sanctioned, bringing the total to 188 in 159 primary schools.[39]

The PERB report supported the statement of policy in relation to multi-denominational education as set out in the Programme for Action 1983–84.[40] O'Rourke was a champion of parents' rights in education and she continued to give government funding to the NPC. Like Wilson, she supported multi-denominational schools, and she granted permission 'for such schemes to be progressed: in Bray and Ranelagh and then Swords, Cork, Sligo, Kilkenny, North Bay Dublin, and Rathfarnham'.[41]

The PERB report gave details of the preferential treatment All-Irish schools received from the government. Like multi-denominational schools, initial recognition for these schools was provisional and was reviewed in the light of enrolment trends. The department assisted All-Irish schools with any rental costs incurred. In the case of permanent buildings, the cost of the site and the building was borne by the State, which then assumed ownership of the school. All-Irish schools also

enjoyed more favourable conditions in relation to pupil–teacher ratios, staff allowances, capitation grants and school transport. As the more favourable treatment
afforded to All-Irish schools was having an unfavourable impact on enrolment
figures in surrounding schools, it was recommended 'That the implications of this
be examined further'.[42]

TEACHER EDUCATION

Historically, the teacher was placed on a pedestal in Irish society.[43] It was clear
from submissions made to the OECD team who reviewed national policies for
education in various countries, that teachers were held in high regard in Ireland,
unlike in other countries. In comparative terms, Irish teachers were well paid, with
92 per cent of expenditure on primary schools and more than 70 per cent of
expenditure on secondary schools going towards teachers' salaries.[44] The primary
teaching profession attracted candidates of high academic quality, whose results
'in their final school examination … would have comfortably guaranteed them a
university place'.[45]

There were two models of teacher education in Ireland, the concurrent model
and the consecutive model. Under the concurrent model, students concentrated
on specific academic subjects and educational theory, and engaged in teaching
practise in the classroom. Under the consecutive model, students first took a
general university degree and then spent 1 year in a College of Education in order
to study educational theory and to undertake teaching practise in the classroom.
The PERB recommended the continuation of the training of the majority of
primary teachers through the concurrent method.[46]

In 1986 Hussey commissioned The International Study Group to consider the
case for a new technological university for Ireland. The group recommended that
the status of the two NIHEs should be raised to that of independent universities,
a recommendation which O'Rourke gave legislative effect to in 1989. This was a
historic event as the government recognised the first two new universities since the
foundation of the State, namely Dublin City University (DCU) and the University
of Limerick (UL).[47] It considered 'that degree options between the Colleges of
Education and these universities might also be explored'.[48] In November 1991,
a memorandum of understanding was issued by Mary Immaculate College,
Limerick and the UL about a future linkage.[49] It was only a matter of time before
St Patrick's College, Drumcondra and DCU would follow a similar course.

The OECD reviewers promoted the idea of career-long education and training,
and suggested a nationwide induction and in-service system using the concept of a

career-long development of teachers.[50] O'Rourke informed them that 'The financial provision for inservice training … would increase again in 1990 to become significantly more than double the 1988 figure'.[51] The increase in in-service funding was long overdue, as expenditure in this area came to a mere 0.004% of the annual education budget.[52] The need was all the greater as an early retirement scheme had been introduced for teachers, as well as a scheme of career breaks in 1985–86.

O'Rourke established a working party in April 1990 under the chairmanship of Liam Ó Laidhin, former secretary of the Department of Education, to examine and report on the setting up of a Council for Teachers.[53] It was expected to issue a report before the end of 1990, but no report was published.

DEPARTMENT OF EDUCATION

Four separate reports passed judgment on the inspectorate in the early 1990s. The Review Body recommended that external inspection of primary schools, both on a 'whole school' basis and on an 'individual teacher' basis, should continue. They also urged internal evaluation by the school staff acting as a team, linked to school plans drawn up under the leadership of the school principal. They recommended that inspector numbers should 'be brought up to full strength' in line with staffing levels recommended in the report of the Department of the Public Service in 1981.[54]

The PERB report observed that a characteristic of the work of the primary inspectorate had been 'the mushrooming complexity of special duties', and they called for expansion of the service to be addressed.[55] They recommended that the inspectors should be fully involved in departmental policy formulation, and that a new style of annual report should be issued by the department incorporating the professional views of the inspectorate.[56]

The OECD review of the Irish education system concurred with these recommendations.[57] However, it suggested that if the inspectorate was to remain at its present size, then it should shed some of its existing duties, such as its involvement with the examinations and the delivery of in-service training for teachers, in order to concentrate on auditing school performance and advising the Minister. O'Rourke's response to the OECD reviewers was that 'as an increase in the number of inspectors was unlikely to occur, this might necessitate a gradual phasing out of their duties in connection with the examinations'.[58]

At this time the EEC was concerned about the role of the inspectorate, and in 1988 it commissioned a report from Dr Clive Hopes of the German Institute for International Research, on the inspectorate in EEC countries. The Country

Report for Ireland was prepared by two inspectors who highlighted the 'under-staffing, poor promotion prospects and the lack of incentives to join the inspectorate' as well as the gender imbalance within the inspectorate.[59]

Hopes' review prompted Noel Lindsay, the secretary of the department, to invite him in April 1990 to conduct a review of the role and functions of the Irish schools inspectorate. The last such appraisal took place in 1927. Hopes presented his report in May 1990, and it was highly critical of an inefficient system of inspection which required reform at every level. His report called for a major increase in staffing, but no further action was taken.

The main criticism of the department by the various review bodies was that there was an absence of systematic policy making. O'Rourke established a Primary Education Policy Unit 'in order to strengthen the policy and planning function of the Department'. The Unit had responsibility for implementing and overseeing a comprehensive strategic plan for the development of primary education.[60]

DRAFT GREEN PAPER

The 1989 coalition government of Fianna Fáil and the Progressive Democrats[61] agreed a Programme for Economic and Social Progress (PESP) with the social partners in January 1991, to follow on from the Programme for National Recovery. As part of the programme, the government committed itself to the preparation of a comprehensive Green Paper on education, to be followed by a White Paper and a wide-ranging Education Act.

The Irish education system was administered by a series of ministerial circulars issued from the department and addressed to schools and school managements, setting out the rules to govern the system. These supplemented the Rules for National Schools and the Rules for Secondary Schools. The primary school framework had no statutory foundation but according to the PERB report, the term 'statutory' was not co-extensive with the term 'legal', and there were 'many instances in which the courts have regarded such circulars as binding'. It nonetheless recommended 'a statutory basis for primary education'.[62]

The OECD reviewers commented on the 'patchwork' character of the Irish education system and observed that 'It was not planned methodically but expanded in piecemeal fashion'. It also noted that 'the department is over-stretched simply to administer the education system'.[63] This resulted from the direct contact between the education partners with the department, which had the effect 'of clogging up the central administrative machinery'.[64] They suggested that the department might devolve some of its routine functions to regionally based administrative units.[65]

In November 1990, O'Rourke issued a press briefing setting out the rationale for an Education Act. In it she mentioned the administrative weaknesses of the centralised system, and she questioned 'whether some of the practices in relation to education conform with Article 42 of the Constitution'.[66] The PERB report posed the same question.[67] The primary curriculum which called for integration of subjects including religion was a case in point.

She set about preparing a draft Green Paper, but she was dissatisfied with the end product. In the summer of 1991 she requested the assistance of John Coolahan, Professor of Education at St Patrick's College, Maynooth, in drawing up a Green Paper. The revised draft Green Paper of 25 October 1991 was a radical document with far-reaching proposals, among which was provision for mandatory boards of management in all post-primary schools.

The draft Green Paper laid down conditions for the receipt of State aid, one of which required schools to establish a representative board of management. It stipulated that one member of the board should be from the local business community.[68] School owners would have the same representation on boards of management as parents and teachers would jointly have.

At the November 1989 meeting with the OECD reviewers, O'Rourke did not accept the arguments made for a regional or local administrative system in education.[69] Two years later she accepted that the establishment of an intermediate tier was timely. She envisaged one that would have a mainly supportive and coordinating role in the case of first- and second-level schools. She accepted the new reality that the country's thirty-eight VECs would be replaced by county committees of education.[70]

CURRICULUM CHOICE

O'Rourke introduced the Leaving Certificate Vocational Programme (LCVP) in 1989, an alternative leaving certificate programme designed to cater for students of varying abilities. Recent research had shown that early school leavers were three times as likely to be unemployed as those who left school with a leaving certificate. In 1989 youth unemployment stood at 21 per cent. She responded to the needs of unqualified 15–18-year-olds by establishing a Youthreach programme in 1988, in collaboration with the Minister for Labour, Bertie Ahern. The programme drew together a number of strands from the education and training spheres. The first Youthreach centres were opened in 1989. In an *Irish Times* interview, she referred to the fact that the government had provided for 17,000 1-year post-leaving certificate courses (PLCs) in order to 'offer students who do not go on to third level a year of further vocational training to equip them to find employment'. Her department devised the Vocational Training Opportunities Scheme (VTOS) to cater for unemployed young people aged 21+. It expanded from 260 places in 1989 to around 5,000 places in 1998, having benefited from the ESF since 1990.[71] She revealed that it was her intention to provide a system of national certification for these groups in the autumn.[72]

On 29 October 1991, she did so by setting up the National Council for Vocational Awards (NCVA) on an ad hoc basis. The function of the council was to structure courses on vocational/technical education and training on a modular basis, and to provide assessment and certification for such courses. Participants in NCVA programmes included those who completed PLCs, Youthreach programmes, and adults with little or no formal educational qualifications who wished to re-enter the workforce with new skills. The council lasted for 10 years.[73]

O'Rourke was pleased to have gained government approval in 1990 'to remove the inequitable requirement whereby students needed four higher level leaving certificate 'Cs' to qualify for a HEA grant, while those who could afford it, could sometimes get a place with just two 'Cs'.[74] She also arrived at the decision to abolish the university matriculation examination, and when she informed the heads of the universities of her plan, it was greeted with a frosty reception.[75]

It was O'Rourke's intention to introduce two bills dealing with the RTCs and the DIT, which she said would be 'the key to greater autonomy ... and more effective interaction with business and industry'.[76] The bills aimed to retain the RTCs and the DIT within the VEC structure while establishing them as self-governing institutions. The bills were enacted into law in 1992 by Séamus Brennan as Minister.[77]

In November 1991, her ministry was brought to a sudden end. A political heave against Haughey's leadership[78] led to a cabinet reshuffle, whereby Noel Davern (1945–2013) from County Tipperary was 'catapulted' into the Education Ministry.[79] His appointment 'baffled and infuriated' Haughey's most loyal supporters who were junior ministers and promising back benchers.[80] Davern held ministerial office briefly from 14 November 1991 to 11 February 1992, but nonetheless he made an important contribution in the vocational education area. First, he appointed John Slattery, the CEO of the County Tipperary South Riding VEC, as his educational advisor, one 'who held strong views on the issue of technical versus academic education'.[81] This was under discussion at the time following the publication of the Culliton report on industrial policy, which claimed that the prestigious leaving certificate had diverted students who would be much better suited to technical training. The report recommended a parallel stream of non-academic, vocationally oriented education at second level.[82]

O'Rourke, who was now Minister for Health and Children, rejected this suggestion, as did FitzGerald, who quoted the relevant statistics, which showed that '8% of students study engineering at leaving certificate level, 14.5% study technical drawing and 9.5% construction studies'.[83] He acknowledged that the Culliton report had 'many excellencies', but he believed that they were 'marred by a badly-researched and ill-argued section on education' as Culliton 'confused education and training'.[84]

Davern inserted a rewritten section in O'Rourke's draft Green Paper on vocational education and training.[85] In it he rejected Culliton's 'non-academic vocational stream' in favour of an expansion of the range of vocational options within the existing leaving certificate vocational programme. His intention was to raise the number of leaving certificate vocational programme participants from 5 per cent of the total in 1991 to at least 30 per cent from 1994. This target was retained in the final version of the Green Paper, which was published on 25 June 1992.[86]

Of all the Ministers for Education, Mary O'Rourke was one of the most politically astute. She displayed her political acumen when, in a move reminiscent of Donogh O'Malley, she won media support for her plan to secure a reversal of educational cuts. She displayed it again when she set up the NCCA, and ensured that the department's power was protected by keeping decisions on curricular issues and responsibility for the public examinations firmly under its control. In the process she warded off adverse publicity by re-instating senior personnel in the CEB to similar positions in the NCCA.

There was nothing haphazard about educational planning from the 1980s onwards. Mary O'Rourke sought professional assistance in the drafting of her Green Paper, and her policies were research-based, having been recommended by the PERB or the OECD review team. One such policy was the HSCLS which was later lauded by the OECD. Another was her decision to set up a Special Education Review Committee. This came in the wake of a declaration she signed along with her European counterparts to pursue a policy of integration. Special education policy came under not only European but international influence at this time.

The areas she bypassed for reform and investment, such as the inspectorate, in-service provision and the establishment of a Council for Teachers, beg the question why she chose to do so. She had three reports which mentioned the understaffing in the Irish inspectorate, and a deeply critical report from the European expert Dr Clive Hopes which called for a major increase in staffing levels. In the case of in-service education, it had been grossly underfunded since the 1970s, but now it accounted for only 0.004 per cent of the annual education budget, at a time when there was an exodus of teachers from the teaching profession as they availed of schemes of early retirement or career breaks. Setting up a Council for Teachers was a difficult challenge, as Dick Burke discovered when he attempted to do so. Perhaps the same difficulties faced O'Rourke's working party when they examined the possibility again in the 1990s.

From the outset O'Rourke prioritised curriculum reform. She presided over the development of the junior certificate, and introduced the LCVP as an alternative to the established leaving certificate. Programmes such as Youthreach and the VTOS went some way towards meeting the needs of early school leavers without qualifications, and the provision of additional PLCs offered a vocational option for those who wished to seek employment. She advanced Hussey's policy of positive discrimination for the educationally disadvantaged, and brought her plans to raise the two NIHEs to university status to a successful conclusion in 1989. In so doing, she enabled the Colleges of Education to make vital linkages to the new universities and to explore degree options.

Mary O'Rourke's ministerial legacy to Irish education lay in her review of primary education and the primary school curriculum, which led to the Revised Primary Curriculum of 1999, and in her draft Green Paper which led to the Education Act of 1998.

Notes

1   OECD, *Reviews of National Policies for Education: Ireland* (Paris, 1991), p.134.

2   The outcome of the election was inconclusive. Haughey negotiated a deal with Independent Deputy Tony Gregory, at an estimated cost of £150 million, to secure his support for the Fianna Fáil government and for his leadership. See FitzGerald, *All in a Life*, p.404.

3   Bertie Ahern appointed O'Rourke as Deputy Leader of Fianna Fáil in 1994 when he took over as leader. In 2002 she lost her seat in the general election and Ahern nominated her to the Seanad, where she became Leader of the Seanad.

4   Stephen Collins, *The Haughey File. The Unprecedented Career and Last Years of The Boss* (Dublin, 1992), pp.95–6.

5   Sweeney, *The Celtic Tiger: Ireland's Continuing Economic Miracle*, p.100. NESC was an advisory body through which employers, trade unions, farmers and senior civil servants analysed policy issues.

6   John Coakley and Michael Gallagher (eds) *Politics in the Republic of Ireland* (London, 2005), p.360.

7   After the general election Dr Garret FitzGerald resigned the leadership of Fine Gael. He took little part thereafter in active politics, from which he retired completely in 1992.

8   Quinn, *Straight Left*, p.243.

9   Circular 20/87, Department of Education, November 1987.

10 Conor Brady, *Up with the Times* (Dublin, 2005), p.97.

11 *The Irish Times*, 23 November 1987. 'Schools compromise'.

12 Collins, *The Haughey File*, p.134.

13 Mary O'Rourke, *Just Mary: A Memoir* (Gill and Macmillan, 2012), p.46.

14 Brady, *Up with the Times*, p.99.

15 *The Irish Times*, 24 August 1990. Christina Murphy interview with Mary O'Rourke TD, Minister for Education.

16 Coolahan and O'Donovan, *A History*, p.210.

17 Hyland, 'The interim curriculum and examinations board 1984–1987; a retrospective view' in McNamara et al. (eds) *Achievement and Aspiration*, p.12.

18 Hyland and Milne, *Irish Educational Documents* 11, p.307.

19 John Coolahan, *Irish Post-primary Education at a Cross-roads*. Inaugural lecture, St Patrick's College, Maynooth, 10 March 1988, p.13.

20 Report of the Review Body on the Primary Curriculum, Dublin, May 1990, p.5. Foreword.

21 Ibid., p.22, p.27.

22 Ibid., pp.92–7.

23 Report of the Primary Education Review Body, Dublin, December 1990, p.108.

24 Ibid., pp.62–5.

25 Concepta Conaty, *Including All: Home School and Community United in Education* (Dublin, 2002), p.81.

26 Centre for Educational Research and Innovation (CERI), *Parents as Partners in Schooling* (Paris, 1997), p.38.

27 Griffin and Shevlin, *Responding to Special Educational Needs*, pp.41–3.

28 *Reviews of National Policies: Ireland*, p.124.

29 PERB report, p.70.

30 Ibid.

31 Ibid., p.60.

32 Griffin and Shevlin, *Responding to Special Educational Needs*, p.44.

33 Commission on Itinerancy, Report of the Commission on Itinerancy (Dublin, 1963), p.64.

34 Anne Ryan, 'The education of Travellers in Ireland 1963-1992: overview and comment' in *Oideas* 40, 1963, pp.61–71, p.61.

35 White Paper on Early Childhood Education, Ready to Learn (Dublin, 1999), p.101.

36 Ryan, 'The education of Travellers', p.65.

37 Ibid., pp.65–6.

38 PERB report, p.67.

39 Coolahan and O'Donovan, *A History*, p.255.

40 Op. cit., p.57.

41 O'Rourke, *Just Mary*, p.67.

42 PERB report, p.55.

43 Antonia McManus, *The Irish Hedge School and its Books, 1695-1831* (Dublin, 2002), p.95.

44 *Reviews of National Policies: Ireland*, pp.46–8.

45 Hyland and Milne, *Irish Educational Documents* 11, p.385.

46 PERB report, p.21.

47 Hyland and Milne, *Irish Educational Documents* 11, p.452.

48 Op. cit.

49 Hyland and Milne, *Irish Educational Documents* 11, p.388.

50 *Reviews of National Policies: Ireland*, p.98.

51 Ibid., p.131.

52 Coolahan, *Irish Post-primary Education at a Cross-roads*, p.34.

53 PERB report, p.28.

54 Report of the Review Body, p.90.

55 PERB report, pp.88–9.

56 Ibid., p.91.

57 *Reviews of National Policies: Ireland*, p.44.

58 Ibid.

59 Coolahan and O'Donovan, *A History*, p.238.

60 PERB report, pp.85–6.

61 Haughey called an unnecessary general election in the hope of achieving an overall majority.
    Fianna Fáil dropped four seats and he was forced to go into coalition with the Progressive
    Democrats' leader Dessie O'Malley, who he had previously expelled from the Fianna Fáil party.

62 Op. cit., pp.11–12.

63 *Reviews of National Policies: Ireland*, p.39.

64 John Coolahan, *Secondary Education in Ireland* (Strasbourg, 1995), p.19.

65 Op. cit., p.41.

66 Press briefing on the question of an Education Act, 26 November 1990, Mary O'Rourke
    TD, Minister for Education, cited in Walshe, *A New Partnership*, p.8.

67 PERB report, pp.11–12.

68 Department of Education, Draft Green Paper 25 October 1991, unpublished. Cited in
    Walshe, *A New Partnership*, p.97.

69 *Reviews of National Policies: Ireland*, p.120.

70 Draft green paper 25 October 1991.

71 O'Rourke, *Just Mary*, p.82.

72 *The Irish Times*, 24 August 1990.

73 Mary-Liz Trant, 'The quest for an inclusive curriculum and assessment culture: the national
    council for vocational awards 1991-2001' in *Irish Educational Studies*, 20:1, spring 2002,
    pp.19–32, pp.19–26. The NCVA was subsumed into the Further Education and Training
    Awards Council in 2001.

74 *The Irish Times*, 24 August 1990.

75 Ed Walsh and Kieran Fagan, *UPSTART Friends, Foes and Founding a University* (Cork, 2011),
    p.259.

76 *Dáil Debates*, vol. 412, col. 265, 5 November 1991.

77 O'Rourke, *Just Mary*, p.69–70.

78 The heave took place against a background of continuing business controversies in which friends
    of Haughey were involved. Reynolds mounted a challenge to Haughey's leadership and lost.

79 Collins, *The Haughey File*, p.223.

80 Keogh, *Twentieth-century Ireland*, p.390.

81 Walshe, *A New Partnership*, pp.19–20.

82 Report of the Industrial Policy Review Group: A time for change: industrial policy for the 1990s (Dublin, 1992), p.54.

83 *Dáil Debates*, vol. 417(b), col. 2187, 27 March 1992.

84 Dr Garret FitzGerald, 'The future of Irish education' in *Irish Education Decision Maker*, 6, autumn 1992, p.7.

85 Department of Education, Draft green paper, 29 January 1992, unpublished, cited in Walshe, *A New Partnership*, p.20.

86 Department of Education, Education for a Changing World. Green paper on Education, (Dublin, 1992), p.78.

21

Séamus Brennan (1992–93): 'One can only hope that a recovery of nerve will take place before the Green Paper turns white'

> The author was education correspondent with *The Irish Times* … and had spent almost a fortnight in mid-February working on a three part series on the Green Paper. During this time … was able to secure leaked drafts of both O'Rourke's and Davern's Green Papers … the newspaper recognised that they would be of considerable public interest.[1]

The coalition government was rocked to its foundations in January 1992 following the revelations of a former Minister in Haughey's 1982 cabinet that Haughey had been complicit in a phone-tapping scandal involving the phones of two well-known journalists. Haughey was forced to resign on 11 February 1992, and he was replaced as Taoiseach by his erstwhile political foe, Albert Reynolds.[2]

Reynolds appointed Séamus Brennan (1948–2008) as Minister for Education. He was a 44-year-old accountant who had been a Minister of State with responsibility for Trade and Marketing in 1987, and was appointed Minister for Tourism and Transport in 1989. In 1991 his brief was widened to include Communications as well. Reynolds regarded the Fianna Fáil coalition with the Progressive Democrats (PDs) as a 'temporary little arrangement'. Relations between himself and the Tánaiste and leader of the PDs, Desmond O'Malley, were strained and 'Cabinet meetings were bruising affairs'.[3]

Despite such tensions, the financial outlay for education in 1992 was 'the highest ever provided by the State at 6.4% of GNP' and was one of the highest in the EC.[4] However, this was 'rather less generous in terms of spending per capita'. It should be remembered also that out of a population of 3½ million, nearly 1 million students were now in the education system.[5]

Reductions were made in the pupil–teacher ratio which stood at 25.2:1 at primary level and 19.25:1 at post-primary level. The provision for educational disadvantage was increased under the PESP by £1 million in 1991, and the 1992 allocation provided a further £250,000. The biggest challenge that faced the government was meeting the demand for third-level places as enrolments had increased by over 66 per cent over the previous decade, just as Gemma Hussey had predicted.

The provision for third-level capital projects in 1992 was nearly £42 million, 'an increase of 81% on the 1991 outturn', £33 million of which was provided to enhance the capability of the third-level education sector to support industry in bridging the technological gap that existed between Ireland and the more advanced regions of the EC. This expenditure would attract support from the European Regional Development Fund. The HEA was given a financial injection, which included '£3 million for the creation of an additional 3,600 places in the universities in line with a government undertaking to provide £15 million over a 5-year period for this purpose'. Not only that, but a programme for the utilisation of spare capacity in the Colleges of Education was well under way. The amalgamation of Thomond College with the UL would provide 600 places and the agreed institutional linkage between the UL and Mary Immaculate College of Education would provide a further 600 undergraduate places.[6]

THE GREEN PAPER –
EDUCATION FOR A CHANGING WORLD

A noted educational historian acknowledged the comprehensive nature of Brennan's Green Paper, Education for a Changing World, when she remarked that 'Never before in the history of Irish education has such a wide-ranging document been issued'. She commended its impressive aims but added, 'The difficulty arises when the how and wherefore of these proposals are spelled out'.[7]

FitzGerald also lavished praise on its statement of aims, but what disturbed him was the emphasis being placed 'on enterprise, together with business and tech-nology'.[8] He was referring to a proposal in the Green Paper to introduce a subject called Enterprise and Technology Studies as an obligatory subject, first at junior certificate level, and then at leaving certificate level.

Brennan, who came from a business background, was aware of the criticism contained in the Culliton report and from the Confederation of Irish Industry, that the Irish education system was not producing students who were imbued with the entrepreneurial spirit or with the capability to create employment. This was what he had intended to foster by introducing Enterprise and Technology Studies. He also intended to incorporate O'Rourke's idea of appointing a business person to boards of management in first- and second-level schools.

However, it was his designation of school principals as chief executives which annoyed educators, who viewed it as yet 'another move redolent of a business type approach to education'.[9] They were deeply concerned at the suggestion in the Green Paper that each school should issue a school report which would 'contain, as an appendix a summary analysis of relevant statistical data'.[10] This might have led to examination results being freely available, thereby enabling the compilation of league tables, which was anathema to educators.

Brennan rejected the proposal in the Culliton Report for a 'parallel stream of non-academic, vocationally-oriented education at second level' in favour of expanding the LCVP. This was now a matter of some urgency as the NESC report revealed that in 1991 there was an increase in the proportion of school leavers who left school without any qualifications whatsoever.[11]

Another worrying proposal in the Green Paper was one suggesting that standardised tests should be given to children aged 7 and 11 years. They had been introduced in Britain and in other countries, but Irish educators had no desire to return to the old primary certificate type examination with its book-centred emphasis. There was also an awareness of the negative effects of too much testing.

The Colleges of Education were very concerned at the proposal in the Green Paper for 'a common form of initial training for all teachers' involving a 3-year university degree, followed by a 1-year postgraduate teacher training diploma that would include teaching practice.[12] This was at variance with the recommendation in the report of the PERB which favoured maintaining the concurrent model. The Church of Ireland College of Education (CICE) together with the CICE Students' Union sent separate submissions on the Green Paper proposals, voicing their strong objections.[13]

Teaching unions and school management bodies were critical of what they perceived to be the utilitarian, instrumentalist view of education presented in the Green Paper. FitzGerald was taken aback at the section on third-level education with its extensive references to rationalisation, modularisation, the efficient use of resources and cost efficiency.[14]

He was disheartened also at Brennan's decision to abandon plans for an inter-mediate tier of county committees of education in favour of executive agencies. FitzGerald hoped 'that a recovery of nerve would take place before the Green Paper turns white'.[15] By taking this decision, Brennan rejected the views of the OECD and the advice offered by his own advisory council.[16]

The Green Paper envisaged a changed role for the inspectorate, which would be reconstituted as a single cohesive unit with statutory powers. It would prepare an annual report on the performance of the school system. A different style of inspection, called a whole school inspection, would be employed 'using a team approach and related to overall school performance'. A new agency would be established to conduct the examinations, and in-service would be conducted by teachers seconded for a fixed period to work with the inspectorate.[17]

IMPACT,[18] the public sector trade union representing inspectors, made a submission on the Green Paper demanding that examinations should remain part of the functions of the inspectorate. It did not favour the secondment of teachers to conduct in-service, nor did it see the need for integration of the inspectorate. Another submission which was made by the Department of Education branch of the Public Service Executive Union, expressed concern about the proposal to set up external executive agencies.[19]

BOARDS OF MANAGEMENT

Proposals concerning the composition of boards of management and the governance of schools disconcerted school authorities. According to the Green Paper, all the powers which were previously vested in the patron were to be transferred to owners or trustees of school property.[20] Not only that, but the proposals meant that the school owners would have a minority of members on the boards. The Church of Ireland had 'grave concerns' about the proposal which removed a voting majority from the patron's representatives, as this had provided them with a safeguard for the preservation of the ethos of their schools.[21]

The CPSMA failed to see the merit in enlarging boards of management for primary schools, especially in light of the fact that the PERB had recommended 'that no change be made in the present composition of the boards'.[22] It took the position that the patron would require as of right that his representatives would constitute a majority on the board of management.[23] Bishop Thomas Flynn, chairman of the Episcopal Commission on Education, said that to exclude the patron from a role in the primary school system would be seen as an attempt to push the Church out of education.[24]

Brennan gave a 6-month deadline for receipt of submissions in response to the Green Paper, but political developments dictated otherwise. In May 1991, a Beef Tribunal had been set up to inquire into allegations of malpractices and fraudulent activities in the beef processing industry. When the leaders of the coalition parties, Reynolds and O'Malley, gave their respective testimonies at the tribunal, they were clearly at odds with one another. As a result the PDs resigned from the government on 5 November 1992 and a general election was called for 26 November.

Séamus Brennan came to office as the government put in place measures to meet the growing demand for third-level places. It also invested heavily in third-level technological courses in order to support Irish industry, which struggled to compete with its technologically advanced European competitors. Once again there was a reliance on Europe to support the government's efforts through its Regional Support Fund.

But it was the Green Paper which attracted most of the headlines, not the Minister's one, but rather the two leaked draft Green Papers of Mary O'Rourke and Noel Davern, which appeared in *The Irish Times*. Séamus Brennan had no option but to produce a new Green Paper bearing his own personal imprint. However, it would appear that he was wearing his business hat when he did so, with the result that the role of enterprise and technology in education was over-emphasised, and the role of the arts in education under-emphasised.

Confusion arose when the recommendations on teacher education and on the composition of boards of management were at odds with the recommendations in the PERB report. The proposal that patrons would have a minority of members on boards of management was never going to be acceptable to school owners, who wished to protect the ethos of their schools. O'Rourke's proposal that patrons would have the same representation as parents and teachers would jointly have, was never likely to be acceptable to parents or teachers either. Brennan's decision to abandon plans to introduce county committees in favour of executive agencies caused further unease, and ran counter to the advice of the OECD and the NESC.

Séamus Brennan's Green Paper was his ministerial legacy to Irish education. It stimulated educational debates, and was set to become one of the most widely discussed documents ever to emanate from the Department of Education.

Notes

1 Walshe, *A New Partnership*, p.23.

2 The Progressive Democrats looked for Haughey's resignation as the price for staying in government with Fianna Fáil.

3 Keogh, *Twentieth-century Ireland*, p.396; Quinn, *Straight Left*, p.287.

4 *Dáil Debates*, vol. 420, col. 1649, 5 June 1992.

5 Gemma Hussey, *Ireland Today: Anatomy of a Changing State* (Dublin, 1993), p.399.

6 *Dáil Debates*, vol. 420, cols 1651–6, 5 June 1992.

7 Dr Áine Hyland, 'A response to the Green Paper' in *Irish Education Decision Maker*, 6, autumn 1992, p.6.

8 Dr Garret FitzGerald, 'The future of Irish education' in *Irish Education Decision Maker*, autumn, 1992, p.6.

9 Walshe, *A New Partnership*, p.27.

10 Education for a Changing World, p.114.

11 National Economic and Social Council, *A Strategy for Competitiveness, Growth and Employment* October 1993, pp.482–4.

12 Education for a Changing World, p.164.

13 Parkes, *Kildare Place*, p.203.

14 FitzGerald, 'The future of Irish education', p.9.

15 Ibid., p.7.

16 *A Strategy for Competitiveness*, p.495.

17 Education for a Changing World, pp.173–4.

18 IMPACT – The Irish Municipal Public and Civil Trade Union.

19 Coolahan and O'Donovan, *A History*, pp.243–4.

20 Hyland, 'A response to the Green Paper', p.38.

21 Church of Ireland Board of Education response to the Green Paper, November 1992.

22 PERB report, p.36.

23 CPSMA response to Education for a Changing World, December 1992.

24 Bishop Thomas Flynn address to seminar on Green Paper, Sligo, 6 November 1992.

Niamh Bhreathnach (1993–97): 'The most significant piece of university legislation since the State was founded'

I am absolutely confident that history will record Niamh as one of the two or three best Ministers for Education the country has ever seen.[1]

Dick Spring, the leader of the Labour Party, labelled the Fianna Fáil election campaign of November 1992 as 'the politics of the gutter' and urged his supporters to give their second preferences to the newly formed Democratic Left party. The Labour Party won thirty-three seats, the PDs 10, Democratic Left 4, Fianna Fáil 68, and Fine Gael 45. It was expected that Spring would join an anti-Fianna Fáil rainbow coalition with Fine Gael, but on 13 January 1993, Labour entered a coalition government with Fianna Fáil. Reynolds served again as Taoiseach and Spring became the new Tánaiste.[2]

Reynolds had no objection to the Education Ministry being given to a Labour deputy for the first time. Spring selected Mervyn Taylor for the post, but he 'swapped jobs with Niamh Bhreathnach with Dick's agreement'.[3] Bhreathnach (1945–), a Froebel-trained teacher and chairwoman of the Labour Party (1990–93), was appointed a cabinet Minister on her first day in the Dáil.[4]

She started by extending the deadline for receipt of submissions to the Green Paper to Easter 1993. In an unprecedented move, she held a National Education Convention (NEC) in Dublin Castle from 11 to 21 October 1993. She invited representatives of forty-two different organisations and educational bodies, as well as the social partners, to participate in discussions on key issues of educational policy. The convention was an extension of the consultative process on the Green Paper and on the Programme for a Partnership Government of January 1993. It was described as 'an unprecedented democratic event in the history of Irish education'.[5]

Professor Coolahan acted as secretary general of the seven-member Secretariat at the convention, and a year later he edited the Report on the National Education Convention. The initial challenge was to gain acceptance for proposals in the Programme for a Partnership Government to introduce 'democratic intermediate structures for the management of first- and second-level education'. Brennan's plans for executive agencies were to be replaced by new structures called regional education councils.[6] Bhreathnach could rely on the support of the CMRS who came out strongly in favour of regionalisation in January 1993.[7]

The issue of regionalisation was discussed at the convention. There was general agreement that the proposed new structures could play a valuable role in 'supporting the quality of educational provision within the system'.[8] It was considered that the new structures would require a much broader remit than the VECs in terms of their powers, composition and functions. In her closing speech at the convention, Bhreathnach undertook to draw up a Position Paper on regional education councils in advance of the White Paper.[9]

One of the key issues addressed at the convention was that of school governance. The Green Paper had proposed that the patrons/trustees should cede many of their powers and functions to schools' boards of management. It intended that the boards would receive the necessary authority to fulfil their duties from the patrons/trustees 'on the basis of clearly defined roles and responsibilities which would be embodied in appropriate instruments and articles of management'. But the Green Paper neglected to spell out what exactly 'appropriate instruments and articles of management' might be, and how they might safeguard the concerns of patrons/trustees.[10]

The composition of boards of management was one of the most contentious issues discussed at the convention. The NPC (Primary) made a strong case for equal representation on boards, as did the teaching unions. Patrons/trustees of Catholic schools considered it essential that they should appoint the majority on boards of management and that they should nominate the chairperson. Nevertheless, the Catholic bishops and the CMRS stated that they were prepared to discuss alternative methods with the department and other relevant bodies, provided the religious ethos of their schools could be protected. The Protestant management bodies defended the right of patrons/trustees to nominate the majority on boards of management on similar grounds. They too indicated a willingness to discuss possible new structures.

The Educate Together movement, representing multi-denominational schools, made a submission to the convention, in which they sought equality of treatment when establishing their schools. According to the Green Paper, the department supported the establishment of such schools on the same terms as were available to denominational schools. This was also in line with the recommendations made by the PERB.[11] It was considered appropriate at the convention for the State to commence discussions with the religious authorities so that vacant school buildings, which were mainly State funded, could be made available on reasonable terms to multi-denominational groups of parents where a clear need arose.

The report on the convention warned that the State needed to take greater responsibility in upholding the rights of minority religions for education facilities which would respect their outlook. The sensitive issue of protecting civil liberties came to the fore when a representative of those seeking a secular education pointed to 'The conscientious dilemma which existed for non-believing parents who had no choice but to attend religiously-run schools'.[12] This question of the lack of choice of schools was addressed in the Report of the Constitution Review Group of 1996.[13] They considered that the issue of right of access to a suitable school was one which required prompt attention.

They also noted that the constitutional guarantee that one could attend a school which was in receipt of public money without attending religious instruction at that school, was undermined in 1971 by the introduction of an integrated curriculum.[14] The report on the convention recommended the establishment of a representative working party by the department to draw up 'good practice' guidelines, and suggested that 'Such a working party might also explore legal and perhaps constitutional issues which may be involved'.[15]

POSITION PAPER ON REGIONAL EDUCATION COUNCILS

Bhreathnach published her Position Paper on Regional Education Councils (RECs) on 11 March 1994.[16] In it she proposed to introduce eight RECs. They would have statutory planning, coordinating, support and service roles for all educational activity with the exception of third-level education. Schools would have their own boards of management and the right to appoint staff. However, the composition of selection boards 'would include one nominee of the REC and one non-voting nominee of the Chief Executive Officers, in the case of larger schools.

It was envisaged that RECs would own new school buildings for leasing to different groups or to patrons/trustees. The trusteeship of schools currently vested in the VECs would be transferred to the relevant local authorities,[17] and the ownership of the buildings would be transferred to the RECs.

The IVEA responded to the Position Paper by pointing out that such proposals could compromise the RECs, as they could be tempted to give preferential treatment to their own schools.[18] It stated also that it would be inappropriate for an education authority to be involved in the direct management of a school.

As the VECs were set up as statutory committees under the 1930 Vocational Education Act, dismantling them would involve complex legislation. Besides, the IVEA had considerable lobbying skills, and it succeeded in enlisting the support of Fianna Fáil backbenchers. One observer noted that 'As time went by, it became obvious that the VECs would be retained although they faced the probability of some form of rationalisation'.[19]

Five days of roundtable discussions took place in Dublin Castle on the Position Paper. Twenty organisations participated under the chairmanship of Professor Coolahan, with senior officials from the department in attendance. The main topic for discussion was the future of the VEC schools in the event of the establishment of the RECs. It transpired that 'All organisations attached to VEC schools were opposed to the proposal to transfer the ownership and trusteeship to local authorities'.[20] No agreed solution emerged at the roundtable discussions.[21]

Bhreathnach circulated her Position Paper on the Governance of Schools in July 1994. It dealt with the composition and functions of boards of management of primary and post-primary schools. It agreed that a single model was not satisfactory and provided illustrative possibilities of boards of eight, ten and twelve members.[22] It stated that 'Receipt of State funding by a school would be conditional on putting in place a board of management consistent with the approach and criteria outlined in this paper'. In bold print the paper warned that 'The management structures in schools should reflect the reality that the State pays most of the capital and current cost of recognised schools'.

It devised a method whereby patrons/trustees/owners/governors could nominate a majority of members on boards of management, and whereby parents and teachers could also have equivalence of membership on boards. It would be achieved through a formula which would require trustees to include in their nominations parents of pupils in the school and teachers (not necessarily teachers in the school). By this means it was intended to guarantee the continuity of ethos in schools and to provide equal representation to all partners involved.[23] It was stipulated that the composition of boards should conform with government policy on gender balance.

It was proposed that, at a minimum, principals would be ex-officio, non-voting members of boards, but that the question of whether or not the principal would be a voting member was one to be determined by the choice of model of school board.[24]

Bhreathnach arranged a meeting of school owners, teachers and parents in Dublin Castle on 12 and 13 September, to engage in roundtable discussions on the Position Paper. Sixteen groups were represented. Teaching unions and parents' representatives came out in favour of equal representation on boards of management. The IVEA and the Association of Community and Comprehensive Schools were mostly supportive of Bhreathnach's proposals, but in general the various churches and school management bodies were strongly opposed to them.

The most trenchant criticism came from Bishop Flynn, who took exception to the suggestion that State funding could be conditional on putting in place a board of management consistent with the approach and criteria outlined in the paper. The Episcopal Commission had sought legal advice which confirmed that the proposal was unconstitutional.[25] The Protestant Church representatives were very unhappy with the Minister's proposals, especially with regard to the composition of boards of management.[26]

Agreement was not reached after the 2 days of talks and Bhreathnach appointed an independent facilitator, Dr Tom McCarthy of TCD, to hold talks with representatives of the churches, teaching unions and parents.

WHITE PAPER – CHARTING OUR EDUCATION FUTURE

Unsurprisingly, the White Paper met with general approval as it resulted from a long consultation process and was informed by the NEC report. It was laid out in seven parts. The first part outlined its philosophical rationale for educational policy and practice. It identified 'The core concerns of the State in relation to education as being the promotion of pluralism, equality, partnership, quality and accountability'.[27] It affirmed the rights of schools, colleges and other institutions to give effect to their own ethos and philosophical approach.

Part two of the White Paper covered all levels of education. The section on primary education included pre-schooling in disadvantaged areas and mainstream schooling. It set a rather aspirational target that there should be no students with serious literacy problems in early primary education within 5 years. Other areas dealt with were the revision of the curriculum, the need for 'Sensitive and systematic assessment of student potential', and the needs of people with disabilities. It repeated the observation that the participation rates of also Traveller children in education were 'unacceptably low for a democratic society'. It set another optimistic target that within 5 years, all Traveller children of primary school age, would participate fully in primary education.[28]

With regard to second-level education, a specified target of 90 per cent completion rate of the senior cycle by the year 2000 was set. There was a presumption in this that the formal education system was best for all students. However, it was planned that students would have access to a more student-centred curriculum, and that there would be a shift of emphasis, with a movement towards school-based assessment methods in the junior cycle, as well as an increased emphasis on oral and aural assessment.

Part two also revealed that the school-leaving age was to be raised to 16, following the completion of 3 years of junior cycle education. In future new school buildings at first- and second-level were to be owned by the education boards and leased to patrons/trustees. Bhreathnach dealt with the issue of school rationalisation and amalgamation at first and second level by leaving it to a Commission on School Accommodation (CSA) to advise her on the issue. In future, full recognition and entitlement to capital grants were to be given to all schools, including multi-denominational and All-Irish schools, from the date of their establishment.

A more cohesive approach between the education sector and other agencies in the provision of PLCs and adult education programmes was to be adopted. A Further Education Authority was to be established to co-ordinate provision at national level. TEASTAS – the Irish National Certification Authority – was in the process of being developed in order to regulate national certification for vocational and adult education and training programmes. In the area of higher education, an advisory authority under the auspices of the HEA was already examining the future needs of higher education. New university legislation was to be introduced, covering the composition of governing bodies and the structure of the NUI, and providing for increased accountability. The RTCs and the DIT were to be brought under the remit of a reconstituted HEA, and more rigorous control procedures were to be introduced for private commercial colleges.

Part three of the White Paper brought welcome news to the teaching profession when it confirmed that the concurrent model for training primary teachers was to be retained. A major programme for in-service education for all teachers was to be carried out with financial assistance from the European Union up to 1999. The conditions of service for teachers and their future pay were to be determined by a single negotiating forum in the context of the relevant provisions of the new social partnership agreement – the Programme for Competitiveness and Work (PCW). A school-based scheme for the appraisal of teachers was to be introduced in consultation with teachers. A long-awaited statutory Teaching Council was to be established for the registration of all teachers, the regulation of the profession, and the promotion of professional standards.

Part four of the White Paper gave official recognition to the status of parents in education as it set out their statutory right to set up parents associations in all schools in receipt of exchequer funding, their statutory right of access to their children's school records, and the right of appeal to education boards. The NPC (Primary and Post-Primary) were to be given statutory rights to be consulted on important education matters. In disadvantaged areas, the HSCLS was to be expanded and specially designed training programmes made available to parents.

Part five confirmed that ten education boards were to be set up. In conjunction with the development of education boards, a rationalisation of existing VECs was to be undertaken by the CSA. Bhreathnach appointed the commission on 1 March 1996, but the IVEA and the Chief Executive Officers Association withdrew from the Steering Group meetings. The commission published its report in October 1996, and it recommended that the existing thirty-eight VECs should be reduced to twenty-one.[29]

The role of the department's inspectorate was to undergo radical change. A small core inspectorate located in the department would be responsible for the evaluation and maintenance of standards at national level. Inspectors would also be assigned to each education board, and their main task would be to evaluate the effectiveness of schools and provide advice on best practice. Teachers were to be seconded on short-term contracts to work with the education boards and the department's inspectorate. Education policy-making in future would be underpinned by national and international research.

Part six committed the Irish education system to continued participation in educational initiatives and programmes within the EU. It agreed that active co-operation between the education systems on the island of Ireland would be promoted systematically, and that the education system in general would promote an awareness of world issues, including development and environmental issues.

Part seven of the White Paper dealt with the legal framework within which statutory provision would be made. It acknowledged that educational legislation would be complex due to the lack of a legislative tradition in education and because of the variety of interest groups directly involved in educational practice and provision.[30]

The White Paper avoided controversy by using the CSA to provide direction on the rationalisation of the VECs and the possible closure or amalgamation of post-primary schools. However, two weaknesses in the White Paper gave rise to comment, one was the absence of any costings for the proposed education boards and the second was the absence of a separate section on information technology.

TIME IN SCHOOL – CIRCULAR M29/95

Bhreathnach was out of office from 17 November to 15 December 1994, and Michael Smyth became Acting Minister. This occurred when Reynolds resigned as Taoiseach amid controversy over the appointment of the Attorney

General, Harry Whelehan, as president of the High Court. Whelehan resigned and the political recriminations which followed led to the fall from office of the coalition government. Following protracted negotiations with Bertie Ahern, who was the new leader of Fianna Fáil, Dick Spring in a surprise move entered into government with a 'rainbow' coalition of Fine Gael and Democratic Left. John Bruton,[31] the leader of Fine Gael, became Taoiseach and Spring continued to hold the position of also Tánaiste.

The length of the school year had been discussed in the Green Paper and the White Paper. It was noted that the school year was being eroded by such factors as early closures, special closures, and days when only part of the student body was present in school.[32] Circular M29/95, Time in School,[33] arrived in schools during the summer holidays of 1995, setting out changes to the length of the school year. It was badly received by the teaching bodies and led to deteriorating relations between them and Bhreathnach.

Her precipitous action made it more difficult to gain consensus on the terms of the new social partnership agreement, the PCW. By February 1996, negotiations were finalised and Bhreathnach made a £66.7 million offer which she hoped would be acceptable to all parties. It proved acceptable to just one union, the INTO, as it stood to gain most from it through the creation of additional promotional posts.

The TUI's objection to the PCW proposals centred around the terms for the early retirement scheme, under which teachers could retire at 55 years of age with 35 years' service. Another area of concern was the requirement that posts of responsibility were to include non-teaching duties which were to be conducted outside of teaching time, for 15 hours annually.[34] A survey conducted by the County Limerick branch of the TUI showed that second-level teachers spent on average 22 hours per week in classroom teaching, and a further 19.25 hours on extra-curricular activities.[35]

The ASTI objected to the terms of the early retirement scheme, and it was opposed to the ending of promotion by seniority to middle management posts in secondary schools. A further irritant to the ASTI was the perception that primary teachers received a better deal, particularly in the area of pension rights.[36]

Morale was low among second-level teachers, and many complained of having to endure disruption in schools due to teacher absences and lack of substitution while in-service education was under way. Funding for in-service education came from the government's National Development Plan (NDP) 1994–99, which received co-funding of £36 million from the ESF over the 5-year period. The government was now in a position to set up an In-Career Development Unit within the department, and in 1995 alone 28,000 teachers underwent in-service training. The White Paper with its plans for rationalisation and amalgamation of schools, created great uncertainty for teachers and the PCW proposals had not 'recognised or valued' the huge changes 'they had faced' and continued to face.[37]

For many teachers it was the department's Time in School circular which caused most resentment. The question being asked at both the ASTI and the TUI conferences was why was Bhreathnach 'insisting on extra productivity when she hasn't given any recognition to the extra workload resulting from the plethora of new programmes in schools'.[38]

Bhreathnach struck the right chord when she addressed the teachers, and the ASTI and the TUI agreed to re-enter negotiations in order to rescue the government's £66.7 million offer on teachers' pay and conditions.[39] An independent facilitator was appointed to broker an agreement in April 1996. Following the completion of talks, the Revised Teachers' PCW Proposals were issued in December 1996.

The Revised PCW proposals reduced the demand made on post holders for 15 hours per year for non-teaching duties to an unspecified amount, which the unions interpreted as a maximum of 6 hours. The number of places available for early retirement was increased and the package was accepted by the ASTI and the TUI. Promotion to middle management posts in secondary schools was to continue to be based on seniority. The TUI demanded an element of seniority for promotion in vocational schools and the facilitator was re-appointed to hold discussions with the TUI and the IVEA on the issue. He reported to Bhreathnach in favour of granting the required concession, and she accepted his recommendation.

The managers of second-level schools who were opposed to promotion on seniority, objected to the latest agreement and inserted advertisements in the newspapers under the heading 'Better Schools, a Lost Opportunity'. Bhreathnach sided with the teachers, thereby avoiding industrial action being taken so close to the summer examinations and to a general election.

LEAKED DRAFT EDUCATION BILL

In March 1996, the draft heads of the Education Bill were presented to cabinet, setting out the composition of the education boards and their functions. A month later, details of the leaked draft Bill appeared in the *Irish Independent* just as the teachers' annual conferences were getting underway. Attention was drawn to the proposal to give statutory powers to school patrons to block the appointment of teachers where they believed that such appointments could prejudice the ethos of their schools. Religious run schools tended to employ teachers of their own religion, but it was now proposed to have this formally enshrined in law.

Bhreathnach was leaving herself open to the charge of discrimination and sectarianism according to Joe O'Toole, the general secretary of the INTO, and Micheál Martin, the Fianna Fáil education spokesman, believed that the proposed legislation seemed 'to fundamentally contradict the forthcoming equality legislation'.[40] She was of course acting on advice received from the Attorney General's office. Under Article 42 of the Constitution, denominational schools had the right to hire teachers of a particular religion, and educational legislation had to reflect this reality pending an amendment to Article 42.

The State's largest ethical minority, the Association of Irish Humanists, issued a strong statement defending the rights of the non-religious community in Ireland. It criticised 'The failure of the State to provide a nationwide network of schools which can accommodate all citizens as pupils and teachers'.[41]

Another section of the draft Bill provided that schools in receipt of public funds would have a board of management.[42] Those who refused to do so would have their annual State grants 'frozen' at the existing level. Gerry Whyte, a senior law lecturer in TCD, gave as his opinion that the very authority of the State to legislate for such issues as the establishment and composition of school boards of management was 'far from assured', at least as far as primary schools were concerned.[43]

The gods were not smiling down on the Minister because in May the draft Deed of Trust was leaked to *The Irish Times*, just as the partners in education were endeavouring to reach consensus on the composition of boards of management. *The Irish Times* revealed that they were considering a 'core' board of management of two elected parents, two teachers and two nominees of the patron. The core board would propose two extra members from the wider community to the patron for appointment. The patron would then formally appoint the eight-member board. In return for ceding majority control, the churches were to be given legal guarantees for the continued ethos of their schools. The two co-opted members of the board were expected to uphold the ethos of the school.[44] Bhreathnach issued a press release clarifying that the core boards would be free to select the two additional members onto the board from the local community without any preconditions.[45]

In November agreement was reached on the composition of boards of management for primary schools and there were no surprises. It allowed for equal representation for parents, teachers, owners and the wider community in return for statements guaranteeing the ethos of schools.[46]

1997 EDUCATION BILL

The 1997 Education Bill caused great consternation when it quickly became clear that the owners'/patrons' powers were diminished in it compared to the leaked 1996 Education Bill, and those of the boards of management and the Minister enhanced. The Episcopal Commission claimed that the Bill did not appear to recognise the rights of patrons as owners of Catholic secondary schools, and that it had eroded the rights of patrons as owners of primary schools.[47] The response from the Church of Ireland captured the sense of frustration felt by the school patrons/trustees at what it called the 'statutory takeover' of a school by a board of management, which was 'contrary to the word and spirit of the White Paper'.[48]

Even though the Bill had been cleared by the Attorney General's office, this did not deter the education partners from seeking their own independent legal advice. Various Senior Counsels agreed that the Bill was unconstitutional in its efforts to freeze funding to schools that refused to set up boards of management. More worrying from the Church's perspective was the removal of the legal provision, initially afforded to protect the ethos of their schools, through a veto on teacher appointments. This was transferred to the Employment Equality Bill.

Such was the level of opposition to the Bill that representatives of almost every faith came together on 10 March 1997 to protest against the Education Bill's proposals on the management of schools. The protest was organised by members of the Church of Ireland and it took place outside the CICE. The government was aware that any attempt to impose reforms on the Protestant community would inevitably be seen by their Northern co-religionists as a restriction on Protestant freedom in the Republic of Ireland.[49]

The Conference of Religious of Ireland[50] (CORI) argued that the Bill might make it impossible for them 'to actively engage in influencing the direction of the school in relation to matters of ethos'. CORI believed that the Bill failed to reflect the White Paper's commitment to a diversity of school types and the rights of patrons to 'protect and promote' the particular religious ethos of their schools.[51]

Micheál Martin fully supported the views of CORI, as did Mary Harney, leader of the Progressive Democrats.[52] Martin promised that a Fianna Fáil government would overturn these provisions if his party was returned to power. However, at the annual conference of the NPC (Primary), its coordinator, Fionnuala Kilfeather, called on parents to 'start shouting' to put pressure on politicians not to dilute the Education Bill by giving more power back to Church-linked school patrons. She defended the rights of parents, and took issue with the teaching unions and others who suggested that the Education Bill's proposed appeal procedures 'would lead to floods of vexatious and frivolous appeals from parents and young people'. She urged Bhreathnach to 'push ahead' with her 'democratic reforms'.[53]

Bhreathnach ignored her call and announced sixty amendments to the Education Bill, which had the effect of restoring power to the owners/patrons of schools. Boards of management were to be accountable to the patron for upholding a school's 'characteristic spirit' or ethos. The composition of school boards of management was to be agreed between the owners/patrons, national parents' bodies, teaching unions and the Minister. There was a broad welcome for these amendments, but ministerial time ran out for Bhreathnach.

EDUCATIONAL DISADVANTAGE

Research undertaken for the HSCLS showed that the individual and social costs of educational failure were great and prevention costs minimal compared to the prospective costs of correcting educational failure.[54] The White Paper, Charting our Education Future indicated that 20 per cent of students in second-level schools were under-achieving or non-achieving. The National Economic and Social Forum's (NESF) Report on Early School Leavers and Youth Unemployment revealed that almost 1,000 students dropped out of full-time education while still at primary school, and at junior cycle 2,600 students left with only the junior certificate and some subsequent vocational qualification.[55]

The majority of early school leavers came from disadvantaged families and communities. In 1990 Schemes of Assistance to Schools in Designated Areas of Disadvantage were devised. The criteria used to indicate whether students were disadvantaged were somewhat crude and focused exclusively on economic indicators of disadvantage. They did not reflect the fact that educational disadvantage was largely concentrated in rural areas. It was estimated that 61 per cent of all disadvantaged students came from rural areas with a population of 10,000 or less. While Dublin had the greatest concentration of educational disadvantage in numerical terms, the problem was primarily a rural phenomenon in that three out of every five disadvantaged students lived in a small town in rural areas.[56]

The department launched its pilot programme Early Start for disadvantaged pre-school children in June 1994. It was introduced free of charge but without sufficient consultation with local groups already providing pre-school services in the targeted areas. It 'resulted in the disempowerment of some of the more active women from disadvantaged communities'.[57]

Early Start was based on the Rutland Street Project and sought to draw on its curriculum and teaching methodologies.[58] The programme was conducted in existing primary schools and consisted of groups of fifteen children aged 3–4 years. Each class was taught by a primary teacher and had the assistance of a childcare worker. The curriculum emphasised the development of cognitive and linguistic skills, but attention was also paid to personal and social development. The first evaluation of the programme conducted by the ERC had disappointing results, but the evaluation of the second cohort of students was encouraging as their 'language performance … was significantly better than the performance of the first cohort'. Difficulties to be overcome included poor attendance and a need for greater clarification of the roles of the parties involved.[59]

In 1995 Bhreathnach commissioned the Combat Poverty Agency[60] to conduct a detailed study of the 'criteria used to determine eligibility for inclusion in the disadvantaged areas scheme'.[61] In the same year, a report on Educational Disadvantage in Ireland by Kellaghan et al. was presented to the Minister. It made specific recommendations on the Schemes of Assistance to Schools in Designated Areas of Disadvantage and on how resources could be deployed more effectively. It recommended the use of revised criteria to identify schools in the most disadvantaged urban and rural areas, along with the provision of additional supports for these schools.[62]

In September 1996, a pilot project, Breaking the Cycle, was introduced into junior classes in primary schools in disadvantaged areas based on studies conducted by the Combat Poverty Agency and on the Kellaghan et al. report. It was hoped that it would assist in identifying means of breaking the cycle of educational disadvantage. The project involved thirty-two urban schools and 121 rural schools, and provided extra staff to allow a maximum class size of 15:1. The department provided additional funding for materials, equipment and out-of-school projects. It also provided a coordinator for the project and access to HSCLS services, as well as in-career development for school staff. Each targeted school had to produce a 5-year plan of action. Particular emphasis was placed on school planning and teaching methodologies.

Early indications were that the programme was generally well received. McCormack and Archer considered that 'The schemes will result in genuine positive discrimination'.[63] They referred to anecdotal evidence which suggested that some disadvantaged schools had been excluded from the scheme although there were 'no great differences between the schools that have been included and some that have not'.[64]

The government's National Anti-Poverty Strategy (NAPS), which involved a commitment from all government departments and agencies to include the reduction and prevention of poverty as prime objectives in their policies, identified

tackling educational disadvantage as a key issue. The NAPS Working Group on Educational Disadvantage questioned the focus of the new initiatives on disadvantaged schools rather than on disadvantaged students. Like McCormack and Archer, it drew attention to a number of anomalies in the designation criteria that still prevailed and which discriminated against disadvantaged students in rural schools in particular. It was only schools with sufficiently large numbers of disadvantaged students who were included in the schemes. In some instances, certain schools were identified as disadvantaged, while neighbouring schools attended by brothers and sisters from the same family were not.[65]

In 1996 the Combat Poverty Agency initiated a Demonstration Programme on Educational Disadvantage, which was planned to run for 3 years. The programme was based on a partnership approach to educational disadvantage at a local or district level, and it had two overall objectives. The first one was the establishment and support of locally based networks to develop an integrated response to educational disadvantage within their area. The second objective was the development of structures which would have the capacity to influence policy at national level, drawing from the local experience. Projects supported by the Demonstration Programme as well as research conducted by the NESF would continue to inform government policy in this area.

CURRICULAR REFORMS

The department's objective was to retain at least 90 per cent of the relevant age cohort in full-time education until the end of senior cycle. In 1997, 80 per cent of students completed the senior cycle. The NESF identified the problem of early school leaving as a central issue for national policy.[66] It called for the total elimination of early school leaving within 5 years.[67] One expert suggested that pursuing such a policy would be impractical as it 'presumes that the formal education system is the best for everyone'. He compared the annual average number of early school leavers for 1992–94 with that for the years 1993–95, and his comparison showed that while more students were 'staying in school up to their Leaving Certificate', a similar number were not passing the examination.

He suggested that the introduction of the Leaving Certificate Applied (LCA) and the LCVP 'may address this problem'[68] but said that the available statistics were not encouraging. He considered that 'those who do not leave school early may become more marginalised with fewer prospects open to them'.[69]

The introduction of the LCVP in 1989 increased the vocational relevance of the leaving certificate examination and recognised a diversity of learner styles.

This was in line with the theory of multiple intelligences put forward by Howard Gardner in the USA in 1983.[70] The LCVP was restructured in 1994. It provided an expanded range of curricular options, along with three mandatory link modules in enterprise education, preparation for work and work experience. The assessment for the LCVP consisted of a written examination, which accounted for 40 per cent of the marks, and a portfolio of coursework, which made up the remaining 60 per cent. The link modules were assessed separately by the NCVA. The programme was commended for adopting authentic assessment approaches whereby a range of goals were identified and assessed.[71]

The same was true of the LCA, which was introduced in 1995 as another alternative to the mainstream leaving certificate. It was modular based and aimed at preparing students for adult and working life. The programme was structured around three main areas: vocational preparation, general education and vocational education. Students had to undertake a number of practical tasks, either individually or in teams, over the 2-year programme. These were externally assessed by examiners appointed by the department. A maximum of 100 credits could be achieved on successful completion of the programme. Students could accumulate two-thirds of their credits over the duration of the programme, and the remaining third in the final year. The LCA was offered in fifty-three schools initially, but that number had risen to 132 schools by September 1996.[72] The programme received the endorsement of specialists in this area.[73]

However, LCA students could not advance to third-level colleges without first completing a PLC. The LCVP, on the other hand, allowed students to gain entry points to third-level colleges on the successful completion of the link modules, and on the results of the leaving certificate examination. In 1995 universities did not allow points for link modules, but in February 1999, the Conference of Heads of Irish Universities[74] announced its intention to recognise the link modules for points purposes.[75] Another welcome addition to the senior cycle was the extra choice offered to schools when Bhreathnach extended the Transition Year option to all second-level schools in 1994. Overall, the restructuring of the senior cycle was regarded as a successful policy achievement.

Success was also achieved in restructuring the junior certificate programme, which was not catering for the needs of students at risk of early school leaving. It was in this context that the Junior Certificate School Programme (JCSP) was introduced in 1996. The programme set short-term learning targets for students to build towards specific statements of knowledge, ability and skill. The statements formed the basis of a school-based student profiling system of the students' achievements. Students were required to take the junior certificate course in English and mathematics and to follow a suitable course in Irish. All students in the JCSP were entered for the

junior certificate examination. In addition to their junior certificate, they received an award based on the student profile, which was validated by the department. A feature of the JCSP was its innovative approach to assessment, which emphasised a range of achievements and acknowledged a multiplicity of intelligences.

SPECIAL EDUCATION

Bhreathnach was familiar with the special educational needs of children, having taught in this specialised area herself. She lauded the recommendations of the Report of the Special Education Review Committee (SERC) when she addressed a Conference on Special Educational Needs in response to the report.[76] The report was regarded as a major publication[77] that would provide a blueprint for the development of special education in Ireland.[78]

Professor T. Desmond Swan, Head of Education at UCD, welcomed the report in his keynote address to the conference.[79] He pointed out, however, that the committee neglected to include post-primary schools in its survey, and relied on research conducted in other countries. Nonetheless, the SERC report contained important data. It revealed 'The presence of 8,000 pupils with various kinds of disability ... in ordinary national school classes ... without any worthwhile support services for these teachers'.

Only 12–14 per cent of students in need of psychological assessment had been referred for assessment, and 70 per cent of parents refused to have their children placed in special schools and classes. Many post-primary schools had no remedial teacher at all, and other schools that had been sanctioned for a remedial post did not use it for this purpose.[80] In 1993 Bhreathnach authorised the appointment of eighty-six remedial teachers at primary level.[81] Further progress was made in this area when an agreement was reached in 1995 with the In-Career Development Unit of the department and the CICE 'to organise a national programme of in-service for remedial education for both primary and post-primary teachers'.[82]

In order to assist children with special needs to integrate into mainstream classes, she appointed a number of resource teachers. She was making arrangements within her department to centralise responsibility for policy in the special needs area, at both primary and post-primary levels, in the Special Education section. She announced at the conference 'that a further 50 child-care assistant posts would be made available in 1994' for special schools.[83]

A key recommendation in the report was that a greatly expanded school psychological service 'should be established on a countrywide basis without delay'.[84] In 1990 O'Rourke had initiated 3-year pilot projects offering an educational

psychological service to primary schools in two areas. Bhreathnach put the service on a permanent basis in these areas, and she planned to extend the scheme on a gradual basis to primary schools generally. As a first step, she appointed ten additional psychologists in 1994–95.[85]

It was government policy 'to ensure a continuum of provision for special educational needs' students'.[86] Meeting this objective posed challenges due to their geographical spread. In the early 1990s, educational provisions for profound and severely handicapped students 'were limited if non-existent'.[87] However, in 1993 the 'High Court judgment in the O'Donoghue case underlined the State's responsibility to provide appropriate educational opportunities for all children, whatever their disabilities or learning needs – as of right'.[88]

THE UNIVERSITIES ACT

Profound changes had taken place in higher education in Ireland. Participation rates had risen dramatically since the IIE report of 1966 showed that only about 4 per cent of the school leavers' cohort studied progressed from second level to university education.[89] Another change occurred with the introduction of a strong binary system, whereby the RTCs, the DIT and the two NIHEs represented the non-university sector. The designation of the NIHEs as universities 'did not impair the binary approach'. The HEA, which was set up in 1968 with specific responsibility for the higher education sector and for the university sector in particular, and the NCEA, which was established in 1971 with academic responsibility for the non-university sector, played a pivotal role in this expansion.[90]

Ireland moved quickly from a situation where a relatively small elite went into higher education to something approaching mass higher education.[91] This was in line with trends in most other developed countries in the 1990s, and the expansion was not confined to the university sector. In 1965–66 there were only 1,007 full-time students in the non-university sector, but by 1993–94 this had grown to 34,673. The growth in the university sector was greater, and it took place mainly in the 1970s and the 1990s. Full-time enrolments rose from 16,007 in the 1965–66 academic year to 52,300 in 1993–94.[92] There was a 50 per cent increase in the number of students transferring to third-level education in 1994–95 and this placed heavy demands on the national exchequer. The current expenditure increased from about £10 million in 1965 to £430 million in 1995. The capital expenditure from public sources increased from £11 million in 1965 to £36 million in 1995.[93]

The government looked for a return on its investment by ensuring that higher education answered the economic and social needs of society. It provided priority funding to science, technology, engineering and business subject areas, and it encouraged higher education institutions to establish links with industry and to seek sponsorship from the private sector. At the post-graduate level, State funding was provided only for students researching in the areas of science and technology, and particular provision was made through an Advanced Technical Skills Programme for students studying subjects deemed relevant to the manpower needs of indigenous industry.[94]

As numbers in higher education steadily increased, Dr Patrick Clancy recorded in his third survey on access to colleges, that there had been some decline in inequality between 1980 and 1992. However, the universities were still dominated by representatives from the highest professional groups. Clancy noted that the more prestigious the sector and field of study, the greater the social inequality in participation levels. He stated that the degree of inequality was significantly less in the RTCs than in the other sectors and that all of the manual socio-economic groups had their highest representation in this sector.[95]

In a further study conducted by Clancy and Wall of the 1998 cohort of students, their findings showed a slowing in the reduction of inequality since 1992. They concluded that relative inequalities between classes were likely to change only when demand for advanced schooling from the privileged classes had been saturated. They believed that the policy of increasing the number of places at third level had the potential to further reduce inequality in higher education.[96]

The provost of TCD expressed his concern at the fact that 'The number of students from semi-skilled or unskilled socio-economic backgrounds attending Trinity' was only around 1.3 per cent. He warned that this level of inequality of educational opportunity 'will entrench social inequality and divisions and will produce a virtual caste system'. He recognised that the problem was not unique to Ireland as in other EU countries the participation rate in third-level education of disadvantaged students was approximately six times lower than the overall rate.[97]

Since the late 1980s, universities had been developing access programmes for second-level students from disadvantaged backgrounds to prepare them for entry to university.[98] Two such intervention programmes were the Limerick Community-Based Educational Initiative, which prepared students for entry to the UL, as it was one of the first three universities to offer special access to disadvantaged students, and the Ballymun Initiative for Third-Level Education (BITE). The BITE initiative prepared students in selected schools for entry to DCU, and since 1993 the Trinity Access Programme (TAP) provided a range of supports to assist disadvantaged students to gain entry to TCD.

In December 1993, Bhreathnach requested the HEA to set up a steering committee to advise on the future development of the higher education sector. A Technical Working Group (TWG) was set up to support the steering committee and it produced an interim report in January 1995. The Report of the Steering Committee on the Future Development of Higher Education was issued in June 1995. It recommended a number of support measures to enhance the participation of disadvantaged students in higher education. Among these was one which had already been indicated in the White Paper,[99] namely that a pool of 500 reserved places nationally should be put in place for disadvantaged students in order to increase the participation of semi-skilled and unskilled manual groups by 50 per cent over 3–4 years. It suggested also that there should be 'an intake of a further 250 places to be designated between DIT, DCU, and TCD'.[100]

In order to increase the number of disadvantaged students who would avail of higher education to 500 nationally, the Higher Education Access Route (HEAR) admissions scheme was introduced by a number of universities and colleges as an alternative route of entry to third-level institutions. The scheme allowed disadvantaged students under the age of 23 from linked schools to apply for reduced points entry to participating higher education institutions.[101] In 1998 the TAP developed an alternative access route by providing a foundation course that helped to develop the skills set necessary for accessing higher education. In 1995 UCD commissioned the Lynch and O'Riordan study to identify barriers to participation in higher education,[102] and in 1998 it launched its New Era programme, which adopted the HEAR scheme.[103]

The HEA consulted with the universities and in 1996, 1997 and 1998 provided funding of £260,000, £475,000 and £695,000, respectively, to a number of them who were engaged in initiatives to improve the participation of disadvantaged school leavers to a level of 2 per cent of all such entrants. In 1994 a special fund called the Disadvantaged Fund was set up, which comprised two elements – The Hardship Fund and the Special Fund for Students with Disabilities. It was administered by the universities and funded by the HEA. In the case of RTCs/ITs and Colleges of Education, funding came directly from the department.[104] Particular attention was paid to access for and the participation of students with disabilities. The steering committee recommended 'that the annual intake of students with disabilities into higher education be doubled from its present level ... by the year 2000'.[105]

A further initiative which followed along similar lines, was taken by a number of colleges and universities who set up the Disability Access Route to Education (DARE). This was an admissions scheme which offered places on a reduced points basis to school leavers under the age of 23 who had disabilities.

ABOLITION OF UNIVERSITY FEES

The Labour Party promised to abolish university tuition fees for undergraduates as part of its 1992 general election manifesto. In July 1994, Bhreathnach took steps to do so without government approval. There were political tensions in government over the pending Beef Tribunal and one civil servant commented that 'she did it because she's scared Labour won't be around after [the] Tribunal Report'.[106]

But Labour formed part of the Rainbow Coalition, and the partners agreed to her proposal in December 1994. Some government TDs expressed their reservations about the abolition of tuition fees, as did the ESRI.[107] The main criticisms of the policy, which was introduced in 1995, were that it was deemed to be socially regressive and that it was unlikely to affect lower income groups. IFUT called for 'the introduction of a much more comprehensive system of grants' as it drew attention to the implications which fee abolition would have on the provision of extra resources and on the financing of universities.[108] Academics argued that this was more likely to benefit the middle classes, and that it ran counter to what was happening in other countries, such as the UK where tuition fees were being re-introduced.

Supporters of the policy, such as Ruairi Quinn, argued that abolishing fees brought Ireland into line with what was happening in most European countries. He believed that it introduced greater equity into the university system as the wealthy and middle classes had been exploiting an old provision in the personal income tax code 'to effectively fund for free, the university education of their sons and daughters'.[109]

Those who opposed the abolition of fees claimed that it would give the government an excuse to defer tackling the inequalities in the existing funding of higher education grants. The provost of TCD thought that the money would have been better spent on providing extra university places, especially for the disadvantaged.[110] An effective campaign for additional funding was conducted by the universities, and on 13 September 1995, Bhreathnach announced the creation of 6,200 additional places in the university sector at a cost of £60 million.[111] However, the universities would have to raise half of the money from private sources.

Bhreathnach did not extend the benefit of free tuition fees to part-time students or to postgraduates. This meant that equal educational opportunities were not available to students who did not follow the traditional route from second-level into third-level education, although it was government policy to improve participation by 'mature' students. The steering committee recommended that the intake of mature students in publicly funded institutions should rise from the then current 3.7 per cent of total intake, to about 15 per cent by the year 2010.[112]

However, the government professed to be committed to providing second chance education as part of a new strategy on lifelong learning. This was very much in evidence during Ireland's Presidency of the EU in 1996, which saw that year designated 'The Year of Lifelong Learning'.

Wide ranging reforms to improve the quality of higher education received attention in the Green Paper of 1992 and the White Paper of 1995, and in the report of the steering committee. Among these reforms was the change to modularisation and semesterisation of courses.[113]

Many higher education institutions had adopted modularisation of programmes and credit transfer arrangements to facilitate student mobility within and between institutions at home and abroad. The steering committee recommended that the HEA should collaborate with TEASTAS and with third-level institutions to establish an appropriate credit accumulation and transfer system, and a monitoring unit to oversee its implementation. The system would be based on the European Course Credit Transfer System which had wide acceptance.[114]

Another pressing issue was that of research. The major policy decisions on research outlined in the White Paper were broadly in line with recommendations from the NEC. It stated that the unified teaching and research budget to colleges should remain in place, and that additional funding for research should be provided in a separate budget which would be open to competitive bidding. Each educational institution would in future be required to publish its policy approach to research.[115] The report of the steering committee dealt lightly with the topic. It commended the involvement of third-level institutions in campus companies related to research output and technological development and transfer.[116]

This was hardly likely to satisfy academics who knew that the international prestige of universities rested on their research achievements. Concern was expressed that research in the humanities and social sciences might be neglected 'In the legitimate concern to promote research in science and technology'.[117]

The HEA commissioned a Management Consultancy Group – CIRCA Group Europe – to carry out a comparative international assessment of the organisation, management and funding of university research in Ireland and Europe. In its report, there was a statement from the HEA confirming that it valued research in basic science and in the social sciences and humanities as much as research that was 'more immediately oriented to product and business development'.[118]

The consultants conducted fieldwork in ten countries, and in their comparative assessment of Irish research, they considered that 'In terms of quality, many areas of Irish university research now appear to be at or above world levels.' But they considered that 'Public funding of higher education research in Ireland' to be 'among the worst in the OECD'.[119]

They recommended a discontinuance of block grants for funding and research. They concluded that the direction of university research owed more to EU research policy and private sector influence than to national science policy, as it was motivated by whatever funding opportunities were available.[120] They supported the proposal for the setting up of two research councils, the further development of a dynamic interface with industry and service, and the establishment of inter-university and multi-disciplinary collaborations.[121]

Bhreathnach issued a confidential Position Paper to university heads in July 1995. This heralded the start of private discussions with them. The document called for the dissolution of the NUI and the creation of four new universities from UCD, UCC, UCG and St Patrick's College, Maynooth, changes in the governance of the universities, and increased powers for the Minister and the HEA with regard to the financing and staffing of the universities. This led to further tension between the university heads and Bhreathnach. Dr T.K. Whitaker, chancellor of the NUI, communicated his displeasure to her and she then gave a written assurance to the NUI that it would be retained if and when the four colleges obtained constituent university status.[122] The Position Paper was leaked to the education editor of the *Irish Independent*, which resulted in months of discussion on university governance 'in which the misgivings of personnel at TCD received a first public airing'.[123]

Two senators from the Progressive Democrats party tabled a motion in the Senate warning Bhreathnach not to interfere with the governing structures of TCD, or to weaken the autonomy of the colleges of the NUI.[124] She presented a briefing note for Senators stating that there would be no such interference. The universities would decide which outside bodies would be represented on the governing authorities, but they would have to ensure gender balance in their selections.

The Rainbow Coalition government did not have a majority of senators in the Senate. If the university and Fianna Fáil senators supported the PDs' motion, then a government defeat was possible. Bruton requested an additional briefing document from Bhreathnach and the Senate agreed to postpone a vote on the motion. This allowed her time to issue a revised Position Paper on 28 November 1995, in which she put forward various models for the composition of governing bodies.[125] The Senate vote was taken on 30 November. The government amendment was carried and a crisis was averted. However, she faced formidable opposition following the publication of the Universities Bill in July 1996.

The Bill dealt with the structures of the governing bodies for the seven universities, the reconstitution of the NUI, and new transparency and accountability procedures. The Bill would allow the Minister to appoint a maximum of four representatives to any governing authority following consultation with the head

of the university. Up to four other members would be chosen by the governing authority from nominations made by outside bodies, such as industrial bodies and trade unions.

FitzGerald[126] submitted two articles critical of the Bill to *The Irish Times*. While he welcomed the fact that there would no attempt at uniformity in the governing structures of the universities, he regretted that academic representation on them would be reduced. The second article referred to the powers which the HEA would have conferred on it, which would give it control over key functions of the universities. Should the universities breach HEA guidelines or fail to comply with requirements, the HEA could report the matter to the Minister, who would publish any such report in the *Iris Oifigiúil*, the government's official gazette. He asked, 'How has our Oireachtas come to be presented with such an extraordinarily authoritarian, indeed Thatcherite Bill'.[127]

Ronan Fanning, Professor of Modern History at UCD, suggested in his article in the *Sunday Independent* of 29 September, that the HEA's 'appetite for power over the universities is insatiable'. Further opposition to the Bill came from the Council of Convocation of the National University,[128] the NUI Senate,[129] IFUT,[130] the Fellows of TCD,[131] the UCG governing body[132] and the governing body of UCC.[133]

The HEA placed an advertisement in the newspaper in which it reviewed its role since 1968. It emphasised 'the positive working relationship built up between the Authority and the Colleges'. It stated that the HEA had consistently asserted the importance of university autonomy. Its statutory role was to allocate funds made available by the government to the universities and to ensure that deficits were not incurred. It considered that the process had worked well and it had not sought the proposed changes. The HEA did well to clarify its position as many universities assumed that it was the driving force behind many of the detailed provisions in the Bill.[134]

In response to a headline in the *Irish Independent* which suggested that the Bill was one that nobody wanted, the presidents of DCU and the UL issued statements supporting the Bill. They would gain from it as under current arrangements the Minister appointed the governing authorities of their colleges.[135] St Patrick's College, Maynooth, which was about to become an independent university, also supported the Bill.[136] Breathnach published over 100 amendments to the Universities Bill in December 1996, which made it acceptable to the Council of Heads of Irish Universities (CHIU). The revised Bill went through the Dáil and on to the Senate in April, but only following an intervention on behalf of TCD, which led to an amendment of the composition of the academic councils.[137] The amendment was carried and the Bill went back to the Dáil.

An order initiating the Universities Act was signed on 13 June 1997 at Maynooth College, which was renamed NUI Maynooth. The college, together with UCD, UCG and UCC, became a constituent university of the NUI. The Act also allowed for a separate Private Member's Bill for the University of Dublin to define a new structure for the board of TCD. This would allow for outside representation on the board of the university for the first time since its foundation. While Bhreathnach's consultation process lacked precision, the Universities Act which followed was generally regarded as a balanced one.[138]

DIT SEEKS UNIVERSITY STATUS

The DIT, the country's largest non-university institute, had been seeking degree-awarding powers for some years, and in November 1995, an International Review Team was appointed by the HEA, at Bhreathnach's request, to evaluate the quality assurance procedures in the DIT. The review team recommended degree-awarding powers for the DIT to take effect from 1998–9.[139] Bhreathnach accepted this recommendation. The team also recommended that the authorities should consider whether key features of the proposed universities legislation should be extended to the DIT. On the basis of this recommendation and other considerations, the DIT sought recognition as a university under Section 9 of the Universities Bill. Bhreathnach agreed that when the Universities Act was passed, she would request the government appoint a review group to advise on whether the DIT should be established as a university.[140]

The commitment to establish a review group was honoured by her successor Micheál Martin in July 1997. He set up an International Review Group. It reported in November 1998, recommending that major academic developments needed to be undertaken before the DIT could become a university. It estimated that this would take between 3 and 5 years to achieve.[141] The HEA published its response within 3 months and accepted the main finding of the review group. It therefore recommended against the establishment of the DIT as a university.[142]

The RTCs formed the main part of the binary system, and one in particular, Waterford RTC, had ambitions to be raised to institute of technology status. In fact, there had been an ongoing campaign in Waterford for a university since 1977, but the steering committee of 1995 recommended that it be upgraded to a Regional Institute of Technology.[143] As a general election approached, Bhreathnach came under political pressure to upgrade Waterford RTC to institute status.[144] She did so on 19 January.[145]

This sparked off protests by the students from Cork RTC,[146] Athlone RTC[147] and Tralee RTC.[148] The RTCs at Sligo and Carlow also called for enhanced status. In response to the protests, Bhreathnach appointed a representative High-Level Group to advise her on the technological sector.[149]

NCEA AND NCVA UNDER THREAT

The future of the NCVA and the NCEA was uncertain since the Green Paper proposed that a new statutory council should be set up to cover all aspects of vocational training, as well as taking over the role of the NCEA in relation to non-university courses.[150] The White Paper proposed that TEASTAS would be responsible for 'all non-university third-level programmes and all further and continuation education and training programmes'.[151]

The NCEA was to be reconstituted as a sub-board of TEASTAS, and Bhreathnach established an interim TEASTAS authority on 18 September 1995. It produced its first report in January 1997, in which it suggested that a single awards body would act on behalf of a consortium of RTCs which until then had received their awards from the NCEA.[152]

The NCEA under its new acting director[153] issued a press release stating that the model proposed ignored the authority and value of the NCEA's validating role accumulated over 25 years.[154] But the position of the NCEA had become untenable following the publication of a leaked report which had been prepared by KPMG consultants for the HEA. The report stated that the NCEA had 'lost its sense of purpose and sense of direction' and that it was 'neither an efficient nor a cost-effective body'.[155] The editor of the *Irish Independent* asked, 'why has it taken so long to discover all the faults listed?'[156]

The TEASTAS report claimed the right to approve, review and audit the awards process, not just of a consortium of RTCs but also of the DIT. The DIT, which could now award its own degrees, was ill-disposed towards submitting them for approval to TEASTAS.[157] Other bodies to be incorporated into the TEASTAS structure included the NCVA, FÁS[158] and CERT.[159] The TEASTAS report was undermined by the announcement to upgrade the DIT and Waterford RTC.[160]

The report of the High-Level Group was presented to Bhreathnach on 2 May 1997. It recommended the upgrading of all eleven RTCs to IT status under a new Irish National Institute of Technology, which would take over the role of the NCEA in relation to the RTCs. It could delegate awarding powers to individual colleges or to a consortia of colleges within a national framework. But there was a lack of clarity over what would happen to the non-RTC colleges

who received their awards from the NCEA. Bhreathnach would not have to resolve this issue as she lost her seat in the 1997 general election.

Niamh Bhreathnach broke new ground by holding the National Education Convention. It was indeed 'an unprecedented democratic event' and a far cry from the days when the leader of one church only was consulted on a policy matter. The outcome of the Convention was a successful White Paper which was well received. Admittedly, the success was partly due to the fact that contentious issues were not dealt with in it but were handed over to the CSA for adjudication.

From the outset the Episcopal Commission warned that threatening to withdraw funding from schools unless they established a board of management along specified lines was unconstitutional. Yet the Position Paper on the Governance of Schools repeated this threat, as did the 1996 and 1997 Education Bills, at which stage an array of Senior Counsels confirmed that this was indeed the case. Bhreathnach had a tendency to rely on facilitators, the CSA and a High-Level Group to resolve her difficulties. Perhaps if she had had more direct contact with the Church leaders prior to the publication of the Education Bill, she would have struck a better balance and saved herself from their clerical wrath.

She displayed political and diplomatic skill following the untimely arrival of Circular M29/95 just as she was trying to gain consensus on the PCW proposals, by winning angry teachers over to her side through conciliatory gestures. When the managers of secondary schools objected to her decision to allow promotion to middle management posts based on seniority to continue, she did not falter.

Her efforts to tackle educational disadvantage were impressive as she introduced research-based pilot programmes at pre-school and first level and the revised LCVP, the LCA and JCSP at second level. Her decision to ring-fence the LCA despite the NCCA's advice to widen access to it was a mistake.

She welcomed the SERC report and implemented many of its recommendations. Although it was government policy to provide a 'continuum of service for special educational needs' students, following the O'Donoghue judgment Bhreathnach had no choice but to prepare the groundwork for the introduction of legislation to comply with this ruling.

The abolition of university fees was intended as a measure to bring a level of equity into the university system, but it discriminated against part-time students and brought into question the Minister's commitment to the policy of lifelong learning. But Niamh Bhreathnach made a major contribution to the Education Act, and she achieved unprecedented success with the enactment of the Universities Act, and therefore left 'a legacy that is real and tangible' to Irish education.[161]

Notes

1 Fergus Finlay, *Snakes and Ladders* (Dublin, 1998), p.320.

2 Keogh, *Twentieth-century Ireland*, p.397.

3 Quinn, *Straight Left*, p.294. In 1927 Labour tried to topple the government but failed. Had it succeeded T.J. O'Connell would have been appointed the first Labour Minister for Education as Tom Johnson offered him the ministry.

4 Katie Hannan, *The Naked Politician* (Dublin, 2004), p.144. Alan Dukes, Dr Noel Browne, Kevin Boland and Martin O'Donoghue were also appointed Ministers on their first day in the Dáil.

5 John Coolahan, Report on the National Education Convention (Dublin, 1994), p.1.

6 Report on the NEC, p.14.

7 CMRS Education Commission, LEC. A Case for their Establishment and a Tentative Proposal, January 1993.

8 Report on the NEC, pp.18–19.

9 Ibid., pp.20–2.

10 Ibid., pp.23–4.

11 PERB report, p.56.

12 Report on the NEC, p.23.

13 Report of the Constitution Review Group, Dublin, June 1996, pp.338–76, p.368, p.375.

14 Ibid., p.374.

15 Report on the NEC, p.33.

16 Position Paper on Regional Education Councils issued by Niamh Bhreathnach TD, Minister for Education, 11 March 1994.

17 Ibid., pp.14–16.

18 IVEA response to Minister's position paper on Regional Education Councils, April 1994.

19 Walshe, *A New Partnership*, p.75.

20 John Coolahan and Séamus McGuinness, Report on the roundtable discussions in Dublin Castle on the Minister for Education's position paper on 'Regional Education Councils', p.10.

21 Ibid., p.29.

22 Position paper on the governance of schools issued by Niamh Bhreathnach TD, Minister for Education, July 1994, pp.12–14.

23 Ibid., pp.8–10.

24 Ibid., pp.19–20.

25 Catholic Bishops presentation to roundtable discussions, Dublin Castle, 12 December 1994.

26 Church of Ireland Board of Education presentation to roundtable discussions, Dublin Castle, 12 September 1994.

27 Department of Education, Charting our Education Future, White Paper on education (Dublin, 1995), pp.3–4; Department of Education Charting our Education Future, summary guide to the White Paper on education, p.2.

28 Charting our Education Future, p.26. The White Paper repeated the conclusion arrived at on Traveller education in the Report on the NEC, p.127.

29 CSA. Rationalisation of Vocational Education Committees. Report of the Steering Group, October 1996, p.43.

30 Charting our Education Future.

31 Alan Dukes was ousted as leader in December 1990 following the Fine Gael candidate's weak showing in the Presidential election. The Fianna Fáil candidate Brian Lenihan was sacked as Tánaiste by Haughey following revelations during the Presidential campaign of his involvement in January 1982 in the making of phone calls to Áras an Uachtaráin in an effort to persuade President Hillery not to grant a request by FitzGerald to dissolve the Dáil, but instead to ask Fianna Fáil to form a government. Labour's candidate Mary Robinson became the first female President in Ireland following the 1990 Presidential election.

32 Charting our Education Future, p.61.

33 Circular M29/95, Department of Education.

34 *The Irish Times*, 10 April 1996. 'Downey wants united front on pay claim'.

35 Ibid., 'Deffely accuses Breathnach of cynicism'.

36 Ibid., 'Actions to be considered after rejection of offer'.

37 *The Irish Times*, 10 April 1996.

38 *The Irish Times*, 12 April 1996.

39 Ibid.

40 *The Irish Times*, 10 April 1996. 'O'Toole says churches cannot get religious veto on hiring teachers' by Anne Byrne.

41 *The Irish Times*, 10 April 1996.

42 Draft Education Bill, pp.83–4, cited in Walshe, *A New Partnership*, p.173.

43 *Irish Independent*, 7 May 1996.

44 *The Irish Times*, 20 May 1996.

45 Press release by Niamh Bhreathnach TD, Minister for Education, 21 May 1996.

46 Press release by Niamh Bhreathnach TD, Minister for Education, 28 November 1996. 'A new and stronger partnership in the running of our schools'.

47 Education Commission of the Episcopal Commission, response to the Education Bill, 19 February 1997.

48 Church of Ireland Board of Education. Education Bill, 1997, submission to the Minister for Education, March 1997.

49 *The Irish Times*, 11 March 1997. 'Churches united in opposing school management reform' by Andy Pollak. Churches had already united in 1974 and 1985 in opposition to regionalisation.

50 CORI was formerly the CMRS, which was formed in 1983 by the merger of previously separate organisations of male and female Catholic religious orders. It currently consists of 138 member congregations, with a membership of 9,000 in the 32 counties.

51 CORI, Education Bill, 1997: an analysis. CORI Education Commission, CORI February 1997, p.26.

52 Harney succeeded O'Malley as party leader in 1993 and was appointed the first female Tánaiste and Minister for Enterprise Trade and Employment in the 1997 coalition government.

53 *The Irish Times*, 7 April 1997. 'Parents urged to oppose dilution of Education Bill'
    by Andy Pollak.

54 Report on the NEC, p.106.

55 National Economic and Social Forum, Early School Leavers and Youth Unemployment
    Forum report no. 11, January 1997, p.39.

56 Thomas Kellaghan, Susan Weir, Séamus Ó hUallacháin, and Mark Morgan, *Educational
    Disadvantage in Ireland* (Dublin, 1995), pp.38–97, p.47.

57 Early School Leavers and Youth Unemployment, p.53.

58 Ready to Learn, White Paper on early Childhood Education (Dublin, 1999), p.99.

59 Ibid., pp.100–01.

60 The Combat Poverty Agency was established under the Combat Poverty Act of 1986.

61 *Dáil Debates*, vol. 458, col. 258, 14 November 1995.

62 Early School Leavers and Youth Unemployment, p.11.

63 Teresa McCormack and Peter Archer, 'Inequality in education: the role of assessment and
    certification' in CORI (ed.) *Inequality in Education. The role of Assessment and Certification.
    Analysis and Options for Change* (Dublin, 1998), p.13.

64 Ibid.

65 NAPS Working Group on Educational Disadvantage draft consultative document,
    October 1996, p.27.

66 Early School Leavers and Youth Unemployment, p.3.

67 Ibid., p.97.

68 Scott Boldt, *Hear My Voice: A Longitudinal Study of Post-school Experiences of Early School
    Leavers in Ireland* (Dublin, 1997), pp.35–7.

69 Scott Boldt and Brendan Devine, 'Educational disadvantage in Ireland: literature review
    and summary report' in Peigín Doyle (ed.) *Educational Disadvantage and Early School Leaving*
    (Dublin, 1998), p.12.

70 Howard Gardner, *Multiple Intelligences: The Theory in Practice – A Reader* (New York, 1993);
    Áine Hyland, 'Primary and second-level education in the early twenty-first century'
    in Fionán Ó Muircheartaigh (ed.) *Ireland in the Coming Times: Essays to Celebrate T.K.
    Whitaker's 80 Years* (Dublin, 1997), pp.177–9.

71 Ibid., p.179.

72 Coolahan and O'Donovan, *A History*, p.259.

73 Scott Boldt, *Unlocking Potential. A Study and an Appraisal of the Leaving Certificate Applied*
    (Dublin, 1998).

74 The Conference of Heads of Irish Universities was a body formed in 1990, consisting of
    the heads of the seven universities in the Republic of Ireland. In 1992 the Conference
    of Rectors of Ireland was formed which includes the heads of universities in Northern
    Ireland and the Republic.

75 The points allotted by the Conference of Heads of Irish Universities for the link modules
    fell short of what was offered by the Institutes of Technology, formerly RTCs.

76 Opening address by Niamh Bhreathnach TD, Minister for Education, in Brendan J. Spelman
    and Seán Griffin (eds) *Special Educational Needs – Issues for the White Paper: A Major Conference*

in Response to the Report of the Special Education Review Committee (Dublin 1994), p.3.

77   Dr David J. Carey, *The Essential Guide to Special Education in Ireland* (Dublin, 2005), p.131.

78   Griffin and Shevlin, *Responding to Special Educational Needs*, p.45.

79   Professor T. Desmond Swan, 'Keynote address – making the ordinary special and the special ordinary' in Spelman and Griffin (eds) *Special Educational Needs*, p.8.

80   Swan, 'Keynote address', pp.13–14.

81   Bhreathnach, Opening address, p.4.

82   Parkes, *Kildare Place*, p.207.

83   Bhreathnach, Opening address, p.5.

84   Report of the Special Education Review Committee (Dublin, 1993), p.226.

85   Coolahan and O'Donovan, *A History*, p.254.

86   Charting our Education Future, p.24.

87   Hyland, 'Primary and second-level education', p.174.

88   Griffin and Shevlin, *Responding to Special Educational Needs*, p.45; Report of the Constitution review group, p.352; O'Donoghue – v – the Minister for Education, 1993 Judgment of Mr Justice R. O'Hanlon.

89   IIE report, pp.172–6.

90   John Coolahan, 'Third-level education in Ireland: change and development in Ireland' in Ó Muircheartaigh (ed.) *Ireland in the Coming Times*, p.192.

91   Walshe, *A New Partnership*, p.117.

92   HEA, Report of the Steering Committee on the Future Development of Higher Education Based on a Study of Needs to the Year 2015, Dublin, June 1995, p.105.

93   Charting our Education Future, p.90.

94   Dr Thomas N. Mitchell, 'Opening address to the 1993 annual conference of the Educational Studies Association of Ireland' in *Irish Educational Studies*, 13, spring 1994, p.3.

95   Patrick Clancy, *Access to College: Patterns of Continuity and Change* (Dublin, 1995), pp.154–5.

96   White, *Investing in People*, p.199; Patrick Clancy and Joy Wall, *Social Background of Higher Education Entrants* (Dublin, 2000), p.68.

97   Mitchell, 'Opening address', pp.10–11.

98   Commission on the Points System. First report and recommendations (Dublin, 1999), p.136.

99   Charting our Education Future, p.100.

100 Report of the Steering Committee on the Future Development of Higher Education, pp.21–2.

101 The Central Applications Office was founded in 1976 as a limited company by the third-level institutions, and as an administrative mechanism for dealing with applications and admissions. In the 1990s the CAO expanded to include Colleges of Education, RTCs and private third-level colleges. A points system was employed whereby applicants were ranked according to their points scored in any single sitting of the leaving certificate. See Commission on the Points System.

102 Kathleen Lynch and Claire O'Riordan, *Social Class, Inequality and Higher Education: Barriers to Equality of Access and Participation among School Leavers* (Dublin, 1996).

103 Patricia O'Reilly, *The Evolution of University Access Programmes in Ireland* (Dublin, 2008), pp.24–5.

104 Commission on the Points System, p.136.

105 Report of the Steering Committee, p.11.

106 Seán Duignan, *One Spin on the Merry-Go-Round* (Dublin, 1996), p.113.

107 The Economic Research Institute was founded in 1960, but was renamed the ESRI
     in 1966 when the State took over the financing of the institute. It is an independent,
     non-profit making body which researches social and economic conditions to provide
     relevant data for policy-makers.

108 Marie Coleman, *IFUT – A History: The Irish Federation of University Teachers 1936–99*
     (Dublin, 2000), p.79.

109 Quinn, *Straight Left*, pp.329–30. Ruairi Quinn was referring to the tax covenant provision
     which enabled a parent to assign 5 per cent of his/her gross income to a child, free of tax,
     and to have their net income assessed for personal income tax. There was no limit on how
     much could be covenanted to a non-relative.

110 *The Irish Times*, 27 July 1994.

111 *Irish Independent*, 14 September 1995.

112 Report of the Steering Committee, p.60.

113 *Education for a Changing World*, p.186.

114 Report of the Steering Committee, p.10.

115 Ibid., p.107.

116 Report of the Steering Committee, pp.13–14.

117 Coolahan, 'Third-level education in Ireland', p.205.

118 CIRCA Group Europe, *A Comparative International Assessment of the Organisation,
     Management and Funding of University Research in Ireland and Europe* (Dublin 1996), p.3.

119 Ibid., p.iv.

120 White, *Investing in People*, p.201.

121 *A Comparative International Assessment*, pp xvii–xix.

122 *Irish Independent*, 27 September 1995.

123 White, *Investing in People*, p.225.

124 Walshe, *A New Partnership*, pp.137–8.

125 Position paper on proposals for university legislation issued by Niamh Bhreathnach TD,
     Minister for Education, November 1995.

126 Dr Garret FitzGerald was formerly a lecturer in UCD and would shortly be nominated as
     Chancellor of the NUI.

127 *The Irish Times*, 24 September 1996.

128 *The Irish Times*, 21 October 1996.

129 *The Irish Times*, 24 October 1996.

130 *The Irish Times*, 25 October 1996.

131 *The Irish Times*, 31 October 1996.

132 *The Irish Times*, 5 November 1996.

133 Walshe, *A New Partnership*, p.145.

134 Ibid., p.148.

135 *Irish Independent*, 12 November 1996.

136 *Irish Independent*, 15 November 1996.

137 *The Irish Times*, 25 April 1997.

138 Coolahan, 'Third-level education in Ireland', p.196.

139 Report of the International Review Team on Quality Assurance Procedures in the DIT (Dublin, 1996), pp.22–3.

140 Press release on DIT by Minister for Education, 10 April 1997.

141 Report of the International Review Group to the Higher Education Authority. Review of the application of the DIT for the establishment of a university under section 9 of the Universities Act, 1997. Dublin, November 1998, p.6.

142 Recommendation of the HEA to government in accordance with the terms of section 9 of the Universities Act, 1997, concerning the application by DIT for establishment as a university. Dublin, February 1999, p.11.

143 Report of the Steering Committee, pp.20–1.

144 *Irish Independent*, 27 January 1997.

145 Department of Education press release, 19 January 1997.

146 *The Irish Times*, 29 January 1997.

147 *The Argus*, 24 January 1997.

148 Walshe, *A New Partnership*, p.159.

149 *The Irish Times*, 31 January 1997.

150 Education for a Changing World, p.115.

151 Charting our Education Future, p.85.

152 TEASTAS – The Irish National Certification Authority, first report January 1997.

153 Séamus Purséil, a former president of the INTO, fulfilled this role. He was not in office during the period covered by the damning report. He was appointed as the first Chief Executive of HETAC when it was established in 2001.

154 NCEA – Press release, January 1997.

155 *Irish Independent*, 19 July 1996. 'Degree body "neither efficient nor effective"' by John Walshe.

156 *Irish Independent*, 19 July 1996. Editorial 'Early alert was needed'.

157 *The Irish Times*, 28 January 1997.

158 FÁS – Foras Áiseanna Saothar or The Training and Employment Authority which replaced AnCO.

159 CERT – The Council for Education, Recruitment and Training for the Hotel Industry, set up 1963.

160 Walshe, *A New Partnership*, p.162.

161 Hyland, 'A legacy to education that is real and tangible'.

23

Micheál Martin (1997–2000): 'Today's one right way is tomorrow's obsolete policy'

He proved to be an energetic minister and performed much better in office than he had in opposition.[1]

Despite the fact that the Rainbow Coalition succeeded in vastly improving the economic fortunes of Ireland, Fianna Fáil won seventy-seven seats in the June 1997 general election and the Labour Party won seventeen seats, which was a decrease of sixteen seats on their 1992 tally.[2] Fianna Fáil and the PDs formed a minority coalition government, with Bertie Ahern, leader of the Fianna Fáil party, as Taoiseach,[3] and Mary Harney, leader of the PDs, as Tánaiste. Ahern appointed front bench spokespersons to the portfolios they had 'shadowed' in opposition. Micheál Martin (1960–) had been spokesperson on Education and the Gaeltacht since early 1995, and he was now appointed to the newly expanded position of Minister for Education and Science.

He took immediate steps to replace the Education Bill he had inherited by making major changes to the original bill,[4] most notably the abandonment of RECs. Two days before Christmas the Education Bill was signed into law. The Education Act consisted of fifty-nine sections divided into nine parts. It introduced executive agencies such as those Séamus Brennan had proposed, in order to perform 'functions in or in relation to the provision of support services'.[5]

Provision was made for the establishment of a committee to advise the Minister on policies and strategies to combat educational disadvantage.[6] The Act defined 'educational disadvantage' in terms of 'the impediments to education arising from social or economic disadvantage which prevent students from deriving appropriate benefit from education in schools'.[7]

Micheál Martin in opposition had promised to defend patrons' rights if his party was elected. Now he delivered on that promise. The Act gave statutory recognition to the role of patrons as owners of schools.[8] Patrons would establish boards of management in a spirit of partnership, and the composition of boards would result from an agreement reached by all the education partners.[9] All boards would be required to 'uphold ... the characteristic spirit of the school' and to be 'accountable to the patron for so upholding'.[10] Boards would have to 'consult with and keep the patron informed of decisions and proposals of the board'.[11]

Teachers' rights were protected under the Act as they would be statutorily entitled to representation on boards of management.[12] Boards would appoint principals based on procedures agreed with the Minister, the patron, school management organisations, 'and any recognised trade union or staff association representing teachers'.[13] Teaching unions now had a right to be consulted by the Minister, which was something unheard of in other countries. Teachers were entitled to request the Chief Inspector to review any inspection carried out by an inspector.[14]

Parents were brought centre-stage as the legislation gave statutory recognition to the NPC, and gave similar status to any parent associations they might set up in schools.[15] They were entitled to access to their children's school records[16] and they had a right to be consulted in relation to the psychological assessment of their children.[17] They were entitled to appeal to a board of management against a decision of a teacher or staff member in the school,[18] and to the secretary general of the Department of Education and Science (DES) against certain actions taken by the board of management.[19]

Students with a disability or with other special educational needs had their rights and entitlements enshrined in law. Each school would be obliged to publish its policy in relation to the 'admission to and participation by students with disabilities or who have other special educational needs'.[20] It would have to alter its buildings if necessary, and it would have to provide appropriate material to accommodate any such students.[21] The Minister had to ensure that among those he/she appointed to the inspectorate, there would be psychologists or educational specialists in the area of special educational needs.[22]

Students aged 18 or over had the right to access their school records.[23] They were entitled to appeal to the board of management against a decision of a teacher or other staff member of a school,[24] and to the secretary general of the DES against certain actions taken by the board of management.[25] Each board of management was obliged to establish and maintain procedures 'for the purposes of informing students in a school of the activities of the school',[26] and, in the case of post-primary schools, boards were expected to encourage students to establish a student council as a means of involving them in the operation of the school.[27]

Students were entitled to be consulted, along with the other education partners, with regard to the school plan.[28]

This was a landmark piece of legislation which took five Ministers and almost a decade to place on the statute books. It clarified the rights and entitlements of all the partners in education, and it set out clearly their roles and responsibilities in the education system.

WHITE PAPER ON EARLY CHILDHOOD EDUCATION – READY TO LEARN

Ireland has an extensive State-funded system of primary education available to all children aged 4–6 years. Practically all 5-year-olds and more than half of 4-year-olds attend primary schools. However, the success of the Rutland Street Project and the Early Start programme demonstrated how pre-schooling could assist efforts to combat socio-economic disadvantage.

It was against this backdrop that Martin produced the first ever White Paper on Early Childhood Education – Ready to Learn. First he engaged in a process of intensive consultation with all interested parties by holding a National Forum for Early Childhood Education. Discussions took place in Dublin Castle from 23 to 27 March 1998, following which a report was published.[29]

The White Paper focused on children from birth to 6 years. It stated that it intended to build on what was best in existing provision. It recognised that young children required both education and care, and that the focus could never be exclusively on either but that needs had to be met in a unified way.[30]

The White Paper set out the government's principal policy objective in relation to early childhood education, which was to provide high-quality early education with particular focus on the target groups of the disadvantaged and those with special needs. Provision would be encouraged 'by offering incentives to schools and also through a broader government strategy to increase supply of childcare places.'[31]

State provision for pre-school children was undeveloped in Ireland. Just over 1 per cent of 3-year-olds were in full-time education in January 1998, and the majority of these were enrolled in private primary schools. The main programmes operated by the DES which had a particular focus on early education, were the Early Start programme, pre-school provision for Traveller children and for children with disabilities, and the Breaking the Cycle pilot project.[32]

The White Paper set out existing provision for children aged 4–5 with Special Needs in the School System. Since November 1998, these children had an entitlement to a range of supports including resource teachers, special needs assistants

(SNAs), special school visiting teachers, special school transport, equipment and assistive technology. The department's visiting teacher provided a service to young children with visual and/or hearing impairment from 2 years of age. Teachers with specialist qualifications taught the young children in their homes. Three pre-school special classes were established on a pilot basis for young children diagnosed with autistic spectrum disorders, two in Dublin and one in Cork.[33] Martin reminded the Dáil in May 1999 that he had appointed forty-six full-time and twenty-six part-time resource teachers as well as 247 SNAs to cater for children with special educational needs. He reduced the pupil–teacher ratio in all special schools down to the level recommended in the SERC report.[34]

Furthermore, he set up the long overdue National Educational Psychological Service (NEPS) in September 1999 and most of the existing psychologists in the department opted to go to the NEPS.[35] There were fifty psychologists in the department, and a further twenty-five were due to take up their appointments in the school year 1999–2000. He saw these developments as representing 'a dramatic move away from an approach which was willing to spend large sums on legal costs, rather than take action'.[36]

The White Paper introduced the concept of the Quality in Education (QE) mark, which would be awarded to providers of early education who met standards set by the DES 'concerning curriculum, methodologies, staff qualifications and training'. The definition of appropriate educational and developmental standards would be undertaken by the proposed Early Childhood Education Agency (ECEA) and the DES following extensive and ongoing consultation.[37] It accepted that the system of training and qualifications for early childhood workers, like the pre-school system generally, had 'developed in a somewhat ad hoc manner in Ireland'.

Tackling this issue would be done within the framework of the recently enacted Qualifications (Education and Training) Act, 1999. The Act provided for the setting up of the National Qualifications Authority of Ireland (NQAI). The national qualifications framework envisaged would include a qualifications framework for the early childhood education sector. It would identify the core competencies required for early childhood education teachers and childcare workers, and would determine which courses would equip participants with these skills.

The White Paper noted that some persons employed in early childhood education might not have acquired formal qualifications. It was believed that placing an emphasis on qualifications as the sole criterion of suitability would place such individuals at a disadvantage and would imply that their experience counted for nothing. It was considered that the NQAI would address this issue.[38]

The importance of parental involvement in early childhood education was emphasised. The White Paper proposed financial supports for parents and more

flexible working arrangements to ensure provision of 'some or all of their children's care and education in the home setting'.[39] Support for the development of a representative body for parents of pre-school children was also envisaged.[40]

It was proposed that the administration of the system would be assigned to the ECEA. The DES would be responsible for policy development and for the establishment of the ECEA. A specific unit, called the Early Years Development Unit, was to be established to oversee implementation strategies and to evaluate the effectiveness of the ECEA in the discharge of its functions.[41] Further structures to assist in the co-ordination of the system were to be put in place, such as a high-level interdepartmental committee and an 'advisory expert group'.[42] The planned new structures were criticised on the grounds that they gave 'a strong sense of perpetuating the current fragmentation of responsibility for early years service'.[43]

GREEN PAPER – ADULT EDUCATION IN AN ERA OF LIFELONG LEARNING

There was growing recognition of the importance of adult education as a vital component in a continuum of lifelong learning. In his introduction to the first Green Paper on adult education – Adult Education in an Era of Lifelong Learning[44] – Martin stated that the concept marked 'a critical departure from the traditional understanding of the role of education in society'.[45]

Willie O'Dea, who was Minister of State for Adult Education, Youth Affairs and Educational Disadvantage, had responsibility for the publication of the Green Paper. He commented that it was now opportune to invest in this sector as the number of young people in full-time education was set to drop in the coming years, so that 'the task of renewing the labour force' would 'rely increasingly on those already within it rather than on new entrants to it'.

In his introduction to the report, Martin's message was that new forms of learning in settings wider than schools and colleges had to be recognised, and that greater links with industry and more flexible provision needed to be developed.[46] This was precisely the same message as the one that had been conveyed in the last report on adult education – the Kenny Report of 1984 entitled 'Lifelong Learning'.

The Green Paper acknowledged the important role which the VECs and, more recently, the community and comprehensive schools had played in the provision of adult education.[47] Section 9 (j) of the Universities Act, 1997 made provision for adult and continuing education, and so too did the 1992 RTCs Act, and the DIT Act.

The Green Paper also recognised the contribution of the voluntary and community sector in providing adult education, in particular the community-based

women's education groups. It recommended a forum for practitioners of adult and community education. AONTAS, the national association for adult education which was established in 1969, noted the changing profile of its members, which reflected the diversification of the adult education sector.[48]

There was another body – the National Adult Literacy Agency (NALA), which was established in 1980 as an umbrella organisation to co-ordinate literacy activities on a national scale. The Green Paper acknowledged the critical role which both AONTAS and NALA played 'in heightening the visibility and priority of literacy and Adult Education issues in Ireland'. It recommended new structures to accommodate the diversity of providers and participants. At national level it proposed the establishment of an executive agency – the National Adult Learning Council – and at local level it proposed the establishment of Local Adult Learning Boards.[49]

The Green Paper gave its approval to government initiatives to introduce national programmes of second-chance education, such as the VTOS. However, the greatest advancement in this area occurred in 1997, when a number of schemes for second and third-level access were consolidated into a new Back to Education Programme.[50]

The Green Paper proposed a National Adult Literacy Programme to combat the major literacy problems as highlighted in the 1997 International Adult Literacy Survey (IALS) conducted by the OECD. The survey noted that Irish adults had lower levels of education and qualifications compared with adults in most other OECD countries, and lower levels of investment and participation in adult education. Drawing on OECD statistics, it showed that of a group of twelve OECD countries, Ireland, with 45 per cent, had the lowest percentage population aged 25–64 with upper secondary education. By comparison, the USA had 85 per cent and Germany 84 per cent.[51] As upper-second-level education was increasingly a pre-requisite for career and educational progression, it proposed the introduction of a national Back to Education Initiative aimed at widening the opportunities for adults to complete second-level education.[52]

Drawing on another OECD report – Education at a Glance, Policy Analysis, 1997 – the Green Paper set out the percentage distribution of first time new entrants into public and private third-level institutions by age group for 1995. It transpired that Ireland was in the lower part of a league table of sixteen countries. Whereas an average 15.7 per cent of new university students were over the age of 25, in Ireland the figure was a mere 2.0 per cent.[53] Even more surprising was the poor performance of the non-university sector, where only 1.1 per cent of new entrants was over 25 years of age, as opposed to an average of 27.9 per cent across the sixteen countries. The Green Paper recommended that universities and Institutes of Technology should introduce a system of mature student quotas in as many faculties as feasible.[54]

In Ireland, not only was there a skills shortage, but there was also an urgent need to up-skill those already in employment. The extent of the problem was obvious from a 1996 survey conducted by Forfás.[55] It showed that 30 per cent of companies saw skills deficiencies as a problem, and 60 per cent saw a need for increasing skill levels in technology and customer service.[56] The Green Paper emphasised that skills deficiencies placed Ireland at a competitive disadvantage.[57]

The Green Paper also dealt with the issue of educational disadvantage and quoted alarming statistics from the EUROSTAT data concerning poverty in twelve member states of the EU. It showed that Ireland had the fourth highest proportion of poor households and of individuals living in poverty, and the second highest proportion of children living in poverty. The Green Paper identified education as central to addressing poverty and disadvantage. As the educationally disadvantaged were most likely to join the ranks of the long-term unemployed, the Green Paper recommended that the part-time options on the VTOS, Youthreach and PLCs should be expanded to cater for them.[58]

The Green Paper emphasised the importance of access to information and communications technology (ICT) training for adults. This training should be accompanied by concerted action to address literacy and basic educational needs. It observed that the development of distance education opportunities had been slower in Ireland than in many other European countries. It attributed this to the high costs of the initial investment, together with institutional barriers in areas of course modularisation and a credit transfer system.[59]

It recommended a comprehensive National Adult Guidance and Counselling Service,[60] and it saw a need for greater provision of childcare services to facilitate access to adult education.

EDUCATIONAL DISADVANTAGE

Social partnership agreements, first entered into in the mid-1980s, had served the country well. In 1999 Ireland achieved the fastest employment growth across the member states of the EU.[61] Nonetheless, there were still significant challenges remaining, particularly with regard to the long-term unemployment of the educationally disadvantaged.

Martin announced in December 1998 that an additional £57 million would be allocated over a 2-year period to tackle educational disadvantage and early school leaving. At this time, Ireland was ranked sixteenth out of twenty-six OECD countries for its retention rates in second-level schools, despite the positive response to new programmes such as the LCVP and the LCA. In 1997–98, 20 per cent of

senior cycle students were enrolled in the LCVP, while 5.0 per cent were enrolled in the LCA.[62] In 1999 the LCVP was offered in approximately 480 of the 770 schools and centres to almost 30,000 participants, and the LCA was offered in 209 schools and centres in the school year 1999–2000.[63]

The LCA was monitored continuously by the NCCA, which in 1998 produced its Review of the Leaving Certificate Applied: Report on Programme Structure. This resulted in some fine tuning of the programme, but in general the review found 'that the existing programme structure and its constituent components did not require a fundamental re-evaluation'. Evaluations and reviews of the LCVP during this period indicated 'that the programme has taken root'. The success of the link modules of the LCVP in addressing key skills such as those in areas of communication, ICT, project management and problem solving, was such as to warrant the question from the NCCA, 'why are the Link Modules not available to all those participating in the Leaving Certificate?'[64]

Both programmes were seen as contributing to higher level retention rates by offering a more appropriate choice of senior cycle study. There was wide agreement that access to both certificate options should be widened.[65]

Two new schemes launched by the DES to encourage students to remain in the education system were welcomed by the NESC in light of the fact that the ESRI annual school leavers' survey for 1997 showed that 69 per cent of the 1995–96 cohort of school-leavers had no qualifications and were not participating in any further education or training programmes.[66] The first scheme was the 8–15-year-olds Early School Leavers Initiative, which was introduced as a 2-year pilot programme in 1998. It was designed to explore area-based responses to early school leaving. The initiative brought together groups of primary and second-level schools which worked in collaboration with statutory, voluntary and community services. Local consortia then developed a range of in-school and out-of-school interventions in support of students at risk of early school leaving. Interventions were also developed to support those students who had dropped out of school with a view to supporting their gradual return to mainstream provision.

The second scheme was the Stay in School Retention Initiative, which was introduced in 1999 with a budget of £4.5 million. At the core of the initiative was a retention plan or agreement drawn up between the school and the DES, with the requirement that the school should operate on a multi-agency basis and establish cross-community links in order to increase the retention rate to completion of the senior cycle. The NESC praised these innovative programmes but recommended that 'other innovative approaches should be developed for schools in rural areas' which had problems with early school leaving which needed to be addressed.[67] At the time, the Education Welfare Bill, which would replace the

School Attendance Acts 1926 to 1967,[68] was making its way through the Houses of the Oireachtas. Its enactment into law would raise the school leaving age to 16.

It was imperative therefore that these students would have a variety of programmes to choose from, especially in light of the fact that the ESRI survey showed that about 19 per cent of the relevant age group left school annually without completing senior cycle. The problem was compounded by the fact that there was a ready availability of work.[69] Consultations conducted by the NCCA as part of its review of the junior cycle curriculum revealed the attractiveness of the labour market for students and the serious impact this had on retention rates.[70]

However, the department's commitment to tackling educational disadvantage was long term in nature. This was evident from the announcement in December 1999 of a further package of measures amounting to £194 million to address educational disadvantage. The programme was called The New Deal – A Plan for Educational Opportunity. It set out investment plans in a range of areas at all levels of the education system to take place over the period 2000–2002.[71]

The Green Paper on adult education brought the plight of mature students seeking second-chance education into sharp focus. The Commission on the Points System, set up by Martin in October 1997 to examine the system of selection for third-level entry, calculated that around 5–7 per cent of all those entering undergraduate third-level education were mature students. This was in marked contrast to other OECD countries, where the equivalent figure could be as high as 40 per cent.[72] The relative neglect of Irish mature students compared to their European counterparts was due mainly to demographic factors. The number of births in Ireland reached a peak of over 74,000 in 1980 and declined by 3 per cent to just under 48,000 in 1994.[73] The emphasis was therefore placed on education provision for school leavers. In addition, the introduction of 'free education' in 1967 meant that the increase in participation at second level in this country occurred later than in Western countries. Ireland was largely playing 'catch up' with many of our competitor nations who made similar investments during the immediate post-war years.[74]

The Review Committee on Post-Secondary Education and Training Places, set up by the government in July 1996 to review the recommendations contained in the HEA Report of the Steering Committee on the Future Development of Higher Education, recommended the provision of an additional stock of up to 10,000 places for mature students to be built up over a period of years.[75] The Points Commission recommended that by the year 2005, each third-level institution should set aside a quota of at least 15 per cent of places for mature students, and that by the year 2015, this target might be raised to 25 per cent. It also suggested that the HEA should develop a fund to support part-time undergraduate third-level courses, and that fees for part-time courses should be abolished.

The Points Commission called for greater flexibility in higher education provision and for major changes in patterns of access to and participation in third-level education. It promoted the merits of distance education in order to meet the demand for part-time study.[76] The Review Committee also believed that flexible provision was essential.[77] Martin accepted the need to promote flexibility and responsiveness in educational structures, as he said, 'Today's one right way is tomorrow's obsolete policy'.[78]

QUALIFICATIONS (EDUCATION AND TRAINING) ACT

He also accepted the need for a more coherent and effective system of certification and accreditation for the non-university sector, which he said had been 'both recognised and endorsed by successive governments and by the EU'.[79] The enactment of the Qualifications (Education and Training) Act, 1999 was therefore important. The Act set out plans for the establishment of the first national system of certification covering the full range of qualifications from basic literacy certificates to specific skills training to further and higher education. The NQAI was to be set up to act as an overall guarantor of the quality of further and higher education.

The Authority would oversee two new bodies. The first one was the Further Education and Training Awards Council (FETAC), which would incorporate the current education and training functions of FÁS, CERT, TEAGASC[80] and the NCVA. The second body was the Higher Education Training and Awards Council (HETAC), which would incorporate the higher education and training certificate functions of the NCEA and other bodies. The Act provided strict criteria for the delegation of authority from the HETAC to Institutes of Technology to make higher education and training awards within the framework of qualifications. Similarly, provision was made for the delegation of authority from the FETAC to FÁS, CERT and TEAGASC. The Act provided that universities would be advised by the NQAI on the implementation of access, transfer and progression arrangements.[81]

A key emphasis of the Act was the importance of ensuring progression pathways within education and training, so that each qualification had the potential to lead to a higher qualification. The new structures would do much to facilitate and promote lifelong learning, and were likely to lead to an even greater demand among mature students for access to further and higher education.[82]

The establishment of the NQAI in 2001 provided a framework to promote international recognition of awards, and international mobility. In June 1999, Ireland was one of forty-six countries to sign the Bologna Declaration with the aim of creating a European Higher Education Area by 2010, which could compete against the best performing systems in the world, notably those of the USA and Asia. Irish students

could now choose from a wide range of high-quality courses in European higher education colleges, and they could benefit from agreed recognition procedures.

THE INFORMATION SOCIETY

In 1995 several companies signalled that there was a problem with the availability of high-skill information technology labour. Forfás, at Mary Harney's request, established the (Interim) Skills Group to examine emerging skills needs. The Group's analytical work provided the basis for the government's 'An Action Plan for Skills'. The Action Plan provided for the 'intake of 3,200 students into software professional, electronic technician and teleservices staff courses run by the universities, Institutes of Technology and PLC Colleges'.[83]

In November 1997, the government launched the £250 million Scientific and Technological Education Investment Fund.[84] Simultaneously, Harney announced the Business/Education and Training Partnership to develop national strategies to tackle the issues of skills needs, manpower forecasting, and education and training for industry and business.[85] The first meeting was held on 18 June 1998 and was jointly chaired by Martin and Harney.

A key element of this initiative was the establishment of the Expert Group on Future Skills Needs. Writing in the Foreword to the First Report of the Expert Group, Martin said that educators had an important role to play in providing the type of skills that would 'enable both students and workers to fully participate in the knowledge economy'.[86] The report focused on the 'high technology' sector and projected a need for an additional 8,300 technologists each year up to 2003, but estimated that the supply would only reach 6,100, leaving a shortfall of 2,200 technologists annually.

The report suggested employee up-skilling, conversion courses, additional full-time undergraduate places for technology students, accelerated technician learning and improved completion rates to meet the shortfall. Arrangements to accommodate the extra full-time technology students needed to be put in place immediately to protect Ireland's competitiveness.[87]

In November 1998, an additional 500 places in computing and manufacturing were announced to address the need for key technician skills. The courses were to be run in nine participating Institutes of Technology. Applicants would be eligible for the Back To Education allowance and would be paid during their 6-month work placement by a sponsoring company. Martin provided for new PLCs in international teleservices. Participants taking the course were required to spend a minimum of 17 weeks on job training, and in language immersion in their chosen European country.[88]

The government made a capital allocation of £20 million for PLCs from the £250 million Investment Fund. Martin announced that maintenance grants would be allocated to all PLC students from September 1998. Furthermore, the DES invested £75 million in providing facilities in third-level institutions for 2,400 technician places and 3,000 degree places, mainly in the engineering and computer hardware and software areas.

A sum of £40 million was provided for the Schools IT 2000 project from the £250 million Investment Fund. In January 1998, the National Centre for Technology in Education (NCTE) was set up to oversee its implementation. The aim of the project was to integrate technology into teaching and learning in Irish schools. It consisted of initiatives such as the Technology Integration Initiative, which provided 60,000 multimedia computers and connection of all schools to the internet, and the Teaching Skills Initiative, which provided information technology skills to at least 20,000 teachers. ScoilNet developed an internet service for schools and the wider community, including the development of content relevant to the Irish curriculum, and a Schools Support Initiative, which included the appointment of information technology advisers to the twenty full-time Education Centres.[89]

RESEARCH AND DEVELOPMENT

Ireland was ranked 10th out of twenty-eight countries in terms of business expenditure on research and development.[90] The ESRI suggested that Ireland's level of public funding for research and development should be significantly increased 'until it is at least in line with the EU average'. The government accepted the expert advice it received, and invested heavily in research and development in third-level institutions.

Included in the £250 million Investment Fund was £30 million for third-level equipment renewal grants, and £15 million for reinforcing the research and development capacity of third-level institutions over a 3-year period. In November 1998, a Programme for Research in Third-Level Institutions was announced by the government. This was a £150 million 3-year investment programme for scientific and other research in universities and Institutes of Technology. The programme was to provide for government capital spending of £75 million with £75 million in matching private funding to be raised by the colleges. The heads of Irish universities sought private funding among the Irish American community in North America, and from the Atlantic Philanthropies foundation of the Irish American Chuck Feeney.[91] This investment was of special significance as research in the humanities and sciences was included for funding.[92]

The Irish Council for Science Technology and Innovation (ICSTI) developed a Technology Foresight exercise in Ireland. The results provided the government with data for the preparation of an NDP to be submitted to the EU Commission in the context of a forthcoming round of structural funds. The ICSTI report showed that there was a need to increase capacity in niche areas of ICT and biotechnology, and it recommended the establishment of world-class centres for research and technology development in both these fields.[93]

Following a similar path, the Expert Group on Future Skills Needs published its second report which covered the main craft areas of the construction industry, chemical and biological sciences at third level, and information technology at third level. They recommended that an extra 1,800 places on degree courses should be provided in relevant science disciplines on a phased basis over 4–5 years. They further recommended that the Accelerated Technician Programme should be extended immediately to cater for 250 science technician students.

Concern was expressed at the falling numbers of school leavers interested in studying science and chemistry. They attributed this trend to the variation in marking between different leaving certificate subjects and to the perception that chemistry was a difficult subject in which to attain high marks. They reiterated the recommendation of the Points Commission that the DES should consider appropriate strategies to ensure a more even distribution of grades across subjects.[94]

Martin had already announced an initiative in 1999 to increase the uptake of physics and chemistry to leaving certificate level. It included additional funding of £15 million for laboratory resources and a special per capita grant for each student studying physics and chemistry at leaving certificate level. New syllabi in leaving certificate physics and chemistry had been finalised and would be introduced in September 2000, and the revision of the junior certificate syllabus would be completed in the summer of 1999. Plans for in-career development for teachers were at an advanced stage.[95]

In November 1999, the NDP was published, and it showed clearly that Ireland placed a high premium on research and development. It included provision for an investment of £550 million over the period 2000–2006 in research, technological development and innovation in the educational sector under the aegis of the DES. Shortly after Martin left office, a £550 million Technology Investment Fund was set up, as well as a Technology Research Foundation to oversee the spending of the fund.[96]

Prior to the publication of the White Paper on Adult Education – Learning for Life by Michael Woods,[97] the NDP, which was co-funded by the EU, set out its programme for investment in projects to promote social inclusion. It covered

early education and Traveller education, and allowed a budget of £95 million for a Third-Level Access Measure, which included supports for students with disabilities. Second-chance education and further education were the main beneficiaries as the Back to Education Initiative received a staggering £1.027 billion for the expansion of part-time options across PLC/Youthreach/Traveller and VTOS programmes. Adult education got a boost also when a sum of £73.8 million was allocated for the National Adult Literacy Strategy, while £35 million was provided for the Further Education Support Measure, which allowed for the establishment of an Adult Education Guidance Service.[98]

The Department of Education took preventative measures to avoid a re-occurrence of adult literacy problems in Ireland. Martin expanded the HSCLS and remedial service to all designated schools in disadvantaged areas. He had already established the NEPS, and legislation to raise the school leaving age to 16 would soon be enacted into law. A stimulus to improve Ireland's literacy levels continues to be supplied by the OECD indicators of comparative education performance across a number of European countries.[99] In 2000 Ireland joined the OECD's new Programme for International Student Assessment (PISA) – a programme of international assessment which focuses on the capabilities of 15-year-olds in reading, mathematics and science.

Willie O'Dea's White Paper on Adult Education – Learning for Life outlined the government's comprehensive strategy for second-chance and further education in its Back to Education Initiative. It included access to information and communications technology training (ICT), electronic technician training, language skills, childcare, the junior and leaving certificate examinations, and other access programmes. It supported the use of ICT in the classroom and for distance education[100] and it launched the first national programme in ICT training for adults.[101]

Learning for Life confirmed that a competitive Targeted Higher Education Mature Student Fund was planned, which would rise on a phased basis to £10 million per annum. This was aimed at increasing mature student participation in higher education, but a general programme of free fees for part-time students was not advocated. However, fees would be abolished for those on nationally certified part-time third-level courses who were medical card holders, recipients of welfare/health payments or in receipt of Family Income Supplement.[10]

COMMISSION ON SCHOOL ACCOMMODATION

The CSA was established by Bhreathnach in March 1996.[103] The steering group of the commission were assisted by a TWG who reported to Martin on 30 January 1998. The commission was asked to 'make recommendations on

appropriate criteria and procedures for the consideration of applications for school recognition at primary level'.[104]

The chairman of the commission observed that the great majority of primary pupils were enrolled in denominational schools, and that all the indications were that the majority of parents would retain this preference. However, with the emergence of a more pluralistic society, there was growing parental demand for access to multi-denominational schooling. There was also a clear demand for education through the medium of Irish.[105]

Different criteria for recognition applied to different types of schools. In the case of primary schools generally, the patron or promoter of the school had to provide a site for a new school and was not entitled to grant aid from the department. In contrast, the full cost of sites for All-Irish schools was provided by the department.[106]

The report pointed to the differences in the application of criteria to the four main categories of schools, particularly regarding enrolment requirements. Denominational schools had to have a significant average daily enrolment, whereas minority denominational schools had to have a minimum enrolment of twenty-four pupils of 4 years of age or over. All-Irish schools needed an enrolment of not fewer than twenty pupils on opening, but in the case of multi-denominational schools no requirements had been laid down.

With regard to special schools, all that was required was that there should be enough children to warrant the establishment of one class. It was the responsibility of the primary inspectorate to investigate the needs of the children concerned, and to make a recommendation regarding required provision.

The four categories of schools had different entitlements conferred by recognition. Denominational schools and special schools received permanent recognition from the department at the time of establishment. Since 1987 the minority denominational schools, All-Irish schools and the multi-denominational schools received provisional recognition, which entitled them to the payment of teachers' salaries but not to capital funding. After the period of provisional recognition, which generally took 2–3 years for All-Irish schools and multi-denominational schools, these schools had to join the queue for capital funding for accommodation. In 1997 a new school could exist in temporary accommodation 'for one to fifteen years' before being established in permanent accommodation.

These schools were entitled to receive financial support for their temporary accommodation, which took the form of a rent refund. There were differences in the level of funding support offered. Denominational and minority denominational schools were entitled to a refund of '50% generally of reasonable rental costs',

All-Irish schools were entitled to 75 per cent, multi-denominational schools to 50 per cent, and special schools got a 100 per cent refund.

The Report of the Steering Group of the CSA was presented to Martin in September 1998. In it the enrolment criteria set the minimum guaranteed enrolment for the first year of operation at seventeen junior infants, and the maximum projected enrolment for the third year of operation at fifty-one pupils. A New Schools Advisory Committee to be established could recommend to the Minister a derogation from the regulated minimum enrolment criteria in exceptional cases.

As Section 31 of the Education (No. 2) Bill provided for the establishment of a body of persons to plan, advise and provide support for the specific needs of Irish medium education, the Steering Group 'strongly supported'[107] the view of the TWG that 'it is preferable to allocate funding to proposers of new schools in an equal and non-discriminatory manner'.[108] From 1 September of the year in which recognition was granted, all schools (excluding special schools) would be entitled to payment of teachers' salaries, capitation and other related grants, a grant for furniture, and a rent refund of 75 per cent. After verification of the third year minimum enrolment requirement, schools would be entitled to eligibility for capital funding and a rent refund of 95 per cent on interim accommodation.

The recommended procedure for the recognition of a new primary school (excluding special schools) was set out in five stages with a firm timescale, and involved a process of consultation. Applications were to be processed by the New Schools Advisory Committee.

Ownership of a new primary school would either rest with the Minister for Education and Science or with the patrons/trustees. If patrons/trustees did not wish to own a new school, the Minister would take up ownership of it and lease the property to them on terms that would facilitate flexibility in the use of the property. If, on the other hand, patrons/trustees wished to own the new school, it would be 'under conditions that may be agreed from time to time' between them and the DES. Initially, planning for new schools was to be conducted by the CSA.

Provision for diversity within existing schools was to be supported by a working party chaired by the inspectorate to be established from 1999 to 2002. Its function would be to develop a model of good practice on the inclusivity of denominational schools, and to report to the Chief Inspector of the department. A further provision was made for the development of a model of transformation to Irish medium schools, and to identify possible schools or areas for transformation. A strategy group chaired by the inspectorate was to be established from 1999 to 2002 for this purpose, which would report to the Chief Inspector. The Steering Group called for 'an adequate level of capital funding ... to provide permanent accommodation for recognised schools' in order to eliminate the building backlog.[109]

Before the report was published, Martin offered to purchase all school sites in future in order to reduce the cost on local communities.[110] This placed a considerable strain on his own department's Planning and Building Unit. The union representing administrative and professional staff in the unit claimed that the department had largely ignored requests for staffing levels to be addressed.[111]

THE INSPECTORATE

Martin supported the introduction of a number of agencies and support teams in order to devolve responsibility for the provision of a range of educational services, and by so doing he lightened the excessive workload of the inspectorate and allowed it to concentrate on its professional work. But some of the agencies still retained close links with the inspectorate, for instance the department's advisory body, the NCCA, had inspectors on its council and sub-committees, and the NCTE, which was set up in 1998, 'drew heavily on the work of the inspectorate'.

A year later Martin established a planning group to prepare the way for the setting up of a National Council for Special Education as an external agency, and plans were underway for a State Examinations Commission.[112] On 4 November 1997, he set up a steering committee on the establishment of a Teaching Council. The TWG reported in April 1998 and the steering committee in June 1998.[113] Plans were now in place to relieve the inspectorate of its most demanding tasks.

Support teams lightened their workload too. In May 1999, the DES launched the School Development Planning Initiative which envisaged a new partnership approach to school planning whereby the school plan would be drawn up collaboratively by the school community. The inspectorate drew on the expertise of skilled teachers to deliver in-service education on devising and implementing the school plan, having first produced Guidelines for School Development Planning for both primary and post-primary schools.

Following publication of the Revised Primary school Curriculum, the inspectorate drew once again on the expertise of a support team called the Primary Curriculum Support Programme (PCSP). The PCSP consisted of rotating cohorts of seconded primary teachers who worked with their peers on various aspects of the curriculum.[114] Curriculum reform at second level was also quite extensive during the 1990s, and post-primary teachers were assisted with the introduction of new programmes by seconded second-level teachers, known as the Second Level Support Service.

By the end of the 1990s, the Department of Education could no longer be referred to disparagingly as that 'stagnant pond' as Section 13 of the Education Act placed it on a statutory footing. It was now a vibrant department with a newly established Evaluation

Support and Research Unit (ESRU) which oversaw the successful pilot project on Whole School Evaluation in a number of first- and second-level schools. The ESRU confirmed the potential of this model of evaluation to successfully combine school self-review and external inspection using common criteria of evaluation.

John Boland had a vision of Ireland as the Silicon Valley of Europe, and he intended to computerise schools and equip students for the 'technological revolution' which was underway. Unlike Boland, Micheál Martin had access to a £250 million Scientific and Technological Education Investment Fund which enabled him to equip all schools with computers.

In the late 1960s Brian Lenihan declared, to the dismay of educators, that 'education has never been adequately geared to the requirements of the economy'. Three decades later, Martin collaborated with Mary Harney in the Business/ Education and Training Partnership, and in the Foreword to the First Report of the Expert Group, he reminded educators of the important role they had to play in supplying the type of skills students and workers would need to fully participate in the knowledge economy. There were few dissenting voices. When the Expert Group identified a shortfall of 2,200 technologists annually, Martin provided the necessary funding and resources to the nine Institutes of Technology, PLC colleges and universities in order to meet market demands. The Second Report of the Expert Group expressed concern at the falling numbers of students interested in studying science and chemistry to leaving certificate level, but Martin was one step ahead as he already had measures in place to stimulate interest in the uptake of these subjects.

Martin continued with the policies of his predecessor even though he dropped her plans for RECs. When he was presented with the CSA report which she had commissioned, he was so enthused by its recommendations that he immediately offered to purchase all school sites in future. The overworked, understaffed Planning and Building Unit did not share his enthusiasm.

European influence was all pervasive in the many reports on Irish education in the 1990s. The White Paper on Early Childhood Education referred to best practice in Europe, but unlike Europe, Ireland had limited pre-school provision. There were no plans in the White Paper to alter this, and the multi-layered structures proposed for a coordinated delivery of the service did not inspire confidence. However, the White Paper highlighted weaknesses in the system of training and qualifications for the delivery of early childhood education, and Martin rectified this weakness by providing a more coherent and effective system of certification and accreditation and a progression pathway not just for this sector but also for the further education and the non-university sectors in the NQAI.

Children with special educational needs had their rights protected in the Education Act, and Martin improved their educational prospects through

the appointment of additional resource teachers, SNAs and as a result of the establishment of the NEPS. In the 1990s, two pilot schemes were introduced to encourage second-level students to remain in the education system, but the NESC rightly called for similar schemes for disadvantaged students in rural schools. As the NCCA confirmed that the LCA and LCVP contributed to higher level retention rates at senior cycle, Martin should have widened access to both these programmes in light of the rising number of early school leavers, and particularly as the school leaving age was being raised to 16.

OECD reports, such as Education at a Glance, and the IALS Survey, enabled Martin to target specific areas for priority funding from the NDP and European structural funds. Even so, part-time students were still only entitled to free tuition fees in exceptional cases. But there were some hopeful signs for the future. In 1999 the Points Commission called for greater flexibility in higher education provision, and it promoted the merits of distance education for part-time students. Martin shared this view, as he told the Senate on 17 December 1998 'To-day's one right way is tomorrow's obsolete policy'.

Micheál Martin's ministerial legacy to Irish education lay in his generous allocations of funding for research in higher education institutions, which benefited not just higher education but also the Irish economy. Other Ministers contributed to the Education Act of 1998, and Niamh Bhreathnach laid the foundations, however shaky, for the introduction of the Qualifications (Education and Training) Act of 1999, but it was Micheál Martin who gave legislative effect to both.

Notes

1   Walshe, *A New Partnership*, p.202.

2   Keogh, *Twentieth-century Ireland*, pp.404–5.

3   Ahern became leader of Fianna Fáil in 1994. In 1997 he became the youngest Taoiseach ever, aged 45. He was widely acclaimed for his role in the Peace Process which led to the signing of the Good Friday Agreement in 1998. He held power during the 'Celtic Tiger' era, but as Ireland entered an economic recession he was forced to resign as Taoiseach in 2008 in the wake of revelations in the Mahon Tribunal that he had received money from developers. His explanations for these payments were considered implausible by the tribunal.

4   Oliver Mahon, Education Act, 1998 (Clare, 2000), p.vii.

5   Education Act, 1998, Part IX, s.14 (8).

6   Part VI, s.32 (i), (2).

7   Part VI, s.32 (9).

8   Part IV, s.14 (i).

9   Part IV, s.14 (5).

10 Part IV, s.15 (2) (b).

11 Part IV, s.15 (2) (c).

12　Part V, s.24 (i).

13　Part V, s.22 (i).

14　Part III, s.13 (9).

15　Part VI, s.26 (i).

16　Part II, s.9 (g).

17　Part III, s.13 (4) (a).

18　Part VI, s.28 (ii) (a).

19　Part VI, s.29 (i).

20　Part IV, s.15 (d).

21　Part IV, s.15 (g).

22　Part III, s.13 (2).

23　Part II, s.9 (g).

24　Part VI, s.28, (i) (a).

25　Part VI, s.29, (i).

26　Part VI, s.27 (i).

27　Part VI, s.27 (3).

28　Part IV, s.21 (3).

29　Report of the National Forum for Early Childhood Education (Dublin, 1998).

30　Ready to Learn, p.3.

31　Ready to Learn, pp.14–16.

32　Ibid., p.21.

33　Ibid., p.86.

34　*Dáil Debates*, vol. 504, col. 1387, 18 May 1999.

35　Coolahan and O'Donovan, *A History*, p.277.

36　Op. cit., cols 1385–7.

37　Ready to Learn, p.55.

38　Ready to Learn, pp.58–9.

39　Ibid., p.115.

40　Ibid., p.135.

41　Ibid., pp.132–3.

42　Ibid., p.135.

43　Nóirín Hayes, Head of the School of Social Services, DIT in *The Irish Times*, 8 February 2000.

44　DES, Green Paper: Adult Education in an Era of Lifelong Learning. Dublin, November 1998.

45　Green Paper: Adult Education, p.2.

46　Ibid., pp.2–3.

47　Ibid., p.9.

48　Ibid., pp.40–2.

49　Ibid., p.11.

50　Ibid., p.41.

51　Ibid., p.28.

52　Ibid., p.8.

53 Ibid., p.30.

54 Ibid., p.8.

55 Forfás is the national policy advisory board for enterprise, trade, science, technology and innovation in Ireland. It was established in 1994 and is run by a board appointed by the Minister for Jobs, Enterprise and Innovation, to whom the agency is responsible.

56 Green Paper: Adult Education, p.34.

57 Ibid., p.33.

58 Ibid., pp.24–7.

59 Ibid., p.23.

60 Ibid., p.8.

61 National Economic and Social Council, *Opportunities, Challenges and Capacities for Choice* (Dublin, 1999), p.263.

62 Ibid., p.277.

63 NCCA, Developing Senior Cycle. Education consultative paper on issues and options (Dublin, 2002), pp.16–7.

64 Ibid. The NCCA was placed on a statutory footing under Part VII, s.39 (2) of the Education Act 1998.

65 *Opportunities, Challenges*, p.275.

66 ESRI, *Annual School Leavers' Survey for 1997* (Dublin, 1998).

67 Op. cit.

68 Education (Welfare) Act, 2000, No. 22 of 2000, p.5. The 1967 Bill shortened the procedure concerning warning notices and court orders, and made provision for increases in the minimum fines previously imposed for offences against the 1926 Act.

69 Report of the Information Society Commission, Building a Capacity for Change: Lifelong Learning in the Information Society, Dublin, July 1999, p.23.

70 NCCA, The Junior Cycle Review: Progress Report, 1999.

71 DES, Learning for Life: White Paper on Adult Education, Dublin, July 2000, pp.59–60.

72 Commission on the Points System, pp.111–14.

73 Report of Review Committee on Post-Secondary Education and Training Places, Dublin, March 1999.

74 Report of the Information Society Commission, p.51.

75 Review Committee on Post-Secondary Education, p.2.

76 Commission on the Points System, pp.112–5.

77 Review Committee on Post-Secondary Education, p.3.

78 Micheál Martin TD, Minister for Education and Science address to Seanad Éireann, 17 December 1998.

79 *Dáil Debates*, vol. 504, col. 1278, 18 May 1999.

80 TEAGASC was the agricultural and food development authority.

81 Op. cit., col. 1285.

82 Commission on the Points System, p.23.

83 Forfás, Responding to Ireland's Growing Skill Needs. The first report of the expert group on future skills needs to the Tánaiste and Minister for Enterprise, Trade and Employment

and the Minister for Education and Science, June 1998. p.13.

84   Report of the Information Society Commission, pp.36–7.

85   Op. cit., p.4.

86   First report of the expert group, p.2.

87   Ibid., pp.7–8.

88   Report of the Information Society Commission, pp.42–3.

89   First report of the expert group, pp.25–6.

90   Forfás, National Competitiveness Council. Annual Competitiveness Report (Dublin, 1999), p.65.

91   *The Irish Times*, 24 January 1997.

92   In the academic year 1929–30, State research grants were awarded for the first time to postgraduate students. See Ó Buachalla, *Education Policy*, p.258, p.421.

93   Forfás, *Technology Foresight Ireland: An ICSTI Overview* (Dublin, 1999), pp.1–3.

94   Forfás, Responding to Ireland's Growing Skills Needs. The Second Report of the Expert Group on Future Skills Needs, 2000, pp.11–12. Commission on the Points System, p.70.

95   *Dáil Debates*, vol. 504, cols 1387–8, 18 May 1999.

96   *The Irish Times*, 9 March 2000.

97   Michael Woods was Minister for Education and Science from 27 January 2000 to 6 June 2002.

98   DES, Learning for Life: White Paper on Adult Education Dublin, July 2000, pp.58–9.

99   OECD, *Education at a Glance* (Paris, 1995).

100 Learning for Life, pp.91–9.

101 Ibid., p.108.

102 Ibid., pp.146–7.

103 CSA, Criteria and procedures for the Recognition of New Primary schools. Report of the Steering Group, Dublin, February 1998.

104 CSA, Criteria and Procedures for the Recognition of New Primary schools. Report of the Technical Working Group, Dublin, January 1998, p.9.

105 Ibid., p.5.

106 Ibid., p.14.

107 CSA, Report of the Steering Group, pp.10–13.

108 CSA, Report of the Technical Working Group, p.103.

109 CSA Report of the Steering Group, pp.39–41.

110 DES. Press release on first year of government, 26 June 1998.

111 Public Services Executive Union. Press release, 15 January 1999, cited in Walshe, *A New Partnership*, pp.202–3.

112 Coolahan and O'Donovan, *A History*, pp.276–8.

113 Report of the Steering Committee on the Establishment of a Teaching Council, Dublin, June 1998, pp.v–vi.

114 Coolahan and O'Donovan, *A History*, p.281.

Conclusion

Throughout this study of ministerial careers spanning eight decades, the most striking feature was the continuity of educational plans, not just from one Minister to the next, but from one generation of Ministers to the next. Successive Ministers refused to hold an education inquiry for the first 30 years, and it was only in 1966, following the publication of the joint OECD/Irish survey team's Investment in Education Report, that research-based policies and reforms were initiated, at which stage the education system underwent a transformation. The much-anticipated White Paper on Educational Development of 1980 did not provide a clear overall educational plan, but Hussey's Programme for Action in Education in 1984 did. Ministers now recognised that there was 'a greater level of confidence in a system where its direction' had 'been clearly signposted'.[1]

New methods of policy making were adopted whereby all the partners in education were consulted and consensus was arrived at. International expert opinion was now sought before major educational decisions were taken, such as the upgrading of the NIHEs. There was nothing haphazard about educational planning from the 1980s onwards. Many of the errors and omissions in policy making in the past were rectified by a new generation of Ministers who were influenced by educational developments abroad, and who were supported by the OECD and the ESF. By 1999 the education system was well funded, more democratic and more equitable, but serious challenges still remained.

For 40 years the Irish language policy was synonymous with the education policy, and the managerial system was held sacrosanct, but all that was soon set to change. From the 1920s to the 1950s, the INTO sought the introduction of LECs from Ministers, but from the 1970s to the 1990s, the impetus came from the Ministers themselves. Intermittent attempts to replace vocational schools were instigated by Ministers, but none succeeded. Over the decades Ministers failed grievously in their neglect of Industrial and Reformatory schools, with devastating consequences. In the earlier decades they failed to include parents in education or

to provide free second-level education when given the opportunity to do so, but even more disturbing was their neglect of remedial education provision, especially after the INTO had alerted them to the need for it.

When the MacPherson Education Bill, 1919–20 proposed setting up LECs, the new structures were seen as a threat to the managerial system. Cardinal Logue issued a pastoral letter calling for a national solemn novena in honour of St Patrick 'to avert from us the threatened calamity'.[2]

In the 1920s, the INTO's general secretary and Labour TD, T.J. O'Connell, called for LECs to take over the maintenance of schools. He repeated his call at the 1945 INTO congress. Bishop Michael Browne, who addressed the congress, regarded his suggestion 'as a threat to the managerial system', which he observed 'has given Ireland, the most satisfactory state of Catholic school control of any country in Christendom'.[3] In 1952 David Kelleher informed Cardinal D'Alton of the INTO policy, and the cardinal replied, expressing the concerns of the bishops, that if school maintenance was removed from managers 'that it would circum-scribe and endanger the rights of managers'.[4] Joint deputations of the INTO and the Clerical Managers to Mulcahy, Lynch and Hillery did not resolve the issue, but a 3-week work stoppage by teachers in five Ardfert National Schools in 1967 focused managerial minds so that school maintenance became their top priority nationwide.

Church opposition to LECs broadened out when Burke and Hussey took tentative steps towards the regionalisation of education. The Catholic and Protestant churches and their respective management bodies united in opposition to Burke's plans, while Hussey's proposals were flatly rejected by the CMCSS and by the Secondary-School Council of Governors. The churches just bided their time as different Ministers proposed different options, such as county committees of education, LECs and regional education councils. In 1997 Martin, who defended patron's rights while in opposition, introduced executive agencies as Minister. The ghost of MacPherson had finally been laid to rest.

By the mid-1970s, the Irish Catholic hierarchy recognised that the winds of change were blowing in the wake of the Second Vatican Council which saw a role for lay involvement in education. It was now possible to replace the 144-year-old managerial system with the more democratic boards of management, even if they had limited powers.

For over two decades a power struggle took place over the composition of boards of management between the teaching unions, religious authorities and the department, and latterly parents joined the fray. Power sharing proved to be difficult for those who had traditionally enjoyed the lion's share of it. In 1978 the INTO withdrew from participation on boards of management for over a year,

and following protracted negotiations with the Catholic Primary School Managers Association, patron's nominees were reduced.

Negotiations between the ASTI and the CMRS in 1977 on the composition of boards of management collapsed. It took 12 years before agreement was finally reached. The composition of boards of management for community schools caused a storm of protest, with Faulkner being accused of sectarianism when he permitted a greater weighting to be given to the representatives of the Catholic Church at the expense of the VECs. Teachers had to wait another 7 years to be represented on boards of community schools.

Bhreathnach's 1997 Education Bill was the last straw for the churches as it diluted the power of patrons. It led to representatives of almost every religious faith in the country coming together on the lawn of the Church of Ireland College of Education to protest against the proposals on the management of schools. Following this display of solidarity, a resolution was found whereby the composition of boards of management would result from an agreement arrived at by all the education partners and the Minister. Martin incorporated this into the Education Act which gave statutory recognition to patrons as owners of schools, and which required all boards to 'uphold … the characteristic spirit of the school' and to be 'accountable to the patron for so upholding'.[5]

This was a great relief to the patrons, but the religious authorities now had to find a way of protecting the religious ethos of their schools as the number of religious vocations continued to decline. In the 1960s, almost half of the teachers in secondary schools were priests or members of religious orders, but by 1990 the proportion had fallen to 12 per cent.[6] In 1999 the religious teaching orders protected the ethos of their schools by setting up trusteeships in the form of companies, with directors consisting of a number of lay Catholics, to carry out the patron's functions. It was to these companies that boards of management reported.[7]

The Irish language policy too had longevity because Ministers refused to hold it up to scrutiny. Consequently, the INTO had no choice but to conduct its own inquiry, and its 1941 report revealed that the policy placed an undue mental strain on children. Dr Johanna Pollak's unpublished report confirmed that with regard to the teaching of Irish 'the children get an overdose of it'.[8]

A very unscientific inquiry was conducted by the Council of Education which gave its imprimatur to the language policy. Next, de Valera set up the Commission on the Restoration of the Irish Language, which reported in 1966, but like its predecessor, it lacked the benefit of empirical research. Doctoral research conducted by Fr John Macnamara at this time confirmed the accuracy of the INTO's report. Macnamara's findings served as a damning indictment of Ministers for Education who were prepared to put their nationalist aspirations before the educational

welfare of Irish children. In 1960 Hillery announced the closure of all but one of the Preparatory Colleges which had been key to the revival efforts, and he ended the 40-year-old compulsory Irish policy by introducing Circular 11/60.

Replacing O'Sullivan's vocational schools formed part of Ministers' plans for 63 years. The first attempt to do so occurred just 4 years after their introduction. Vocational schools operated in unfair competition with secondary schools until the late-1960s, and were regarded as 'just dead-end schools for dead-end kids'.[9] In the late 1970s, as the community schools grew, VECs became alarmed at what they saw as an erosion of their traditional role in providing non-denominational vocational schools. To counteract this, they set up community colleges, which were in effect renamed vocational schools. They invited representatives of the Catholic bishops to participate in them to raise their status, and the bishops duly obliged. This was not the end of their travails. Burke had already failed to replace them with his regionalisation plans, but Hussey tried again in the 1980s, O'Rourke planned to do so in the 1990s, and so too did Bhreathnach, but the sturdy vocational schools survived, and their plans did not.

The greatest failure of successive Ministers for Education was their denial that there was excessive use of corporal punishment in Industrial and Reformatory Schools, even when individual cases were brought to their attention. It was unthinkable to them, and indeed to most Irish people, that religious orders could countenance such levels of violence and abuse of children in their care. It was to O'Malley's credit that he set up the Kennedy Committee. However, when the committee received an open admission by the highly respected manager of Daingean Reformatory School that boys were punished while stripped naked, District Justice Kennedy had to insist that the department would close the school down. The report on the school made no reference to this incident lest it 'cause a great public scandal'.[10] When the extent of the abuse of children in these schools was revealed in the television documentary *States of Fear*, it did indeed 'cause a great public scandal', and the Minister of the day disclosed the contents of depart-mental records which supported the programme's claims.

Another great failure of the earlier Ministers for Education was their inability to recognise the value of secondary education, or to take stock of parental demand for it. Moylan did not 'agree with this ideal of equal opportunities for all'.[11] Derrig missed two opportunities to provide free second-level education at a time when 'for nine out of every ten Irish people, the primary school' was 'their only centre of learning'.[12] Mulcahy's Council of Education concluded in 1960 that free secondary education was 'untenable and utopian'. Seven years later the education system was prepared for the introduction of 'free education', and O'Malley was in a position to make his historic announcement. In doing so, he paid tribute to Hillery and

Colley for having prepared the way, and to the Taoiseach, who gave 'a government assurance that education' was 'to receive priority'.[13] With this one magnanimous gesture, O'Malley opened up new avenues for all Irish children to explore. It is reasonable to attribute our unprecedented economic success of the 1990s, when Ireland was placed 'top in Europe for its educated workforce and second (after Germany) for the skills of the workers',[14] to O'Malley's 'free education' scheme.

For over four decades, parents were all but excluded from the education system, and some would argue that this was deliberate 'because it suited the interests of powerful sections of society – the middle classes, the churches, the politicians – to keep it so'.[15] O'Sullivan and Moylan accused parents of educational apathy, but they made no effort to find a way to consult parents on educational matters. De Valera, who drew up Article 42 of the Constitution, offered lip-service to the idea when he said, 'I wish there was some way … in which the parents could be represented but I cannot honestly see how you can set up such a committee that will be in any big real way representative'.[16] Derrig believed that he knew more about education than parents did, and Hillery would not consult 'outside bodies'.[17]

But change came about when Hussey gave parents real power through the National Parents' Council (NPC), and when she designated a range of issues on which the department would formally consult them. An OECD report observed in 1997 that when planned reforms were introduced, 'Ireland would have one of the most parent-participative systems in the world'.[18] The Education Act, which gave statutory rights to the NPC and which gave similar status to any parent associations they might set up in schools,[19] brought parents centre-stage in Irish education.

There were occasions over the 80 years when parents provided the lead for Ministers. This was the case in the 1950s, when a mother who had a son with learning disabilities established the Association of Parents and Friends of Mentally Handicapped Children, later called St Michael's House. In 1960 they founded and managed their own special school.[20] It was due to parental demand that All-Irish primary schools grew in the 1960s, and they had official support. Parents were instrumental in setting up the first multi-denominational school in Ireland in the mid-1970s, and they did so in the face of strong official resistance, but Wilson supported them, as did Hussey, and O'Rourke sanctioned eight new multi-denominational schools.

The CSA confirmed that there was growing demand for multi-denominational schools in Ireland, but the influx of immigrant families since the late 1990s, coupled with the decline in the number of practising Catholics, strengthened the case for greater diversity in school provision. The 1996 Report of the Constitution Review Group considered the issue of right of access to a suitable school to be one which required prompt attention.[21] The Association of Humanists was critical

of 'The failure of the State to provide a nationwide network of schools' which could 'accommodate all citizens as pupils and teachers'.[22]

The teaching unions became a powerful pressure group over the 80 years. O'Connell, who was the INTO's general secretary for 32 years, was a towering figure who led the Dublin Teachers' 1946 strike, the first significant teachers' strike in 26 years.[23] He managed to keep McQuaid on side, and he won public support. In 1964 public sympathy was with Hillery because the ASTI had rejected the arbitrator's decision and had boycotted the pubic examinations. The religious authorities supported the teachers, just as they did during the 3-week strike in 1969, because it 'was more than a strike of the teachers: it was a revolt of the schools'.[24] In the end the ASTI suffered a humiliating defeat in the Ryan Tribunal negotiations, but they had proved that they were a force to be reckoned with.

When the three teaching unions united in pay negotiations, the outcome was positive. This happened in the landmark pay settlement of 1980. It happened again in 1985 when the three unions formed a 'Teachers United' campaign. They held a spectacular protest in Croke Park with 20,000 protesting teachers drawn from the three unions. Even before a final settlement was reached, it was reported that teachers believed they had 'already secured a moral victory in effectively toppling the former Minister for Education, Mrs. Hussey'.[25]

Special education had been neglected in the past because Ministers did not see the need for widespread remedial education provision. Seán Brosnahan, the general secretary of the INTO, did and he denounced what he called 'one of the greatest crimes of our system ... the callous disregard for subnormal and backward children', many of whom were 'condemned as fools and dunces'.[26] Hillery raised the status of special education by giving it formal recognition as a distinctive sector.

But it took another two decades before the government's official policy on special education was confirmed in the White Paper on Educational Development. In the late 1980s, special education policy came under European and international influences, and while the government signed up to the United Nations Convention on the Rights of the Child in 1992, the truth of the matter was that education provisions in Ireland for profound and severely handicapped children 'were limited if non-existent'.[27] But following the High Court judgment in the O'Donoghue case, the onus was on the Minister to provide educational opportunities for all students, whatever their disabilities. This ruling was complied with in the Education Act. Commenting on recent advancements in special education, Martin said they represented 'a dramatic move away from an approach which was willing to spend large sums on legal costs, rather than take action'.[28]

In 1963 the Report of the Commission on Itinerancy recorded that 'almost no itinerant children attend school'.[29] Since then, the government adopted a

policy of 'flexible integration' of Traveller children into mainstream classes and provided special schools and pre-schools for them. Traveller resource teachers were appointed, and there was great optimism in the early 1990s when the department appointed visiting teachers, a National Education Officer and thirty-one new special teachers for Traveller children. This optimism was short lived as the White Paper Charting our Education Future concluded that participation rates in education by Traveller children were 'unacceptably low for a democratic society'.[30]

In the late 1960s, Lenihan responded to the needs of socially and educationally disadvantaged children when he and the government sponsored pioneering research in the Rutland Street Project. Fortunately, the project was allowed to continue after the Van Leer Foundation's funding ceased because Burke secured government funding for its continuation.[31] He did so at a time when several worthwhile educational schemes had to be shelved due to the oil crisis. The project became an invaluable resource for those involved in similar programmes in the 1990s.[32]

Following Ireland's accession to the EEC, department officials were quick to take the opportunity to avail of the ESF for pre-employment programmes, as youth unemployment was a European-wide problem at the time. They devised the programmes for second-level students as an alternative to the mainstream leaving certificate, and they proved highly popular. Two of them, the LCVP and the LCA, contributed to higher level retention rates at senior cycle, and the NCCA advised that access to them should be widened, but this did not happen.

This was surprising in light of the fact that the number of early school leavers continued to rise and as plans were in train to raise the school leaving age to 16. Youth unemployment stood at 21 per cent in 1989, and programmes such as Youthreach and the VTOS went some way towards meeting the needs of early school leavers without qualifications, and the provision of PLCs offered a vocational option for those who wished to seek employment. Despite the fact that Ireland achieved the fastest employment growth across the member states of the EU in 1999,[33] and that the government invested heavily in programmes to combat educational disadvantage, the country still faced big challenges regarding the long-term unemployment of the educationally disadvantaged.

Profound changes took place in higher education over 80 years. Participation rates rose dramatically, and Ireland moved quickly from a situation where only one in ten advanced to higher education prior to 1986 to something approaching mass higher education. Expansion was not confined to the university sector, since numbers in the non-university sector swelled as these students benefited from the ESF.

In April 1967, O'Malley caused a sensation when he announced the merger of TCD and UCD in order to meet a projected rise of 25,000 students by

1975.[34] The HEA restored stability when they rejected the merger proposals. In December 1974, higher education was thrown into a tailspin again, when Burke announced the replacement of the binary system of higher education with a comprehensive model. After three chaotic years, the binary system was restored. In 1979 the HEA came to the rescue of the cash-starved universities when it co-operated with the MCC for funding for university courses that met market needs. By 1981 the university sector was mirroring what was happening in the non-university sector, and was playing an equally important role in meeting the country's economic and industrial needs.

However, universities had difficulty coping with increasing numbers when Bhreathnach announced the abolition of university tuition fees for undergraduates. An effective campaign for additional funding was conducted by the universities, who were smarting from the recent announcement. She allowed them over 6,000 additional places, but they would have to pay half the cost. As the international prestige of universities depended on their research achievements, it was a source of disquiet to universities to have it confirmed by CIRCA Group Europe in their comparative assessment of Irish higher education research, that 'Public funding of higher education research in Ireland' was 'among the worst in Europe'.[35]

A buoyant economy allowed Martin to introduce a Programme for Research in Third-Level Institutions, which was a £150 million 3-year investment programme for scientific and other research in universities and ITs. The NDP also made provision for a £500 million investment over the period 2000–2006 in research and technological development in the education sector. Third-level colleges benefited enormously from these investments, and so too did the Irish economy as it improved Ireland's competitive advantage. One of the finest achievements over the 80 years was Bhreathnach's Universities Act of 1997. She had gone where no other Minister was prepared to go.

The non-university sector was thrown into turmoil by the December 1974 announcement, and its awards body, the NCEA, was left wounded by it. When Bhreathnach raised Waterford RTC to IT status, the floodgates were opened and the remaining RTCs sought a similar upgrading. But it was when her interim TEASTAS authority recommended that a single awards body would act on behalf of a consortium of RTCs, which had previously received their awards from the NCEA, that confusion reigned supreme. The question remained as to who would grant awards to the non-RTC colleges who currently received their awards from the NCEA. It was left to Martin to provide a more coherent and effective system of certification and accreditation for this sector, which he did by introducing the Qualifications (Education and Training) Act in 1999 that set out plans for the NQAI.

The NDP provided substantial funding for a vast array of education programmes to promote social inclusion. It targeted second-chance and further education in particular by allowing £1.027 billion for the expansion of part-time courses, which was commendable. However, when it came to the university sector, 'A general programme of free fees for part-time students' was not advocated.[36] But there were some hopeful signs for the future. In 1999 the Points Commission called for greater flexibility in higher education provision, and it promoted the merits of distance learning to meet the demand for part-time study.[37] Martin accepted the need to promote flexibility and responsiveness in educational structures, as he told the Senate on 17 December 1998 'To-day's one right way is tomorrow's obsolete policy'.[38]

The 1990s was a decade of reform. The department itself underwent a radical overhaul of its structures and was renamed the DES in 1997. Six years previously, the OECD observed that 'The Department is over-stretched simply to administer the system', but within less than a decade, a broad range of agencies and a number of support teams assisted the inspectorate and lightened its workload. It was now issuing reports after a lapse of almost 40 years, and 15 years after Hussey provided annual progress reports. Its professional profile was raised by the establishment of the ESRU, and Section 13 of the Education Act placed it on a statutory footing. It could no longer be referred to disparagingly as 'that stagnant pond which is the Department of Education'.[39]

The Education Act of 1998 was a tour de force to which five Ministers made a contribution, namely O'Rourke, Brennan, Davern, Bhreathnach and Martin. It was undoubtedly long overdue as the primary school system had no legislative foundation whatsoever. The Education Act was therefore a vital piece of legislation which clarified the rights and entitlements of all the education partners, and it set out their roles and responsibilities in the education system.

Ministers faced daunting challenges over the 80 years over which they had little control. This was the case in the early 1920s with the War of Independence, the Civil War and the grinding poverty which followed. In the 1930s, the Economies Bill reduced teachers' salaries, and this was followed by the Second World War. In the mid-1950s, capitation grants to secondary schools had to be cut by 10 per cent and annual grants to VECs by 6 per cent. The oil crisis, which peaked between 1973 and 1975, meant that the in-service education budget was reduced from £77,000 in 1974 to £12,000 in 1975.[40]

The White Paper on Educational Development referred to eleven special-ised committees whose reports had to be shelved. In the 1980s, the worldwide economic recession, together with the poor state of the country's finances, forced the introduction of charges for the previously free school transport service, as well as cuts to teacher allocations in post-primary schools.[41] Political instability had a

deeply unsettling effect as there was a change of government three times in 1982, two heaves against Charles Haughey and five different Ministers for Education, including Haughey himself who was acting Minister for 21 days.

The Irish education system was now a vibrant, modern system. There was international recognition of our educated workforce, yet many challenges persisted, such as early school leaving and youth unemployment. The National Educational Psychological Service provided a service which fell far short of demand, and the participation rates in education by Traveller children was still worryingly low. Provision of extra places for part-time students in universities and the abolition of fees for part-time courses were called for. Greater diversity in school provision needed prompt attention to reflect changing demographics as Ireland was now a multi-cultural society.

The modernisation of Irish education was due in large measure to the vision of two Ministers for Education from the 1960s – Patrick Hillery, who allowed the OECD to study our run-down education system and who catered for 'The Modern Third Estate', and Donogh O'Malley, who removed the 'dark stain on the national conscience' and enhanced the future prospects of generations of Irish children. Since Hillery took that courageous step, OECD studies of Irish education have continued, and their reports which provide indicators of comparative educational performance across a number of European countries, ensure that Ministers can never return to the complacency of the past.

Ireland's membership of the EEC brought untold benefits to Irish education as financial support from the ESF provided welcome funding during years of austerity in the 1970s, through the economic recession of the 1980s, and for co-funding of large-scale educational reforms in the 1990s. Finally, credit must surely go to those Ministers who introduced a measure of equity into the education system by employing a partnership approach to policy making, by catering for the needs of the educationally disadvantaged, students with special needs and those with disabilities, and by giving massive funding to programmes promoting social inclusion. They left a proud ministerial legacy to Irish education in the 1997 Universities Act, the 1998 Education Act and the 1999 Qualifications (Education and Training) Act.

Notes

1   The Fourth Annual John Marcus O'Sullivan Memorial Lecture, p.36.
2   O'Connell, *History of the INTO*, pp.318–20.
3   *Catholic Herald*, 20 April 1945.
4   O'Connell, *History of the INTO*, pp.440–2.
5   Education Act, 1998, Part IV, s. 15(2) (b).
6   Hyland, 'Primary and second-level education in the early twenty-first century', p.187.

7 In 1999 the Irish Spiritans Holy Ghost Fathers, Brothers and Associates set up the Des Places Education Association as one such company.

8 NAI *S7801* Dr Johanna Pollak, 'On teaching Irish', 1943.

9 *Sunday Independent*, 22 December 1957.

10 *Dáil Debates*, vol. 504, cols 1181–2, 13 May 1999.

11 *Dáil Debates*, vol. 126, col. 1743, 17 July 1951.

12 *Dáil Debates*, vol. 80, col. 1566, 6 June 1940.

13 Speech by Donogh O'Malley in Browne, *Unfulfilled Promise*, p.187.

14 Sweeney, *The Celtic Tiger*, p.117.

15 *Tuairim*, pamphlet 8, 'Educating towards a united Europe', pp.6–7.

16 *Dáil Debates*, vol. 96, col. 2171, 18 April 1945.

17 *Dáil Debates*, vol. 203, col. 598, 30 May 1963.

18 CERI/OECD, *Parents as Partners in Schooling*, p.141.

19 Education Act, 1998, Part VI, s.26 (i).

20 Griffin and Shevlin, *Responding to Special Educational Needs*, pp.39–40.

21 Report of the Constitution Review Group, p.368, p.375.

22 *The Irish Times*, 10 April 1996.

23 There was a 1-day national strike in 1933.

24 McCarthy, *The Decade of Upheavel*, p.211.

25 *The Irish Times,* 20 February 1986.

26 *Irish School Weekly*, 15 and 22 March 1952, p.27.

27 Hyland, 'Primary and second-level education', p.174.

28 *Dáil Debates*, vol. 1385–7, 18 May 1999.

29 Report of the Commission on Itinerancy, p.64.

30 Charting our Education Future, p.26; Report on the NEC, p.127.

31 NAI *DT 2006/515* Rutland Street Educational Project Memorandum, 11 May 1976.

32 Ready to Learn, p.99.

33 NESC, *Opportunities, Challenges and Capacities for Choice*, p.263.

34 *Dáil Debates*, vol. 227, col. 2190, 20 April 1967.

35 CIRCA Group Europe, *A Comparative International Assessment*, p.iv.

36 Learning for Life, pp.146–7.

37 Commission on the Points System, pp.112–5.

38 Micheál Martin TD, Minister for Education and Science, Address to Seanad Éireann, 17 December 1998.

39 O'Meara, *Reform in Education*, p.6.

40 *Dáil Debates*, vol. 282, col. 1134, 19 June 1975.

41 Hussey, *At the Cutting Edge*, p.23.

Bibliography

OFFICIAL PUBLICATIONS

Dáil Reports

Senate Reports

Reports of the Department of Education

Report of Aireacht na Gaedhilge, June 1920

Report on Ministry of the National Language, August 1921

National Programme of Primary Instruction: The National Programme Conference
(Dublin, 1922)

Report and Programme of the Second National Programme Conference 1925-26
(Dublin, 1926)

Coimisiún na Gaeltachta, Report (Dublin, 1926)

Report of the Commission on Technical Education (Dublin, 1927)

Report of the Committee on Inspection of Primary schools (Dublin, 1927)

Department of Education, Revised Programme of Primary Instruction (Dublin, 1934)

Report of the Inter-departmental Committee on the Raising of the School Leaving Age
(Dublin, 1935)

Report of the Commission of Inquiry into the Reformatory and Industrial
School System

1934-1936 (Dublin, 1936)

Report of the Commission on Vocational Organisation (Dublin, 1944)

Department of Education, A Council of Education: Terms of Reference and General
Regulations (Dublin, 1950)

Report of the Commission on Youth Unemployment (Dublin, 1951)

Report of the Council of Education on the Function and Curriculum of the
Primary school (Dublin, 1954)

Report of the Council of Education: the Curriculum of the Secondary School
(Dublin, 1962)

Commission on Itinerancy, Report of the Commission on Itinerancy (Dublin, 1963)

Investment in Education, Report of the Survey Team Appointed by the Minister for
     Education in October 1962 (Dublin, 1965)
Commission on Higher Education 1960–67, Presentation and Summary of Report
     (Dublin, 1967)
Steering Committee on Technical Education. Report to the Minister on Regional
     Technical Colleges (Dublin, 1967)
Rialtas na hÉireann. Ár nDaltaí Uile – All Our Children (Dublin, 1969)
Reformatory and Industrial Schools Systems Report (Dublin, 1970)
Report of the Committee on Adult Education in Ireland (Dublin, 1973)
The ICE Report, Final Report of the Committee on the Form and Function of the
     Intermediate Certificate Examination (Dublin, 1974)
White Paper on Educational Development (Dublin, 1980)
Programme for Action in Education (Dublin, 1984)
Green Paper, Partners in Education Serving Community Needs (Dublin, 1985)
Report of the Review Body on the Primary Curriculum (Dublin, 1990)
Report of the Primary Education Review Body (Dublin, 1990)
Department of Education, Education for a Changing World. Green Paper on Education
     (Dublin, 1992)
Report of the Special Education Review Committee (Dublin, 1993)
Department of Education, Charting Our Education Future. White Paper on Education
     (Dublin, 1995)
Commission on School Accommodation. Rationalisation of Vocational Education
     Committees. Report of the Steering Group (Dublin, 1996)
Report to the Minister for Education Niamh Bhreathnach TD, on Discipline in Schools
     by Dr Maeve Martin (Dublin, 1997)
Report of the National Forum for Early Childhood Education (Dublin, 1998)
Department of Education and Science, Green Paper: Adult Education in an Era of
     Lifelong Learning (Dublin, 1998)
Commission on School Accommodation, Criteria and Procedures for the Recognition
     of New Primary Schools. Report of the Steering Group (Dublin, 1998)
Commission on School Accommodation, Criteria and Procedures for the Recognition
     of New Primary Schools. Report of the Technical Working Group (Dublin 1998)
Report of the Steering Committee on the Establishment of a Teaching Council
     (Dublin, 1998)
Commission on the Points System. Final Report and Recommendations (Dublin, 1999)
Report of the Information Society Commission. Building a Capacity for Change:
     Lifelong Learning in the Information Society (Dublin, 1999)
Evaluation Support & Research Unit, Whole School Evaluation, Report on the
     1998/1999 Pilot Project (Dublin, 1999)
Annual Report of the Department of Education and Science, 1999
Department of Education and Science, Learning for Life: White Paper on Adult
     Education (Dublin, 2000)

NEWSPAPERS AND JOURNALS

Administration

Education Times

European Journal of Education

Freeman's Journal

Gairm

Hibernia

Irish Catholic Directory

Irish Ecclesiastical Record

Irish Education Decision Maker

Irish Educational Studies

Irish Examiner

Irish Monthly

Irish Press

Irish School Weekly

Irish Independent

Times Education Supplement

The Irish Journal of Education

The Irish Times

The Secondary Teacher

The Vocational Education Bulletin

NATIONAL ARCHIVES OF IRELAND – DEPARTMENT OF THE TAOISEACH

S6369A Proposed new training college for women teachers, 16 November 1932

S6369 Coláiste Éinde to be training college

S9271 Educational reconstruction, S. O'Neill, 21 July 1933

S9271 Copy of minutes of the meeting of the hierarchy, 9 October 1934

S11258 Newspaper cuttings on Irish language

S2512 Higher primary schools in the Gaeltacht

S7801A Irish language development in schools, 1941

S12891A Post-war planning education, 16 July 1942

S12891A Memorandum on vocational education, 15 October 1942

S7801 'On teaching Irish', Dr Johanna Pollak, 26 May 1943

S13180A Irish language 1943, 1949, 1950

S12891B Submission by Department of Education, 1944-45

S12891B Report of the Departmental Committee on Education Provision, June 1947

S12891B Notes on continuation schools, J.P. Hackett, 18 July 1947

96/6/36 S12891E Lemass to Colley, 25 September 1965

96/6/36 S12891E Donogh O'Malley, Minister for Education – education developments 1966-67, 12 September 1966

BOOKS AND ARTICLES

Education

Akenson et al., 'Pre-university education 1921–1984' in J.R. Hill (ed.) A New History of Ireland VII. Ireland 1921-1984, pp. 720–56 (Oxford, 2003)

Coolahan, J., 'Higher education in Ireland 1908-1984' in J.R. Hill (ed.) A New History of Ireland, pp. 757–89.

Coolahan, J. and T. O'Donovan, *A History of Ireland's School Inspectorate, 1831–2008* (Dublin, 2009)

Jones, V., *A Gaelic Experiment: The Preparatory System 1926–1961 and Coláiste Moibhí* (Dublin, 2006)

Ó Buachalla, S., *Education Policy in Twentieth Century Ireland* (Dublin, 1988)

O'Connell, T., *History of the Irish National Teachers' Organisation 1868–1968* (Dublin, 1969)

O'Flaherty, L., *Management and Control in Irish Education: The Post-Primary Experience* (Dublin, 1992)

Raftery, M. and E. O'Sullivan, *Suffer the Little Children: The Inside Story of Ireland's Industrial Schools* (Dublin, 1999)

White, T., *Investing in People: Higher Education in Ireland from 1960 to 2000* (Dublin, 2001)

History, Politics, Religion

Browne, P.J., *Unfulfilled Promise: Memories of Donogh O'Malley* (Dublin, 2008)

Carroll, A., *Seán Moylan Rebel Leader* (Cork, 2010)

Downey, J., *Lenihan: His Life and Loyalties* (Dublin, 1998)

Faulkner, P., *As I Saw It: Reviewing over 30 years of Fianna Fáil and Irish Politics* (Dublin, 2005)

Ferriter, D., *The Transformation of Ireland 1900–2000* (London, 2005)

_____ *Judging Dev, A Reassessment of the Life and Legacy of Éamon de Valera* (Dublin, 2007)

Finnegan, R.B., *Ireland: The Challenge of Conflict and Change* (Boulder: Westview, 1983)

FitzGerald, G., *Reflections on the Irish State* (Dublin, 2003)

_____ *All in a Life, Garret FitzGerald, An Autobiography* (Dublin, 1994)

Garvin, T., *Judging Lemass: The Measure of the Man* (Dublin, 2009)

_____ *Preventing the Future: Why was Ireland So Poor for So Long?* (Dublin, 2005)

Hussey, G., *At the Cutting Edge, Cabinet Diaries 1982–85* (Dublin, 1990)

Keogh, D., *Twentieth-Century: Ireland: Revolution and State Building* (Dublin, 2005)

Lane, J. (ed.) *Seán Moylan in His Own Words, Statements by Seán Moylan T.D. Minister for Education* (Cork, 2004)

Mulcahy, R., *Richard Mulcahy (1886–1971): A Family Memoir* (Dublin, 1999)

O'Rourke, M., *Just Mary: A Memoir* (Dublin, 2012)

Quinn, R., *Straight Left: A Journey in Politics* (Dublin, 2005)

Walsh, J., *Patrick Hillery: The Official Biography* (Dublin, 2008)

Walshe, J., *A New Partnership in Education: From Consultation to Legislation in the Nineties* (Dublin, 1999)

Index